Laws of Shabbat

Volume II

הר ברכה
HAR BRACHA

מגיד
MAGGID

Rabbi Eliezer Melamed

PENINEI HALAKHA

פניני הלכה

LAWS OF SHABBAT

VOLUME II

Yeshivat Har Bracha Maggid Books

Laws of Shabbat: Volume II

First Maggid Edition, 2015

Maggid Books
An imprint of Koren Publishers Jerusalem Ltd.

POB 8531, New Milford, CT 06776-8531, USA
& POB 4044, Jerusalem 91040, Israel
www.korenpub.com

Translation from Hebrew: Yocheved Cohen
Series Editor: Rabbi Elli Fischer
Halakhic Editor: Rabbi Maor Cayam
Editors: Elli Fischer, Daniel Landman, Nechama Unterman
Director: Rabbi Yogev Cohen

Published in Cooperation with Yeshivat Har Bracha

ISBN 978-1-59264-448-3, *hardcover*

A CIP catalogue record for this title is available from the British Library

Printed in the United States

In Loving Memory of Our Parents

אריה בן ר׳ נתן

מלכה פייגא בת ר׳ יוסף

Whose exemplary Shmirat Mitzvot,
Dedication to a Torah life and respect for Gedolim,
Along with Chesed to individuals and
community were outstanding.

Dedicated by
Moshe and Shoshanna Schilit

Dedicated in honor of Sarah Kestenbaum,
the ultimate eshet chayil whose faith has inspired her
children, grandchildren, and all those around her.

In Loving Memory of
Mayer Luden

לעילוי נשמת

מאיר בן אברהם יהודה הלוי ז״ל

Adored husband, daddy, papa, son, uncle, and brother.
He inspired all with his love of life, family, and Israel.

Barry and Aviva Luden

In loving tribute to our father,
Henry B. Levi, of blessed memory

ר׳ אברהם ז״ל בן רפאל הלוי נ״י לעווי, נפטר בכ״ט תשרי תשע״ב

Dedicated by the Levi-Dreyfus family (Atlanta/New York)

May Hashem grant an Aliyah LNeshama for our
Grandparents Lewis, Perloff, Goldberg and Rotstein

May our learning and keeping Shabbat merit
the strengthening of Am Yisrael

In honor of a great Talmid Chacham – Rav Eliezer Melamed
Jonathan & Paula Gold & Family

In loving memory of my dear Father,
Yisrael (Cyril) ben Betzalel & Yenta Blima Newman, z"l,
(Niftar 20 Kislev 5775) and my dear Mother,
Chana Rivka (Helen-Honey) bat Azreil Shimshon haLevy
and Batsheva Minna, z"l, (Nift'ra 18 Elul, 5760).

In honor of my dear Father, Elazar (Leo), YL"A, ben Yekutiel
Yehuda & Frieda, z"l, and my dear Mother,
Hinda Leah (Hilda), TL"A, bat Yeshaya & Chaya, z"l

Chaviva & Yeshaya Leib (Steve) Braun

Contents

List of Abbreviations

Note: Throughout this volume, unless otherwise indicated, citations of *Tur, Shulḥan Arukh,* and Rema refer to the *Oraḥ Ḥayim* section. A full list, with descriptions, of the sources and authorities cited in this volume is available at bit.ly/PenineiHalakhaWorksCited

AHS	*Arukh Ha-shulḥan*
AZ	*Avoda Zara*
Baḥ	*Bayit Ḥadash*
BB	*Bava Batra*
Behag	*Halakhot Gedolot*
BHL	*Bi'ur Halakha*
BM	*Bava Metzi'a*
ḤM	*Ḥoshen Mishpat*
m.	Mishna
MA	*Magen Avraham*
MB	*Mishna Berura*
MK	*Mo'ed Katan*
MT	*Mishneh Torah*
OḤ	*Oraḥ Hayim*
RH	*Rosh Ha-shana*
SA	*Shulḥan Arukh*
SAH	*Shulḥan Arukh Ha-Rav*
San.	*Sanhedrin*
Shakh	*Siftei Kohen*
SHT	*Sha'ar Ha-tziyun*
Smag	*Sefer Mitzvot Gadol*
SSK	*Shemirat Shabbat Ke-hilkhata*
t.	Tosefta
Taz	*Turei Zahav*
y.	Yerushalmi
YD	*Yoreh De'a*

Chapter Fifteen

Boneh and *Soter*

1. THE PRINCIPLES OF *BONEH, SOTER,* AND *MAKEH BE-PATISH*

The *melakha* of *Boneh* (building) is the *melakha* through which the *Mishkan* was constructed. The *melakha* includes leveling the ground in preparation for erecting the *Mishkan* upon it and so that people can walk easily in its courtyard. It also includes putting up the walls of the *Mishkan,* its roofing, and its courtyard gate.

Building anything on the ground or in a house, or adding anything onto a pre-existing structure, is a transgression of a Torah prohibition. Therefore, if one fills in a small hole in a wall or a yard, adds cement or plaster to a wall, or adds water to freshly poured concrete to strengthen it (a process known as curing), he has transgressed a Torah prohibition (*Shabbat* 102b; 73b).

Any activity that is forbidden on account of *Boneh* may not be undone, on account of the *melakha* of *Soter* (demolishing), assuming that there is a purpose to the demolition. If the act of undoing is destructive, it is rabbinically prohibited. Examples of purposeful demolition include destroying something in order to rebuild it more effectively, digging a hole in the ground in order to lay foundations, or drilling a hole in a wall in order to insert a screw (*Shabbat* 31b; MT 10:15).

At times, demolition may be purposeful in itself. In such cases, even if there is no intention to build, one still transgresses *Boneh.*

Examples of this include removing extra cement that is stuck on the floor or wall, digging a hole in order to hide things in it, or creating a hole in a wall in order to conceal things there (*Shabbat* 102b).

Another *melakha* connected to building is *Makeh Be-patish* (applying the finishing touch). For example, after completing the construction of a house, sometimes there are stones protruding from the wall. They are then often hammered down to make the wall's surface uniform. Similarly, after completing the manufacture of a metal tool, there are sometimes rough edges remaining that are smoothed out using a hammer. Both of these actions are prohibited on account of *Makeh Be-patish*. *Toladot* of this *melakha* include fixing broken tools, improving tools whose manufacture is complete, and installing a window to allow air to circulate and light to enter (MT 10:16). There are different opinions in the Gemara regarding whether certain construction-related activities are prohibited on account of *Boneh* or on account of *Makeh Be-patish* (*Shabbat* 102b). We will not explore these types of disagreements, since the primary purpose of this work is to teach people what is permitted and prohibited rabbinically and by Torah law.

Making cheese on Shabbat is prohibited by Torah law because it causes component parts to solidify and coalesce, in the manner of construction (MT 7:6). Making snowballs or snowmen is also prohibited; but since these do not last, the prohibition is rabbinic.

2. *BONEH* ON THE GROUND, AND SAFEGUARDS AGAINST IT

As we have seen, *Boneh* includes the prohibition of leveling the ground, whether in order to make it easier to walk on, enable chairs and benches to be placed upon it, or to build upon it. Therefore, one who levels a mound of earth or fills in a hole transgresses a Torah prohibition.

If a yard was flooded by rain, one may not spread sand or gravel over it in order to cover the mud. Since those materials are normally left in the ground, this is considered leveling the ground, a violation of *Boneh*. However, one may spread straw that is designated for animal food over the mud, since he does not intend to leave it there. This is on condition that the straw is spread with a *shinui*, such as using the back of a shovel to distribute it. Otherwise, the act of spreading looks like a weekday activity (*Eruvin* 104a; SA 313:10).

One may cover excrement or saliva with sand, since one who does this does not intend to improve the yard, but only to cover the filth (*Beitza* 8b; MB 313:55). Similarly, if oil spilled on the sidewalk or the floor, one may cover it with sand to prevent people from slipping. This is on condition that the sand was designated for this purpose and thus is not *muktzeh* (below 23:3). One may similarly spread salt on ice in order to prevent people from slipping (SSK 25:10).

One may not sweep the yard lest he level indentations and thereby transgress a Torah prohibition. However, if the yard is floored with tiles or pavement, he may sweep it.[1]

One who has clay stuck to his shoes should not try to rub it off against the ground, because he may end up leveling the ground (SA 302:6). Some are not worried about this possibility, and permit rubbing off the clay (Rema, *Taz*). One who so wishes may be lenient, but it is preferable to be stringent. In contrast, one may rub off the clay against a grate, tiles, or stones even *le-khatḥila* (MB 302:28).

One should not rub saliva that is on the ground into the dirt with one's shoes, to avoid leveling the ground. If one finds the saliva disgusting, he may step on it in the natural course of his walking, as long as his intention is not to spread it and level the ground (SA 316:11).

One may not play marbles on the ground lest he level the ground so that the marbles roll smoothly. Similarly, one may not play any game on the ground that requires completely flat ground, lest he end up

1. Rif maintains that one may sweep the unfloored ground because one will not necessarily level the ground, and thus if one does so it is unintentional, a *davar she-eino mitkaven*. Rambam permits sweeping an area that is floored. However, if it is unfloored, he is concerned that one might intend to level the ground. Rosh maintains that even a floored area may not be swept because one may come to sweep an unfloored area and level the ground. SA 337:2 rules in accordance with Rambam, while Rema follows Rosh. However, BHL s.v. "ve-yesh" states that in a place where all homes have flooring, Rosh's prohibition does not apply. R. Shlomo Zalman Auerbach adds that a paved area outside a house, even if it is not covered by a roof, is considered part of the house, and even the Rema would permit sweeping such an area (SSK ch. 23 n. 10). See below, ch. 23 n. 14 and *Harḥavot* 23:14:6 regarding why there is no problem of *muktzeh* when sweeping dust from the floor.

leveling it. Even if the ground is paved, one may not play there, as there is a concern that one might then end up playing on unpaved ground (SA 338:5 and MB *ad loc.* 20; MB 308:158). However, one may play on the floor inside one's home; since all homes today have flooring, we are not worried that, as a result of playing there, anyone will end up playing outside on unpaved ground (SSK 16:5).

Children may play in a sandbox containing fine, dry sand, for as long as the sand is dry, the sand will pour back into any indentations made. However, if the sand is wet enough to make holes in it, one may not to play with it (MB 308:143). Wetting the sand is also forbidden, as it constitutes *Lash* (MB 321:50). If the sand has not been designated for play it is *muktzeh*, and thus playing with it is forbidden (SA 308:38; MB *ad loc.* 144).

3. ATTACHING THINGS TO A HOUSE OR THE GROUND

Permanently affixing something useful to a house or the ground violates the Torah prohibition of *Boneh*. Removing such fixtures violates the Torah prohibition of *Soter*. This is the case even if the attachment is not tight and the objects can easily be detached and reattached, as is the case with hinged or sliding windows or doors. Since these are permanently attached to the house, they become part of it, and installing them or removing them is a transgression of a Torah prohibition. Therefore, even if a room is hot, one may not remove a window from the wall or from its frame (*Shabbat* 122b; SA 308:9; MB *ad loc.* 39). Similarly, one may not attach or detach a filter that is screwed onto a faucet, rubber pipes attached to the sink, or light bulbs screwed into their sockets, since their attachment to the house is permanent. Similarly, pounding a nail into the wall or gluing a hook to the wall violates a Torah prohibition, since these additions are permanent (*Shabbat* 103a; MB 314:8).

One may similarly not attach curtain hooks to a curtain track or the curtains themselves to the hooks on the track. Fastening a curtain rod to brackets that protrude from the wall is also prohibited. Even though all these attachments are loose, since the items are being attached to the building, these actions are prohibited by Torah law. If the rod is not truly attached to the brackets, but rather simply rests upon or inside them and can move back and forth easily, then the rod may be placed on the brackets. In such a case, one may also thread the loops at the top of the curtain through the rod.

If the object being attached to the house or the ground will not last long, the prohibition is rabbinic. For example, it is only rabbinically forbidden to attach a vacuum hook to a wall, since its suction cup will not keep the hook anchored for long.

When something may not be attached to the ground or a house, it is also forbidden to tighten its existing attachment. Therefore, one may not tighten the loose screws of a sink, door handle, or closet handle.

In contrast, objects that are not really attached and do not become part of the house may be put up or taken down. For example, one may hang a picture on a nail, because the picture is not considered part of the wall. If a window breaks and cold wind is blowing through the house, the broken window may be covered with cloth to keep out the wind. This is because the cloth does not become part of the wall, but is placed there only temporarily (MB 313:3 and 315:7; SSK 23:41 and 23:44). Similarly, one may stick papers to a refrigerator using magnets, because the magnets are not considered part of the refrigerator. For the same reason, one may hang a colander over the lip of the sink. Inserting a plug in a socket or removing it is also not considered *Boneh* or *Soter*, because the plug is not considered part of the house.[2]

It is self-evident that one may open and close doors, windows, and faucets. This is the case even when the door is not usually opened, or when the faucet in question is the water main, which is rarely shut off. Since they remain attached to the building and this type of opening or closing is the way they are normally used, it is not considered *Boneh* or *Soter*. Similarly, one may open and close a porch's sliding roof that is attached with hinges or that slides on a track, as it is considered the same as a window (Rema 626:3).

---

2. Some are stringent in the case of a plug that is plugged or unplugged only infrequently, such as a refrigerator plug (*Ḥut Shani* 36:1). However, it would seem that all plugs should be treated in the same way, since plugs in general are plugged and unplugged frequently. Furthermore, their primary connection is to the electrical appliance, and thus they are not considered part of the wall. (See SSK 13:33, n. 112; *Orḥot Shabbat* 8:17; *Menuḥat Ahava* 1:24:20.) However, because a plug is *muktzeh*, it should be grasped using a *shinui*.

It is prohibited by Torah law to use a nail or a screw to reattach a door handle that has fallen off. Reattaching it without a nail or a screw in a way that joins the handles of both sides of the door to each other is rabbinically prohibited, since the attachment is only temporary. In contrast, one may insert one of the two handles into the door without using nails or screws. This is not considered an attachment at all, since the handle is just resting there with nothing to support it. However, there is still a concern that one might forget that it is Shabbat and decide to reattach it properly with nails. Therefore, the door handle should be replaced awkwardly, tilted upward or downward, so there is no concern that anyone will tighten the connection. A handle that has begun to come loose from its attachment to the corresponding handle may not be pushed back into place.[3]

4. MAKING A TENT (*OHEL*)

Making an *ohel* is a *tolada* of *Boneh*. In contrast to the *melakha* of *Boneh*, which involves attaching different components, such as stone, wood, cement, and metal, to construct a house or implement, making an *ohel* does not involve the attachment of various components but the erection of something that separates between different areas. The roof of a tent serves as a barrier between the sky and those who are inside the tent, protecting them from the elements. Therefore, pitching a tent on Shabbat using sheets or other things that are not considered construction materials is prohibited by Torah law if the tent is stable and will last for a long time (at least eight days). This is the case even if one tied no knots and used no screws or nails, but only loops and pegs. Even if

3. If the handle had already fallen off multiple times before Shabbat, and everyone is accustomed to using the door with only one of the two handles attached, one may push that one handle back into its normal place, with no awkwardness (*Menuḥat Ahava* vol. 3 ch. 23 n. 71). The permissive rationale of attaching it awkwardly is cited in *Ḥut Shani* 36:4:7. When it is impossible to insert even one handle, one may open the door with the help of a screwdriver or the like (SSK 23:37). Water tanks, septic tanks, and electrical or telephone junction panels boxes are considered part of the building, and thus it is rabbinically prohibited to place a permanent cover on such a structure or to open such a cover. If the tank's cover has a handle, one may open and close it on Shabbat (*Shabbat* 126b; SA 308:10; MB *ad loc.* 42; SSK ch. 23 n. 146).

he only made a roof or a wall, or even simply added a *tefaḥ* to an existing roof or wall, he has transgressed a Torah prohibition (*Pri Megadim, Mishbetzot Zahav* 315:8; MB *ad loc.* 1; SHT *ad loc.* 6).

The Torah prohibition is limited to a permanent, durable *ohel*. The Sages further forbid making a temporary *ohel*. Therefore, one may not spread a curtain or netting over a bed, whether for privacy or for protection against insects.

Since the critical part of an *ohel* is the roof, one may not make any sort of temporary roof to protect a person beneath it, even if it is only a *tefaḥ* wide. But one may put up a temporary *meḥitza*. For example, one may erect a *meḥitza* between men and women attending a Torah lecture. However, one may not erect a *meḥitza* that serves to render something halakhically permitted (*meḥitza ha-materet*) even on a temporary basis. For example, if a *sukka* has only two walls, a third wall may not be erected, even if it is temporary, since erecting this *meḥitza* renders the *sukka* kosher. Similarly, one may not erect a temporary *meḥitza* in order to close a gap in an *eruv*, because this renders the *eruv* kosher (SA 315:1; below 29:8).

The rabbinic prohibition of making a temporary *ohel* is limited to the case of a new *ohel*, but one may make a temporary addition to a pre-existing *ohel*. Therefore, one who wishes to spread an awning in his garden on Shabbat to protect himself from the sun should make sure to spread it at least a *tefaḥ* before Shabbat. He may then extend it fully on Shabbat. Similarly, if the beginning of a permanent roof is already in place, one may put up an awning to serve as a temporary continuation of the roof. One may also take down whatever was temporarily added on Shabbat (SA 315:2; MB *ad loc.* 38).

Even if no one had actually begun to spread out the awning before Shabbat, but it contains a pull-string that is designed for extending it, this string is considered the beginning of the extension, and thus one may complete the extension of the awning on Shabbat (MB 315:37).

A porch's sliding roof that is attached with hinges or that slides on a track may be opened and closed on Shabbat. This is because it is not considered an *ohel*, but rather is comparable to opening and closing a door (Rema 626:3). Similarly, one may open a patio umbrella that is permanently affixed in the yard.

The hinged hood or canopy of a baby carriage or stroller may be opened and closed on Shabbat. Furthermore, since it may be opened, it is considered the beginning of an *ohel*, and one may add to it as well. Thus, if one wishes to protect more of the carriage by extending the hood using a cloth diaper or a plastic sheet, he may do so (SSK 24:13).

5. ADDITIONAL LAWS PERTAINING TO *OHEL*

As we have seen, making even a temporary *ohel* is rabbinically prohibited. Included in this prohibition is placing a wide board or a sheet across vertical supports to protect oneself from the elements. However, when the supports are not permanent, this can be permitted if the *ohel* is erected in a manner that differs significantly from the normal way of doing it. The Sages forbade putting up a temporary *ohel* in the usual order – first putting up the walls or supports, and only then putting up the roof. However, if the order is reversed, the Sages permit one to put up a temporary *ohel*. Thus, if the roof is first held up in the air and then walls or supports are placed underneath it, this would be permitted. Usually a second person is necessary in order to erect a tent in this way (*Shabbat* 43b; SA 311:6; *Bi'ur Ha-Gra ad loc.*).

These rules apply to children's games as well. Children who are of an age where they can understand the laws of Shabbat may not spread blankets over chairs in order to create a tent in which to play, but they may hold the blanket in the air and then place chairs underneath it. Similarly, they may not use interlocking toy bricks (like Lego) to build a house or garage whose inside area is a square *tefaḥ* or more, but they may hold the roof up and then attach the walls from underneath.

Just as one may not put up a temporary *ohel*, one may not take one down. Just as one may put up a temporary *ohel* if he changes the order of construction, so too he may take one down if he changes the order. The walls must be removed first, and only afterward the roof (SSK 24:22).

Even if there is no intention to erect an *ohel* in order to take shelter under it, nevertheless, if in actuality one makes something in the form of an *ohel* and the space underneath serves a purpose, it may not be erected in that form. For example, one may not take two barrels of wine and place a third one across the top. Since it is necessary to have airflow between the barrels so that the wine will not get overheated and spoil, this structure is considered a temporary *ohel*: the two barrels are considered walls, and the barrel atop them is considered a roof. However, the Sages permit doing so if the order is reversed; one person may hold up the top barrel while someone else slips the other two barrels underneath.

One may place a tabletop on legs as long as each leg is less than a *tefaḥ* wide. In such a case, the legs are not considered *meḥitzot*, and one may set the legs first and then place the tabletop on top of them. If each of the legs is a *tefaḥ* wide, they are considered *meḥitzot*. If one wishes to set up such a table, he must hold the tabletop in the air and then have someone else slip the legs underneath it.[4] In contrast, when opening a folding crib, one may place the board and mattress normally, as there are no walls beneath them and there is no purpose served by the space underneath them.

One may open a baby carriage or stroller, a folding table, a folding chair, a cot, or a playpen on Shabbat because the entire structure is already completed and connected before Shabbat. The only part that is done on Shabbat is opening it (SA 315:5).

One may not cover a very large barrel (whose diameter is close to a meter), as this resembles making an *ohel* if a *tefaḥ* of open space remains (*Shabbat* 139b; SA 315:13). However, if the cover of the barrel has a handle on it, then it is clear that this is simply the cover of a receptacle and not the roof of a tent, and thus one may place it on top of the barrel (SSK ch. 24 n. 72). One may overturn a large pot and use it to cover

4. According to Rabbeinu Tam, Rosh, *Smak*, and *Hagahot Maimoniyot*, if the *meḥitzot* (that is, legs that are more than a *tefaḥ* wide) were set up before Shabbat, it is not forbidden to place the tabletop on them. If the legs were set up on Shabbat, then one may not place the tabletop on them even if the space underneath is not being used. However, according to Rashba, Ran, and *Magid Mishneh*, even when the legs are narrower than a *tefaḥ*, if the space underneath is needed then one may not place the tabletop on them. According to *Tosafot* (as quoted by Rashba) and Tur, two conditions must be met in order for the placement to be prohibited: 1) the *meḥitzot* must be put into place on Shabbat; and 2) the space underneath must serve a purpose. Since this law is rabbinic, SA 315:3 follows this lenient position. Therefore, if the legs are less than a *tefaḥ* wide, even if the space underneath it is used, for example, as a place for people to put their feet, one may set the table up in the usual way. Some, however, beautify Shabbat by changing the order of the setup even in this case, as explained in *Harḥavot*.

food and protect it from the sun or insects, because overturning a pot is not considered making an *ohel*. Similarly, one may overturn a recliner or couch even though space is created underneath it, because overturning furniture is not considered making an *ohel* (BHL 315:5, s.v. "kisei").

Many maintain that it is rabbinically forbidden to put on a hat with a hard brim a *tefaḥ* wide, because doing so is considered making a temporary *ohel*. This is despite the fact that one may use a hand fan to shield himself from the sun and hold a *talit* horizontally over one who is called up to the Torah in honor of his marriage. Nevertheless, a hat that remains on one's head without moving is more similar to a temporary *ohel* (*Shabbat* 138b; Rabbeinu Ḥananel; Rambam; SA 301:40). The custom, though, is to be lenient and to allow one to wear a black hat, since it is worn primarily for the sake of honor and not to provide shade. It is also possible that the brims of today's hats are not considered hard (MB 301:151). Alternatively, perhaps the custom relies on Rashi, who maintains that a hat is never comparable to an *ohel*; the only concern is that if one's hat is blown off, people might chase after it and end up carrying it.

The universal custom is to forbid using an umbrella on Shabbat because it resembles an *ohel* (see BHL 315:8, s.v. "tefaḥ"; SSK 24:15).

6. PERMITTED AND PROHIBITED IMPLEMENTS

Just as *Boneh* and *Soter* apply to building or demolishing a house, the ground, or an *ohel*, they also apply to building or demolishing an implement.[5] Therefore, one may not insert the handle of a hammer into

5. *Beitza* 22a states that "Beit Shammai maintains that *Boneh* and *Soter* apply to *kelim*, while Beit Hillel maintains that *Boneh* and *Soter* do not apply to *kelim*." The *halakha* follows Beit Hillel, as Rava rules in *Shabbat* 122b. However, we find in *Shabbat* 102b that according to Rav, one may not insert the wooden handle into the metal blade of a scythe as it constitutes *Boneh*. *Tosafot ad loc.* (s.v. "hai") explain that in a case of bona fide assembly, *Boneh* and *Soter* apply to implements as well. The statement that *Boneh* does not apply to implements refers to loose attachments, as I wrote in the main text. This is also the opinion of *Smag*, Rosh, and Tur. Ramban, Rashba, and Ritva (on *Shabbat* 102b) maintain that one may not build an implement in its entirety because of *Boneh*, but adding onto an implement is prohibited because of *Makeh Be-patish*. Rashi *Shabbat* 74b and *Yere'im* maintain that even creating an implement is prohibited on account of *Makeh Be-patish*, not *Boneh*. The practical significance of this halakhic

the hammer head or a broom handle into the broom shaft. A permanent insertion is prohibited by Torah law, while a temporary insertion is forbidden rabbinically. Similarly, it is prohibited by Torah law to put together a bed or chair using nails, screws, or glue, since such attachments are full and permanent. Fixing a chair leg or table leg that has fallen off is also forbidden, as is attaching or removing a rubber chair tip or table tip (a rubber protector that goes underneath a chair leg or table leg).

If there is a possibility that people will forget it is Shabbat and end up fixing the implement, the Sages forbid moving it. For example, if a leg falls off a chair or table, one may not move the item and prop it up on another piece of furniture, because someone might see it and decide to repair it. However, if the implement would be complicated to fix, or if it had already been used in this manner before Shabbat, there is no concern that he will forget and repair it on Shabbat, so it may be moved (SA 313:8; Rema 308:16; MB *ad loc.* 69; SSK 20:44).

One may use implements on Shabbat whose normal usage involves screwing or unscrewing. Thus, one may screw a lid on a jar, salt shaker, or pressure cooker, put on jewelry whose ends screw together, or look through binoculars that are focused by turning a knob. Since this is the normal way of using these devices, screwing and unscrewing them

---

disagreement is when it comes to *Soter*. If the prohibition is on account of *Makeh Be-patish*, then undoing one's actions is not prohibited by Torah law, as *Soter* is defined as undoing an act of *Boneh*. Therefore, if undoing what was done to an implement is necessary for Shabbat, according to Ramban and those who follow his approach one may do so, while according to Rashi and those who follow his approach it would even be permitted to take the entire implement apart. However, according to *Tosafot* and Rosh, this would be forbidden even for a Shabbat need. Only when dealing with a low-quality implement (such as a *mustekei* – a barrel made of an inferior material) would it be permissible to take it apart for a Shabbat need, as explained below in section 11. SA 314:1 rules in accordance with *Tosafot* and Rosh. However, in 314:7, in the context of asking a non-Jew to break a vessel for a Shabbat need, it is lenient in accordance with Rashi and those who follow him. The justification for this leniency is that two mitigating factors are involved: asking a non-Jew to do *melakha* on Shabbat (which is only a rabbinic prohibition) and a Shabbat need (for example, if the fruits in the vessel are otherwise inaccessible). See *Menuḥat Ahava* 3:23:32. Rambam (MT 10:13) follows *Tosafot*, maintaining that *Boneh* applies to implements. On the other hand, he permits breaking a barrel to get to the food inside it, even if the barrel is not considered a *mustekei* (MT 23:2). See *Kaf Ha-ḥayim* 314:5.

is not considered a *melakha*. However, one may not unscrew something if it unusual to do so. For example, one may not unscrew the knob of a pot cover (SHT 313:32; MA states that the prohibition is by Torah law, while *Taz* maintains that it is rabbinic).

Most *poskim* allow adjusting the height of a lectern ("*shtender*") by loosening a knob and tightening it at the desired height, as this is the normal usage and the lectern remains usable at every stage of the adjustment (*Orḥot Shabbat* 8:9 citing R. Shlomo Zalman Auerbach and R. Yosef Shalom Elyashiv; *Yalkut Yosef* 314:2).

One may adjust a baby carriage or stroller with hinges or latches from an upright position to a horizontal one and vice versa. However, if doing so involves removing screws that hold the seat in position and then screwing them back in, it is forbidden because it entails making a strong attachment that is adjusted only infrequently (SSK 28:50).

7. PERMISSIBLE ASSEMBLY AND DISASSEMBLY OF IMPLEMENTS

There is a difference between attaching things to a house and attaching things to an implement. One may not add anything to (or remove anything from) a house even if it is attached loosely, since the house is considered permanent. For example, one may not install a window on its hinges or remove it from its hinges. Although it is attached loosely and it is easy to make or break this attachment, it is forbidden because the window is part of the house. Note that if a wardrobe or free-standing closet has a volume of forty *se'ah* (three cubic *amot*, or just over ten cubic feet) it has the same status as a house. Thus, one may not connect anything to a large wardrobe, even loosely (Rema 314:1).

In contrast, devices, which are less permanent, may be assembled using temporary attachments that do not require craftsmanship or strength. Therefore, one may assemble and disassemble a portable cot of the type travelers use, which can be assembled and disassembled daily, and which is loosely attached (*Shabbat* 47a-b; SA 313:6). Similarly, one may remove the door of an implement that is easily assembled and disassembled and that turns easily on its hinges. Technically, one should be permitted to place this door on its hinges as well. However if the hinge is attached to the implement with nails or screws, the Sages forbid it out of concern lest one tighten the attachment and thereby transgress a Torah prohibition. Only if nothing can be tightened, such as if the hinge is part of the implement, may the door then be attached to the implement (*Shabbat* 122b; SA 308:9).

The general principle here is that if an implement is normally assembled with a firm attachment, the Sages forbid even attaching it loosely. They were concerned that one might forget and attach it firmly, thus transgressing a Torah prohibition. However, if an implement is assembled with temporary and easy attachments, there is no reason to fear that one will attach it firmly and thus transgress a Torah prohibition, and it may be assembled and disassembled. Therefore, one may extend a table by adding a leaf designed for this purpose, and one may remove a leaf as well, since the leaves are clearly temporary. Similarly, the feeding tray on a child's high chair, which is constantly attached and detached, may be used freely on Shabbat, since the attachment is loose.

Based on this, many maintain that the prohibitions of *Boneh* and *Soter* do not apply to building with interlocking toy bricks (like Lego) and the like, since the pieces are attached to each other temporarily and are designed to be disassembled (*Tzitz Eliezer* 13:31; *Yeḥaveh Da'at* 2:55; but SSK 16:19 is stringent).

Some Aḥaronim maintain that it is rabbinically forbidden to make paper airplanes or boats or to fold napkins into special shapes because this resembles *Boneh* (R. Shlomo Zalman Auerbach cited in SSK 11:41; 16:21). Others permit this on the basis that the prohibition of *Boneh* does not apply to things that are temporary and will soon be disassembled (*Rivevot Ephraim* 1:223:8 quoting R. Moshe Feinstein). One who is lenient has an opinion to rely on, and one who is stringent is commendable. Children may be lenient even *le-khatḥila* (see *Harḥavot*).

8. FIXING BROKEN IMPLEMENTS

Some items are sturdily assembled initially but loosen over time. If people are used to using these items in their loosened state, it is not prohibited to assemble or disassemble them. As noted, assembling implements loosely is not considered *Boneh*. Furthermore, since people are used to using them this way, we are not concerned that they will end up fixing them with nails or glue (see Rema 308:16; SA 313:6).

Thus, if a wheel falls off a baby's crib and people are comfortable using the crib after replacing the wheel loosely, it may be replaced. Similarly, rubber chair tips and table tips may be replaced if they are only loosely attached. This is also the case if the leg of a child's doll has come off: if the leg is attached to the doll tightly, it may not be snapped back into place, but if it is connected loosely, it may be replaced.

If a temple fell off a pair of glasses, it may not be screwed back into place, since generally it is screwed on tightly. One may not even attach it loosely, because one may forget and tighten it, thus transgressing a Torah prohibition. However, if the screw is lost, there is no longer a concern that anyone will tighten it. Thus, one may reattach the temple using a safety pin, as this is a weak attachment that is permitted for implements (*Shulḥan Shlomo* 314:11:2).

If a lens fell out of the glasses' frame and replacing it requires screwing it back in, it may not be replaced at all, even if the screw is left loose. This is because we are concerned that later on one will forget and tighten it. But if there is no screw, but rather the frame has expanded a bit so that the lens sometimes falls out, then the lens may be replaced in the frame. We are not concerned that one will permanently reattach it, as that would require expertise (*Menuḥat Ahava* 3:23:35; *Orḥot Shabbat* 8:49-50).

One may not straighten a spoon, knife, or glasses temple on Shabbat by hand, because this is considered *Makeh Be-patish* (MA 340:11; MB 509:1, 7; see *Harḥavot*).

The prohibition of *Boneh* does not apply to compressing a spring on a toy car so that the car will move forward. One may do so as long as the car does not make noise or light up (see SSK 16:14).

One may inflate an air mattress, air pillow, or rubber ball that had been previously inflated. Since this is permissible, it may be done in the usual fashion, using a manual pump. However, one may not inflate these items for the first time on Shabbat, because many *poskim* maintain that inflating them for the first time makes them into viable implements for the first time, which is prohibited. One may not blow up a balloon even if it had previously been inflated, lest one tie a knot at the bottom. However, if the balloon is sealed with a valve instead of a knot, and it had previously been inflated, it may be inflated on Shabbat (SSK 15:89; 16:7; 34:24).

9. CLEANING THE FLOOR AND MAKING REPAIRS

If the floor is dirty, and leaving it in such a state dishonors Shabbat, one may sweep the floor. A yard, though, may not be swept, because one may end up leveling the ground and thus transgressing *Boneh* (see section 2 above, n. 1).

In contrast, one may not wash the floor, since leaving the floor unwashed does not dishonor Shabbat as leaving it unswept does, and there is concern that one who washed an area with a hard floor will end up washing a dirt floor as well, which would involve leveling the ground and thus transgressing *Boneh* (SA 337:3; MB *ad loc.* 3). However, if water spilled on the floor, one may remove the water using a squeegee (SSK 23:7).

If a particular spot on the floor has become especially filthy, for example, if juice spilled on it, one may pour a bit of water on it and then either wipe it away with a squeegee or soak it up with something that would not normally be wrung out (R. Shlomo Zalman Auerbach cited in SSK ch. 23 n. 30; *Yalkut Yosef* 337:2). If the entire floor is filthy, one who is lenient and pours water on it and wipes it away with a squeegee has an opinion upon which to rely (*Or Le-Tziyon* 43:8).

If clumps of grass are blocking a drainage pipe, causing water to back up onto the roof and leak into the house, the Sages permit stepping on the clump to break up and remove the blockage. Normally, even fixing something with a *shinui* is rabbinically prohibited, but in this case, where otherwise a loss will be incurred, the Sages permit (*Ketubot* 60a; SA 336:9).

Based on this, some prohibit unclogging a sink using a plunger. They maintain that the Sages permit removing blockages only if a *shinui* is used, but using a plunger to break up a blockage is the normal way to deal with this problem. Thus it is forbidden by Torah law, and even in a time of need one may not be lenient (*Yabi'a Omer* 5:33; R. Yosef Shalom Elyashiv). In contrast, others permit this, maintaining that a blockage that can be broken up using a plunger is not a total blockage, and thus breaking it up is not considered a true repair. Furthermore, the improvement that is made is not to the pipe itself. Rather, one is simply dislodging the sludge that clogged it (*Minḥat Yitzḥak* 5:75; R. Shlomo Zalman Auerbach cited in SSK 12:18; *Menuḥat Ahava* 3:24:29). In practice, in a case of need, it is proper for two people to hold the plunger and unclog the drain together. This way, even according to the stringent opinion, the prohibition would only be rabbinic; and when in doubt about a rabbinic mitzva, the *halakha* follows the lenient position. (See above 9:3 and n. 1.)

All agree that one may not remove a blockage using professional equipment like a plumber's snake. It is also forbidden by Torah law to take apart the pipe under the sink in order to empty it of sludge and then reassemble it.

One may remove garbage that accumulates in the sink strainer. It is not necessary to do this with a *shinui*, because this action does not fix anything; one is simply removing filth (SA 308:34; SSK 12:17; below 22:12).

One may not oil a door's squeaky hinge or a baby carriage's wheel, as this is considered a repair (SSK 23:43; 28:53). If pantyhose start to tear (or "run"), one may not put nail polish or soap at the tip of the run to prevent further ripping, because this reinforces the hose (SSK 15:77).

10. *MEḤATEKH*

The *melakha* of *Meḥatekh* is instrumental in transforming raw material into houses, implements, clothing, etc. For example, if one wishes to make leather clothing, he must first cut the leather to the right size. If one wishes to build a house, he must cut the stones, metal, and panels to the right size. If one wishes to install a window, he must cut the glass to the right size. The general principle is that one who cuts something to a specific size on Shabbat transgresses the Torah prohibition of *Meḥatekh*. Similarly, it is forbidden by Torah law to cut off the soft part of feathers in order to make pillows and blankets, since one must cut precisely between the hard and soft sections (*Shabbat* 74b). This is the distinction between *Meḥatekh* and *Kore'a*: the primary purpose of *Kore'a* is to separate two distinct parts, whereas the primary purpose of *Meḥatekh* is to cut with precision in order to create something new.

The *melakha* of *Meḥatekh* does not apply to foods. Therefore one may cut a cake into equal-sized pieces. Similarly, one may cut grooves into an orange in order to peel it. Pills and suppositories used by sick people are also considered food for this purpose, and may be cut where scored (SSK 33:4).

Items that animals would consume are considered food and thus not subject to *Meḥatekh*. Therefore, one may use a knife to cut straw or hay to use as a toothpick. However, one may not fashion a toothpick from hard wood. Since it is inedible to animals, cutting it to size constitutes *Meḥatekh*: if by means of a tool, one violates a Torah prohibition, and if by hand, which is considered a *shinui*, a rabbinic prohibition (*Beitza* 33a-b; MT 11:7; SA 322:4; MB 322:13, 18).

One may take fragrant branches of hard wood that were harvested before Shabbat and trim or rub them so that their aroma spreads. One may also break them into smaller pieces so that more people can smell them. Even though the branches are hard and animals would not eat them, one may break them, since the size of the pieces does not matter. One may only do so on condition that they are broken by hand. If he uses a tool, we are concerned that he will forget and fashion a toothpick, thus transgressing Torah law (*Beitza, loc. cit.*; SA 322:5; MB *ad loc.* 17-18; Rema 336:8).

11. OPENING CANS

One may open cans on Shabbat in order to eat the food inside them. Since cans are disposable and meant for single use, they are not considered true receptacles and are more akin to shells that are broken to get at the nut within.

Similarly, we read in the Mishna: "One may break a barrel in order to eat the dried figs inside it, as long as he does not intend to create a receptacle" (*Shabbat* 146a). Many explain that this *mishna* refers to a *mustekei*, an inferior sort of barrel meant for a single use. Because the barrel was unimportant, it was secondary to the food inside it, just as a nutshell is secondary to the nut inside it. Thus, one may break the barrel in order to eat its figs. They would not break the barrel in a way that scatters the figs; rather they would break off the top, and the figs would remain within for several days, until they were all eaten. The Sages did make one condition: "As long as he does not intend to create a receptacle." If one makes a neat opening and plans to reuse the barrel to store other things, then he is truly creating a receptacle when he opens it, and is thus transgressing (SA 314:1).

The same applies to cans. One may open them on Shabbat if one plans to eat their contents, even if it will take several days to finish the food. Once the food is finished, the can is thrown out; therefore it is considered unimportant and may be opened on Shabbat. However, one who intends to reuse the can for other items may not open the can on Shabbat, since he is creating an opening and rendering it usable, which amounts to creating a receptacle.

Some are stringent and do not open cans on Shabbat even when they intend to throw them out. Since the can is in fact capable of storing additional items, creating an opening for it essentially makes it into a receptacle (*Ḥazon Ish* 51:11). However, in practice the *halakha* follows the lenient position. Since we are dealing with cans and containers that are designed to be disposable, it is not forbidden to open them. Those who wish to be stringent should open cans before Shabbat. If they need to open a can on Shabbat, they should immediately empty it of its contents.[6]

6. Along the same lines as the dispensation quoted in the *mishna* above, a *beraita* cites R. Shimon b. Gamliel as stating: "One may bring a barrel of wine and chop off the top with a sword" (*Shabbat* 146a). This is because the person does not intend to make a neat opening. He simply wants to get to the wine. This is the ruling of SA 314:1 and 314:6. However, Rishonim disagree regarding the type of barrel to which the dispensation applies. *Tosafot* and Rosh understand that the dispensation refers to a *mustekei* barrel, which broke and was then put back together using tar. In contrast, Ran maintains that even a high-quality barrel may be broken in order to reach the food inside it. This would also seem to be the opinion of Rambam (MT 23:2). SA 314:1 is stringent like *Tosafot* and Rosh. In any event, even according to the more stringent opinion, today's cans would not be considered better than the *mustekei* barrels of the Talmud, which were meant to be used only once. For example, the *mustekei* barrel that was broken open could not be reused. In order to store dried figs or wine in the barrel, its top would have to be reattached.

   Ḥazon Ish 51:11 is concerned that a can becomes a receptacle upon being opened. If so, opening it is not breaking it but rather creating a receptacle (*kli*), because it can now be used repeatedly. However, many maintain that the can was already a *kli* prior to being opened, as in fact it preserved the food within it (*Tehila Le-David* 314:12). Opening it thus destroys it, as it can no longer be used. Even if, 60 years ago, many people used cans to store nails and the like, today almost no one does this (*Or Le-Tziyon* 1:24). Those who are lenient here include R. Shlomo Zalman Auerbach (SSK 9:3 and *Shulḥan Shlomo* 314:5); *Minḥat Yitzḥak* 4:82; R. Ovadia Yosef (*Halikhot Olam* vol. 4, p. 250); and R. Mordechai Eliyahu. However, in order to avoid the problem raised by *Ḥazon Ish* that one might be creating a receptacle, some suggest puncturing the bottom of a can before opening it. Then, when it is opened, it does not become a receptacle because there is a hole in the bottom (SSK 9:3). On the other hand, many who follow *Ḥazon Ish* feel that one may not even make this first hole (*Minḥat Ish* 17:3).

12. OPENING BAGS AND WRAPPERS

Many dairy products are sold in plastic containers. One may peel the cover of such a plastic container. Similarly, packages of wafers and chocolate bars may be opened. Since the wrapper is meant to be disposable, it is secondary to the food inside it, just as an orange peel is secondary to the orange and may be removed in order to eat the orange.

One may make a hole in the top of a bag of milk or juice in order to pour out the liquid, open the top of a bag of sugar that is glued shut, and rip open bags of candies or other foods.

Similarly, we find that the Sages permitted cutting open *ḥotalot* (palm leaves used to protect unripe dates) on Shabbat. They permitted this because these leaves lacked importance, as they were considered entirely secondary to the dates inside them, similar to an orange peel. (*Shabbat* 146a; *Kol Bo*; SA 314:8).

Some are stringent and do not open bags or packages if the food will remain inside for a while, as is the case with a bag of sugar. They maintain that one who makes a neat opening is not ruining the bag, but rather is creating a receptacle (*Ḥazon Ish* 51:10). According to this approach, the only way to open such bags is to tear them apart entirely and transfer their contents to a different container.

In practice the *halakha* follows the lenient position, because these bags have no importance and are thrown out after the food they contain is finished. Therefore, one may open them in whatever way enables easy removal of their contents, and he may use them until the food inside is used up.[7]

Additionally, those who feel one may open a can should not make the hole because it is a destructive act, which is rabbinically forbidden. Moreover, sometimes puncturing the can may cause a violation of *Borer*. Thus, it is preferable to open a can in the normal way. One who wishes to comply with the stringent opinion as well should open cans before Shabbat, or at least empty them out immediately after opening them.

7. The dispensation to tear *ḥotalot* (*Shabbat* 146a) is not limited, so even if the opening allows the dates to be removed easily, there is no prohibition. Even in the case of a *mustekei* barrel (*Shabbat* 146a; *Beitza* 33b), one may make an opening through which the contents can be removed over the course of a few days, on condition that there is no possibility that it is a neat opening, which would allow the barrel to be used repeatedly. Therefore, the *mishna* in *Shabbat* allows making an opening in the top of a barrel even if it is made to pour out wine. Only if the hole is made in the side of the barrel,

It should also be mentioned that when opening these bags, one should try not to tear any letters. However, if necessary, one may open the bag even if it is clear that doing so will tear letters (as explained below, 18:3).

Similarly, one may open packages that contain items that are necessary for Shabbat, such as tissues and diapers. It is proper to open them more messily than one would during the week. Those who follow the stringent opinion would need to destroy the packaging so that it can no longer hold its original contents. The *halakha* is in accordance with those who are lenient.[8]

---

where it is clear that the opening is meant to be used multiple times, is it forbidden (*Shabbat* 146a). Indeed, this is the ruling of SA 314:6. The reasoning behind all these permissive rulings is that since we are dealing with packaging that is meant to be used only once, the container is secondary to the food within it. Thus, it is comparable to the peel of a fruit, which may be cut up and removed with no limitations. Even when the package is large and it will take days to finish up what is inside, as is the case with a milk carton or a bag of sugar, there is no prohibition, as the Sages permitted opening a wine barrel or *ḥotalot* even though they were not immediately emptied out. (This is also implied in *m. Kelim* 16:5, according to the explanation of Rash.) It is only if a neat hole is made in the package, in order to allow multiple uses after the current contents of the package are finished, that there is a prohibition. In contrast, when dealing with containers of milk, packages of sugar, and the like, it would never dawn on anyone to reuse them, so there is no issue of *Boneh* or *Kore'a* when opening them. Those who are stringent maintain that the dispensation to make an opening is limited to something that is not part of the packaging itself but only adheres to it, like the lid of a barrel; but if one makes a neat opening in the package itself to pour the milk or measure out the sugar, it is like making a receptacle. However, the prohibition is only rabbinic, since the opening only serves for the contents' removal, not their reinsertion (*Ḥazon Ish* 51:10; see *Orḥot Shabbat* 12:6). They are also concerned about *Kore'a* when opening a bag of sugar, since many maintain that tearing is prohibited if it serves a constructive purpose. However, we have already seen that the law pertaining to a package of food is the same as that of *ḥotalot,* where the prohibition of *Kore'a* is completely irrelevant. Some of the lenient opinions concede that ideally one should comply with the stringent position and open packages before Shabbat. If it is necessary to open a bag of milk on Shabbat, *le-khatḥila* it is better to make a smaller opening than one normally would during the week or to tear the plastic with one's teeth, so that it is clear that one does not mean to make a neat opening. This way, even some of the stringent opinions would concede that it is permissible.

8. The law of opening packages of clothing and the like is the same as that of packages of food (R. Shlomo Zalman Auerbach, *Shulḥan Shlomo* 314:7:6). Just as one may

13. OPENING BOTTLES

Poskim disagree about whether one may open a wine bottle that has a metal screw cap. Some prohibit opening it, maintaining that before the bottle is opened, the cap is simply a cover, but after it is opened and separated from the little metal rim that is left behind on the bottle, it becomes an implement, because it has become a screw cap that aids in opening and closing the bottle (R. Shlomo Zalman Auerbach).

However, most *poskim* are not concerned about opening such a cap. They maintain that even before it is opened it is already considered a bottle cap. Opening it does not create a new entity. Separating the metal rim from the cap is comparable to cracking open a nutshell in order to eat the nut. Additionally, the one who opens the bottle has no intention of making an implement; he just wants to open the bottle. Even though it happens to be that a screw cap is created, there is no prohibition.

Although one who wishes may be lenient may do so, and there are many who are lenient in practice, *le-khatḥila* it is preferable to defer to the stringent opinion and open such a bottle before Shabbat. An additional solution is to keep around old bottle caps and then immediately throw out the new cap after opening a bottle on Shabbat. Since in this case there is no intention to use the bottle cap that was opened on Shabbat, even those who are stringent would concede that one may open it.

If no old bottle cap is available and a bottle was not opened before Shabbat, another solution for those who are stringent is to puncture the bottle cap before opening it. This effectively ruins the bottle cap

---

use packages of food until their contents have been finished, so too when opening packages of tissues or diapers he may use the packages until their contents have been finished. Those who are stringent require destroying the packaging entirely (*Minḥat Ish* 17:22; *Orḥot Shabbat* 12:23). According to *Yalkut Yosef* 314 n. 22, one should not rip the wrapping paper off a book or picture, because those who are lenient only permit tearing a package when the item is needed for Shabbat, and that is not the case here. It would seem in practice that one may do so if there is a need. However, MB 340:41 and BHL s.v. "ha-niyar" prohibit opening a letter even if there is a great need. On the other hand, Maharil, MA 519:4, and *Taz ad loc.* 5 permit it. Since the prohibition is rabbinic and there is a need, one may be lenient.

so that after it is opened it is not considered an implement (SSK 9:18). According to those who are lenient, it is preferable to open the cap without puncturing it.

Even most of those who are stringent regarding a metal bottle cap maintain that a plastic cap may be opened, as this is considered a bottle cap even before it is opened. Thus, opening a plastic bottle cap does not make it an implement (SSK 9:21). This is the custom. One may also use a corkscrew to remove a cork on Shabbat.[9]

---

9. The stringent opinion of R. Shlomo Zalman Auerbach regarding the removal of metal bottle caps is quoted in *Shulḥan Shlomo* (314:9:4-5). It is also recorded in SSK 9:18 and *Orḥot Shabbat* 12:17. *Responsa Devar Yehoshua* 2:45 disagrees with R. Shlomo Zalman Auerbach, based on *Magid Mishneh* 12:2, which explains that as long as one does not intend to create an implement, we do not consider it a *psik reisha*. Therefore, one may pour a large quantity of cold water into a very hot kettle. Since he does not intend to temper the kettle and thus apply one of the final stages of the metal forging process, it is not prohibited even though in fact he is doing so. MA 318:36, *Bi'ur Ha-Gra* 314:11, and MB 318:80 follow this position. Here too, one's intention is to open the bottle, not to produce a bottle cap. R. Shlomo Zalman Auerbach disagrees with this position, maintaining that even though one's primary intention is to open the bottle, he also wishes to produce a bottle cap. However, many believe that the bottle cap was considered functional even before the bottle is opened, but could not be used in practice because it was attached to the bottle by the metal rim. This is the approach of *Tzitz Eliezer* 14:45:1, *Yeḥaveh Da'at* 2:42, and *Or Le-Tziyon* 2:27:8; R. Mordechai Eliyahu ruled this way as well. If one intends to throw away the bottle cap, R. Shlomo Zalman Auerbach agrees that one may open the bottle (as explained by *Devar Yehoshua ad loc.*). If one needs the cap, R. Shlomo Zalman Auerbach allows him to puncture it and then open it, because by doing so he renders it less functional as a bottle cap. However, according to those who are lenient, since it is not necessary to puncture the cap, it is questionable whether one may do so. If it is considered an implement even before it is opened, it is rabbinically prohibited to destroy it. If it is comparable to a *mustekei*, it might be permitted to destroy it (even if it is not necessary). Those who take into account the opinion of R. Auerbach and his followers do so in an attempt to avoid a possible Torah prohibition.

According to R. Shlomo Zalman Auerbach, one may remove the ring that remains on a metal or plastic bottle cap, since the cap is already functional without it. Others forbid this on account of *Makeh Be-patish*. R. Yosef Shalom Elyashiv maintains that this is forbidden because of *Meḥatekh* (*Orḥot Shabbat* 12:19-20). It would seem that even those who prohibit this would agree that the prohibition is rabbinic.

14. OPENING SODA CANS AND SEPARATING ATTACHED PLASTIC CONTAINERS

Some forbid opening a pop-top can on Shabbat. They are concerned that this action may constitute *Boneh,* because it creates a neat opening that allows one to drink. They are also concerned that one may be transgressing *Meḥatekh,* because the tab is pre-scored and produces a very precise opening.

However, many permit this, maintaining that because the can is meant to be disposable, opening the top does not create a receptacle. Rather, it is comparable to breaking a barrel in order to remove the wine inside it. *Meḥatekh* is also not an issue, because that applies only when material must be cut to an exact size. Since it does not matter where a cut is made on the can, and the only goal is to create an opening for drinking, the can may be opened in the most convenient way possible – by lifting the tab.

One may be lenient if he wishes. If one wishes to be stringent, he should not drink from the opening formed by popping the top, but rather should pour the drink from the can into his cup. This makes it clear that he is not interested in the neat opening of the can. If one wishes to be more stringent, he should be careful to lift the tab only slightly, less than he would on a weekday. This way the act of cutting is not completed, and the opening is not as good as it is usually.[10]

There is another case that is subject to debate. Many dairy products (yogurts, puddings, and the like) come in containers that are loosely connected to each other. May one separate them by applying light pressure to that connection?

Some maintain that breaking the containers apart along score lines that are made for this purpose is a violation of the Torah prohibition

---

10. *Orḥot Shabbat* 11:43 and 12:5 cite R. Yosef Shalom Elyashiv as forbidding opening a pop-top can in the normal manner and R. Shlomo Zalman Auerbach as permitting this. R. Meir Mazuz and *Menuḥat Ahava* 3:24:5 permit this on condition that one pours the drink into the cup. This approach is also recorded in *Eshmera Shabbat* 1:1:17. *Or Le-Tziyon* 2:27:6 permits this on condition that the pop top is not opened entirely, so that the can will not be easily usable. Accordingly, even those who are stringent would concede that a complete *melakha* was not performed. *Yalkut Yosef* 314:23 states in the name of R. Ovadia Yosef that technically one may open a pop top, but it is proper to be stringent and not open it entirely.

of *Meḥatekh*. They are also concerned that this might be *Makeh Be-patish*, since separating the containers makes them usable.

Others are lenient, maintaining that cutting is forbidden only when it is precise, and here the goal is simply to separate the containers from one another. No one cares exactly how precise the cut is. Furthermore, it is not *Makeh Be-patish*, since the containers were completely ready for use even beforehand. Separating them simply removes an external impediment.

In practice, one who wishes to be lenient has an opinion to rely upon, and one who chooses to be stringent should be commended. It is proper to separate such containers before Shabbat.[11]

---

11. Included among the permissive *poskim* are: R. Shlomo Zalman Auerbach (*Shulḥan Shlomo* 314:13:3); *Or Le-Tziyon* 2:27, n. 7; *Halikhot Olam* vol. 4, p. 254; and *Binyan Shabbat* 11:3. Included among the stringent *poskim* are: R. Yosef Shalom Elyashiv (quoted in *Orḥot Shabbat* ch. 12 n. 22); *Ḥut Shani* vol. 1, pp. 128-129; R. Mordechai Eliyahu; and *Menuḥat Ahava* 3:16:14. Even though some state that this is a Torah prohibition, it seems that Rambam (MT Laws of Yom Tov 4:8) maintains that if there is a prohibition at all, it is only rabbinic. Therefore, I wrote in the main text that one who wishes to be lenient has an opinion to rely upon.

There is a debate about tearing open small sugar packets that are often perforated to facilitate tearing them. According to R. Shlomo Zalman Auerbach, one may tear along the dotted lines, because no one cares exactly where the cut is; the point of the perforation is to make it easier to tear open. R. Yosef Shalom Elyashiv, however, maintains that the prohibition of *Meḥatekh* applies because one is cutting precisely. Therefore, the packet must be torn at a different place (*Orḥot Shabbat* 11:41).

Chapter Sixteen

Mav'ir and *Mekhabeh*

1. THE *MELAKHA* OF *HAV'ARA*

The Torah states: "But the seventh day is Shabbat of the Lord your God; you shall not do any *melakha*" (Shemot 20:9). The Sages explain that the intent of this verse is to forbid all 39 *melakhot* that were instrumental in erecting the *Mishkan*. One of these *melakhot* is *Hav'ara* (kindling a fire), which was necessary to prepare dyes for the *Mishkan*'s curtains. Nevertheless, the Torah explicitly mentions the prohibition of *Hav'ara*: "You shall kindle no fire throughout your settlements on Shabbat" (Shemot 35:3). The Sages ask why it was necessary for the Torah to single out *Hav'ara*. R. Natan explains that the Torah was using one *melakha* to serve as an example, to teach us that while all 39 prohibited *melakhot* are derived from one verse ("You shall not do any *melakha*"), nevertheless each and every *melakha* is an independent prohibition. Therefore, if one unknowingly performs multiple *melakhot*, he must bring a sin offering for each one of them (*Shabbat* 70a).

The awesome power of fire allows man to rule over the forces of nature and harness them in his service. Through the use of fire, people created metal tools, improved food, and later created powerful machines. Perhaps this is why *Hav'ara* was chosen out of all the *melakhot* to express man's tremendous ability to improve the world. However, on Shabbat every Jew must rest and rise above all creative activity. We must remember our Creator who took us out of Egypt, and we must enjoy Shabbat via Torah study and festive meals.

At first glance, there is a basic question about the *melakha* of *Hav'ara*. We have a ruling: "All destructive acts are exempt [by Torah law, but liable rabbinically]" (*Shabbat* 105b). Therefore, if one tore an item of clothing or broke a utensil, he is not obligated to bring a sin offering. To be sure, he transgresses rabbinically, but not by Torah law. In light of this, and given that burning an item generally ruins it, why is lighting a fire on Shabbat considered a transgression of a Torah prohibition? The answer is that any time the positive elements provided by the fire (heating or lighting one's home) outweigh the loss of the burned item, it is classified as a constructive rather than a destructive act (MT 12:1; see *Kesef Mishneh*).

2. THE LAWS OF *HAV'ARA*

One who lights a fire of any size that meets some need violates a Torah prohibition. It makes no difference whether he starts the fire by rubbing stones together, using a magnifying glass to focus the sun's rays on straw, lighting a match, or turning on the electricity. It also does not matter if the fire is fueled by oil, kerosene, or electricity. Anytime one intends to start a fire and succeeds in doing so, he transgresses a Torah prohibition.

However, one who merely causes sparks to be released does not violate Torah law. Furthermore, if the sparks were released unintentionally, there is no prohibition at all. Therefore, one may wear woolen or synthetic clothes, even though sometimes sparks are released when putting them on or taking them off. Since these sparks are released unintentionally and to no purpose, there is no prohibition (SSK 15:76; *Yeḥaveh Da'at* 2:46).

Just as it is prohibited by Torah law to kindle a new fire, it is also prohibited by Torah law to increase a pre-existing flame. The law on Yom Tov is different; while one may not kindle a new fire then either, one may turn up an existing flame. On Shabbat, however, one may not even raise a flame. For example, one may not increase the flame on a gas burner by turning the knob controlling the gas flow. Likewise, one may not increase the flow of kerosene to a heater in order to raise the flame or add oil to a burning lamp on Shabbat (*Beitza* 22a).

Similarly, one may not stoke coals, since this intensifies the fire (*Kereitot* 20a). Likewise, one may not open the door of a wood-fired oven because doing so allows air to enter the oven and fan the embers, thus increasing the fire (MB 259:21). If the oven door is already open, or there is a fire in an enclosed area (such as a fireplace), one may not open a window or door facing the fire, because a strong wind may enter and fan the flames. If there is no breeze, one may open the door or window (SA 277:2).

While an oil lamp is on a table, one must try to avoid shaking the table, because the oil may move closer to the wick and increase the flame, a violation of *Hav'ara*. However, if it is a wax candle on the table, or if the oil lamp has a floating wick, he does not need to worry that shaking the table will cause the flame to increase (MB 277:18).

3. READING BY CANDLELIGHT

The Sages ordained that one may not read by the light of an oil lamp on Shabbat, lest the flame become dim and the reader absent-mindedly tip the lamp so that more oil reaches the wick, thus transgressing the Torah prohibition of *Hav'ara*. To be sure, the Sages also ordained the kindling of Shabbat lamps, but this serves a different purpose. Shabbat candles are meant to provide light for the meal, not for careful examination of texts, and to allow one to walk around in his home without bumping into furniture. In contrast, the Sages forbade doing things that require careful examination by lamplight, out of concern that in such a case one might end up tipping the lamp in order to see better. One who wishes to study by the light of an oil lamp should ask a friend to keep him company, to ensure that he will not tilt it. Alternatively, he may learn together with a friend so that they can look out for each other (*Shabbat* 11a; SA 275:1-3).

Many *poskim* maintain that a lone individual may read by the light of a wax or paraffin candle because there is no concern that he will tilt the candle. Unlike an oil lamp, where the point of tilting is to move oil up the wick to the flame, the wax in a candle is attached to the wick and already close to the flame, so tilting would serve no purpose. Similarly, there is no concern that one might come to adjust the wick, since candles burn well on their own, and there is no need to adjust them at all once they are lit (MB 275:4; *Kaf Ha-ḥayim* 275:11).

An individual may study by the light of an electric lamp, even if only one of two bulbs in the lamp is turned on, and even when the intensity of the light can be adjusted by means of a dimmer; the ordinance regarding oil lamps was because of concern that if the light grew dim, one might tilt the lamp to restore the light. There was no concern that one might light an additional lamp or add oil to an existing one. Since electric lights do not grow dim, we are not concerned that one might turn on an additional light or turn up an existing one. Nevertheless, *le-khatḥila* it is advisable to cover the dimmer knob with a note that says "Shabbat" so that no one will accidentally adjust the light (SSK 13:37; *Yeḥaveh Da'at* 6:20).

4. SHABBAT CANDLES

While a candle is burning at home, one must be careful not to open a window or door facing it, as the wind may blow out the flame. Even if the wind outside is currently too weak to put out a candle, one still may not open a window, since it might happen that at the very moment when the window is opened, the wind will become stronger and blow out the candle. If this happens, it would mean that the act of opening the window blew out the candle. When there is no wind whatsoever, some permit opening the window, while others forbid it. In a case of necessity, such as when it is hot inside the room, one may follow the lenient position, and the window may be opened (MB 277:3).

One may open a window or door if even a strong wind would be unable to extinguish the candle; for example, if the candle is at a great distance from the window or door, or if the window is at such an angle that very little wind comes through it. Even if the wind is likely to affect the flame and cause it to flicker, as long as it is not powerful enough to blow it out, one may open the door or window (SA 277:1; *Menuḥat Ahava* 3:26 n. 6).

If Shabbat candles were lit in front of an open window and then the wind started blowing, the window may be closed in order to protect the flame. By closing the window, one is not acting directly on the flame itself; one is merely preventing the wind from blowing it out (Rema 277:1).

Similarly, one may close a door in a place where a fire is burning (such as a room with a fireplace), even if the wind coming in is blowing on the coals and fanning the flame, and closing the door will weaken the fire. Closing the door is not considered an act of extinguishing, since it merely prevents more wind from entering and feeding the flame (SA 277:2). In contrast, if the fire is fueled by gas or kerosene, one may not turn down the flow of the fuel. This truly qualifies as extinguishing, since one is acting directly on the fuel itself (SA 265:1).[1]

5. THE *MELAKHA* OF *MEKHABEH* AND THE MEANING OF *MELAKHA SHE-EINA TZERIKHA LE-GUFAH*

Extinguishing a fire in order to produce charcoal is one of the 39 *melakhot* prohibited on Shabbat. In the *Mishkan* they would turn wood into charcoal by setting fire to wood and then extinguishing it. They would then use this charcoal to build a steady and long-lasting fire for preparing the dyes used to color the curtains in the *Mishkan*. Similarly, if one extinguishes the flame of a candle so that its wick will light more easily later on, he transgresses a Torah prohibition.

---

1. *Beitza* 22a states: "One who adds oil to a lamp is liable on account of *Mav'ir*, and one who takes some away is liable on account of *Mekhabeh*." According to *Tosafot*, the reason one is liable for removing oil is that when he does this, the flame is immediately weakened. In contrast, if adding or removing oil has an effect only after a while, this is considered *grama*; one is not extinguishing a flame but only causing a flame to be extinguished indirectly. However, according to Rosh (*Beitza* 2:17), even if adding or removing oil does not have an immediate impact, since ultimately it will cause the lamp to stay lit for a longer or shorter amount of time, it is considered *Mav'ir* and *Mekhabeh* by Torah law. In his opinion, *grama* only applies in a case where the action is not done directly to the item in question. An example of this would be filling pitchers with water that will burst when a fire reaches them, thereby releasing the water and extinguishing the fire. However, in our case, one is acting on the fuel itself, directly changing the amount of time the fire will stay lit. It follows that if one adds kerosene to an oven or oil to a lamp, and the strength of the fire immediately increases, all agree that he has transgressed a Torah prohibition. However, if the fire does not show the effect of his actions immediately, but will ultimately stay lit for longer, according to Rosh this is prohibited by Torah law, whereas according to *Tosafot* the prohibition is rabbinic.

What about one who extinguishes a fire not because he wants the charcoal, but because he wants to conserve fuel, or because the light produced by the flame is bothering him? In other words, he is not essentially interested in putting out the fire; he simply does not want the candle to keep burning. The Tanna'im disagree about this. According to R. Shimon, since this is a *melakha she-eina tzerikha le-gufah* (a *melakha* that is not needed for its own sake) it is only prohibited rabbinically. However, according to R. Yehuda, even if one's objective is not the performance of the *melakha* itself, since he does in fact intend to extinguish the flame, he has performed a *melakha* and violated Torah law (*Shabbat* 31b and 93b).

Practically speaking, Rambam maintains that a *melakha she-eina tzerikha le-gufah* is prohibited by Torah law (MT 1:7), while according to most Rishonim it is rabbinically prohibited (R. Hai Gaon, Rabbeinu Ḥananel, *Ha-ma'or*, Ramban, and others; see also SA 334:27 and MB *ad loc.* 85). Since the only difference between a *melakha she-eina tzerikha le-gufah* and a regular *melakha* is the intention behind it, performing a *melakha she-eina tzerikha le-gufah* is considered more severe than violating a standard rabbinic prohibition. (See above 9:6.)

6. FIRE THAT CAUSES PROPERTY DAMAGE

If a fire breaks out on Shabbat, the first question that must be addressed is whether it presents a danger to human life. If it does, there is a mitzva to do whatever is necessary to extinguish it. However, if it is clear that there is no danger to human life, then even if the fire may cause extensive property damage, as is the case when an entire house goes up in flames, one may not put it out, because monetary loss does not override Shabbat.

Furthermore, the Sages prohibited moving items from a burning house to the street or courtyard even when there is an *eruv*. Their concern was that people might be so panicked about saving their property that they may either put out the fire or carry objects from a private domain to a public domain, thereby violating the *melakha* of *Hotza'ah*. Only food, clothing, and receptacles/implements needed for that Shabbat may be removed from a burning home (assuming it is within the *eruv*). If there is a large receptacle in the home, one may fill it with food even if it is more than will be needed for that Shabbat, as long as it can be carried out of the home in one trip. The same principle applies to clothing: as long as one is wearing them as he leaves the house, he may save many items of clothing, even more than are necessary for that Shabbat. This prohibition only applies to moving things into a shared courtyard; but one may salvage any quantity of food and non-*muktzeh* objects into a private yard where an *eruv* is not required, or into another apartment in the same building where there is an *eruv* (SA 334:11, MB *ad loc.* 28).[2]

2. According to Rambam and those who follow his approach, who maintain that performing a *melakha she-eina tzerikha le-gufah* is prohibited by Torah law, it is clear that there is no way to permit putting out a fire to save one's possessions. It is also obvious why the Sages ordained that one may not save more than what is necessary for Shabbat. However, according to most *poskim*, who maintain that a *melakha she-eina tzerikha le-gufah* is only rabbinically prohibited, why does this rabbinic prohibition apply even in a case where following it would lead to a massive loss? After all, the Sages permitted stamping on the grass clogging up a pipe in order to prevent a loss (*Ketubot* 60a; SA 336:9). Even though many maintain that fixing the pipe would be prohibited by Torah law, the Sages permitted fixing it with a *shinui* to prevent a loss (*Livyat Ḥen* §103). Similarly, they were lenient in allowing one to carry valuable possessions into a public thoroughfare with a *shinui* to prevent their possible theft (Rema 301:33). Some even permit moving *muktzeh* objects in order to save possessions from fire or theft (SA 334:2). So why didn't the Sages allow one to put out a fire in order to save all of his possessions?

   It would seem that the answer is that, as Ran writes (on Rif, 61a, s.v. "u-vimkom"), a *melakha she-eina tzerikha le-gufah* is more severe than other rabbinic prohibitions. Ran suggests that since performing a *melakha she-eina tzerikha le-gufah* looks the same as performing an act prohibited by Torah law, and only the intent differs, the Sages were concerned that people would be unable to distinguish between the two and would end up being lenient even with Torah prohibitions. Therefore, the Sages forbade putting out a fire even in the case of a *melakha she-eina tzerikha le-gufah*. A similar approach appears in *Ḥayei Adam* 46:1 and BHL §278 at the end of s.v. "mutar." (A parallel idea appears in the laws of *bein ha-shmashot*, as explained in MB 342:1.) It also may be that because having a fire in one's home can make one extremely distressed, one who is worried about his possessions might perform several *melakhot* in his distressed state. Because of this, the Sages felt a need to reinforce the observance of the *melakhot* and did not permit even rabbinic transgressions. They allowed rescuing possessions only under very limited circumstances, so as to eliminate the concern that it would cause people to transgress other prohibitions as well.

   R. Shlomo Zalman Auerbach, cited in SSK ch. 41 n. 8, wonders why we do not seem to be concerned about the emotional state of the homeowner and his family, who might lose their minds upon seeing their home and possessions going up in flames. In fact, it is possible for one to die or to go insane as a result of this kind of

Just as a homeowner may save items that he needs for Shabbat, he may also tell his neighbors that they can take whatever they need. Each neighbor can then take food for himself for Shabbat and put on as many items of clothing as he can. After Shabbat, the custom of the pious is to return the salvaged clothing and items to the original owner (SA 334:9; SSK 41:3-13).

The *poskim* disagree about whether one may salvage money and valuables that are not necessary for Shabbat from a burning building. One who is lenient has an opinion on which to rely. However, this is all on condition that he not transgress a Torah prohibition. If, in order to salvage his money, he would need to carry it from a private domain to a public domain, thus violating Torah law, he may not do so. However, he may carry the money out with a *shinui*, as this is only rabbinically prohibited (SA 334:2; *Taz*; see MB *ad loc.* 4-5, SHT *ad loc.* 3, and BHL s.v. "ve-yesh").

Residents of neighboring buildings may remove everything they own from their homes. As long as the fire has not yet spread to their homes, we can assume that they are not so panicked, and so we are not worried that they will end up putting out the fire (SA 334:1).

Although a Jew may not extinguish the fire, he may hint to a non-Jew to do so. For example, he may say: "Whoever extinguishes this fire will not lose out." Or he could call to the non-Jew urgently and tell him that a fire has broken out and that it is forbidden for a Jew to put it out. The non-Jew will then figure out on his own that the Jew wants him to put out the fire, and perhaps will even pay him for doing so (SA 334:26).

Similarly, one may indirectly cause the fire to go out, since according to Torah law it is only acting directly that is forbidden. Normally the Sages forbid causing *melakha* to be done indirectly, but in a case of loss, *grama* is permitted. Therefore, if one side of a cabinet catches fire, one may cover the other side with wet rags so that the fire will go out when it

---

trauma. Elsewhere in SSK (ch. 32 n. 83), R. Auerbach points out that some allow the transgression of Torah prohibitions to protect one's mental and emotional health. In practice it would seem that when there is a real possibility of a family member experiencing psychological trauma, the fire may be extinguished, but when there is no such concern, even if tremendous suffering is involved, one may not extinguish the fire.

reaches them. Similarly, one may place bags full of water on a spot where the fire has not yet reached, so that they will burst open and extinguish the fire when it reaches them (SA 334:22). One may also pour water on a spot that is not burning, as long as it is far enough away from the fire that the water will only reach the fire and begin extinguishing it after a while (See SA 334:24; SSK 41:16).

7. PUTTING OUT A FIRE WHEN THERE IS DANGER TO HUMAN LIFE

In a situation where human life might be endangered by a fire, it is a mitzva for anyone who can put it out to do so as soon as possible, since danger to human life overrides Shabbat. Even if the danger is uncertain, it is still a mitzva to put out the fire. For example, if a fire breaks out in a large building, even if it seems that all the residents managed to get out, one must put out the fire as long as there is a possibility that someone may still be inside. Even if the odds are that anyone left inside has already died, since there is still a chance that a rescue is possible, everything must be done to put out the fire (SA 329:3; below 27:1).

Everything necessary must be done as efficiently as possible on all fronts: Those able to rescue people from the fire should try to do so, and those able to extinguish or control the fire should try to do so with whatever means are at their disposal. At the same time, others should call the fire department. If an observer is uncertain whether the fire department has been called already, even if it seems likely that they have been, he too must call to make sure that they come, because the possibility of saving lives overrides Shabbat. At such a time one must not ask a rabbi what to do, but rather move as quickly as possible to help.

In practice, nowadays we treat any large fire that breaks out in a residential building as a life-threatening one that must be extinguished even on Shabbat. For example, if a fire breaks out in an apartment building, there is a concern that it may spread to additional apartments and there may not be time to evacuate the residents. Besides, when there is a large fire there is no time to check if there are apartments with babies or disabled people who cannot make their way out on their own. Additionally, some homes contain explosive gas canisters that endanger people outside the building, especially considering that fires often attract large numbers of gawkers. Sometimes it takes longer to clear people out of the area than to put out the fire. If the fire is near other homes, it might spread and endanger those residents. Sometimes a fire breaks out in a storage area containing chemicals whose poisonous fumes may endanger area residents.

R. Shlomo Goren ruled that if anti-Israel terrorists start a fire that will damage property, it may be extinguished on Shabbat even if there is no danger to life, because if we do not put it out, the terrorists will feel they have succeeded and will be motivated to undertake similar attacks that could endanger lives (this is based on SA 329:6 and R. Goren's expansion of the category of a "border town," which may be defended against even property damage on Shabbat, to all cities in Israel, where low-grade conflict can break out; see below 27:12).

8. PUTTING OUT A FIRE TO PREVENT PEOPLE FROM BEING INJURED

As we have seen (section 5), one who puts out a fire only transgresses rabbinically, according to most *poskim*. Only one who extinguishes a fire in order to produce charcoal is doing so *le-tzorekh gufo*. When one puts out a fire in order to prevent damage from occurring, he is not interested in the act of extinguishing, but in creating a situation in which the fire is gone. Accordingly, this is considered a *melakha she-eina tzerikha le-gufah*.

Therefore, even though the Sages insisted that one may not put out a fire in order to salvage property, they permitted extinguishing a fire that has the potential to cause mass injury. For example, if there is a burning ember in a public domain, where many people are liable to be harmed by it, one may remove it even though it is *muktzeh*. If it is impossible to move it, the Sages permitted extinguishing it in order to prevent harm to the public, even though there is no danger to human life. However, in Israel, one may not call the fire department, because their travel involves Torah prohibitions, and one may not violate Torah law in order to prevent possible harm that does not involve potential loss of life. In the Diaspora, where firefighters are non-Jews, one may call the fire department, as this only involves the violation of a rabbinic prohibition (SA 334:27; see below 27:16).

To summarize, we have discussed three situations in which one may put out a fire directly or indirectly:

1. In a situation of danger to human life, it is a mitzva to do everything possible to save lives.
2. In a situation where there is a danger of harm to the public, one may put out the fire (as the Sages did not apply rabbinic rules in such a case), but one still may not violate Torah prohibitions to do so.
3. In a situation where there is financial loss but no threat of physical harm to humans, one may not extinguish the fire. Nevertheless, one may do so via *grama*. One may also hint to a non-Jew to put out the fire.

Chapter Seventeen

Electricity and Electrical Appliances

1. TURNING ON ELECTRIC LIGHTS AND APPLIANCES

It is prohibited by Torah law to turn on an electric light bulb or activate an electric heating element, because when the bulb is turned on or a heating element activated, the filament incandesces (see above, 4:5 and n. 3, regarding fluorescent bulbs), and this is a form of *Hav'ara* prohibited by the Torah. While it is true that in the past, people did not generally produce heat or light by heating metal, we nevertheless find that heating metal for any purpose was prohibited by Torah law. Thus Rambam writes that if one heats metal with the intention of tempering it afterward by plunging it into cold water, he transgresses the Torah prohibition of *Mav'ir* (MT 12:1). Clearly, then, heating metal is forbidden by Torah law if it accomplishes some purpose.

Extinguishing a light bulb or heating element is only rabbinically prohibited. It is different from a normal act of *Mekhabeh*, whose purpose is to create charcoal (as explained above 16:5). In contrast, turning off an electrical appliance creates nothing, so its prohibition is rabbinic.

The Torah forbids performing prohibited *melakhot* by means of electrical appliances. Thus, activating an electric flour mill on Shabbat constitutes a violation of *Toḥen*, operating an electric mixer on Shabbat violates *Lash*, and so forth for all *melakhot*. Although the person is not manually grinding or kneading, since he presses the button or flips the switch to turn the appliance on, all *melakhot* performed by the appliance are viewed as *melakhot* performed by him (*Oraḥ Mishpat* §70; *Aḥiezer* 3:60).

Just as one may not turn on an electrical appliance by pressing a button, so too one may not activate something by remote control. Even though there is no direct contact between the finger pressing a button on the remote control and the appliance, since this is the normal way to turn on such appliances, it is forbidden just as manual activation is forbidden.

2. IS USING ELECTRICITY A TORAH PROHIBITION OR A RABBINIC PROHIBITION?

One may not activate electrical appliances and devices such as telephones, microphones, alarms, doorbells, fans, air conditioners, and computers on Shabbat. Even if these appliances do not contain an incandescent filament or heating element and do not perform any of the 39 *melakhot*, it is still forbidden to use them on Shabbat. Aḥaronim disagree, however, whether the prohibition is by Torah law or rabbinic.

Some maintain that using any electrical appliance violates the Torah prohibition of *Mav'ir*. They maintain that electricity has the same status as fire since, like fire, it has energy and power that can be harnessed. Rav Kook favors this position, arguing that the key aspect of fire is not its appearance, but rather its power to illuminate, heat, and provide power. Indeed, the Sages state that there are different types of fire (*Yoma* 21b), including some that do not burn and destroy. One example of this is the fire that Moshe saw at the burning bush (Rav Kook, *Oraḥ Mishpat* §71). R. Uziel agrees with this approach, adding that turning on electricity is also prohibited as a form of *Metaken Mana* since activating an electrical appliance renders it useful (*Mishpetei Uziel*, OḤ 2:36:2). *Ḥazon Ish* (OḤ 50:9) maintains that turning on an electrical appliance is prohibited on account of *Boneh*, because completing a circuit creates a *kli*: when electricity flows through a device, an electrical wire within comes to life and activates the device. Thus, one who completes a circuit builds an implement, and one who breaks a circuit demolishes it.

Many others maintain, however, that using electrical appliances that do not contain an incandescent filament and do not perform one of the 39 *melakhot* is only prohibited rabbinically, as it is considered a weekday activity. Additionally, some maintain that turning on appliances is prohibited because it is creating a new entity on Shabbat (*Molid*), as it creates a new electrical current in the wires (*Beit Yitzḥak*). No Torah prohibition is involved, because there is no "fire" in appliances without an incandescent filament. There is no problem of *Boneh*, because an electrical circuit cannot be considered a *kli*, that is, an implement or receptacle. This is the opinion of R. Shlomo Zalman Auerbach (*Minḥat Shlomo* 1:9-12) and R. Eliezer Waldenberg (*Tzitz Eliezer* 1:20:10).

In practice, *le-khatḥila* we defer to the opinion that using electricity is a Torah prohibition. In times of need, when there are additional reasons to be lenient, we rely upon those who believe that using electricity is only a rabbinic violation.[1]

---

1. According to Rav Kook, using electricity is prohibited on account of *Mav'ir*. Therefore, one may not speak into a microphone, as this increases the electric current. His responsa on the subject are not so well known, since *Responsa Oraḥ Mishpat*, in which they appear (§70-71) was printed in 1979, thirty years after the main debates among contemporary Aḥaronim. At the time, Ḥazon Ish was inclined to say that use of electricity is prohibited by Torah law on account of *Boneh*, but many disagreed with him, including R. Shlomo Zalman Auerbach and R. Eliezer Waldenberg. Nevertheless, other Aḥaronim share Rav Kook's opinion that the prohibition on electricity is due to *Mav'ir*. These include *Mishpetei Uziel*, OḤ 2:36:2; *Yaskil Avdi* 5:38; *Brit Olam, Ha-mav'ir Ve-hamekhabeh* 1; R. Yosef Messas's *Responsa Mayim Ḥayim*, OḤ §134. Also see the entry on "*ḥashmal*" in the *Encyclopedia Talmudit*, which focuses on the opinions that disagree with Ḥazon Ish and maintain that the prohibition is rabbinic. One should be aware that according to Ḥazon Ish, if an appliance is already on, increasing the current to amplify the power of the appliance is not prohibited by Torah law. However, according to Rav Kook, who believes using electricity is prohibited because of *Mav'ir*, increasing the current is prohibited by Torah law as well.

Many contemporary authorities accept the opinion of R. Shlomo Zalman Auerbach that there is no Torah prohibition involved in using electricity. However, *le-khatḥila* they still take into account the opinion that maintains it is prohibited by Torah law (see *Yabi'a Omer* 1:20; *Minḥat Yitzḥak* 2:112; and many additional works). *Igrot Moshe* (OḤ 3:42, 3:55, and 4:84) maintains that the status of the prohibition is unclear. In practice, although many state that in principle the prohibition on using electricity is rabbinic, in fact they relate to the prohibition of turning on electrical appliances as if it were prohibited by Torah law. Thus, even in cases of uncertainty and cases where electricity is required for the sake of a mitzva, to avoid substantial loss, or to help someone who is bothered by a minor illness, they are not lenient and prohibit using electricity via a non-Jew or when activated with a *shinui*, despite the fact that

3. ELECTRICAL APPLIANCES THAT PRODUCE SOUND (TELEPHONES AND MICROPHONES)

As we have seen, the prohibition on using electrical appliances on Shabbat includes microphones and telephones.

Even if a phone is in use before Shabbat, or if a microphone is turned on before Shabbat, one may not speak on the phone or use a microphone on Shabbat, because doing so increases the electric current running through it and violates a Torah or rabbinic prohibition. In addition, the Sages banned *hashma'at kol* (producing sound) with an object specifically designed for this purpose. Many maintain that one who speaks into a microphone transgresses this prohibition (based on Rema 338:1). Furthermore, using a microphone resembles a weekday activity. It also may seem to belittle Shabbat, as those who hear the amplified sound are likely to think that the microphone was activated on Shabbat (*Igrot Moshe*, OḤ 3:55).[2]

Nevertheless, one who is hard of hearing may use an electric hearing aid that rests on or inside the ear on Shabbat as long as it is turned on before Shabbat and he does not adjust the volume on Shabbat. When he wants to go to sleep, he should remove the device without shutting it off. In the morning, he may put it back in without turning it on. Although we stated that one may not use a microphone or telephone because speaking into it increases the electric current, this prohibition applies

---

each of these scenarios would constitute a *shvut di-shvut* (see above 9:11). Only in cases of true necessity do they take into account the opinion that the prohibition is rabbinic. Therefore, the only way these appliances can be used on Shabbat is if they are turned on before Shabbat. In times of true necessity they can be used through *grama* (above 9:9), meaning that one's actions will not directly or immediately cause the appliance to turn on. Examples of the permitted use of electricity on Shabbat include wearing a hearing aid (section 3 below) and adjusting the setting on a timer (as explained below in n. 6). For appliances that appear to work normally but have a built-in *grama* mechanism, see section 18 below. Regarding the use of computers, see below 18:1 and *Harḥavot*.

2. If a Jew in the United States who does not observe Shabbat calls a Jewish friend in Israel when Shabbat is over in Israel but while it is still Shabbat in the U.S., the latter may not speak with him, because he is benefiting from his friend's Shabbat desecration. However, a Jew in Israel may speak with a non-Jew who calls him when it is Shabbat in the U.S., since a non-Jew is not obligated to keep Shabbat (SSK 31:27).

only when someone speaks directly into them. However, when speaking normally, the activation of the device in the wearer's ear is secondary and therefore a form of *grama*, which is permitted when truly necessary. Furthermore, there is no problem of producing sound on Shabbat or belittling Shabbat since the sound is heard only by the wearer.[3]

Just as one may not turn on a microphone before Shabbat with the intention of using it on Shabbat, so is leaving on an intercom over Shabbat to hear the voices of people coming to visit, or to hear what is going on in the children's room. To be sure, if one simply speaks normally in the room and not directly into the intercom, the prohibition is less severe since it is then a case of *grama*. It is nevertheless prohibited, because it is a weekday activity, it belittles Shabbat, and it produces sound with an object designed for that purpose. However, if the intercom was accidentally left on over Shabbat, as long as one does not intend to use it he may speak in a normal fashion in the room with the intercom.[4]

---

3. There is no problem of *hashma'at kol* since the sound is only heard by the wearer of the device. The only problem is the electrical operations of the hearing aid. Indeed, some prohibit the use of hearing aids (*Dovev Meisharim, Levushei Yom Tov* §15; R. Yosef Shalom Elyashiv cited in *Orḥot Shabbat* 26:23). However, in practice many have permitted the hearing-impaired to use hearing aids, including *Igrot Moshe*, OḤ 4:85. Those who maintain that turning on an electrical appliance without an incandescent filament is rabbinically prohibited because it creates a new flow of electricity in the wires do not view increasing the current as a new creative act. At worst, it might be deemed a weekday activity, in which case one may be lenient in the case of a great need. Similarly, for those who believe that turning on an appliance is prohibited on account of *Boneh* or because it is creating a *kli*, there is no problem here; since the hearing aid is already on, increasing the current creates nothing new. Based on these rationales, the following authorities permit the use of a hearing aid: R. Shlomo Zalman Auerbach; *Tzitz Eliezer* 6:6; SSK 34:28; *Yabi'a Omer* 1:19:19; *Minḥat Yitzḥak* 2:17. See *Encyclopedia Talmudit* vol. 18, pp. 731-732. It is true that Rav Kook in *Oraḥ Mishpat* §71 prohibits speaking into a microphone, because the speech causes electric current to flow. He explains that this cannot be considered *grama* since the result is direct and immediate. It seems, though, that since the sound waves resulting from normal speech are only converted to electric current once they reach the hearing aid, this can be considered *ko'aḥ sheni* ("secondary power"), a form of *grama*, as explained in *San.* 77b and *Ḥullin* 16a. *Grama* is permitted under pressing circumstances, as explained in *Shabbat* 120a, SA 334:20, and Rema *ad loc.*; see above, 9:9.
4. One who uses a microphone fully intends to speak into it, and this is the normal way to amplify a voice, so it is not considered *grama*. In contrast, if one simply speaks

4. ELEVATORS

One may not operate an elevator on Shabbat. Pressing the elevator buttons involves Torah prohibitions or, minimally, rabbinic prohibitions. However, some "Shabbat elevators" are set to operate automatically, meaning that they are set before Shabbat to stop on every floor or every other floor, at which point the doors open on their own for a predetermined amount of time and then close on their own. The elevator then continues on its way. There is a difference of opinion among the *poskim* regarding these elevators.

Some prohibit using a Shabbat elevator, maintaining that using it is a weekday activity. Additionally, entering the elevator causes its motor to use more electricity when the elevator goes up and down (*Ḥelkat Yaakov*, OḤ §144; *Minḥat Yitzḥak* 3:60; *Ḥut Shani* vol. 1, p. 206; R. Shmuel Wosner).

Others maintain that one may go up in a Shabbat elevator but not down. This is because when the elevator goes down, the extra weight helps produce electricity. Thus one who rides the elevator has a hand in generating electricity (R. Levi Yitzḥak Halperin, *Ma'aliyot Be-Shabbat*).

A third opinion maintains that a Shabbat elevator may be used. Since the settings are in place before Shabbat, and no action needs to be taken on Shabbat to make the elevator work, there is no prohibition. The fact that the elevator has a system that determines the weight of the passenger, which in turn tells the motor how much power to use, and even makes use of the additional weight to produce electricity, is of no interest to the rider. As long as the elevator goes up and down according

---

normally in a room that has a baby monitor and thereby projects his voice over the intercom, since this is not the normal way to converse and his mouth is far from the intercom, it is considered *ko'aḥ sheni* and thus *grama*, as in the case of a hearing aid (though this requires further study; see *Harḥavot*). However, since the sound can be heard in the room with the receiver, it is a weekday activity and belittles Shabbat. It might also be considered *hashma'at kol* (Rema 338:1; *Oraḥ Mishpat* §71; also see Rema 252:5). In contrast, if the intercom was left on accidentally, then since one who speaks in that room is using it only via *grama*, and he is not interested in making his voice heard, this is a case of *psik reisha de-lo niḥa lei* in the case of a rabbinic prohibition, where one may be lenient in a case of need. In pressing circumstances, such as when one is sick, one may be lenient and leave an intercom on. See *Terumat Ha-goren* §79. *Yalkut Yosef* (vol. 5, pp. 403-405) permits this even *le-khatḥila*. One should only rely on this leniency under pressing circumstances.

to its settings, the passenger does not care about the elevator's electricity-conserving mechanisms. Therefore, the actions caused indirectly by his entry into the elevator are not attributable to him at all (it is a *psik reisha de-lo niḥa lei* via *grama*; this is the position of R. Yosef Eliyahu Henkin; R. Isser Yehuda Unterman; R. Shlomo Zalman Auerbach in SSK 23:58; Prof. Ze'ev Lev in *Teḥumin* 2; and R. Yisrael Rosen in *Teḥumin* 5.)

In practice, the lenient position is the primary one, while those who are stringent are commendable. In a case of need, even those who are normally stringent may be lenient. Those who are lenient must be careful not to enter or exit the Shabbat elevator when the door is about to close, so as to avoid causing it to reopen. Even for those who are lenient, it is better if the automatic system is programmed under the supervision of an organization that specializes in *halakha* and technology, as this can help ensure that entering the elevator does not turn on a light or the like and minimize the prohibitions involved according to the stringent view.[5]

5. USING ELECTRICITY THAT WAS PRODUCED ON SHABBAT

Power supply is a vital need of the State of Israel all week, including Shabbat. Interrupting or impairing the supply can endanger human life. Hospitals are full of devices that depend on the supply of power, and even in private homes there are people who are dangerously ill who rely on electrical devices to stay alive. Police officers and security forces use electrical equipment, and without electricity they would be unable to respond properly to emergencies. On cold days, many homes are heated using electricity. If the electricity were to be withheld on Shabbat, babies and sick people

5. The lenient position is the primary one, as its reasoning is compelling. Furthermore, it does not seem reasonable to view entering an elevator as worse than *grama* (as this is not a direct action but *ko'aḥ sheni*). Some are lenient even *le-khatḥila* in a case of *grama* (*Taz* 514:7). To be sure, most *poskim* permit *grama* only in cases of need (SA 334:22), but here the *grama* is combined with a *psik reisha*, so it is permitted even *le-khatḥila* (*Minḥat Shlomo* 1:10:6; see above 9:9 and *Harḥavot*). In any case, even according to those who do not allow entering a Shabbat elevator, the prohibition is rabbinic, since one who enters the elevator does not intend to do a *melakha*. Since the *poskim* disagree, the law follows the principle that we are lenient in cases of doubt about a rabbinic rule.

would likely be at risk. Very hot days can also pose a certain risk for those who are ill and require air conditioning. In addition, since nowadays we store food for an extended amount of time in refrigerators and freezers, this food may spoil if the electricity is cut off. In a large population, some would likely contract food poisoning, which can be life-threatening.

Therefore, it is necessary for the Israel Electric Corporation (IEC) – whose employees are predominantly Jewish – to supply electricity nonstop, even on Shabbat. If there is some impairment to the supply of electricity in a particular location, whatever is needed to fix it must be done. Since technicians may fix the grid on Shabbat, everyone may benefit from the electricity that is subsequently generated, even though it was restored on Shabbat. The only exception is if a power outage takes place in a small area where it is known for certain that there is no risk to human life involved, in which case the repair may not be made on Shabbat. If it was nevertheless repaired by Jews on Shabbat, one may not benefit from the electricity until an hour after Shabbat. (R. Shlomo Zalman Auerbach, quoted in SSK ch. 32 n. 182; below, 26:6).

Much to our dismay, it is known that IEC workers perform activities on Shabbat that are not essential to guaranteeing the electricity supply, but that are for the purpose of saving money. Furthermore, if there were greater awareness of Shabbat observance, it would be possible to automate the entire electricity-generating system and eliminate the need for human intervention without extra expenses. It would only be necessary to have a few workers in the power stations, monitoring the system and troubleshooting emergencies. However, since in fact the IEC does not try to avoid performing *melakha* on Shabbat, several leading rabbis ruled that one should not use its electricity on Shabbat (but rather use a local generator) to avoid benefiting from Shabbat desecration or supporting it in any way. (See *Ḥazon Ish*, OḤ 38:4.)

In practice, though, this electricity may be used on Shabbat, even in Israel. It is true that the IEC could take measures before Shabbat to avoid some of the Shabbat violations. Nevertheless, when its technicians do what is necessary to guarantee the electricity supply, they are not desecrating Shabbat, since electricity is necessary for people to live. Because of this, everyone may benefit from the electricity. Since the consumers do not benefit from the *melakhot* performed by the IEC technicians for the sole purpose of saving money, and from their perspective it would be better if the procedures were automated, they may benefit from the electricity on Shabbat (see *Ha-ḥashmal Ba-halakha* vol. 2 ch. 1; *Menuḥat Ahava* 1:24:1). We have recently learned of efforts to automate the grid and prevent Shabbat desecration.

6. TIMERS

Shabbat prohibitions become forbidden at the onset of Shabbat, but before Shabbat begins, one may take actions whose effects will continue into Shabbat. A prominent example of this is using a timer ("Shabbos clock"). Such timers are connected to the power supply and to an appliance, and its settings control the flow of electricity, determining when the device will turn on and off. This is how, nowadays, we can set electric lights to go on and off over the course of Shabbat. One may leave on lights before Shabbat and set the timer to turn them off at bedtime, on again at lunch time, and off again for the afternoon before turning on again for *se'uda shlishit*. Similarly, one can use a timer to turn on an electric oven or fan, setting it so that the appliance will go on and off at the desired times.

If one sets a timer to turn off the lights at 11 PM, but then decides that he would like to study Torah until midnight, some say that he may not delay the time that the lights will be extinguished by adjusting the timer's settings, as in their opinion, the timer is an integral part of the lighting system, and the Sages forbade taking any action that effects a change in the duration of the lights' operation. This can be inferred from the talmudic case of attaching an oil-filled container to an oil lamp, which the Sages forbid out of concern that one might remove some of the oil on Shabbat (*Shabbat* 29b; *Beitza* 22:1).

Others, including R. Shlomo Zalman Auerbach, offer a different perspective. They maintain that delaying the time the lights will go out is comparable to the case of one who is sitting in a room with a lit oil lamp. If the wind starts to blow though his window, threatening to extinguish the light, everyone agrees that he may close the window, even though this allows the lamp to burn longer. Since he is not doing anything to the lamp itself, but merely preventing the wind from blowing it out, there is no prohibition. Similarly, one who extends the settings of a timer is not doing anything to the light itself or to the electrical appliance, but merely preventing the timer from turning them off. Assuming that this action is permitted, the switches on the timer are not *muktzeh*, and they may be adjusted.

Since the rationale of those who are lenient is compelling and also accords with the widespread practice, one may rely on their opinion even *le-khatḥila*. Therefore, one may take action to extend the current state of affairs. If the electricity is off, one may extend the time that it will remain off and have the lights go on later. If the electricity is on, he may lengthen the time that it will remain on, and have the lights go out later. Similarly, if the lights are off, one can move the light switch to the off position, so that when the timer eventually restores the power, those lights will not go back on (SSK 13:26-33).[6]

However, one may not change the timer so that lights or appliances will go on or off earlier. For example, if the timer was set so that the lights would go off at midnight, but it turns out that people want to go to sleep earlier, one may not adjust the timer's settings to make the lights go off earlier. Although he is not turning them off directly because his actions will not have any effect until later, nevertheless indirectly

---

6. Some maintain that making any change to the settings of an electric timer is prohibited by Torah law (*Yaskil Avdi* 7:23), while others maintain that only certain kinds of changes are prohibited by Torah law (*Igrot Moshe*, YD 3:47:4; *Az Nidberu* 3:25 and 8:32). If this opinion is correct, then the problem of *muktzeh* also comes into play. Nevertheless, the logic of those who are lenient is very compelling, as explained in *Harḥavot*. First, the stringent position is based on the opinion of Rosh and those who follow him, with which many disagree (above ch. 16 n. 1). Second, it would seem that even Rosh would permit in this case, as the action of adjusting the timer is not done directly to the lights. Indeed, R. Shlomo Zalman Auerbach writes thus in *Minḥat Shlomo* §13, as does R. Ovadia Yosef in *Yabi'a Omer*, OḤ 3:18.

It should be added that when the lights are off, one may increase the time they will remain off, even if they will go on in the interim period. In other words, if the lights are off during the night, and are set to go back on at 10 AM and turn off again at noon, one may adjust the timer so that the lights will go off at 11 AM. The principle is that while the lights are off, one may cause them to be off for a longer period of time. This is true whether the current state is being extended, or whether the future state is being extended following a period when the lights will be on. Similarly, while the lights are on, one may cause them to be on for a longer period of time, even if in the interim they will turn off for a certain amount of time (SSK 13:30).

causing lights to go off is rabbinically forbidden. Similarly, if the timer was set to turn the lights on at 10 AM, it may not be adjusted to make the lights come on earlier, as indirectly causing lights to go on is rabbinically prohibited.[7]

7. THERMOSTAT CONTROLS

The laws of thermostat controls are the same as those of an electric timer. Some *poskim* maintain that one may not adjust a thermostat. According to R. Shlomo Zalman Auerbach and others, one may change the setting if it will lead to the extension of the current state.

For example, if one set the thermostat of an electric oil-filled radiator to medium before Shabbat, but on Shabbat realizes that it is hotter than he had expected, he may lower the setting of the thermostat once it has switched the radiator off. Thus, he ensures that the radiator will remain off for a longer period of time, and the heating element will work for a shorter period of time. However, one may not lower the thermostat while the radiator is on, because this changes the current state by causing the heating element to cycle off sooner.

If, during the course of Shabbat, one wants a radiator to stay on for longer, he must wait until the radiator has cycled on, and the temperature of the radiator has reached at least *yad soledet bo* (at least 160 degrees Fahrenheit or 71 degrees Celsius). Then he may turn up the thermostat so that the radiator will stay on for longer. However, if he does this when the temperature is below *yad soledet bo*, he transgresses

7. This applies under normal circumstances. However, in cases of need, those who are lenient allow causing a timer to turn the lights on earlier. According to most *poskim*, using a timer is considered *grama*, which some permit even *le-khatḥila* (*Taz*), and most permit in times of need (as explained above 9:9). This is the position of R. Shlomo Zalman Auerbach as cited in SSK 13:29, and of R. Ovadia Yosef in *Yabi'a Omer*, OḤ 3:18. Therefore, when one is sick (even if he is not dangerously ill), if the lights are disturbing his sleep and the timer is set to turn off the lights in a couple of hours, the settings may be changed so that the lights will go out in half an hour instead. An additional reason to be lenient is that turning off lights is only a rabbinic prohibition (above, section 1). In a case of dire necessity, one may make the lights turn on earlier for the sake of a mitzva, such as if the lack of light would cause one to waste much time that would have been spent learning Torah. In deference to the stringent position, however, it is proper to use a *shinui* when making the adjustment.

Bishul, because he is causing the oil inside the radiator to heat up. Once the radiator has cycled off, it is not permissible under any circumstances to turn up the thermostat, because this will change the current state and may lead to the radiator turning on immediately.

The same rules apply to air conditioners and refrigerators that have manual thermostats. When the compressor has cycled on, one may turn down the temperature, which will keep the refrigerator or air conditioner on longer. When the compressor has cycled off, one may turn up the temperature, which will keep the machine off longer (*Minḥat Shlomo* §10; SSK 23:24).

Of course, all of this assumes that there is no display recording the temperature. However, if the thermostat is adjusted by pressing buttons to change the temperature, and this is shown in an electronic display (as is the case with many air conditioners), then it is prohibited, both on account of *Kotev*, and because each press of a button makes direct use of electricity.

8. OPENING A REFRIGERATOR OR OVEN, AND ENTERING AN AIR-CONDITIONED ROOM

If opening the door of a refrigerator causes an electrical event to occur, one may not open the door on Shabbat. Most refrigerators have an electric light inside that goes on automatically when the refrigerator door is opened. Thus, if the light has not been removed before Shabbat, one may not open the refrigerator on Shabbat. There are also refrigerators where a fan turns on or off whenever the door is opened. These refrigerators and any with similar electrical mechanisms may not be opened on Shabbat.

In contrast, if it has been ensured that opening the refrigerator will not turn anything on or off, one may open the door on Shabbat. Indeed, some permit opening a refrigerator when the compressor has cycled on but prohibit opening the refrigerator when the compressor is off, as opening the door causes warm air to enter the refrigerator. Since the compressor is activated by an internal thermostat, opening the refrigerator may cause the compressor to go on immediately, or at least sooner than it would have otherwise.

However, in practice one may open the refrigerator even when the compressor is off. There are a number of reasons for this. First, it is unintentional: The person opening the door does not intend to turn on the compressor. Second, it is uncertain whether opening the door will cause the compressor to turn on, as it is possible that the compressor was about to cycle on anyway. Third, even if opening the door does cause the compressor to cycle on, this was only done indirectly, via *grama,* as opening the door does not itself turn on the compressor. It simply causes warm air to enter, which may in turn affect the compressor. Accordingly, one does not need to worry about a case where there is uncertainty regarding *grama* combined with lack of intent.

For the same reason, one may drink cold water from a water cooler without checking whether or not the compressor has cycled on. One may also enter a room that has a working air conditioner that is controlled by a thermostat, even though opening the door may cause the air conditioner to cycle on. First, it is not certain that opening the door will cause the air conditioner to cycle on. Even if it does cycle on, this was accomplished via *grama.* Similarly, one may open a door or window in a room that has a thermostat-regulated heater or air conditioner. This is because the person opening the door or window does not intend to affect the machine, it is not certain that opening the door or window will in fact do so, and if the machine is affected it will have been accomplished through *grama.*

However, many are stringent regarding an oven that is controlled by a thermostat and will not open such an oven when the heating element has cycled off. Since it is a small appliance, opening the door is more likely to cause it to cycle on. To avoid this problem, some ovens have a Shabbat setting in which the oven produces a steady heat and does not respond to a thermostat. When the oven is on this setting, all agree that it may be opened and shut at will.[8]

8. As explained in 9:9 above, some permit *grama* even *le-khatḥila,* while most only permit it in cases of need. Here, even if the act of opening the oven door will definitely turn on the heating element, since he does not intend to turn it on, it is simply a *psik reisha de-lo niḥa lei,* which is permitted even under normal circumstances. This point is even more relevant if it is possible that the oven would have cycled on even if left alone. In that case, opening the door accomplishes nothing. R. Shlomo Zalman Auerbach writes this regarding a refrigerator (*Minḥat Shlomo* 1:10), as do R. Ovadia Yosef (*Yabi'a Omer,* OḤ 1:21) and R. Eliezer Waldenberg (*Tzitz Eliezer* 8:12).

9. WHEN THE REFRIGERATOR LIGHT BULB WAS NOT DISCONNECTED

If one did not remove or disable the light bulb of a refrigerator before Shabbat, he may not open or close the door on Shabbat, as this will turn the light on or off. If one needs the food in the refrigerator for Shabbat, he may seek the help of a nearby non-Jew. In order to avoid the prohibition of benefiting from a *melakha* performed by a non-Jew, one should offer him food from the refrigerator, at which point he will open the door for his own benefit. Once the non-Jew has opened the refrigerator for himself, the Jew may take whatever he needs out of the refrigerator as well. Although generally one may not ask a non-Jew to perform a *melakha* on Shabbat, here one is not asking him to perform a *melakha*. Rather, one is asking him to open the refrigerator, which also happens to turn on the light. Afterward, in order to continue opening and closing the refrigerator permissibly, one may ask the non-Jew to remove the

---

However, many recommend being stringent and opening the refrigerator only when the compressor is already on; only then is it impossible for opening the door to cause the compressor to turn on, as it is already on. Even though the influx of warm air will lead the compressor to stay on for longer, this is not prohibited (*Responsa Har Tzvi*, OḤ 1:151; *Ḥelkat Yaakov* 3:179). Nevertheless, the bottom line is that one may open a refrigerator without checking whether or not the compressor is on.

The law regarding opening a refrigerator is more lenient than the law regarding opening an electric oven. There are two reasons for this distinction. First, an oven is small, and thus opening the door is likely to cause it to cycle on. There is a slight possibility that this would not be considered *grama*, but rather a direct action. In contrast, a refrigerator is large, and it is unlikely that opening the door will affect it immediately. If this were to happen, it would definitely be considered *grama*. Second, according to many *poskim*, turning on the refrigerator's compressor is only a rabbinic prohibition, since there is no heating element (above, n. 1). In contrast, turning on the oven's heating element is prohibited by Torah law according to all opinions. Reflecting this distinction, SSK 1:35 is stringent about opening the door of an electric oven, while when it comes to a refrigerator he records the lenient position as well. In contrast, *Igrot Moshe*, OḤ 4:74, *Bishul* 28 is lenient even in the case of an electric oven with a thermostat. He maintains that one may open the door even when the oven has cycled off, because it is an uncertain *psik reisha* in the case of a rabbinic prohibition (as it is performed via *grama*), and such a combination is permitted. Regarding opening the door of a room that has a radiator or air conditioner, almost no one is stringent. Since there is a relatively large distance between the door and the air conditioner or radiator, even those who are stringent would agree that this is considered *grama*. See above 10:17.

bulb, because turning off electric lights is only prohibited rabbinically, and one may ask a non-Jew to transgress a rabbinic prohibition for the sake of Shabbat (above 9:11; below 25:2, 5).

If no non-Jew is available, and the food is truly needed, then when the compressor has cycled off, the refrigerator may be unplugged using a *shinui*, such as by prying the plug out of the socket using a thin piece of wood or plastic. Since the plug is *muktzeh*, it may not be moved in the normal fashion (below 23:14).[9]

In a case where one is uncertain whether or not the bulb was removed, many *poskim* maintain that one may open the refrigerator. First, he does not intend to turn on the light, but only to open the refrigerator. If the light does go on, it is a case of *psik reisha* – he is performing a permitted action, and a second prohibited action takes place collaterally – which is normally prohibited. However, since the prohibited action might not occur, this is a case of an uncertain (*safek*) *psik reisha*, which is not prohibited. Although some are stringent in such cases, the lenient position is the primary one.

---

9. SSK 10:14 permits one to pull the plug using a *shinui*, but only if it often plugged and unplugged. If this is not the case, he is concerned that unplugging it might qualify as *Soter*. In 15:3 above I write that even if a particular appliance is not plugged and unplugged regularly, the law follows the majority of plugs (which are plugged and unplugged regularly), and we do not distinguish between types of plug. Therefore, there is no problem of *Boneh* or *Soter*. *Menuḥat Ahava* 1:24:20 is not concerned about this and allows one to remove the plug with a *shinui*. In any case, as long as a *shinui* is used, then even concerns of *Boneh* and *Soter* amount to a doubt about a rabbinic law, and when necessary one may be lenient. However, it is still forbidden to plug the appliance back in. See *Harḥavot* for what to do in a case of dire necessity.

Nowadays, most refrigerators have near-constant electrical activity, and pulling the plug puts an immediately stop to this activity, resulting in an act of *Mekhabeh*. Nevertheless, as long as one pulls the plug with a *shinui*, since the prohibition of turning off electricity is rabbinic, it is a *shvut di-shvut*, which is permitted for the sake of a mitzva, as explained above in 9:11.

Asking a minor: In cases of necessity, when the food is needed to feed a minor, one may ask the child to open the refrigerator. Since he has no intention of turning the light on, his act of opening the door is only prohibited rabbinically, and several Rishonim maintain that one may instruct a minor to transgress a rabbinic prohibition for his own needs. Some extend this leniency to cases of great need, and when necessary one may rely on them, as explained below 24:5 and in *Harḥavot* here.

If the refrigerator was opened and the light went on, food that is needed may be removed. The refrigerator should not be closed. Rather, a towel or some other object should be positioned in a way that prevents the refrigerator from closing and turning off the light. This way, the refrigerator can also be reopened.[10]

10. DISHWASHERS

A dishwasher may not be activated on Shabbat. This is because one may not use electricity, and additionally because the dishwasher heats water to wash the dishes. This heating is a transgression of *Bishul.*

One who always clears off dirty dishes from the table and places them directly in the dishwasher may do so on Shabbat as well. Then after Shabbat he can run the dishwasher. However, if he does not generally do this, then he may not do so on Shabbat, as it would amount to preparing on Shabbat for the weekdays, which is forbidden.

One may not even turn on a dishwasher via a timer, because the dishwasher is designed so that it will not go on unless the door is closed. This means that the person who closes the door to the dishwasher after the dishes have been loaded causes it to turn on (SSK 12:37). However, in times of need, when there will be a great need to wash many dishes on Shabbat and it would be extremely difficult to wash them by hand, one may set the dishwasher with a timer. This is because causing it to turn on by closing the door is considered *grama*. Since an action performed via *grama* is not a true *melakha*, in times of need it is permitted (above 9:9; *Responsa Me-rosh Tzurim* §30).

---

10. The status of a *safek psik reisha* is subject to dispute. *Taz* permits it, while R. Akiva Eger forbids it. The *poskim* tend to be lenient in times of necessity, especially when it is a *psik reisha de-lo niḥa lei,* in which case it is a case of doubt about a rabbinic law, as explained in BHL 316:3 s.v. "ve-lakhen." SSK 10:15 applies this rule to the case of a refrigerator, as does *Menuḥat Ahava* 1:24:20. See above, 9:5 and n. 2 and *Harḥavot* 9:5:8. If the refrigerator has been opened and the light is already on, and one is desperate to close the refrigerator door so that the food will not spoil, he should push the door in the opposite direction and then let it swing shut on its own. This way it is closed via *grama*. As *San.* 77b explains, if one throws a rock upward, and it then falls straight down, such an action is considered *grama* (*Orḥot Shabbat* ch. 29 n. 38).

If one can disable the system that makes the dishwasher's activation dependent on closing the door, so that the dishwasher will go on at the set time even if the door is not shut, then even in ordinary circumstances one may load the dirty dishes and have the dishwasher wash them during Shabbat (R. Yeḥiel Faust, *Le-ohavai Yesh* 1).

11. AUTOMATIC DOORS

One may not approach a door that automatically opens when it senses someone near it. One who does so is viewed as directly triggering the electricity that opens the door. It is immaterial whether the system works through floor sensors, an electric eye, a motion detector, or the like. As we have seen (section 2), according to many, including Rav Kook, turning on an electrical appliance is prohibited by Torah law.

One who finds himself in a hotel or hospital with automatic doors must find an alternative way to enter that does not involve using electricity. If a non-Jew approaches the door in order to enter, a Jew may follow him through (below 25:1-2). But if the person approaching the door is a Jew who does not observe Shabbat, a Shabbat observer may not follow him in, because the Shabbat observer may not benefit from the Shabbat desecration of a fellow Jew. Furthermore, when an observant Jew takes advantage of Shabbat desecration and benefits from it, it is considered a desecration of God's name. Even though some are lenient in this case, it is proper to be stringent. Only under pressing circumstances, when there is no alternative, may one rely on those who are lenient.[11]

---

11. Some are lenient and allow an observant Jew to follow a non-observant Jew through an automatic door, maintaining that this is not considered benefiting from *melakha* performed on Shabbat, since opening the door is merely removing an obstacle (R. Shlomo Zalman Auerbach in SSK 18:63). Furthermore, if the person who opens the door is considered an unintentional transgressor, in times of necessity one may rely on the opinion of R. Meir that one may benefit from *melakha* performed by such a person on Shabbat (MB 318:7). In contrast, there are reasons to be stringent. First, many maintain that opening such a door is considered a *melakha* performed on Shabbat (*Igrot Moshe*, OḤ 2:77). Second, the scenario of an observant Jew waiting for a non-observant Jew in order to benefit from his Shabbat desecration constitutes a desecration of God's name. Therefore, one may be lenient only under pressing circumstances.

Doctors and nurses may enter a hospital through an automatic door, as their work entails saving lives. Others may then follow them through the door. Ideally, the hospital administration should try to minimize the need for Shabbat desecration and arrange alternative entrances for visitors and staff to enter without activating any electrical devices.

Some say that if one unintentionally came too close to an automatic door, thus causing it to open, he must remain in place, because moving away will cause the door to close. They maintain that he should wait until a non-Jew arrives and ask the non-Jew to stand near him, at which point he can leave. Afterward, when the non-Jew leaves as well, the non-Jew will be the one who causes the door to close. However, if remaining in place causes the Jew anguish, he may simply leave, as he is just walking normally and does not care if the door is open or closed. His act of leaving is a *psik reisha de-lo niḥa lei* brought about via *grama*, which is not forbidden. Even if the person who mistakenly caused the automatic door to open did in fact want to enter, in a time of need he may still enter, since the *melakha* was unintentional. In contrast, if he intended for the door to open but forgot, and only later remembered, that it is forbidden, he should not enter, because one may not benefit from a *melakha* that was unknowingly (albeit intentionally) performed on Shabbat (SA 318:1; see n. 11 above and 26:4 below).

12. WHEN ENTERING A ROOM CAUSES THE LIGHTS TO TURN ON

One may not enter a room where doing so automatically turns on the lights or air conditioning. While one might claim that he did not intend to turn on the lights or air conditioning by entering the room, the fact is that everyone knows how the system works in such places.

This problem is common in hotel rooms and bathrooms. One who stays in such a hotel must make sure that the system is switched off before Shabbat. If he did not take care of this in advance and is outside his room when Shabbat begins, he may ask a non-Jew to open the door for him. He should further ask the non-Jew to stay for a bit so that the non-Jew will benefit from the lights or air conditioning, since he is then viewed as having turned them on for his own sake, and the Jew may then benefit from them (below, 25:2).

What if the hotel guest is inside such a room when Shabbat begins, and he knows that if he leaves he will cause the lights or air conditioning to shut off? If he can easily stay inside until after Shabbat, or if a non-Jew is due to come shortly to disable the system, it is preferable to wait inside. However, if doing so causes him anguish, he may leave the room or bathroom because the purpose of this system is to save the hotel money by conserving electricity. The hotel guest does not care about that, so it is a case of *psik reisha de-lo niḥa lei* regarding a rabbinic prohibition (since all agree that the prohibition of turning off the lights or air conditioning is rabbinic). When necessary, in such a case, one may be lenient (above, ch. 9 n. 2).

However, as we saw earlier, once the guest has left his room he will not be able to return to it, because doing so will turn on the lights and air conditioning. The only way for him to re-enter would be with the help of a non-Jew. Therefore, the proper course of action in this case is to ask a non-Jew to disable the system. Then the guest will be able to enter and exit the room as needed.[12]

13. INTERCOMS, SECURITY MONITORS, AND DOORBELLS AT BUILDING ENTRANCES

Some buildings use closed-circuit television (CCTV), in which surveillance cameras transmit images to monitors. A non-Jewish security guard stationed at the entrance keeps an eye on the people who come and go by watching the monitors. When people whom the guard recognizes as residents of the building or their guests arrive at the front door, he pushes an electric button that unlocks the door, allowing them to enter. Since this system is beneficial to the Jewish residents and guests of the building, a Jew may not stand where his image will be captured on the monitor. Similarly, if a Jew wishes to enter the building, he may not press

12. The claim that one may enter a room where the lights and air conditioning will automatically turn on since one is not interested in this happening is not legitimate. Part of the reason the system was put into place to begin with was to make one's life easier by relieving him of the need to turn on the lights and air conditioning every time he enters the room. Just because he does not want it to happen on account of a Shabbat prohibition does not make this a *psik reisha de-lo niḥa lei*. See *Orḥot Shabbat* 26:28, n. 41 and *Yalkut Yosef* vol. 3, pp. 55-56.

the intercom button to request that the guard unlock the door for him, since using electricity is prohibited.[13]

Therefore, one should make certain that the place where the guard sits is not far from the front door. Then, when a Jew wishes to enter, he can knock on the door while standing out of camera range, so that the guard can see him and unlock the door for him. If the non-Jew elects to open it using the electric release button, the Jew may still enter, since it is also possible for the non-Jew to open the door manually. If the non-Jew prefers to use the door release button, he is doing so for his own convenience, and not for the benefit of the Jew.

If there is a non-Jew entering the building at the same time as the Jew, even if the non-Jew makes use of the electricity, the Jew can follow him in, since the non-Jew is doing this for his own benefit. If it is a non-observant Jew who makes use of the electricity in order to enter, one may not follow him in, since he may not benefit from *melakha* done by a fellow Jew on Shabbat. Additionally, this constitutes a desecration of God's name. Although some are lenient in this regard, it is proper to be stringent. Only under pressing circumstances, when there is no alternative, may one rely on those who are lenient (as explained above, ch. 11 n. 11).

If one wishes to enter a building, but no one inside the building hears him knocking and calling out, may he ring an electric doorbell to gain admission? Some maintain that under pressing circumstances one may ring the bell using a *shinui*, while others forbid this. Under pressing circumstances, when there is no other solution, one who wishes to may rely on the lenient opinion provided that this leniency is not used regularly, as doing so regularly belittles Shabbat.[14]

13. In addition to causing electrical activity, one who stands in a place where his image will be captured on the monitor transgresses *Kotev* as well (on the rabbinic level, since the image is not permanent). See *Orḥot Shabbat* 15:35 and 26:27. However, when one has no interest in this happening, he may walk where there are cameras or sensors installed, even though his movements cause electrical activity, as explained in the next section.

14. According to R. Shlomo Zalman Auerbach and those who follow him in stating that using electricity is prohibited rabbinically, ringing the bell with a *shinui* renders his action a *shvut di-shvut*, and under pressing circumstances he may be lenient. However, for those who maintain that using electricity is prohibited by Torah law, even with a *shinui* it is still only a single *shvut*, which remains forbidden. Since according to all

14. MOTION DETECTORS IN PUBLIC DOMAINS AND IN THE HOME

One may walk where security cameras record images of passersby. Since the pedestrian has no interest in being videoed, he is not held responsible for his image being recorded, and there is no prohibition. Similarly, one may pass through a metal detector, since one who goes through is not interested in its electrical activity. One may also walk on a street where there are motion detectors that detect the movements of passersby. Even if a security system turns a light on when it senses movement, one may walk past it, because he is innocently walking through and is not interested in turning on the light. However, if it is not difficult, it is preferable to use an alternate route, since indirectly causing an electric light to go on is not properly respectful of Shabbat.

A private home might have a security system in which the burglar alarm has been disarmed, but the sensors continue working. Consequently, whenever one passes by certain places, LED security lights go on, or images are recorded. Some forbid walking around in such a house on Shabbat since doing so will cause electrical activity. They maintain that if one wishes to walk there, he must either disable the entire system or cover all the sensors so they will not detect a person's movements. (See R. Mordechai Eliyahu, *She'elot U-teshuvot Ha-Rav Ha-Rashi*, 5750-5753, p. 174.)

Others permit walking there. This is because one simply wishes to walk, and has no interest in triggering sensors or having his image captured; the only reason he does not deactivate them is because it is so difficult to do (*Si'aḥ Naḥum* §25). This is the primary position. Nevertheless, if possible, it is preferable to disable the sensors.

---

opinions, ringing the bell with a *shinui* renders the prohibition rabbinic, there is a rabbinic doubt about whether this is a case of *shvut di-shvut* or not. Accordingly, one who wishes may be lenient. As I have written above (ch. 9 n. 7), the entire leniency of *shvut di-shvut* may be utilized only rarely, under pressing circumstances.

If one accidentally presses a doorbell, he should stop pressing as soon as he realizes what he has done, because this act of stopping is not considered an action. If a light will turn on when he stops ringing the bell, some prohibit this (SSK 23:56). Others permit it, insisting that letting go of the bell is not considered an action. (See *Kedushat Ha-Shabbat* vol. 2, p. 27.) Under pressing circumstances, one may be lenient.

One must disable a light that automatically turns on when one approaches the entrance to one's house, because he benefits from the light in this case. Even if he does not benefit, it is not properly respectful to Shabbat to cause the light to go on. In a case of need, when the system is activated and there is no other way to enter the house, one can crawl through in such a way that the light might not turn on. Even if it is almost certain that the light will still turn on, turning it on by crawling constitutes a *shinui*. Additionally, he should keep his eyes closed so that he will not benefit from the light when it goes on.

15. SECURITY SYSTEMS

When a home security system is necessary for protection against thieves, there are two possible ways to set it up in a halakhically acceptable fashion. The best way is to use a timer. One may set the timer to arm the system during the hours when people are in bed or out of the house and disarm the system during the hours when people are awake and going in and out of the house. The problem with this is that if schedules change, the system needs to be changed, and if doing this involves using electricity, it is absolutely forbidden on Shabbat. If the system has an external timer, one may extend the current state, as explained above (section 6; under pressing circumstances one may also shorten the time, as explained in n. 7).

The second possibility is to use a special key that works via *grama*. Such a key disarms the security system when turned in one direction and arms it when turned in the other direction. To avoid transgression, the key must not cause any immediate electrical activity. Rather, it activates a mechanism that will eventually activate or disconnect electricity powering the alarm. Even though performing *melakha* through *grama* is normally prohibited *le-khatḥila*, when the only alternative will result in loss, one may be lenient.[15]

15. Within this second possibility, there are two permissible options. The first is to set it up so that when the system is shut off via *grama*, all the sensors stop working, and when it is re-armed the sensors resume working. The advantage of this option is that while people are home, no sensors are activated. The disadvantage is that every turn of the key causes the electrical system to turn on or off. The second option is to arrange that the sensors are always working, while the key simply serves to

Another question regarding security systems relates to monitoring services. In many cases, if a burglar alarms for a home or a car is triggered, the system signals a central monitoring station. Operators at the station see the signal and contact the owner to find out what happened. If the owner does not answer, the operators dispatch security personnel to apprehend the thieves. May one maintain a security system that involves such a service?

Some are stringent and require the owner to demand that the monitoring service refrain from desecrating Shabbat on his behalf. This approach would require the service to use non-Jewish security personnel on Shabbat. Others permit using a monitoring service even if it is staffed by Jews, maintaining that every theft nowadays involves an element of danger to human life. Therefore one may hire a service that employs and sends out Jewish security personnel on Shabbat. In practice, it is proper to use a company that tries to use non-Jewish security personnel on Shabbat. If that is not an option, one may use a company that is not particular in this regard. If the alarm goes off and the service calls to find out if a dispatch is necessary, even if the personnel are non-Jews, one should answer the phone, in order to prevent them from making an unnecessary trip.[16]

---

connect and disconnect the alarm system. The disadvantage of this option is that every movement in the house activates the sensors (see the previous section). The advantage is that turning the key does not cause any recognizable electrical activity. Even when the system is armed, if no thief enters, the alarm will not go off.

16. *Orḥot Shabbat* 23:208 maintains that one may not hire a security service that is under Jewish ownership or hires Jewish workers. In contrast, R. Shaul Yisraeli (*Amud Ha-yemini* §17) maintains that police may take action against thieves on Shabbat because it prevents danger to human life. *Be-mar'eh Ha-bazak* 4:43 applies this approach to monitoring services as well. Nowadays, there is an additional reason to be lenient. Thieves in Israel are often connected with terrorists. Just as the Sages allowed people in border towns to defend themselves on Shabbat against robbers of straw and hay (SA 329:6), so, too, people who live anywhere in Israel may defend themselves against the thievery of terrorists (below 27:12). In practice, one should give preference to a monitoring service that tries to hire non-Jewish guards. Nevertheless, this is not absolutely necessary, because the primary position is that preventing theft involves preserving lives as well. Not only that, but one may answer the phone when the monitoring service calls to check if there was a break-in. This is similar to the case of ambulances, which we discuss in 27:10 below. All false alarms cause danger to human life. See *Harḥavot*.

16. TURNING OFF AN ALARM THAT WENT OFF ON SHABBAT

If an alarm goes off on Shabbat because one touched one's car or entered one's house carelessly, what should be done? If the alarm goes off during the day and will stop relatively soon, one may not take any action to turn it off. However, what if it will continue to make noise for an extended period during the day or for even a short period at night? If the alarm disturbs people and causes them anguish because it prevents them from sleeping, sets them on edge, and ruins their enjoyment of Shabbat, one may turn it off, as long as one does so via a *shvut di-shvut* (above 9:11). This is because turning off the alarm is only prohibited rabbinically (see section 1 above), so if one turns it off with a *shinui* such as by pressing the appropriate button on the remote control with a spoon or the back of his finger, then the action taken is considered a *shvut di-shvut*. Even if turning off the alarm will make a light go on temporarily, since he does not need this light, it is considered a *psik reisha de-lo niḥa lei* (above 9:5).

It is true that some forbid this, only allowing one to be lenient if a non-Jew is available to turn off the alarm. For one who follows this position, if his non-observant Jewish neighbors threaten to call the police (which will lead to additional Shabbat desecration), he should tell the neighbors where the remote control is. Then the neighbors can choose to turn the alarm off themselves rather than call the police (*Melakhim Omnayikh* 10:6).

However, in practice, since this is a case of great necessity for the sake of a mitzva, one may turn off the alarm via a *shvut di-shvut* (see *Be-ohalah shel Torah*, OH §23; R. Dov Lior in R. Moshe Harari's *Kedushat Ha-Shabbat* vol. 1, p. 303).

Connecting a synagogue ark to an alarm system and disconnecting it when the Torah scrolls are taken out to be read must be done by means of *grama*, that is, using a key that activates or deactivates the system only a few minutes after the key is turned. In *Teḥumin* 1, Rav Dasberg proposed an excellent solution that does not even require *grama*. See *Harḥavot*.

17. ALARM CLOCKS, WATCHES, AND DIGITAL PHOTO FRAMES

If an electric alarm clock goes off on Shabbat, one may not turn it off, because doing so involves the use of electricity. If the noise is disturbing, the clock may be wrapped in blankets and moved where it will not be heard. If there is no way to minimize the noise, and the ringing is so loud that it is difficult to rest, one may turn off the alarm using a *shinui*. This follows the principle that a *shvut di-shvut* is permitted for the sake of a mitzva (as explained in the previous section).

Before the alarm actually goes off, one may press a button to deactivate it. Similarly, one may move an analog clock's hands in order to delay the time that the alarm will go off. However, one may change the time to an earlier time only for the sake of a mitzva or when there is a great need (above, 6:7). One may not change the time if it involves typing words or digits or any other use of electricity.

One may wear an electronic watch that displays the time. Even if there is a computer inside, one may wear it, since its primary purpose – displaying the time – is permitted (below, 22:8). However, if one knows that he is likely to end up using the computer, he may not wear this watch on Shabbat. Of course, one may not wear a watch that requires him to press a button to see the time, as it is *muktzeh*.

One may not wear a watch that measures the room temperature and displays it, because the movements of the wearer cause the watch to work. The claim that one is not interested in this feature is patently false; if this were the case such watches would not be made, and if they were made, no one would buy them. However, if the watch detects the temperature but does not display it unless one presses the appropriate button, one may wear the watch. The reason is that the measurement is done via *grama*, and it is a case of a *psik reisha* where the person is indifferent toward the result (see above, ch. 9 n. 3).[17]

---

17. See SSK 28:20, 22 and *Yeḥaveh Da'at* 2:49, which state that if one need not press an electric button to see the time, one may wear it on Shabbat, and even if it has a calculator built in, it is not considered a base for a forbidden object (*basis le-davar ha-asur*; *Tzitz Eliezer* 6:6; *Orḥot Shabbat* 19:43). Regarding a thermometer and the

Some are stringent and avoid wearing a solar-powered watch or an automatic quartz watch that is powered by movement. They are concerned that whenever the wearer moves his hand or enters a well-lit place, he causes the watch to recharge. Others are lenient on condition that the watch would be able to function for a few days without being charged, so that the charging that takes place on Shabbat is not really necessary. One who wishes may be lenient, and one who is stringent should be commended.[18]

A digital photo frame, which stays on all week and cycles through a slideshow of family pictures or scenic views, does not need to be turned off before Shabbat. This is because everyone knows that it is automatic and is on nonstop throughout the week.

---

like, the relevant principle is the one described above in section 14, namely, that causing the activation of sensors that have no present purpose is permitted, but is forbidden if they have a present purpose. Regarding the adjustment of an alarm clock to an earlier or later time, see SSK 28:33; *Orḥot Shabbat* 8:90-91.

18. Those who are lenient maintain that when there is no need to charge the battery, doing so is considered *mitasek*, as he is moving his arm for entirely different purposes, and the clock is recharged incidentally and without any purpose. This is even more lenient than a *psik reisha de-lo niḥa lei*; in a *psik reisha*, one plans to do a particular activity, but in the present case, moving one's arm is not even an intentional activity. Moreover, there are some who maintain that a *psik reisha de-lo niḥa lei* is permitted if the activity is rabbinically prohibited, and certainly according to those who maintain that electricity is a rabbinic prohibition, in which case the present example is a rabbinic prohibition on a rabbinic prohibition, as explained above (9:2). Moreover, it is possible that his movements will not generate electricity because the internal battery is already full. Thus, wearing it is a *davar she-eino mitkaven* that does not reach the level of a *psik reisha*. See SSK 28:28. However, when the battery needs to be full for Shabbat or even Sunday, he wants it to recharge, and it is therefore forbidden. According to those who maintain that electricity is forbidden by Torah law, one should be concerned that this is a violation of Torah law. According to those who maintain that electricity is forbidden by rabbinic law or on account of *Boneh*, there are grounds to say that even if the watch cannot continue for much longer on its own, one may still wear it, as carrying the watch or exposing it to light merely adds to the current, which is not forbidden, especially when it is done unintentionally. However, if the watch has already stopped, it is forbidden for anyone to activate it, as stated with regard to winding up the spring of a watch in SA 338:15 and MB *ad loc.* 15 (see also *Ḥelkat Yaakov* 1:75; *Yabi'a Omer* 6:35:8; *Tzitz Eliezer* 9:20). See *Orḥot Shabbat* 26:50.

18. *GRAMA* SOLUTIONS TO HALAKHIC PROBLEMS ON SHABBAT

Several organizations specialize in *halakha* and technology, devoting themselves to engineering electrical appliances to turn on via *grama* so that they may be used in cases of need. One such method is called "removing an impediment" (*hasarat ha-mone'a*). A second method uses a type of scanner that performs a scan every few seconds and turns an appliance on if it determines that a switch has been flipped. Thus, flipping the switch does not turn on the appliance but only causes it to be turned on indirectly. A third method is based on the principle that one may extend the present state: the appliance is set to turn on for one second every few seconds. When the switch is flipped, the next time the appliance turns on, it will not turn off after a second but will remain activated.

Others maintain that one may not use any of these clever stratagems. If an appliance is set to be activated electronically, causing its activation is not considered *grama* but the normal way of activating it.

In practice, it would seem that if one's action causes an appliance to turn on within a short time, like it would be turned on during the week, then even if the appliance has been programmed to turn on in a *grama*-like way, one may not turn it on. The internal workings of the machine are not important; if it turns on in a way that looks normal, then that is not considered *grama*. Therefore, elevators and automatic doors may not be turned on via *grama*; since the goal is for them to function in their normal way soon after being turned on, it would not be considered *grama*. Similarly, one may not travel using a "*kalno'it*" (an electrical wheelchair or gold cart specially designed for use by the sick, disabled, and elderly on Shabbat), since it operates in the way that one would operate a similar device during the week.

In contrast, when one's action causes an appliance to turn on only with a significant delay, then if it is brought about indirectly – whether by *hasarat ha-mone'a*, scanning, or extending the present state – it is considered *grama*, and such a system may be used when needed. This is the practice regarding arming a security system: if turning a key will cause the system to work via *grama*, and it will only actually arm itself ten minutes after the key is turned, it is considered *grama,* and one may do so in cases of great need.[19]

19. R. Levi Yitzḥak Halperin, the head of the Institute for Science and Halakha, maintains that in case of need, one may activate devices by "impeding an impediment." For example, consider a device that is in working order, but a beam of light hitting a particular spot prevents the device from working. When one blocks the light beam, the device begins to work again. Thus, blocking the beam "impedes an impediment" and is considered a *grama.* According to R. Halperin, technically this is even less severe than *grama,* but many disagree with him.

The Zomet Institute has developed three strategies: 1) *Grama* by means of a scanner that performs a scan every few seconds. When it detects that a switch has been moved, it activates the device. 2) Extending a state: every few seconds, the device is activated for a second before turning off. If the switch is moved, then the device will not turn off after a second, and the "on" state is thus extended. 3) The device operates constantly at a certain level of power consumption. Flipping the switch merely increases the electrical current. This relies on the numerous *poskim* who maintain that electricity is forbidden on account of *Molid,* and consequently adding to the current is not forbidden. Moreover, according to Ḥazon Ish, the prohibition of electricity is based on *Boneh,* and if the electrical current already exists, it is not prohibited to add to the current. Based on this, they permitted use of a *kalno'it.* However, according to Rav Kook and those who agree with him, as described above in section 2, increasing a current is forbidden by Torah law. In general, the Zomet Institute relies on the rulings of R. Shlomo Zalman Auerbach, R. Yehoshua Neuwirth, and R. Ovadia Yosef, as detailed in several essays that have appeared in *Teḥumin* (the journal of contemporary halakhic issues published by the Zomet Institute).

Some say that since these devices were developed for this purpose, the leniency of *grama* does not apply to them at all. Rather, operating them has the same status as operating normal electrical devices. Moreover, these devices breach the walls that safeguard Shabbat. This is the position of *Tzitz Eliezer* 21:13; *Orḥot Shabbat* 29:27; *Shvut Yitzḥak, Grama* 15:15 in the name of R. Elyashiv; *Ḥut Shani* vol. 1, p. 206; *Binyan Av* 4:17. It is also implied in *Responsa Aḥiezer* 3:60. Certainly all of the reasons to be stringent apply to the *kalno'it*: according to Rav Kook and those who agree with him (above, section 2), increasing a current is forbidden by Torah law, and according to the remaining *poskim,* since it moves just as it would move during the week, one may not operate it on Shabbat. They also forbid the *kalno'it* because it breaches the walls safeguarding Shabbat and belittles its honor.

The proper approach seems to be the one we learned in 9:9 above. That is, a precondition for *grama* is that the action is done in a way that differs from the normal way of performing the *melakha.* As long as people perceive the device to be operating normally, it should not be permitted. Therefore, only if the delay is obvious and of significant duration does the device operate in a manner that sufficiently differs from the normal mode of operation on a weekday. Once the mode of operation is considered different, if the activation takes place via *grama,* that is, by means of a scanner, the removal of an impediment, or the extension of the present state, will it be permissible in a case of need, as is the rule in cases of *grama.* See *Harḥavot.*

Chapter Eighteen

Kotev, Moḥek, and *Tzove'a*

In addition to *Kotev* (writing), *Moḥek* (erasing), and *Tzove'a* (dyeing), this chapter will also explain the *melakhot* of *Mafshit* (skinning), *Me'abed* (tanning), *Memaḥek* (smoothing), and *Mesartet* (marking).

1. *KOTEV* AND *MOḤEK*

Kotev is the *melakha* of expressing ideas precisely using letters, numbers, or meaningful pictures in a manner that allows the idea to last a long time. In the *Mishkan*, letters were written on the posts that formed its walls so that the order, position, and orientation of each post would always be clear. Sometimes mistakes would be made, so there was a need to erase the letters and replace them with the correct ones. This is the *melakha* of *Moḥek*, erasing in order to write other letters (*Shabbat* 103a; Rashi on *Shabbat* 73a).

At first glance, *Kotev* seems to be a trivial and insubstantial *melakha* that should not have been included on the list of serious *melakhot* prohibited on Shabbat. However, in truth, writing is the basis for human activity. No matter how smart one was or how good a memory one had, he would still have had difficulty remembering exactly where to place each individual post in the *Mishkan*. This is the case with all complex matters: if one does not write them down, he will not remember them precisely and he will lose the ability to reconstruct the knowledge he has accumulated and the achievements he has already attained. Through writing, mankind was able to develop scientifically and improve human life.

In order to ensure that information is precise, sometimes it is necessary to erase a mistake in order to replace it with accurate information. Even if a piece of paper has a stain on it and one erases it so he can write letters instead, he transgresses *Moḥek*, as his erasure prepares the writing surface (SA 340:3).

Sometimes erasing is considered a *melakha* even if one does not plan to write in the place of the erasure; for example, if there is an extra letter in a Torah scroll which must be erased in order to render the Torah kosher (*Shabbat* 104b; BHL 340:3, s.v. "ha-moḥek").

Using a rubber stamp is also considered *Kotev*. It makes no difference whether the stamp is held with the right or left hand, because the stamp can be easily used with either hand. Similarly, using a printer, photocopier, or fax machine is prohibited by Torah law on Shabbat, since doing so commits meaningful symbols or letters to writing (see MA, OḤ 32:57; *Taz*, YD 271:8; *Igrot Moshe*, OḤ 4:40:10).

One may not type letters or characters on a computer or save them to a computer's memory. It is also forbidden to take photographs, or to record voices or sounds. However, since these actions do not produce stable forms or letters, many maintain that the prohibition is rabbinic.[1]

2. DEFINING THE PROHIBITION OF WRITING AND EXPLORING LENIENCIES FOR LIFE-THREATENING SITUATIONS

It is critically important to define each *melakha* precisely and establish what is rabbinically prohibited and what is prohibited by Torah law, and moreover these determinations have practical consequences. For example, when writing is necessary in a hospital or in the army in

1. R. Yosef Shalom Elyashiv and R. Mordechai Eliyahu maintain that typing on a computer is prohibited by Torah law. This would also be the position of those who maintain that using electricity is prohibited by Torah law, as explained above in 17:2. See *Harḥavot* here and there.

order to save lives, *le-khatḥila* one should minimize the prohibitions one violates and write in a manner that is only rabbinically prohibited. We shall first clarify what is prohibited by Torah law and what is rabbinically prohibited, and then detail how one should write in cases where there is danger to human life.

The Torah prohibition of *Kotev* refers to writing normally with the right hand, though one who writes irregularly with the left hand violates a rabbinic prohibition. A lefty who writes with his left hand violates Torah law, and if he uses his right hand he violates rabbinic law. One who is ambidextrous violates Torah law by writing with either hand (*Shabbat* 103a).

If one holds the pen with a *shinui* – in his mouth, with his foot, or with the back of his hand – he violates a rabbinic prohibition (MT 11:14).

The Torah prohibition of *Kotev* also refers to writing that lasts for a significant amount of time. Therefore, if one writes with a pencil or pen on paper, he violates Torah law. However, if he writes using fruit juice, which will quickly fade, or with a regular pen but on a leaf that will dry out and crumble, he violates a rabbinic prohibition.

According to the vast majority of *poskim*, the Torah prohibition of *Kotev* applies to all languages (MT 11:10; BHL 306:11). A few *poskim* maintain that the Torah prohibition applies only to letters that may appear in a Torah scroll, but writing in any other script, in a foreign language, or in cursive Hebrew, constitutes a rabbinic transgression (*Or Zaru'a*).

If writing is necessary to save lives, and it is clear that a slight delay will not cause any further danger, the prohibition should be minimized by writing with a *shinui*, using the left hand. If one is ambidextrous, he should grasp the writing utensil with the back of his hand or between his little finger and ring finger. Ideally, a medical professional should buy a "Shabbat pen" whose ink disappears within a few days and with which writing is only rabbinically forbidden. If something must be typed on a computer, a *shinui* should be used if possible, such as typing with the knuckles, with a teaspoon, or the like. It is also preferable to write in cursive rather than in block letters.

To summarize, if one must write because of a life-threatening situation, it is preferable to use a Shabbat pen, since everyone agrees this is only rabbinically prohibited. Even with a Shabbat pen, it is proper to write using a *shinui* if possible. When a Shabbat pen is not available, one may write or type as needed, but in cursive and using a *shinui* when possible.

3. INCIDENTAL WRITING AND ERASING

One may not cut through letters that are written on a cake in frosting, candy, or the like. Similarly, if a cake is decorated with a meaningful picture, like a tree or a house, one may not cut through the picture. Even though one's intention in cutting the cake is to eat it, since the letters or pictures have meaning and it is very clear that they are being "erased" when the cake is cut, it is rabbinically prohibited (*Mordechai*; Rema 340:3). However, one may cut between the letters. Even though this separates a word into its component parts, one does not violate *Moḥek* as long as each letter remains whole. Therefore, if a cake that one plans to serve on Shabbat is being decorated, it should be done in such a way that one will be able to cut between the letters and pictures. Afterward, the slices of cake may be eaten even though eating them will destroy the letters. Since one is engaged in the process of eating, it is not considered *Moḥek*.

When letters or pictures appear on cookies as a result of having been stamped into the cookie dough, as with petits beurres cookies, there is no prohibition against cutting or breaking them. Since these letters have no significance, erasing them incidentally is not prohibited (MB 340:15).

Some maintain that it is rabbinically prohibited to read a book that has letters stamped or written on the edges of the pages (such as a library stamp) because when one opens the book the letters break apart, and when it is closed they are reconstructed (*Levush*; MA). In practice, if no other book is available, one may read such a book, because many maintain that bringing the different parts of a letter together is not considered *Kotev*, nor is separating them considered *Moḥek*. Additionally, since a book is meant to be opened and closed repeatedly, this is not considered even short-term *Kotev* and *Moḥek*, and thus involves no prohibition (Rema 340:3; *Taz*; MB *ad loc.* 17).

Some rule that if opening a package of food will definitely tear letters or pictures, it may not be opened on Shabbat. They permit opening the package only if it is possible that the letters or pictures will not be torn in the process (based on *Taz*). Others maintain that one may open such a package, since all parts of the letters actually remain, but have simply been separated from each other (based on Rema). *Le-khatḥila* it is proper to be stringent, but when there is no way to open a package without tearing letters, one may be lenient. One who opens the package has no interest in "erasing" the letters, and the action is not constructive but destructive.

One may wear shoes whose soles are stamped with letters or pictures, even though walking in these shoes may leave impressions of these letters or pictures on mud or similar surfaces.[2]

One who wrote on himself with a pen may still wash his hands and dry them in the usual way, since ink generally does not come off as a result of washing and drying one's hands one time. However, if he

2. According to Rema (*Responsa Rema* §119), tearing a letter is not considered erasing, since all parts of the letter remain but have simply been separated from one another. However, according to *Taz* 340:2, it is considered erasing and is prohibited. Based on this, SSK 9:13 prohibits opening packages if this will involve tearing letters. However, even within *Taz*'s approach, one may be lenient *be-di'avad*; as we have seen (ch. 9 n. 2), a *psik reisha de-lo niḥa lei* in a case of a double rabbinic prohibition is permitted. This case is considered a *psik reisha de-lo niḥa lei* as well, since one has no interest in the letters. All he is interested in is opening the package. There are two factors that render the entire prohibition rabbinic. First, one is not erasing to enable writing in that space. Second, the erasing is done with a *shinui* (or destructively). This is, in fact, the position of *Or Le-Tziyon* 2:27:7 and *Yalkut Yosef* 314:19. For the same reasons, one may walk in shoes that will leave impressions of letters or pictures on the ground. Here, too, there are two factors that render the prohibitions rabbinic. First, the "writing" will disappear fairly quickly. Second, this is not the normal way to write. Furthermore, since one has no interest in leaving impressions of letters in the ground, it is permitted.

Based on this, it would seem at first glance that one should also be allowed to cut a cake with writing on it, as this is a *psik reisha de-lo niḥa lei* in the case of a double rabbinic prohibition as well. Furthermore, according to Rema, it is not an act of erasure but of separation. Indeed, *Taz* is inclined to rule this way in 340:2. *Dagul Me-revava* and a number of other Aḥaronim also rule this way (cited in *Livyat Ḥen* §119). Nevertheless, many *poskim* are stringent. The reason for this would seem to be that the letters on a cake are noticeable and significant, and it is very clear that they are being erased when the cake is cut. This is what I wrote in the main text. One may cut between the letters because most *poskim* maintain that separating letters is not considered *Moḥek* (*Ma'amar Mordechai*; *Avnei Nezer*; SSK ch. 9 n. 51). In times of necessity, if it is very important to eat the cake and it cannot be cut without cutting through the letters, one may rely on those who are lenient. The status of a book with lettering on the edge is more complicated, as explained in *Harḥavot*.

would like the letters to come off, he must be careful to wash and dry his hands gently, so that he does not assist in the removal of the letters.

4. TEMPORARY WRITING, WORD GAMES, AND JIGSAW PUZZLES

As we have seen, temporary writing is rabbinically prohibited. Erasing something when one does not plan to write something else in its place is rabbinically prohibited as well. Therefore, one may not write in the condensation on a window or erase such writing. Similarly, one may not form letters in the sand or erase them (MB 340:20-21).

One may not mark a page using his fingernail to remind oneself that the page contains something notable or something that needs to be corrected. Since he is creating a lasting mark, it is rabbinically prohibited (MB 340:25; *Kaf Ha-ḥayim ad loc.* 51). However, one may dog-ear the page, because there his goal is not to "engrave" a mark in the paper. Rather, the fold itself is the mark.

Some allow a sick person to use a thermometer strip. They maintain that it is not really writing since the numbers are already imprinted on the strip, and the temperature only makes them visible for a short time, after which they disappear (*Yeḥaveh Da'at* 4:29). Others forbid this, considering it temporary writing (SSK 40:2). Since the issue is rabbinic, one may be lenient in times of need (*Tzitz Eliezer* 14:30; below 28:11). Similarly, *le-khatḥila* one should not perform any medical tests that cause colors to appear, but in times of need, one may be lenient (*ibid.*).

Colorful blocks may be put next to each other to form a letter, and thread may be laid down in the shape of a letter. This is because the blocks or thread already exist; one is simply arranging them. Similarly, he may juxtapose two cards that together form a picture, letter, or word. This is because all the forms already exist; they are simply being brought together.

This applies when the different parts do not connect to each other or to a board. However, if they do connect, most contemporary *poskim* maintain that it is rabbinically forbidden to put them together and that therefore one may not pin parts of letters to a board to form a whole letter, on account of *Kotev*. Similarly, one may not assemble a jigsaw puzzle, since creating meaningful pictures also constitutes *Kotev*. Others permit these activities, maintaining that they are not considered writing since all the writing already exists, and the activity merely brings the letters or puzzle pieces into proximity. However, even according to the lenient position, one may not complete a jigsaw puzzle in order to preserve it as a portrait.

In practice, those who wish may be lenient and allow their children to engage in these activities, but it is proper for adults to be stringent, as most *poskim* are stringent here. More generally, it is important to realize that Shabbat is meant to be dedicated to Torah, and some therefore say that adults may not play games on Shabbat at all (below 22:13, 24:7; and *Harḥavot*).[3]

One may use a multiple-dial combination lock on Shabbat, because turning the discs to align the numbers is not considered writing. The numbers are already there; one is merely realigning them temporarily to form the correct combination and open the lock (*Tzitz Eliezer* 13:44).

5. DYEING

Tzove'a is a *melakha* with the objective of making something more beautiful. In the *Mishkan*, the woolen threads of the curtains were dyed indigo, royal purple, and scarlet. Even though the *melakha* of *Kotev* can be described as "dyeing" a page with letters, there is a difference between *Kotev* and *Tzove'a*. The goal of writing is to express an idea. Even when the "writing" is a picture of a house or a tree, the goal is still to express an idea, and that is how one transgresses *Kotev*. In contrast, the goal of dyeing is not to express an idea, but to beautify an item. Therefore, one who creates a meaningful image on paper or on a wall transgresses *Kotev*, and if he then colors it to beautify it he transgresses *Tzove'a* (*y. Shabbat* 7:2).

Therefore, it is prohibited by Torah law to paint, color, or dye walls, cabinets, utensils, fabric, or clothing on Shabbat. The specific color is irrelevant; any color that beautifies is prohibited by Torah law. Even if the paint is colorless and merely adds glaze or shine, it is prohibited,

3. SSK 16:24 rules stringently but states in n. 66 that one does not have to stop a child from playing games on Shabbat, relying on those who are lenient. This is the opinion of the majority of *poskim*. *Or Le-Tziyon* 2:42:6 permits little girls to play games but not little boys, so they do not grow accustomed to wasting time that could be used for Torah study. He insists, however, that for adults, games are *muktzeh*. See *Harḥavot*.

because shine is considered color. It is prohibited by Torah law to paint a wall even if it was previously painted with the same or a different color.

It is also prohibited by Torah law to polish shoes. Even if the polish is neutral or colorless, it is prohibited by Torah law, because it makes the shoes shine. If the polish is a cream that is spread on the shoes, then one who applies it also transgresses *Memare'aḥ* (section 6 below). If the polish improves the leather, then one transgresses *Me'abed* as well (MB 327:12, 16; see section 6 below). Even if the polish was applied before Shabbat, one may not buff the shoes on Shabbat to make them shine, because shine is considered color. However, if there is dust on the shoes, one may gently remove it with a rag (SSK 15:40).

The Torah prohibition of *Tzove'a* is limited to permanent dyes. If the color will come off by itself within a short time, the prohibition is rabbinic (MT 9:13).

If one's hands become stained with fruit, blood, or any other substance, *le-khatḥila* he should first wash his hands and only afterward dry them with a towel, to avoid "dyeing" the towel. Similarly, if juice spills on a tablecloth, the one who wipes it off should be careful not to drag the juice along the cloth as that will dye the tablecloth. Even though such "dyeing" dirties the tablecloth rather than beautifying it, those who are stringent maintain that since it is normal to dye such a cloth, it is rabbinically prohibited (SA 320:20). In times of need one may be lenient, since many *poskim* say that adding color in a way that dirties the object is not prohibited (MB 320:59; *Kaf Ha-ḥayim ad loc.* 122).

Since bandages or tissues are not normally dyed, they may be used to clean up blood or other colored substances. Since the color added dirties material that is not normally dyed, there is no prohibition (SAH §302, *Kuntres Aḥaron*).

Everyone agrees that there is no issue of staining the hands or mouth when eating strawberries or other brightly colored foods, because this is not the normal way to color skin, and any such coloring is actually dirtying the skin (MB 320:58). However, one may not put on makeup, as we explained earlier (14:4).

If a toilet has an automatic toilet bowl cleaner that colors the water with every flush, *poskim* disagree whether one may flush the toilet on Shabbat. Some maintain that since people are interested in the water being colored, it is rabbinically prohibited even though the color is present only briefly. Others maintain that since the primary goal is to clean the toilet, and the color is just incidental, one may flush the toilet. In practice, it is preferable to use a clear toilet bowl cleaner. However, if one finds himself in a place where the cleaning material is colored, he may flush the toilet. Those who wish to be lenient and use a colored toilet bowl cleaner have an opinion to rely upon.[4]

6. *MAFSHIT, ME'ABED, MEMAḤEK,* AND *MESARTET*

There are four *melakhot* that relate to preparing animal skins for writing: *Mafshit, Me'abed, Memaḥek,* and *Mesartet* (as explained below). When parchment was the standard writing surface, everyday things were written on it. Nowadays, however, only Torah scrolls, *tefilin,* and *mezuzot* are written on parchment. Additionally, nowadays, animal skins are used to make leather clothing, shoes, satchels, and upholstery. In the *Mishkan,* skins were prepared to be used as curtains as well. *Mesartet* was performed not only on skins, but on wood as well – to designate a place on the boards for writing.

Mafshit refers to removing the skin from an animal that was slaughtered. This skin has two layers. The outer layer, or *klaf,* is the

---

4. This disagreement hinges on several issues: 1) Is it forbidden to color water? According to *Pri Megadim* and MB 320:56, it is forbidden. However, since in this case the dye is not long-lasting, the prohibition is rabbinic. This is the opinion of most *poskim.* Others maintain that it is permitted, either because the color does not become absorbed anywhere specific (*Or Le-Tziyon* 1:29), or because water is a liquid, and *Tzove'a* does not apply to liquids (*Tzitz Eliezer* 14:47). 2) Even if *Tzove'a* applies to water, some maintain that since the dyeing is done indirectly – flushing the toilet involves lifting the flush valve, which is considered removing an impediment to the water going down through the cleaner – it is a case of *grama.* If this is correct, then this is a *psik reisha* in a case of a double rabbinic prohibition (*Halikhot Olam* vol. 4, p. 286). Others maintain that this is not considered *grama,* and is therefore prohibited (*Shulḥan Shlomo* 320:31:3). 3) There is also a disagreement regarding the facts of the case. What is the purpose of the cleaning material – cleaning or coloring?

In practice, those who are stringent include *Shulḥan Shlomo, Menuḥat Ahava* 3:13:4 and n. 9, and *Orḥot Shabbat* 15:64. The latter adds that if one forgot to remove the container of the toilet bowl cleaner before Shabbat, he should do so on Shabbat with his foot, because it is *muktzeh.* Those who are lenient include *Tzitz Eliezer, Or Le-Tziyon,* and *Halikhot Olam.* If one knows that he cares about the color of the water, he should be stringent.

material upon which Torah scrolls, *tefilin,* and *mezuzot* are written. The inner layer, or *dokhsostos,* may only be used for *mezuzot.* One who separates the two layers transgresses a *tolada* of *Mafshit.* Although one may not remove an animal's skin, one may skin a cooked chicken, because the prohibition of *Mafshit* does not apply to edible meat.

Me'abed refers to placing the skin in salt, lime, or other substances that draw out the skin's juices and acids. This allows the skin to last for hundreds of years. Any action that prepares skins for use is included in this *melakha.* Therefore, one may not to stomp on skins to harden them, use one's hands to soften them, or spread oil on them to make them soft and pliant (MT 11:6). We explained above the laws of *Me'abed* as they pertain to food (12:9).

Memaḥek refers to smoothing the skins by removing hairs and irregularities. This *melakha* also includes smoothing any rough surface, such as wood or stone, by means of sandpaper or a file (*Shabbat* 75b). It is also forbidden to scour silver items with a material that smooths their surface (SA 323:9). One may not scour metal with steel wool or sharpen knives (MB 323:40).

The *melakha* of *Memaḥek* has a *tolada* called *Memare'aḥ,* which refers both to spreading a substance evenly upon an object and to spreading a substance on an object in order to smooth out the object. Therefore, one who spreads ointment on a poultice transgresses Torah law (*Shabbat* 75b; see below 28:8). It is also forbidden to spread lotions and creams on one's body, as explained above (14:5). Similarly, one may not polish shoes by spreading cream on them. Even without a cream, one may not rub leather shoes in order to shine them (see AHS 327:4; SSK 15:40). As we explained above (12:11), according to most *poskim,* the prohibition of *Memaḥek* does not apply to foods.

Mesartet refers to scoring a line to facilitate writing in a straight line. This *melakha* also includes drawing a straight line on leather, wood, or stone in order to mark where to cut these materials. However, one may use a knife to draw lines on a cake or to score an orange, to help one cut with precision. Since the prohibition of *Meḥatekh* does not apply to food (as explained above in 15:10), *Mesartet* does not apply to food either (MB 322:12, 18; SSK 11:15).

Chapter Nineteen

Agricultural *Melakhot* (*Ḥoresh, Zore'a, Kotzer,* and *Me'amer*)

1. ḤORESH

The *melakha* of *Ḥoresh* refers to preparing ground for sowing or planting, by making furrows or holes in the soil in order to plant seeds or seedlings. Plowing also loosens and softens the soil, making it easier for roots to spread out and absorb nutrients.

Thus, one who levels the surface of the ground violates *Ḥoresh*, because doing so softens the soil and makes it easier to prepare for sowing and planting. Making even a small hole is a transgression of *Ḥoresh* because a seed can be planted in it. Similarly, clearing rocks from a field, fertilizing it, and weeding are all *toladot* of *Ḥoresh*, since these actions improve the soil and make it easier to sow and plant. Anyone who undertakes any activity in order to improve the ground prior to sowing or planting violates Torah law (*Shabbat* 103a; *y. Shabbat* 7:2). Even if he does not intend to sow or plant there, he has still violated *Ḥoresh*, since in fact he has improved the land for sowing or planting (*Eglei Tal, Ḥoresh* 16).

One may not make a hole in the dirt of a flowerpot or even stake something into the dirt of a flowerpot, thereby making a hole in which one can plant, as these violate the *melakha* of *Ḥoresh* (MB 498:91; see n. 4 below).

The Sages prohibited sweeping the ground in the yard, out of concern that one would end up leveling the ground, thus transgressing a Torah prohibition. If it is arable land, he violates *Ḥoresh*. If it is land that serves simply as a yard, he transgresses *Boneh*. However, one may sweep a part of the yard that has a hard, paved floor.[1]

One may not kick dirt and sand, or move it around with one's foot, because this both loosens soil and levels the ground. Saliva that is on the ground should not be rubbed into the dirt with one's shoes, to avoid leveling the ground. However, if one finds the saliva disgusting, he may step on it in the natural course of his walking, as long as his intention is not to spread it and level the ground (SA 316:11).

One who has mud stuck to his shoes should not try to rub it off against the ground, because he may end up leveling the ground (SA 302:6). Some are not concerned about this possibility, and allow rubbing off the mud (Rema, *Taz*). One who wishes may be lenient, but *le-khatḥila* it is preferable to be stringent. In contrast one may rub off the mud against a grate, tiles, or stones even *le-khatḥila* (MB 302:28; also see above 15:2).

2. DRAGGING OBJECTS AND PUSHING A BABY CARRIAGE

One may drag a bed, chair, or bench on the ground, since it is not certain that doing so will make a furrow. Even if the item could easily be lifted off the ground, thus avoiding the possibility of creating a furrow, it may still be dragged on the ground. As long as the person dragging the item does not intend to make a furrow, and there is no certainty that one will be formed, this is permitted, as it is considered a *davar she-eino mitkaven* (SA 337:1). However, if it is certain that a furrow will be made, one may not drag the item, as it constitutes *Ḥoresh*. Even if one does

1. See above 15:2 and n. 1 for the laws about sweeping floors. In practice, one may sweep all paved floors in the home and all paved areas outside. See below 23:14 and n. 14 on why doing so presents no problem of *muktzeh*.

not intend to plant there, making the land cultivatable is in fact an act of *Ḥoresh* (via the principle of *psik reisha*; see above 9:5).[2]

In an area with an *eruv*, one may push a baby carriage or stroller even if it is clear that the wheels will make grooves in the dirt. This is because the wheels do not dig in and loosen the earth as a plow does. Rather, they pack down the earth, which actually does not effectively prepare it for sowing or planting. One may even pivot in the dirt with the carriage, because even then it is not certain that earth will be turned over and prepared for planting (SSK 28:48; *Yeḥaveh Da'at* 2:52).

3. *ZORE'A*

The *melakha* of *Zore'a* refers to causing plants or trees to grow by, for example, planting seeds or saplings or by grafting trees. All actions that improve the growth of branches or fruit are forbidden by Torah law as well. Thus, pruning and weeding are forbidden, because these actions promote plant growth. Similarly, one may not water plants or fertilize the soil surrounding them. It is also forbidden to apply dressings (such as tar or paint) to a tree's wounds in order to heal it (*Shabbat* 73b; MT 7:3, 8:2).[3]

---

2. *Davar she-eino mitkaven* refers to a case where it is not certain that a *melakha* will be performed. It is permitted in accordance with the opinion of R. Shimon in *Shabbat* 22a. However, if it is certain that a *melakha* will be performed, it is considered a *psik reisha*, which R. Shimon agrees is prohibited (*Shabbat* 103a; MT 1:5-6). According to most *poskim*, *psik reisha* is prohibited even when the *melakha* performed is rabbinic. Their proof for this is derived from the prohibition on dragging. Even though the furrow is made with a *shinui* and not by an instrument normally used to plow, it is still prohibited (*Shabbat* 46b). Others maintain that making a furrow by dragging a heavy object over the ground is prohibited by Torah law, because it is not considered a *shinui*. Rather, it is extremely similar to the classic way of plowing. This is the opinion of Rabbeinu Tam and R. Avraham ben Ha-Rambam. See *Menuḥat Ahava* 2:1:6. If a furrow would actually be detrimental to the yard, it would seem that one may drag items, as the action would be considered a *psik reisha de-lo niḥa lei* in a case of a double rabbinic prohibition (according to many), since the furrow is made in a way that is irregular as well as destructive. See above, ch. 9 n. 2.
3. If one plants a seed on Shabbat but removes the seed from the ground before it takes root, then according to Rashash, he has not violated Torah law, because the

One may not leave an avocado pit in a dish of water so that it will take root and begin to grow. Likewise, one may not put a branch in water so that it will take root and start growing.

Included in the prohibition is germinating seeds in water so that the sprouts can then either be eaten or transferred to soil. It is also forbidden to soak seeds in water to soften them, preparing them to take root and grow (SA 336:11).[4] However, one may soak barley to soften it before feeding it to animals. This is because one does not desire for the barley to grow; besides, the barley is removed from the water and fed to the animals before the roots emerge (MB 336:51).

One should not toss seeds onto damp ground. Since they could start growing, one who tossed them would be guilty of planting on Shabbat. However, one may throw seeds somewhere they probably will not grow. Therefore, one may throw seeds in a place where people walk regularly, or in front of animals who will eat them within a day or two (SA 336:4).

One may not open or close the windows or doors of a greenhouse in order to encourage the growth of the plants inside. However, if there is a houseplant in the room, one may still open the shades and the windows for one's own sake, even though the sunlight and air that enter will indirectly help the potted plant grow. Since he did not open the shades and windows for this purpose, and the benefit to the plant is remote, it is not prohibited (as it is a *psik reisha* in a case of a double rabbinic prohibition, since the *melakha* is done both with a *shinui* and via *grama*; *Har Tzvi*, OḤ §133 and *Yeḥaveh Da'at* 5:29).

---

prohibition takes place only when the seed takes root. According to *Minḥat Ḥinukh* and *Eglei Tal, Zore'a* 8, simply placing the seeds is already a Torah prohibition.

4. According to *Nishmat Adam* 11:1 and AHS 336:30, planting seeds even in a planter that does not have holes is prohibited by Torah law. In contrast, according to Mahari Ḥagiz and *Eglei Tal, Zore'a* 9, the prohibition is rabbinic, since normally people do not plant using such a flowerpot. The reason that soaking seeds is prohibited by Torah law is because that is the way it is generally done (see *Menuḥat Ahava* vol. 2 ch. 3 n. 33). Recently, people have begun growing seeds and plants hydroponically, using water and a combination of chemicals to substitute for the nutrients normally found in soil. It would seem that all would agree that one who plants seeds hydroponically violates Torah law, since nowadays this is a normal way of planting, similar to the case of planting in dirt on a roof (*Responsa Rosh* 2:4).

4. IRRIGATION

One may not water plants, as it helps them grow and thus constitutes *Zore'a*. However, one may open irrigation pipes or turn on sprinklers before Shabbat even if they will water plants during Shabbat. Similarly, one may program a computer before Shabbat to activate sprinklers on Shabbat, as on Shabbat no action will be done by a Jew. One who opened irrigation pipes before Shabbat may close them on Shabbat, as this involves no *melakha* (see above 2:9).

One who eats in a yard must be careful not to wash his hands over plants or their roots (SA 336:3). If the plants are small and their roots are short, the prohibition applies only in the immediate vicinity of the plants, but if the plants are large, the prohibition applies to the entire garden bed around them.

One may pour water on the ground if there are no plants or roots nearby. Even though it is possible that eventually the water will reach roots or that wild flowers will subsequently grow there, this is not prohibited since one does not intend this to happen (*Kaf Ha-ḥayim* 336:27).

One may not pour water on his own soil if it is suitable for planting. Since this softens the ground, preparing it for planting, it is considered *Ḥoresh* (MB 336:26; SHT *ad loc.* 18).

5. USING A SINK WHOSE WATER DRAINS INTO THE YARD

If a sink's drainpipe empties onto soil where plants grow, it may not be used on Shabbat by anyone who has an interest in the plants being watered. It goes without saying that one may not use this sink on Shabbat if it was intentionally set up to water the plants.

Nevertheless, many *poskim* maintain that one who does not care about watering the plants may use such a sink on Shabbat – for example, if the plants do not belong to him and he has no interest in their growth. In a time of need, one may rely on these *poskim*. To be sure, one who pours water directly onto plants violates a prohibition, even if he does not intend to water them, because he is helping them grow. In contrast, here the water is poured indirectly and is therefore a case of *grama* and permitted (SSK 12:19). If the water from the sink reaches plants that have already been adequately watered, whether through heavy rains or water that drained from the sink before Shabbat, then even one who is interested in the plants growing may use the sink on Shabbat, since he is not helping them at all.

Rain sometimes falls on Sukkot, and in order to prevent one's *sukka* from getting wet one might extend a sliding roof over it. When the rain stops, he will want to retract the roof, but he knows that if he does so, water that accumulated on the rooftop will spill onto the nearby plants. May he retract the roof anyway on Shabbat and Yom Tov? It depends: If the rain was hard enough and long enough to saturate the ground, one may retract the roof, because the extra water serves no purpose. However, if there was only a little rain, the roof may not be retracted, because this will water the plants and violate *Zore'a*.[5]

6. *KOTZER*

Kotzer refers to cutting something off from its source of growth, and it includes harvesting grain, picking grapes, dates, olives, or figs, and pulling off any other fruit or branch from a tree. Cutting down trees to use for heating or building is included in this prohibition as well. It is also forbidden to pull grass out of a crevice in a wall or to remove fungi

5. This is the approach of *Ḥut Shani* (*melekhet Zore'a*) and *Orḥot Shabbat* ch. 18 n. 10; see *Kaf Ha-ḥayim* 336:29. Concerning the sink, I followed the position of those who are lenient and maintain that as long as one is not interested in watering the plants, one may use the sink. However, some are stringent and maintain that even if one is not interested in watering the plants, one may not spill water in the sink. This is the position of *Az Nidberu* 4:17 and R. Levi Yitzḥak Halperin (*Ma'aseh U-grama Ba-halakha* 4:2:5). According to them, the water that flows into the yard via the drainpipe is not viewed as arriving there through *grama* and *ko'aḥ sheni*, but rather it is as if the person is pouring it directly. However, in practice, when necessary one may rely on those who are lenient, as I write in the main text in the name of SSK. A *psik resiha de-lo niḥa lei* is only rabbinically prohibited (and according to *Arukh* it is permitted), so when it is unclear whether it is also *grama* and permitted, the *halakha* follows the lenient position. Indeed, *Yalkut Yosef* 336, *Zore'a* 9 and *Menuḥat Ahava* 2:3:8 say as much. If the water that flows from the sink reaches plants that have no need of water – whether because there was heavy rainfall and the ground is saturated, or a large amount of water flowed from the sink before Shabbat – watering these plants is not prohibited on account of *Zore'a* (*Petaḥ Ha-devir* as quoted by *Kaf Ha-ḥayim* 336:29). It would seem that in such a case, even those who are otherwise stringent would be lenient.

from bucket handles (*Shabbat* 73b and 107b). Taking an avocado pit or a branch out of water is forbidden as well, if it has started growing roots.

According to Torah law, there is no prohibition on picking fruits, branches, or leaves from a tree that has completely dried out. Since the tree is not absorbing nourishment from the soil, one who pulls off a part of it is not detaching it from the source of its growth. However, since this resembles harvesting, the Sages forbade it. (See SA 336:12.)

In contrast, if a branch was cut off a tree before Shabbat, since it is clear that the branch has already been detached from its source of nourishment, the prohibition of *Kotzer* no longer applies to it, and one may pull off its fruits on Shabbat. If it is a fragrant branch, one may pick twigs or leaves from it in order to smell them (Rema 336:8).

7. USING A TREE

As a precaution, the Sages prohibited using a tree on Shabbat, out of concern that one may end up breaking off a branch or leaf. Therefore, one may not climb or lean against a tree[6] and may not place items on trees or remove items from them. If the wind blows an item of clothing into a tree on Shabbat, one may not remove it. Similarly, one may not recover a ball that fell into a tree nor shake the tree so that the ball will fall out (SA 336:1; MB *ad loc.* 3). One should take care not to place things on a tree before Shabbat if they will be needed on Shabbat (MB 336:12). However, one may touch a tree if he is not using or moving it (Rema 336:13).

---

6. The prohibition of leaning against a tree applies only when one puts all his weight on it. In contrast, a healthy person may lean a bit on a strong tree, since leaning on it slightly is not considered using the tree. This is on condition that the tree is strong enough that it will not move. Furthermore, a weak person may not lean even slightly on the tree, since due to his weakness he may end up shifting all his weight onto the tree and thus violate the prohibition of using it (MB 336:63).

   One who unknowingly climbed a tree may descend even though he will be using the tree again, because remaining in the tree would also be considered using it. However, if he purposely climbed a tree on Shabbat, the Sages mandated as a penalty that he may not descend until Shabbat is over (SA 336:1). If he can get down by simply jumping, without using the tree, he should do so (R. Shlomo Zalman Auerbach cited in SSK ch. 26 n. 45).

Not only is using a tree prohibited, it is also prohibited to use items resting directly on a tree. For example, one may not use a swing that is attached to a tree, even if only one side is attached. One may not remove an item of clothing from a clothesline that is tied to a tree. Similarly, one may not climb a ladder that is resting against a tree, and one may not remove things from a basket hanging from a tree.

However, if a peg was driven into a tree and a swing was hung from the peg, one may use the swing. This is because only the peg is considered resting on the tree, while the swing is resting on the peg. Since the swing is two steps removed from the tree, this was not included in the rabbinic prohibition. Similarly, one may remove an item of clothing from a clothesline that is tied to a peg stuck into a tree, because the clothesline is two steps removed from the tree. If before Shabbat one rested a ladder against a peg embedded in a tree, one may climb the ladder on Shabbat, because the ladder is two steps removed from the tree. If before Shabbat items were placed in a basket hanging from a hook stuck in a tree, one may put items into it and remove them on Shabbat, because this too is two steps removed from the tree. However, on Shabbat one may not rest the ladder against the peg or hang the basket on the hook, because that would be making use of an item resting directly on a tree (SA 336:13; MB *ad loc.* 63).

Regarding the roots of an old tree that protrude above the ground, if they protrude less than three *tefaḥim* from the ground (about 9 in or 23 cm), then they are considered equivalent to the ground, and one may sit upon them. However, if the roots protrude above this height, they are considered equivalent to a tree, and one may not sit upon them (SA 336:2).

8. ADDITIONAL LAWS

The Sages' enactment against using trees applies to shrubs and vines that have hard branches or yield hard fruit, like pumpkins. However, the enactment does not include soft weeds, bushes, or branches. Therefore, one may sit on a lawn on Shabbat, even if it moves the grass slightly.

One may not smell an edible fruit while it is attached to its tree, lest one end up plucking the fruit in order to eat it. However, one may smell fragrant flowers where they grow. This is because he has no reason to pick them, as they can be smelled while still attached to the ground.

If tree branches themselves are fragrant, one may not grasp them and move them closer to smell them, because one may not move them, just as one may not move a tree. If the branches are soft and pliant, as are myrtle branches, one may grasp them and move them closer to smell them. One must, of course, be careful not to pluck the branches.[7]

One may walk on a lawn even though walking on it may uproot some grass. This is because he does not intend to do this, and it is not necessarily going to happen. But if the grass is high and it is certain that walking on it will cause some of it to be torn up, one may not walk on it (SA 336:3; BHL *ad loc.*).

Not only did the Sages prohibit using a tree, they also prohibited riding on an animal, lest the rider break a branch to use as a riding crop to direct the animal. The Sages also prohibited extracting honey from honeycombs, because this resembles picking produce (SA 321:13).

One may bring his animals to a grassy area so that they may graze. This is not considered *Kotzer* because the animals are eating for themselves. We are not commanded to ensure that animals keep Shabbat; we simply must ensure that they do not perform *melakhot* on our behalf (*Shabbat* 122a; SA 324:13).

9. FLOWERS AND BRANCHES IN A VASE

Flowers, branches, or stems that were picked before Shabbat for their beauty or fragrance, are not *muktzeh* on Shabbat. Therefore, a vase containing branches that are used for their beauty or fragrance may be moved. Similarly, they may be removed from the water for viewing or smelling. There is no problem of *Kotzer,* since there are no roots. One may also return stems to the water if they do not have flowers, or if they have fully-developed flowers. There is no problem of *Zore'a,* since the water will not cause any further growth but will only preserve their freshness so they do not wither.

---

7. Some say that the prohibition on using a tree includes moving soft grass or weeds (*Baḥ* and *Taz*). Alternatively, some prohibit moving grass on account of *muktzeh* (MA to SA 311:6; *Kaf Ha-ḥayim* 336:62). However, most are permissive, as Rema writes in 336:1 and SA implies in 336:10 and 312:6. This approach is also followed by MB 312:19; 336:15, 48 and *Livyat Ḥen* 104:6. The grass is not *muktzeh* because they maintain that *muktzeh* does not apply to anything attached to the ground.

However, one may not place in water any stems with flowers that are budding or that have not yet fully opened, because placing them in the water causes further growth. Nevertheless, one may remove them from the water. This is not considered *Kotzer*, because they have not put down roots in the water. Once removed, though, one may not replace them. Therefore, if one receives a bouquet of flowers as a gift on Shabbat and it contains flowers that have not yet fully opened, one may not place them in water, as this will cause the flowers to grow and open. Rather, one should put the bouquet in a vase that does not contain water.[8]

10. A FLOWERPOT

Just as one may not break off a branch or leaf from a plant growing in soil, so too one may not break off anything from a potted plant. If the flowerpot has holes in the bottom, it is considered connected to the ground. Thus one who plucks anything from it transgresses *Kotzer* by Torah law. If the flower pot does not have holes in the bottom, it is not considered connected to the ground, as this is not the way plants normally grow. Thus one who plucks anything from it transgresses only rabbinically (SA 336:7; MB *ad loc.* 42). Similarly, one may not water potted plants (MB 336:41; see n. 4 above).

8. Rema 336:11. According to Maharikash, one may put flowers in water as well, since even if they open it is not considered new growth. His opinion is not accepted. SHT 336:48 even states that a Torah prohibition may be involved. It is generally agreed that one who removed branches from water may put them back. Aḥaronim disagree, however, whether one may put them in water to begin with. *Tosefet Shabbat* and *Ḥayei Adam* prohibit doing so, while SAH and *Pri Megadim* permit it, as is quoted by MB 336:54. SHT *ad loc.* 48 states that one may be lenient, as the law in question is rabbinic. This is on condition that he prepared a container of water before Shabbat. However, on Shabbat, one may not fill a container with water in which to place the branches. This is because it involves exerting effort for the sake of the branches, which is prohibited, as explained in *Sukka* 42a in the context of a *lulav*. *Yeḥaveh Da'at* 2:53 is lenient, based on Rashba, and allows one to fill a container with water on Shabbat. The reason is that while we are stringent regarding a *lulav* because it is *muktzeh*, this stringency does not apply to other branches. As SA 321:11 states: "One may water a detached plant to prevent it from withering." This is also the position of *Menuḥat Ahava* vol. 2 ch. 3 n. 18. It would seem that one may rely on the lenient position, since this is a dispute regarding a rabbinic prohibition.

One may not move a potted plant from its place on Shabbat, because it is *muktzeh*. It is considered a *kli she-melakhto le-isur* (see ch. 23) since watering its contents or picking them is prohibited. However, one may move it if he needs the space it occupies (below 23:8). If the potted plant is frequently moved from place to place for aesthetic reasons or so that it can be smelled, it is not *muktzeh*, since its primary use is a permissible one.

Sometimes moving a potted plant is prohibited on account of *Zore'a* or *Kotzer*. For example, if the flowerpot has a hole in the bottom the size of a small root and it is resting on the ground, the hole allows the plant to draw sustenance from the ground, and thus it is considered connected to the ground. Thus, one may not move the pot from the ground and place it on a hard plastic surface, because that would violate *Kotzer*. Conversely, if the plant is on a hard plastic saucer, it may not be moved from there and placed on the ground, because that would violate *Zore'a*. Thus, if one needs to move the flower pot to use the space it is occupying, he must be careful to move it together with the saucer underneath it.[9]

If a flower pot tipped over and some of its dirt spilled out, one may not put the dirt back in the pot, because doing so helps the plant grow and thus transgresses both *Ḥoresh* and *Zore'a*. Additionally, soil is *muktzeh* and may not be moved. Even if no dirt spilled, but the flowerpot's fall exposed the roots of the plant and they will be covered back up if the plant is restored to a standing state, one may not do so even

9. This law is explained in SA 336:7-8. If a flower pot has a hole in the bottom, one may not lift it from the ground and place it on pegs. Even if it is only removed for a short period of time, and even if there is no object coming between it and the ground, it has nevertheless been distanced from its life source. Similarly, one may not remove the flower pot from the pegs and return it to the ground (SA 336:8 and MB *ad loc.*)

There are many opinions about how big the hole must be. The standard ruling is about an inch (2-2.5 cm). There is disagreement whether floor tiles are viewed as separating the hole from the ground. *Brit Olam* and *Menuḥat Ahava* 2:4:7 maintain that they do. R. Shlomo Zalman Auerbach says that floor tiles only separate the hole from the ground when they are on the second floor or higher. Ḥazon Ish maintains that ceramic tiles do not separate, but marble tiles do. If a flower pot is on a plastic saucer, it is equivalent to a flower pot that does not have holes. (See *Orḥot Shabbat* 18:18 and *Harḥavot*.) Thus, as long as the flower pot has a saucer underneath it, it may be moved from place to place.

using one's foot (such that *muktzeh* is not an issue), because covering the roots violates both *Ḥoresh* and *Zore'a*. (One may open a window in a room containing a plant, as explained above at the end of section 3.)

11. *ME'AMER*

Me'amer refers to gathering harvested grain into sheaves or piles. Similarly, one who gathers picked fruit and places them in boxes or piles transgresses *Me'amer*, as does one who gathers cut branches or reeds to use as fuel.

This *melakha*, as a rule, relates to objects that grow in the ground and are still located in the area where they grew. This is because the harvest is generally gathered where it grows. However, some types of produce are gathered in two stages. For such produce, both stages are prohibited by Torah law, even if the second stage does not take place in the field. This is the case, for example, when producing a pressed fig cake. The first stage in this process involves gathering figs from the field, which is prohibited on Shabbat on account of *Me'amer*. The second stage involves pressing them together to produce a cake. Doing this even at home is prohibited by Torah law as a *tolada* of *Me'amer*, since this is the standard way to form these cakes (SA 340:10; MB *ad loc.* 38; see *Menuḥat Ahava* 2:5:2).

Gathering fruit scattered in a yard is not prohibited by Torah law, because they are not located where they grew, yet the Sages nevertheless prohibited gathering them because it resembles a weekday activity. However, one may collect a few pieces of fruit and eat them. If the fruit fell in one place and did not scatter very much, one may collect them and put them in a basket. If they fell into gravel or dirt, even if they are all in one place, one may not gather them and place them in a basket, because doing so resembles *Borer*. However, one may pick them up one at a time and eat them (SA 335:5).

One may collect fruit that is scattered inside one's home, because gathering items inside does not resemble *Me'amer* (MB 340:37).[10]

10. However, some prohibit gathering fruit even inside, maintaining that it requires just as much effort in one's home as in the yard (*Az Nidberu* 14:17; *Menuḥat Ahava* 2:5:6). MB 340:37 implies that this is permitted inside. *Or Le-Tziyon* 2:43:7 also permits,

Although according to Torah law, *Me'amer* applies only to things that grow in the ground, the Sages forbade collecting salt from salt mines. Since this salt looks like it grows from the ground, collecting it resembles *Me'amer* (SA 340:9). Based on this, several Aḥaronim rule that one may not gather eggs that were laid before Shabbat (*Ketzot Ha-shulḥan*; however, *Shevet Ha-Levi* 4:39 is lenient). Eggs that were laid on Shabbat are *muktzeh*, and therefore one may not pick up even one egg.

Me'amer does not apply to items that have undergone major transformations. Thus, one may gather cooked fruits together. Similarly, gathering clothing made from natural fibers is not a problem, since they have been transformed from their original state (AHS 340:3).

---

maintaining that fruit inside is viewed as having already been gathered, and thus *Me'amer* is irrelevant. Even those who are stringent regarding gathering inside would still allow throwing candies or almonds at a groom in the synagogue. Even though children will collect them and put them into bags, it is an effortless expression of happiness and not a weekday activity (*Menuḥat Ahava* 2:5:7).

Chapter Twenty

Animals

1. REST FOR ANIMALS

Just as a Jew is commanded to rest on Shabbat, so too, he is commanded to allow his animals to rest. There are two commandments that address this issue, one positive (*aseh*), as the Torah states (Shemot 23:12): "Six days you shall do your work, but on the seventh day you shall cease, so that your **ox** and your **donkey** may rest, and the son of your maidservant and the stranger may be refreshed." And one negative (*lo ta'aseh*), as the Torah states (Shemot 20:10): "But the seventh day is a Shabbat of the Lord your God; you shall not do any *melakha* – you, your son or daughter, your male or female slave, or your **beast**, or the stranger who is within your settlements." The mitzva of allowing animals to rest is not one of the 39 *melakhot* but a mitzva in its own right; its violation is not punishable by death or lashes (*Shabbat* 154a; MT 20:1-2).

Even though the Torah in those verses mentions beasts, oxen, and donkeys, the prohibition applies to all animals, including birds and fish (MB 305:1). Therefore, one may not release carrier pigeons on Shabbat, and one may not use trained dolphins to pull a boat. The Torah specifies the ox and the donkey because they are the beasts of burden most commonly used for plowing and carrying heavy loads.

One who causes an animal carrying a load to move from one place to another on Shabbat, whether by striking, pulling, or ordering it, transgresses Torah law. This prohibition is referred to as *Meḥamer*.

Even if the animal belongs to a non-Jew or is ownerless, one may not cause it to walk with a burden. If one causes his own animal to do so, then in addition to transgressing the *lo ta'aseh* against doing work, he has also violated the *aseh* of allowing animals to rest (SA 266:1-2; MB *ad loc.* 7-8). The latter commandment applies on Yom Kippur as well (there is disagreement about whether it applies on Yom Tov; see MB 246:19).

A Jew may not rent his animal to a non-Jew who will use it to do work like plowing or carrying burdens in the public domain on Shabbat. If a Jew rents out an animal with the understanding that it will be returned before Shabbat, but it is not, he should declare the animal ownerless before Shabbat to avoid violating Torah law (SA 246:3). If a Jew and a non-Jew are co-owners of an animal, the Jew may not permit the non-Jew to work the animal on Shabbat. However, if when they first bought the animal they specified that the non-Jew would be the sole owner on Shabbat, while the Jew would be the sole owner on a different day of the week, then the non-Jew may work the animal on Shabbat, because on Shabbat it is his alone (SA 246:5).

A Jew may allow a non-Jew to ride his horse or other animal on Shabbat, in accordance with the principle that "a living being carries itself" (*he-ḥai nosei et atzmo*). Therefore, the non-Jew who rides the animal is not considered a burden (nor are the clothes he wears, as they are secondary to his body). However, the Sages enacted that a Jew may not use an animal at all. He may not lean on it, place an object on it, or sit in a wagon hitched to it, even if a non-Jew is driving the wagon for his own purposes (SA 305:18). The reason for this enactment is to avoid burdening the animal on Shabbat (*y. Beitza* 5:2). Another reason is that while riding an animal, one may come to break off a tree branch in order to goad the animal, thus transgressing *Kotzer* (*Beitza* 36b).

A Jew may not take another Jew's animal outside of *teḥum Shabbat*. This *teḥum* is based on the *teḥum* of the animal's owner (see below, 30:3). If the owner entrusted the animal to a shepherd, whether Jew or non-Jew, the *teḥum* is based on that of the shepherd (SA 397:3-5). The prohibition is only for the animal to leave the *teḥum* at the initiative of its owner; it is not prohibited for the animal to leave of its own volition or for a non-Jewish shepherd to take it outside the *teḥum* (Rema 305:23; MB *ad loc.* 79).

2. ANIMALS AND CARRYING

As we have seen, one must allow animals to rest on Shabbat. This includes making sure that one's animal does not enter a semipublic (*karmelit*) or public domain with a burden on its back. However, not everything an animal carries is defined as a burden. Just as one may enter a different domain wearing his clothes because they are secondary to his body, so too a donkey suffering from the cold may be taken outside wearing a pack saddle that is meant to warm it. Other animals, though, which do not suffer from the cold, may not be taken outside with a saddle (SA 305:7). Similarly, a dog that is wrapped in an article of clothing may not be taken outside. Since it does not truly need this, the clothing is considered a burden. If one is not taking the dog outside, one may dress it, as there is no prohibition to carry in a private domain.

One may take out an animal that is wearing a bandage to protect an injury or a sheep that is wearing a cover designed to keep its wool from getting dirty. This is on condition that they are tightly bound to the animal, with no possibility that they will fall off, thus ensuring that no one will end up carrying them in a semipublic or public domain (SA 305:6). One may not take out an animal with a muzzle that is meant to prevent the animal from grazing in other people's fields. This is because the muzzle is not worn for the animal's sake, but for the sake of the fields' owners (SA 305:11).

One may not lead an animal with a bell around its neck, as doing so generates sound, and it is rabbinically prohibited to generate sound with an object specifically designed for this purpose, such as a musical instrument. However, if the bell is silenced and makes no sound, the animal may be led around in a private domain but not a public domain. If the animal were to be led around in a public domain, it would seem like it was being taken to market for sale (*Shabbat* 53a and 54b; MB 305:42-43). The bell itself is not considered a burden as it is secondary to the animal's halter.

One may take out a horse wearing a bridle or a donkey wearing a halter since these items are used to direct the animals and to prevent them from running away. However, a donkey may not be taken out wearing a bridle, as this would be an excessive precaution, far more than is necessary to ensure that the donkey will not run away. The general principle is that anything normally used to ensure that an animal will not run away is not considered a burden, but anything excessive is considered a burden (SA 305:1; MB *ad loc.* 8).

A dog may be allowed out in a public domain wearing its collar, because that is the normal way for it to go out since it allows one to restrain the dog if necessary by grabbing its collar or attaching a leash to it (SA 305:5; MB *ad loc.* 12). The person holding the leash is not considered carrying the leash, since it is secondary to the dog's body. However, he must take care to grasp the leash within a *tefaḥ* of its end. He also must make sure that the leash does not droop to within a *tefaḥ* of the ground at any point. If either of these things happens, it looks like he is carrying the leash. If the leash is too long, he may wrap it around the dog's neck so it is less likely to droop (SA 305:16).

A blind person may enter a public domain with a seeing-eye dog, even though he is holding the harness attached to the dog. Since the harness is always attached to the dog, it is secondary to its body, and there is no problem of carrying. (Although *Orḥot Shabbat* 31:17 is stringent, it seems reasonable to permit, as explained in *Harḥavot*; this is also the position of *Mikveh Ha-mayim* 4:39; *Menuḥat Ahava* 3:27:49; and *Yalkut Yosef* 305:59.)

A dog may be taken out into a public domain wearing dog tags connected to its collar or ear and on which is engraved the name of the dog's owner. The tags make it clear that the dog has an owner, and thus people are more likely to leave it alone.[1]

---

1. AHS 305:5 forbids taking out a dog wearing dog tags as a sign for people to leave it alone. He brings a proof from the rule that forbids taking out roosters wearing strings as a similar sign to people (SA 305:17). However, SSK ch. 27 n. 34 cites R. Shlomo Zalman Auerbach as permitting it, since this sign is for the dog's benefit and protection. In contrast, if the goal is simply to avoid paying a fine, the dog tags are prohibited. It would also seem that if the sign is permanently attached to the animal's collar, then it is secondary to the collar and is not considered a burden, as explained in *Tosafot, Shabbat* 54b, s.v. "mishum"; MA 305:6; and *Eliya Rabba*.

According to Rashi and Ran, one may take out a dog or other animal with a collar whose purpose is solely decorative, on condition that doing so is the common practice. *Tosafot* and Rabbeinu Yeruḥam maintain that if the collar does not serve a protective purpose, it is forbidden. *Baḥ* rules stringently (MA 305:1; MB *ad loc.* 12).

3. FEEDING ANIMALS

An animal may be led to graze in a grassy area, and it does not constitute *Kotzer* since the animal is eating for its own sake. We are not commanded to make sure that animals keep Shabbat, only that they do not labor for our benefit (*Shabbat* 122:1; SA 324:13).

One may provide food and water to animals in his possession that depend on him, like cows, chickens, and cats. Food and water may also be provided to animals belonging to another Jew. However, one may not feed or water self-sufficient animals like bees and doves. Even though feeding them is not a *melakha*, the Sages prohibited it because it is seen as requiring excessive effort (SA 324:11; BHL s.v. "ve-yonei").

One may put food out for hungry animals like stray dogs and cats. As we know, God shows mercy to all His creatures, as it is written: "His mercy is upon all His works" (Tehilim 145:9). It is proper to emulate His ways (AHS 324:2-3; see MB *ad loc.* 31).

Animals are *muktzeh*. Therefore, they may not be picked up, nor may their limbs be lifted up. However, when it is necessary for their well-being (for example, in order to get them to their food), one may take hold of them and move their limbs to prevent them from suffering (*tza'ar ba'alei ḥayim*), as long as one does not lift them off the ground (SA 308:39-40; MB *ad loc.* 151).

If animals have difficulty eating unless the food is placed directly in their mouths, one may feed them in this way as long as he does not force-feed them. Force-feeding refers to shoving the food so far down their throats that they are unable to spit it up. This requires excessive effort (*Shabbat* 155b; SA 324:9-10).

One may ask a non-Jew to feed geese that have been force-fed for so long that they are unable to eat otherwise and would suffer hunger and pain if they were not fed on Shabbat. In such a case, one may ask a non-Jew to feed them one time on Shabbat. If there is no non-Jew available, the *poskim* disagree whether a Jew may feed them to minimize their suffering (MB 324:27). It is better not to force-feed geese at all, as doing so causes them pain and entails multiple prohibitions (see BHL *ad loc.*; SSK 27:26).

One may cut up food for animals if they would not be able to readily eat it otherwise. This includes cutting up pumpkins that are fed to animals and tough carcasses that are fed to dogs and that they have trouble eating. However, one may not cut up any food for them that they could eat by themselves. Even if cutting makes it easier for them to eat, it is excessive effort and thus forbidden on Shabbat (SA 324:3-8).

4. MILKING ON SHABBAT

Torah law forbids milking a cow or any other animal on Shabbat, as doing so separates the milk from the cow's body and constitutes *Mefarek* (separating something from its source), a *tolada* of *Dash*. Just as one may not separate grain from its husk, so too, one may not separate milk from its source (*Shabbat* 95a).

The problem is that if a dairy cow, which produces great quantities of milk, is not milked on Shabbat, it suffers greatly. Therefore, the Sages permitted asking a non-Jew to milk a cow on Shabbat. Even though, generally speaking, it is rabbinically prohibited to ask a non-Jew to do *melakha* for us on Shabbat, here they suspended the prohibition in order to avoid *tza'ar ba'alei ḥayim*. It is true that this milk is *muktzeh* on Shabbat. However, after Shabbat a Jew may drink or sell it (SA 305:20).

If there is no non-Jew available, a Jew may milk the cow, as long as the milk goes to waste. For example, it may be milked directly onto the ground, or into a bucket that contains an agent that will ruin the milk. This is because milking to make use of the milk is prohibited by Torah law, whereas milking for another reason, in which the milk goes to waste, is only rabbinically prohibited. A Torah prohibition may not be transgressed in order to prevent animals' suffering, but the Sages suspended their own enactment.[2]

2. Even though according to Ramban, milking is only prohibited rabbinically, *halakha* follows the opinion of Rif, Rambam, and Rashi that milking is prohibited by Torah law. On account of the animals' suffering, the Sages permitted asking a non-Jew to milk on Shabbat (most *poskim* maintain that *tza'ar ba'alei ḥayim* is Torah law; see *Peninei Halakha: Collected Essays Likutim III* 10:6.) If no non-Jew is available, a Jew may milk the cows, but in such a way that the milk will go to waste, since according to Rabbeinu Tam (cited in *Tosafot, Ketubot* 6a) one may milk wastefully on Shabbat. Even though Ri (cited *ad loc.*) maintains that one may not milk in such a manner, in order to prevent animal suffering we permit it (SSK 27:49; *Ḥazon Ish* 56:4).

Nowadays, dairy farming has been modernized, and milking is automated. A cup is placed on the teat and connected to a pump via a tube. If there is a non-Jew available, one may ask him to turn on the machine and place the cups on the cow on Shabbat, because otherwise the cows would suffer. If no non-Jew is available, common practice is for a Jew to use a timer or a delay mechanism that is set before Shabbat to turn on the machine. On Shabbat, before the machine turns on, the cups are attached to the cow's teats, and then the machine turns on and automatically pumps out the milk. Thus, the Jew has not performed any *melakha* directly, for when he attached the cups, the machine was not on. Even though placing the cups on the teats causes a *melakha* to take place, this is not prohibited by Torah law. The Torah only forbids direct action, as it states: "You shall not do any *melakha*" (Shemot 20:10). The Sages forbade indirectly causing a *melakha* to be performed. Here, to prevent the cows from becoming painfully engorged, the Sages permitted acting via *grama*. After Shabbat, a Jew may benefit from this milk.

If the cups must be attached to the teats while the machine is operating, then doing so in order to save the milk violates Torah law. Therefore, the milk should spill directly onto the ground, making the action rabbinically prohibited and thus permissible to prevent *tza'ar ba'alei ḥayim* (SSK 27:50; for the laws relevant to a woman who is engorged, see above 11:17).

5. CARRYING PETS AND SICK ANIMALS

As we will see later on (23:5), anything that has no practical use on Shabbat is *muktzeh* and may not be carried. Animals are included in this category and thus may not be carried on Shabbat. If, in order to prevent them from being hurt, it is necessary to move them, the Sages permitted pulling them but not picking them up (SA 308:39-40). At first glance, this would seem to pertain to house pets like cats and dogs, and indeed, this is the position of *Yalkut Yosef* (vol. 2, p. 383) and *Orḥot Shabbat* (19:124). However, it seems more reasonable to assume that *muktzeh* pertains only to animals with which one does not normally play. Pets whose owners play with them and pick them up all week long would not be *muktzeh*, and their owners may thus touch them and pick them up on Shabbat. Similarly, seeing-eye dogs are not *muktzeh* (*Igrot Moshe*, OḤ

5:22:21; *Shulḥan Shlomo* 308:74). Although some are stringent, *muktzeh* is a rabbinic prohibition so the *halakha* follows those who are lenient.[3]

A fish that jumped out of an aquarium and will presumably stay alive if it is returned may be put back even though it is *muktzeh*. This is because, when necessary, and when there is no other solution, one may move a *muktzeh* object to prevent *tza'ar ba'alei ḥayim*. Even though some are stringent in this case, one may rely on the lenient approach (See SA 305:19; MB *ad loc.* 70; SSK 27:28).

If a fish in an aquarium dies, and it is possible that if it is left in the aquarium other fish will catch whatever terminal disease it had, then even though the dead fish is *muktzeh*, it may be removed from the tank to save the remaining fish. If there is a dog or cat in the vicinity, the fish should be fed to them (see SSK 27:29).

6. THE *MELAKHA* OF *TZAD*

Trapping animals was one of the *melakhot* performed for the *Mishkan*. They would trap *teḥashim* to make curtains from their skins and the *ḥilazon* to produce *tekhelet* to dye the curtains (*Shabbat* 73a; Rashi *ad loc.*; *Shabbat* 75a).

The Torah prohibition of *Tzad* is limited to those animals – beasts, birds, or fish – that are normally trapped or hunted for a purpose, whether to eat their meat, use their skins, or enjoy their beauty (as is the case with parrots). In contrast, one who traps species that are not

3. *Maharaḥ Or Zaru'a* §81 permits carrying pet birds in their cage, maintaining that they are not *muktzeh*, albeit while noting that Rosh disagrees and maintains that all animals are *muktzeh*. Indeed, this is the opinion of the majority of *poskim* according to MB 308:146 and SSK 27:27 (*Yabi'a Omer* 5:26 states that if one wishes to move birds in order to prevent their suffering, such as if the sun is beating down on them, one may rely on *Maharaḥ Or Zaru'a*). However, all these discussions relate to birds, which are not commonly carried. In contrast, today people keep house pets and carry them around all week. For this reason, *Igrot Moshe* states that birds are *muktzeh* (OḤ 4:16) and succinctly that pets are not (OḤ 5:22:21). This is also the position of R. Shlomo Zalman Auerbach in *Shulḥan Shlomo* 308:74. Others are stringent (*Yalkut Yosef* vol. 2, p. 383; *Orḥot Shabbat* 19:124). As I have written above, the *halakha* follows those who are lenient. Bird cages and aquariums, which are not normally carried, are *muktzeh*. If one normally moves them around during the week for decorative purposes, then according to R. Shlomo Zalman Auerbach they are not *muktzeh* (*Shulḥan Shlomo* 308:74:2).

normally hunted, such as flies and other insects, violates rabbinic law (*Shabbat* 106b; SA 316:3).

The prohibition of *Tzad* does not apply to tame animals that do not run away from their owners, such as cows, donkeys, and dogs. Since in any case they stay with their owners, there is no such thing as trapping them (Rema 316:12; MB *ad loc.* 59). Nevertheless, carrying these animals is prohibited, as they are *muktzeh*. When necessary they may be grabbed and dragged into their pen or kennel, as long as they are not picked up (SA 308:40; see section 3 above).

If an animal is partially tame in that it runs away when a human tries to grab it but returns to its cage at night, its trapping is rabbinically prohibited (Rema 316:12: MB *ad loc.* 57, 59). When necessary, in order to avoid monetary loss or *tza'ar ba'alei ḥayim*, one may rely on those who are lenient and trap a partially tame animal. (See SA *ad loc.*; SSK 27:36.)

The Torah prohibition refers to completely trapping an animal; that is, holding it in hand, with ropes, or in a cage such that one can do with it as he pleases. Similarly, one who shepherds an animal into an area small enough that he can chase and catch it in one motion, he violates Torah law. In contrast, if one herds an animal into a large area where he would still need to chase it down in order to capture it, he does not violate Torah law, as the animal is not well and truly trapped. However, this is rabbinically prohibited, because the animal can now be more easily trapped. If he subsequently captures it, even though doing so is easier than usual, he is still violates Torah law, as this is the *Tzad* that the Torah forbids (*Shabbat* 106b; SA 316:1).

Hunting with the aid of a dog is forbidden. However, if one commands the dog with his voice and does not actually touch it, the prohibition is rabbinic. If he takes any action to help with the capture, he violates Torah law (Rema 316:2; MB *ad loc.* 10).

A mouse trap may be put out on Friday, since no action is taken on Shabbat. However, it is rabbinically prohibited to put out a trap on Shabbat. This is not prohibited by Torah law, as it is not certain that the trap will succeed in catching anything (MB 316:18).

An animal may be freed from a trap on Shabbat. While there is a prohibition to trap an animal, there is no prohibition to free an animal from a trap on Shabbat (MB 316:25).

One who wishes to feed a caged animal or bird whose nature is to try to escape must take care not to open the cage even briefly. If he mistakenly opened the cage, then if the cage is so small that confining the animal or bird to it would be considered *Tzad* by Torah law, then the cage may not be closed even *be-di'avad*. If the cage is large enough that confining the animal or bird to it would only be rabbinically prohibited, *be-di'avad* one may close it, since the animal or bird was inside when Shabbat began (*Pri Megadim*; BHL 316:6 s.v. "ve-halakh").

7. UNINTENTIONAL TRAPPING

Just as one may not chase an animal in order to trap it, so too one may not exploit the opportunity to catch an animal that got stuck in a confined space. Therefore, if a deer enters a house, the door may not be closed behind it. If a bird flies in through a window, the window may not be shut behind it (*Shabbat* 106b; SA 316:5). If one wishes to close the door or window in order to protect against thieves or the cold, the animal must first be chased out of the house.

If the household members are having trouble chasing out the animal or bird because it is hiding and eluding pursuit, if necessary the door or window may be closed. This is because the person doing so does not intend to trap the animal or bird, but only to protect the house from thieves or the cold. Besides, even after the door or window is closed, the animal is not truly trapped, because capturing it is still an effort.

Similarly, if a window screen has flies on it, and one wishes to close the window beyond it in order to prevent the heat or cold from entering, he must first chase away the flies so that they are not trapped between the window and the screen. If it is difficult to do so, the window may be closed even while they are still there, since one does not intend to trap the flies, only to protect against the heat or cold. Besides, the flies are not truly trapped; even if he wants to catch them, he would have to make an effort to do so.

Similarly, one who wants to close a small box that has flies in it should chase them away before closing it. If it is difficult to chase them all away, he should leave something between the cover and the box in order to create an escape hatch for the flies. If necessary, the box may be closed even though a fly will be trapped inside it, since his intention is not to trap the fly, but only to close the box. Besides, the fly is not truly trapped; even if he wants to catch it, when he opens the box it may very well escape.[4]

8. SLAUGHTERING (*SHOḤET*)

Shoḥet refers to the *melakha* of taking the life of a living being. For the *Mishkan*, they slaughtered *teḥashim* and goats in order to use their skins for the curtains (*Shabbat* 73a, 75a).

It is not only slaughtering that is prohibited. Rather, killing a living being in any fashion is forbidden by Torah law. It does not matter whether death is brought about by striking, strangling, or any other method. One who kills a tiny ant violates Torah law, as does one who removes a fish from water, since this kills the fish. Similarly,

---

4. In order to explain this *halakha*, we must first point out that in all the cases mentioned here, the trapping involved is only rabbinically prohibited, for the following reasons:
   1. The area is large enough that the animals are not truly trapped there. (If the box is very small, then *Sefer Ha-Teruma* maintains that the flies are considered trapped, while *Tur* maintains that they are not trapped since they can escape when the box is opened.)
   2. Flies and the like are not species that are hunted. Thus doing so is only rabbinically prohibited
   3. Since the goal is to close the house or box and not to trap anything, this is a *melakha she-eina tzerikha le-gufah*, which according to most *poskim* is only rabbinically prohibited.

   In all the cases mentioned above, the intention is not to trap but simply to close the window. As a result, these are examples of *psik reisha de-lo niḥa lei* in cases of a double rabbinic prohibition. It is generally agreed that in such instances, one can be lenient when necessary. In cases of true necessity, we are lenient for a *psik reisha* even if there is only one rabbinic prohibition (as explained above in ch. 9 n. 2; see MB 316:15, SHT *ad loc.* 18, and the upcoming footnote). Accordingly, *Ḥayei Adam* 30:2 and MB 316:5 state that if a bird flies into a house and is located in an area large enough that trapping the bird would only be rabbinically prohibited, one may close a window or door on account of the cold. Additionally, one may bring into consideration the following opinion of Rashba (*Shabbat* 107a) based on the Yerushalmi. Even though the Sages state: "If a deer enters a house and one locks it in, he is liable" (*Shabbat* 106b), nevertheless Rashba writes that as long as his intention in closing the door is to protect the house, it is not prohibited. Even though we do not follow this Rashba, we can combine his opinion with other mitigating factors to support leniency. See *Harḥavot*.

one who reaches his hand into an animal's womb and aborts its fetus on Shabbat violates Torah law (*Shabbat* 107b).

The Torah prohibition applies when the animal is killed for its corpse, i.e., to make use of its meat, skin, or blood. In contrast, one who kills destructively, such as stamping on ants because he wants them dead, transgresses rabbinically.

If one is walking and comes across ants, he should jump over them in order to avoid killing them and violating a rabbinic prohibition. If there is a colony of ants in his path and it is impossible to step there without killing ants, he should walk around them. If he is in a place where he cannot pass without walking on them, he may continue walking, since he does not intend to kill them. It is preferable that he walk on the sides of his feet and do his best to avoid killing ants.

Similarly, if there are insects in a toilet and there is a reasonable chance that flushing the toilet will kill them, it is preferable, when possible, to wait until they fly or crawl away. However, if they do not emerge, or if one must flush for the sake of human dignity, he may do so.

If ants are in a sink and can be blown out of the way, that is best. If it is difficult to do so, dishes or hands may still be washed, even though this will probably drown the ants. Since the one washing is not interested in killing them, and he needs the water, it is not prohibited.[5]

---

5. Even if it is clear that the ants or other insects will be killed, it is a *psik reisha de-lo niḥa lei* in a case of a double rabbinic prohibition, as the act is destructive and is being done with a *shinui*. We saw above (ch. 9 n. 2) that when necessary we are lenient in such cases. Even if one insists that the killing here is not done with a *shinui*, it is still a case of *psik reisha de-lo niḥa lei* applying to a rabbinic prohibition. In cases of true necessity, we are lenient even in such a case (MB 316:5; SHT 321:68, 337:10). Some maintain that we may be lenient in such a case even *le-khatḥila* (*Yeḥaveh Da'at* 2:46). If one walks on the sides of his feet, then the killing is definitely done with a *shinui*. Besides, it is possible that this will not kill them. Even though *Menuḥat Ahava* 3:18:10 and *Orḥot Shabbat* 14:27 are stringent, the primary position is the lenient one, as is recorded in *Minḥat Ish* 19:9. For a toilet infested with gnats, *Minḥat Yitzḥak* 10:27 offers additional factors to permit flushing: human dignity, *grama, melakha she-eina tzerikha le-gufah,* and maybe even *mitasek*. *Shevet Ha-Levi* 6:94 is in agreement.

9. WOUNDING (ḤOVEL)

Just as it is prohibited by Torah law to kill any living being, it is also prohibited by Torah law to cause a loss of blood. After all, "blood is life" (Devarim 12:23). Additionally, with the release of a little blood, there is a localized loss of life. This prohibition applies even when the blood does not exit the body, but simply hemorrhages from blood vessels and accumulates under the skin. This too is viewed as a localized loss of life (SA 316:8; BHL s.v. "ve-haḥovel").[6]

Accordingly, if one strikes another person on Shabbat with intent to injure and causes a hemorrhage or hematoma, he is not only guilty of an interpersonal transgression but also desecrates Shabbat. This is also true of one who angrily strikes an animal and causes a hemorrhage or hematoma. In addition to violating *tza'ar ba'alei ḥayim*, he transgresses the prohibition of *Ḥovel*.

One may not do a blood test on Shabbat. Since the goal is to use the blood, taking it is prohibited by Torah law. In cases of danger to life, of course, it is permitted. It is also forbidden to scratch or pick at a scab if doing so will cause it to bleed, or to brush one's teeth in a way that will cause the gums to bleed (as explained in 14:2).

A Jew may administer a shot to one who is ill, even if not dangerously so, as long as the injection is into flesh, since this will not necessarily cause the sick person to bleed. In contrast, if the shot or infusion is done into a vein, it is prohibited for a Jew to administer it to one who is not dangerously ill, since there will definitely be at least a little blood. However, a non-Jew may be asked to give this injection. If the sick person is dangerously ill, even a Jew may give the injection (below 28:7).

Killing lice: *Shabbat* 12a records a disagreement about killing lice on Shabbat. The conclusion reached there is that killing them involves no prohibition, as they spontaneously generate from inanimate matter. Now, however, since we know that lice do reproduce, it is forbidden to kill them. *Halakha* is determined in accordance with current knowledge. See *Harḥavot*.

6. Rashi maintains that *Ḥovel* is a *tolada* of *Shoḥet*. Several other Rishonim (such as Ran) discuss the issue but do not make it clear whether *Ḥovel* is a *tolada* of *Shoḥet* or part of the *av melakha*. Rambam maintains that *Ḥovel* is liable because of *Mefarek*, a *tolada* of *Dash*.

10. TRAPPING AND KILLING SNAKES, SCORPIONS, MOSQUITOES, AND OTHER PESTS

Danger to life overrides Shabbat. Therefore, animals likely to endanger human life may be killed even on Shabbat, like poisonous snakes and scorpions. Even if one is unsure whether a particular animal is poisonous, he may kill it. Similarly, a dangerous dog or rabid animal may be killed.

It is prohibited on Shabbat to kill animals whose bites hurt a great deal but are not life-threatening. This applies to snakes and scorpions that are definitely not poisonous. It is only forbidden to kill them the way one would kill them during the week, so one may kill them in the course of walking; one walks in their direction and in the course of walking steps on them and kills them. The reason for this dispensation is that killing an animal in a destructive manner, when one does not have any use for the cadaver, is only prohibited rabbinically. Thus, in order to avoid great suffering, the Sages permitted killing such animals in the course of walking. However, it is prohibited to kill them directly, out of concern that people will conclude that one may kill animals even when there is no concern that they will cause harm. If such animals are chasing a person, they may be killed even without a *shinui*.

Even if they are not chasing anyone, a receptacle may be placed over them in order to neutralize the threat. This does not need to be done with a *shinui*, because the person's goal is not to trap them, only to prevent them from stinging or biting (SA 316:7; MB *ad loc.* 27).

Animals whose stings are not so painful, such as mosquitoes and fleas, may not be killed in any manner on Shabbat. If the mosquito or flea is clinging to one's skin and cannot be removed without being grabbed, the Sages permitted grabbing it in order to remove it. This is on condition that he not kill it or even squeeze it, which might kill it. Even though grabbing an animal without intending to use it is rabbinically prohibited, the Sages were lenient here since the goal is to avoid suffering (SA 316:9). If one wishes to grab a flea and remove it from under his clothing rather than from his skin need not be dissuaded from doing so (MB 316:37; SHT *ad loc.* 63).

If there are mosquitoes or other pests in a room, one may spray insecticide to repel them as long as he does not spray the bugs directly and leaves open a window through which they can escape. This way he will not necessarily kill any of them. However, one may not spray them directly or to spray in a place where they have no means of escape, because then he will definitely kill them and transgress a prohibition (*Yabi'a Omer* 3:20; see SSK 25:6).

One may apply liquid mosquito repellent on Shabbat, but not an ointment (see above, 14:5).

One may place tablets into a plug-in device that contains a heating element that causes the tablets to heat up and release a mosquito-repellent vapor. It is proper to place the tablets at a short distance from the heating element so that they do not reach the temperature of *yad soledet bo,* which might present a problem of *Bishul* (*Ha-ḥashmal Ba-halakha* vol. 2, p. 364; above 10:4). However, if one is uncertain whether the tablets will reach *yad soledet bo,* he may place them.

Chapter Twenty-One

Hotza'ah

1. THE *MELAKHA* OF *HOTZA'AH*

The *melakha* of *Hotza'ah* consists of transporting an object from a private domain (*reshut ha-yaḥid*) to a public domain (*reshut ha-rabim*) or vice versa, or transporting an object more than four *amot* in a public domain.

During the six weekdays, man's role is to perform *melakhot* in order to improve and develop the world; to craft tools and instruments, build houses, and cultivate crops for food and textiles. The highest purpose of each and every *melakha* is to build the *Mishkan* and *Mikdash*, in which God's presence can dwell. Despite the tremendous value of work, the Torah commands us to refrain from all *melakha* on Shabbat in order to explore the foundations of faith and to study Torah. In this way, the work that we do all week long is imbued with deeper significance. It has the power to bring the world closer to perfection and establish within it a *Mikdash* for the Lord, God of Israel.

The novelty of *Hotza'ah* is that an act that does not physically alter an object can still be considered a *melakha*. Even changing its location in some substantive way is considered a *melakha*. Location is thus of paramount importance. There is nothing in the world that does not have a location, a place. When an item is in its place, it has a purpose; when it is not, it is unimportant. For example, in a place with no water, water is very valuable, while in a place with plenty of water, its value declines. Furthermore, nothing can exist without a place to be. This explains why God is referred to as *Makom* (Place) – because He ensures the world's continued existence and provides a place for it to be. When the Sages discussed each type of place, they used the word "*reshut*" (property, authority, domain), since every object exists by the authority of the place where it rests.

We find in the Torah that the donations for the *Mishkan* were collected from each individual's private domain (*reshut ha-yaḥid*) and were brought to the public domain (*reshut ha-rabim*) where the *Mishkan* was built. This was considered a *melakha,* as the verse states explicitly: "Moshe then ordered that the proclamation be made throughout the encampment: 'Let no man or woman make further effort (*melakha*) on behalf of the donations for the sanctuary!' And the people stopped bringing" (Shemot 36:6).

According to Torah law, there are three types of domains: a private domain (*reshut ha-yaḥid*), a public domain (*reshut ha-rabim*), and an exempt area (*mekom petur*). The Sages decreed that most places defined by Torah law as a *mekom petur* would have the status of a public domain. Such a rabbinically defined public domain is called a *karmelit.*

2. PRIVATE AND PUBLIC DOMAINS

A *reshut ha-yaḥid* is an area enclosed by walls, which render it a single place, and one may carry objects in this enclosed area. Even a large area surrounded by walls is considered one place, and there is no fundamental difference whether an object is located on its east or west side.

The classic example of a *reshut ha-yaḥid* is a house, though an area may be considered a *reshut ha-yaḥid* even without a roof. As long as it is enclosed by a barrier ten *tefaḥim* high (30 in or 76 cm), it is a *reshut ha-yaḥid.* A pit that is ten *tefaḥim* deep is also considered a *reshut ha-yaḥid,* as is a rock or hill that is ten *tefaḥim* high. Even if there are no walls surrounding the rock or hill, the fact that they are raised ten *tefaḥim* from the ground puts them in the same category as something walled. We treat them as if they have walls that extend upward beyond the top of the rock or hill. To be defined as a *reshut ha-yaḥid,* an area must be at least four *tefaḥim* wide (about a foot or 30 cm). Lacking this width, the area is not significant enough to be deemed a *reshut ha-yaḥid,* only a *mekom petur*. It should be noted that a sharp incline is considered a wall as well.[1]

A *reshut ha-rabim* is an area that serves public needs such as streets, squares, markets, and intercity roads. To qualify as a *reshut ha-rabim,* an area must be at least 16 *amot* wide, and unroofed. Some add an additional condition: every day it must be traversed by 600,000 people, equivalent to the number of Israelites during our ancestors' travels in the desert, according to the Torah (see section 8 below). In principle, all prohibitions on carrying are connected to *reshut ha-rabim*. Formulated in the negative, there is no Torah prohibition on carrying where there is no *reshut ha-rabim*. Within a *reshut ha-rabim,* one may not carry an object more than four *amot* (see sections 3-4 below), and one may not transport an object from a *reshut ha-yaḥid* to a *reshut ha-rabim* and vice versa.

3. *MEKOM PETUR* AND *KARMELIT*

The third type of domain is a *mekom petur* (an exempt area). According to Torah law, this includes fields, deserts, oceans, lakes, and other places

1. If the slope surrounding a hill is steep enough (it declines ten *tefaḥim* vertically within four *amot* [6 ft or 182.4 cm] horizontally), it is considered a wall, which makes everything atop the slope into a *reshut ha-yaḥid*. The Sages refer to such a hill as a *tel ha-mitlaket* (MB 345:5; there is disagreement about whether the slope itself is considered a part of the *reshut ha-yaḥid,* as explained in BHL 352:2 s.v. "be-inyan"). The same rule applies to a valley that is surrounded by a slope of such steepness.

   The Sages ordained that if a place surrounded by walls is larger than *beit satayim,* even though according to Torah law it is still a *reshut ha-yaḥid,* one may carry within it only if its walls were made for residential purposes. If they are natural walls, one must put up a new wall that is wider than ten *amot* and at a distance of less than ten *amot* from the natural wall, so that people have participated in the surrounding wall. Then one may carry in the entire area (SA 358:8; MB *ad loc.* 62). *Beit satayim* is the size of the courtyard of the *Mishkan,* the dimensions of which were 50 *amot* by 100 *amot* (5,000 square *amot*). That translates into 1039.68 square meters, or a little more than a dunam (about a quarter of an acre).

   The exact size of a *tefaḥ* is the width of the hand across the knuckles that connect the four fingers (excluding the thumb) to the palm, or approximately 3 in (7.6 cm, see below ch. 29 n. 1). Accordingly, three *tefaḥim* are 8.98 in (22.8 cm). I rounded it off to 9 in (23 cm) the text of this chapter (sections 3 and 7) to make it easier to remember. Four *tefaḥim* are 0.99 ft (30.4 cm), and I rounded it off to 30 (or a foot). Similarly, 16 *amot* are 23.937 ft (7.296 m), which I round off to 24 ft (7.3).

not enclosed by walls (and thus not deemed *reshut ha-yaḥid*) and also not used by the masses on a regular basis (and thus are not deemed *reshut ha-rabim*). Since these are undefined places, they have no significance as a location. An object in a *mekom petur* is not located in a place that establishes a connection with it. Therefore, Torah law permits carrying an object from a *mekom petur* to a *reshut ha-yaḥid* or a *reshut ha-rabim*, and vice versa. Similarly, one may carry objects within a *mekom petur* for as long and far as he wishes.

However, since a *mekom petur* is in some ways similar to a *reshut ha-rabim* – as the masses may make use of both types of areas – the Sages safeguarded the Torah and declared that any open area that is not a *reshut ha-yaḥid* shall be called a *karmelit* and have a status akin to that of a *reshut ha-rabim*. Thus it is prohibited to carry an object more than four *amot* in a *karmelit*, and one may not carry anything from a *karmelit* to a *reshut ha-yaḥid* or *reshut ha-rabim*, and vice versa.

The only places that are still called a *mekom petur* are those that are not fit for significant use, such as rocks that are higher than three *tefaḥim* (about 9 in or 23 cm) and also less than four *tefaḥim* wide (about a foot or 30 cm). One may carry something from a *mekom petur* into a *reshut ha-yaḥid* or *reshut ha-rabim*, and vice versa. Such a *mekom petur* was not included in the decree because it is fundamentally different from the other domains. Since it is over three *tefaḥim* high, it is distinct from the ground, and since it is less than four *tefaḥim* wide, it is not big enough to be significant. Therefore, no one will make the mistake of thinking that if one may carry in an insignificant *mekom petur*, one may also carry in a larger and more significant place.[2]

2. A *mekom petur* can be within a *reshut ha-rabim*. The *poskim* disagree whether a *mekom petur* can be within a *karmelit*. Some say that since a *karmelit* started out as a *mekom petur* but the Sages categorized it as a *karmelit*, any *mekom petur* within it is subsumed by its *karmelit* status, and is treated as a *karmelit* (Ran, *Hagahot Maimoniyot*, *Tur*, and *Beit Yosef* quoting Rambam). Others maintain that since a *karmelit* has the status of *reshut ha-rabim*, if there is an area within it that is more than three *tefaḥim* high and less than four *tefaḥim* wide, that area is a *mekom petur* (Rashi, *Magid Mishneh* quoting Rashba, Me'iri, and Rabbeinu Yeruḥam). But, within a *reshut ha-yaḥid*, all agree there cannot be a *mekom petur*, because the fence that surrounds the *reshut ha-yaḥid* makes everything within it part of the *reshut ha-yaḥid* (Rema 345:19; BHL s.v. "Ran" and "ve-yesh ḥolkim").

4. THE REASON BEHIND THE PROHIBITION OF CARRYING FOUR *AMOT* IN A *RESHUT HA-RABIM*

As we have seen, one may not transport objects from one domain to another. Within a private domain, even in a large house with many rooms, one may move objects around freely, because the entire *reshut ha-yaḥid* is considered one domain. Moving items within it is not considered transporting them from one domain to another. In contrast, in a *reshut ha-rabim,* one may move an object within his four *amot.* Since a *reshut ha-rabim* is communal, each individual may make use of only the four *amot* he occupies. Four *amot* is enough space for one to lie down with arms and legs outstretched. If one moves an item outside his four *amot,* he has moved it from his space to the communal *reshut ha-rabim.* This is prohibited by Torah law.

From a spiritual perspective, it should be noted that all the confusion and corruption in the world stems from division and dissension. Nations fight one another, people compete with each other, and ideological movements struggle with one another. Thus, tremendous amounts of energy are wasted on strife and contention. Even an individual is often torn between his seemingly contradictory desires. The way to rectify these tensions is to reveal the unity underlying all existence. With belief that one God created the entire world, we can understand that all the different desires in the world are directed toward one goal. Only by following the Torah's directions can we harmonize them, and thus improve and perfect the world. Now we can understand why the commandment to "Love your neighbor as yourself" is considered a major

---

A *reshut ha-rabim* extends only to the height of ten *tefaḥim.* If one takes an object in hand and walks on a tightrope or beam that is set up above a *reshut ha-rabim,* he is not transgressing the prohibition of carrying, because the space above ten *tefaḥim* is considered a *mekom petur.* However, there is a disagreement regarding the law relating to a table that is over ten *tefaḥim* high and four *tefaḥim* wide that is standing in a *reshut ha-rabim* or a *karmelit.* According to SA 345:16, since there are no walls to turn it into a *reshut ha-yaḥid,* it is considered a *karmelit,* while according to MB 345:66 and the Vilna Gaon (based on a number of Rishonim), it is defined as a *mekom petur* because there is no such thing as a *karmelit* or a *reshut ha-rabim* above ten *tefaḥim.* SHT *ad loc.* 68 states that R. Yosef Karo recanted (R. Elimelech Lange, *Hilkhot Eruvin,* p. 20).

Torah principle: it bridges the world's fissures and helps us reveal its fundamental unity.

We are now in a position to understand why objects may be carried in a *reshut ha-yaḥid*. In a sense, a *reshut ha-yaḥid* is a perfected place. The walls that enclose it give it a unity of purpose. Thus all its rooms and the areas within it are considered in one place, within which items may be carried. In contrast, a *reshut ha-rabim* has yet to be perfected. It still expresses the different interests of many different people, and the objects found within it are not yet considered in one place. This is why carrying anything more than four *amot* in a *reshut ha-rabim* is considered a *melakha*.

As for a *karmelit*, on the one hand it is not set aside for public use and does not obviously express different interests. Thus, according to Torah law it is the same as a *mekom petur*, and carrying in it is not prohibited. On the other hand, since a *karmelit* is used in a variety of ways by a variety of people, it has something in common with a *reshut ha-rabim*. Therefore, the Sages decided that a *karmelit* should be treated like a *reshut ha-rabim*, and carrying in it is prohibited.

If a *reshut ha-rabim* is enclosed by a wall or fence, and it has gates that are closed at night, its fundamental unity and common denominator is thus revealed, and it is perfected like a *reshut ha-yaḥid*. One may thus carry throughout. A *karmelit* can be perfected even without being enclosed by a fence or wall. A *tzurat ha-petaḥ* alone suffices to make it the equivalent of a *reshut ha-yaḥid* in which items may be carried (as explained below, 29:2).

5. THE PROHIBITIONS OF CARRYING ON SHABBAT

We have seen that the prohibition of *Hotza'ah* applies to carrying objects from a *reshut ha-yaḥid* to a *reshut ha-rabim* or *karmelit* (which rabbinically is considered a *reshut ha-rabim*), and vice versa. We have also seen that it is prohibited for one to carry an object four *amot* within a *reshut ha-rabim* or a *karmelit*. Now let us see more precisely how this Torah prohibition is defined.

The *melakha* of *Hotza'ah* has three stages:

1. picking up an object in one domain (*akira*, [lit. "uprooting"]);
2. transporting it to a different domain (*ha'avara*);
3. putting it down in that domain (*hanaḥa*).

Even if one accomplishes all three of these with one action, for example, by throwing an object from a *reshut ha-yaḥid* to a *reshut ha-rabim,* or throwing it four *amot* within a *reshut ha-rabim,* he has violated *Hotza'ah.* Similarly, if one is holding an object or has one in his pocket as he walks from a *reshut ha-yaḥid* to a *reshut ha-rabim,* he violates *Hotza'ah.* When he begins to walk, he "uproots" the object; when he walks from one domain to the other, he transports it to a different domain; and when he stops walking in the second domain, he is putting it down.[3]

In order to transgress a Torah prohibition, one person must complete all three stages. Thus, if one picks up an item in a *reshut ha-yaḥid* and extends his arm with the item into a *reshut ha-rabim,* he has not transgressed by Torah law unless he puts down the item in the *reshut ha-rabim.* If someone else, standing in the *reshut ha-rabim,* removes the item from his hand, the item has been transported from a *reshut ha-yaḥid* to a *reshut ha-rabim,* but neither person has performed an entire *melakha* by Torah law, since the first person performed *akira* and *ha'avara* while the second person performed *hanaḥa.*

The Sages nevertheless prohibited transporting objects in this way, lest people circumvent the Torah prohibition, grow accustomed to taking it lightly, and ultimately transgress Torah law by performing all three stages (SA 347:1).

It is important to be aware that, according to Torah law, the prohibition on *Hotza'ah* applies only when it is performed in the usual fashion. For example, if one takes an item in his hand, slips it in his

---

3. One may not carry while walking nonstop from a *reshut ha-yaḥid* through a *reshut ha-rabim* into another *reshut ha-yaḥid.* Some say that this is prohibited by Torah law (*Tosafot, Eruvin* 33a, s.v. "de-ha"). However, many maintain that as long as one did not stop walking while in the *reshut ha-rabim,* the prohibition is only rabbinic, because as long as he is walking he has not performed a *hanaḥa* in the *reshut ha-rabim* (Rashba and Ritva, *Eruvin* 33a; *Taz* 346:2). Indeed, practical *halakha* follows this position (SAH 347:9; R. Shlomo Zalman Auerbach cited in SSK ch. 30 n. 134). Therefore, where there is uncertainty about the validity of the local *eruv,* one may carry while walking nonstop from a *reshut ha-yaḥid* to another *reshut ha-yaḥid* via a *reshut ha-rabim.* As long as he does not stop, his carrying involves an uncertainty about a doubly rabbinic law: first, most *poskim* maintain that what we call a *reshut ha-rabim* is in fact a rabbinic *karmelit;* second, walking nonstop from a *reshut ha-yaḥid* into another *reshut ha-yaḥid* via *reshut ha-rabim* is also prohibited rabbinically.

pocket, or puts it in his backpack, he is carrying normally and is thus transgressing Torah law. In contrast, if he uses a *shinui*, such as carrying a handkerchief in his shoe or on his head, he has not violated Torah law. Nevertheless, the Sages prohibited carrying with a *shinui* lest people end up carrying without a *shinui*.

In sum, the Torah prohibition of *Hotza'ah* is limited to the performance of the entire *melakha* by one individual in the way it is normally done during the week. Additionally, the Sages prohibited any action that causes the same result as the *melakha*, even if it is done with a *shinui* or undertaken by more than one person. If the goal is accomplished – transferring the item to the desired place – the action is prohibited. It is important to note that even in a *karmelit*, the Sages prohibited carrying an item with a *shinui* or by more than one person.[4]

6. CARRYING LESS THAN FOUR *AMOT* IN A *RESHUT HA-RABIM*

We have seen in the previous sections that the prohibition of *Hotza'ah* includes transporting an object more than four *amot* in a public domain, since one's personal space within the public domain is defined as four *amot*. If he transports an object further, he is deemed to have moved it to a different domain and transgressed Torah law. But within a square of four *amot* by four *amot* one may carry. Therefore, only one who carries something a distance greater than the diagonal of a four-*amot* square

4. The distinction between a rabbinic and a Torah prohibition lies in the severity of the punishment. One who knowingly violates Shabbat by Torah law is punished with *karet* (extirpation); if the violation is unknowing, he is liable to bring a sin offering. If he does the *melakha* with a *shinui*, which means the prohibition is rabbinic, then if he did so knowingly, he is given rabbinically-ordained lashes; if it is unknowing, there is no punishment. An additional difference is that when it comes to a Torah prohibition, we are only lenient if danger to life is involved; in contrast, when a prohibition is rabbinic, there are certain times of necessity when we may be lenient even if there is no danger to life. For example, one who is sick may violate certain rabbinic prohibitions (below 28:2). Additionally, one who stands to lose a great deal of money may disregard certain rabbinic prohibitions in order to salvage his money by, for example, carrying money with a *shinui* from a *reshut ha-rabim* to a *reshut ha-yaḥid* (Rema 301:33; MB 266:17). The Sages also permitted violating rabbinic prohibitions in order to save *tefilin*, as explained in SA 301:42. See also the next section.

(2.58 m) has violated a Torah prohibition, because only then is it clear that he carried outside the permissible area.

By Torah law, one who wants to transport an object within a *reshut ha-rabim* may carry it a bit less than four *amot,* stand still in order to establish a new location for the object, then walk again for less than four *amot.* He can continue in this way – starting and stopping – until he has transported the object wherever he wants it. However, the Sages forbade this lest one end up carrying more than four *amot* and thus violate Torah law. Even in a *karmelit,* which is considered a *reshut ha-rabim* only rabbinically, they forbade carrying an object less than four *amot* out of concern that one might come to carry more than four *amot* in a *reshut ha-rabim.*[5]

However, one who stands to lose his money, such as one who is traveling with a large sum of money when Shabbat begins and has no safe place to hide it, and no non-Jew is available to guard the money or transport it to his home, then in order to prevent his suffering a financial loss the Sages permit the Jew to carry his backpack in the manner discussed in the previous paragraph – starting and stopping, and making sure to walk less than four *amot* each time (*paḥot paḥot mi-daled amot*). He may continue this way until he reaches a place where he can safely leave the money. This permission applies even in a *reshut ha-rabim.* In a *karmelit,* one may generally carry this way for the sake of a mitzva (SA 266:7, 8; BHL 349:5).[6]

5. According to many *poskim* (Raavad, *Ha-Ma'or,* Rosh, and others), if many people are there, it is permitted *le-khatḥila* for each one to carry an item fewer than four *amot* and pass it to the next person, who will also carry it less than four *amot.* Using this method, they can transport the object across great distances. *Pri Megadim* allows this even when there are only two people involved, as long as each one carries the item less than four *amot* before passing it back to the other person. In contrast, some Rishonim prohibit doing this even with many people (Ramban). These positions are cited by SA 349:3 and BHL s.v. "va-ḥavero." The Sages permitted carrying *tefilin* on Shabbat in this manner, if it is necessary in order to keep them safe (SA 301:42).
6. If the person who did not make it home before the start of Shabbat was walking nonstop from before Shabbat began, there is another possible solution. He can run until he arrives at his home. Since the *akira* of the object was done before Shabbat began, in any case he will not violate Torah law. In order to save his money, the Sages allowed him to run to his house, even though this involves transporting an item to a

7. CARRYING IN A *MEKOM PETUR*

As we have seen (section 3), a *mekom petur* is an area within a *reshut ha-rabim* like a stone taller than three *tefaḥim* (about 9 in or 23 cm) but less than four *tefaḥim* wide (about a foot or 30 cm). Since a *mekom petur* is not deemed significant, one may transport an object from a *reshut ha-rabim* or a *reshut ha-yaḥid* and place it on a *mekom petur*, and vice versa.

According to Torah law one may move an object from a *reshut ha-yaḥid* to a *reshut ha-rabim* by first removing it from the *reshut ha-yaḥid* and placing it on the *mekom petur* and then picking it up from the *mekom petur* and placing it in the *reshut ha-rabim*. However, the Sages forbade this lest people make light of *Hotza'ah* that is prohibited by Torah law as well.

Poskim disagree about whether one may use a *mekom petur* to transfer an item from a *reshut ha-yaḥid* to a *karmelit* or vice versa. Some maintain that it is rabbinically prohibited to transfer items by means of a *mekom petur* even to a *karmelit*. Even though all the prohibitions of carrying in a *karmelit* are rabbinic, the Sages did not differentiate here (*Ha-Ma'or*, Raavad, and Rosh). Others maintain that only when there is a concern that people will end up violating Torah law by carrying from a *reshut ha-yaḥid* to a *reshut ha-rabim* or vice versa is it forbidden to transfer items via a *mekom petur*, but one may transfer them from a *reshut ha-yaḥid* to a *karmelit* in this fashion (Rif and Rambam).

In practice, at times of necessity one may rely on those who are lenient and carry from a *reshut ha-yaḥid* or a *karmelit* and vice versa via a *mekom petur*. This is important for soldiers who are stuck in a place with no *eruv* on Shabbat. If they want to move something from their tent (which is a *reshut ha-yaḥid*) to the common area of the encampment (which is a *karmelit*), they should leave their tent and keep moving until they find a *mekom petur* on which to place the item. Afterward, they can take it from the *mekom petur* and put it down in the common area, and

---

different *reshut* (*ha'avara*) and setting it down there (*hanaḥa*), which are normally prohibited. They ruled that he should run, to ensure that he does not make the mistake of stopping (*Shabbat* 153b: "He should run, not go gently [i.e., walk]. Why? Since there is nothing to remind him, he may end up performing *akira* and *hanaḥa*"). If possible, upon arrival in the *reshut ha-yaḥid*, he should take off his backpack with a *shinui*, so as to minimize the prohibition as much as possible (SA 266:11).

vice versa. This should also be the procedure for transferring items from one tent to the next via the common area. The item should be removed from the tent, left on a *mekom petur* in the common area, and then taken wherever it needs to go.[7]

8. *RESHUT HA-RABIM* AS DEFINED BY TORAH LAW

The most pressing practical question when dealing with issues of *Hotza'ah* on Shabbat is whether streets in cities and towns are considered a *reshut ha-rabim* or *karmelit*. If streets today are considered a *reshut ha-rabim*, then it is very difficult to do what is necessary to transform them into a *reshut ha-yaḥid*. This transformation involves surrounding the entire city with a fence, installing doors in every entranceway, and ensuring that they are all closed at night. Barring this, it would be prohibited to carry in our cities and towns.

In contrast, if streets today are defined as a *karmelit* (i.e., only rabbinically are they treated as a *reshut ha-rabim*), then it is relatively easy to transform them into a *reshut ha-yaḥid* where carrying would be permitted. This transformation involves surrounding the city with a *tzurat ha-petaḥ* (halakhic doorway), by erecting poles and extending strings between them to form a sort of doorway between every pole (below 29:2-3).

---

7. This is the most practical solution for soldiers in the Israeli army. The best *mekom petur* is a rock or a pole that is higher than ten *tefaḥim* (30 in or 76 cm) and narrower than four *tefaḥim* (about a foot or 30 cm). However, if this pole or rock is lower than ten *tefaḥim*, as we saw in n. 2, the *poskim* disagree about whether it is deemed a *mekom petur*. Some say that there is no such thing as a *mekom petur* within a *karmelit*, while others maintain that it can exist. In times of necessity, soldiers in the army may be lenient (*Meshiv Milḥama* §5 and §60). Sometimes the only way to arrange a *mekom petur* is by using a bench that is narrower than four *tefaḥim* . The problem is that another doubt arises in this case, because Me'iri states that a finished product (*kli*) cannot be considered a *mekom petur* (SHT 345:15). But in times of necessity when there is no other solution, a *kli* that is lower than ten *tefaḥim* in a *karmelit* can be considered a *mekom petur* (*Sho'el U-meshiv* 4:3:2; *Hilkhot Eruvin* ch. 1 n. 16).

A person's shoulder: According to Rashba and *Tosafot*, another person's body can be considered a *mekom petur*, on condition that it is higher than ten *tefaḥim*; a person's shoulder generally fits this condition. Others say that a person's body cannot be considered a place, and therefore cannot be a *mekom petur* (see MB 347:10). In times of necessity when there is no other solution, one may rely upon the lenient position.

Let us preface our discussion by recalling that the prohibitions of Shabbat are derived from the types of labor performed for the *Mishkan*. When the Torah commands us to refrain from *melakha* on Shabbat, it means refraining from *Mishkan* work, in which the Jews were involved in the desert. If so, then the definition of *reshut ha-rabim* should also be derived from the Israelites' desert existence. Since the main thoroughfare in the Israelite camp was sixteen *amot* wide (7.30 m) in order to enable the passage of the two wagons that transported the different parts of the *Mishkan*, it follows that only a street equally wide is deemed a *reshut ha-rabim*. However, Rishonim disagree whether, in order to qualify an area as a *reshut ha-rabim*, there is also a minimum requirement for the number of people who make use of the street.

Some maintain that any street or marketplace that is open to the public and is sixteen *amot* wide is considered a *reshut ha-rabim* by Torah law. It makes no difference how many people pass through each day. According to this opinion, the *eruvin* that we construct nowadays (namely, the type known as *tzurat ha-petaḥ*) are ineffective, because our cities have streets wider than sixteen *amot*. Furthermore, according to this position, as long as a city has streets that are sixteen *amot* wide, a *tzurat ha-petaḥ* is not effective for the smaller streets either; the existence of a *reshut ha-rabim* within an area encompassed by a *tzurat ha-petaḥ* invalidates it. This is the opinion of Rambam, Rabbeinu Tam, Ramban, Rashba, and many others.

Others maintain that since the camp of the Israelites in the desert consisted of 600,000 men, all of whom needed to walk to the *Mishkan* in order to help build it and to hear the Torah taught by our teacher Moshe, the Kohanim, and the Levi'im, it follows that a *reshut ha-rabim* is defined as a road or marketplace that is at least sixteen *amot* wide, and through which 600,000 people pass daily. If fewer people traverse it daily, it is considered a *karmelit*. This is the opinion of *Behag*, Rashi, *Smag*, Rosh, and many others. Within this position, there is an additional debate. Some maintain that an area still qualifies as a *reshut ha-rabim* even if it is not used by 600,000 daily, but only frequently or even just occasionally. For in the desert, not all the men traveled on the path to the *Mishkan* every day. In practice, only in megacities such as New York City and Mexico City are there streets traversed by 600,000 people every day. Even most big cities do not have that many people passing through daily. Thus according to this opinion, most streets are not considered a *reshut ha-rabim* but rather a *karmelit*. Therefore, carrying there on Shabbat can be permitted with an *eruv* of the *tzurat ha-petaḥ* type. According to this opinion, today the streets considered a *reshut ha-rabim* by Torah law are mainly intercity highways. Since these roads are meant to serve everybody, and their use is not limited to people of one city alone, they are considered *reshut ha-rabim* even if fewer than 600,000 people pass through each day.[8]

8. BHL 345:7 lists twelve Rishonim who are lenient and twelve who are stringent. According to the simple reading of SA, one should be stringent. Based on this, a number of Aḥaronim write that *le-khatḥila* Sephardim must be stringent and not rely on an *eruv* of the *tzurat ha-petaḥ* type (*Yalkut Yosef* 345:4; *Menuḥat Ahava* 3:27:10, 59). In contrast, some Aḥaronim (MA, AHS) argue that R. Yosef Karo did not reach a decision, since SA in multiple places seems to follow the lenient position (303:18; 325:2). In the introduction to the second volume of *Or Le-Tziyon* 1:1:1-2, R. Ben-Zion Abba Shaul explains that R. Karo is stringent in a case of doubt about a Torah law and lenient in a case of doubt about a rabbinic law. Based on this principle, R. Abba Shaul resolves the apparent contradictions in SA. MA and *Taz* observe that most *poskim* tend to be lenient here. Therefore, they continue, one may rely on an *eruv* of the *tzurat ha-petaḥ* type to permit carrying in our cities. Many Ashkenazim follow this. Other Aḥaronim write that even though we cannot dissuade those who are lenient, nevertheless it is proper for a one who wishes to act virtuously in the eyes of his Creator to be stringent, since this is a doubt about a Torah law. MB 345:23 states similarly.

Regarding the lenient position, some questions have been raised. First, if, indeed, it is necessary to have 600,000 use an area in order for it to be deemed a *reshut ha-rabim*, how is it possible that this criterion is nowhere mentioned in the Gemara? Second, the Sages decreed that we should not blow the shofar on Rosh Ha-shana if it falls on Shabbat and that we should not shake the *lulav* on the first day of Sukkot if it falls on Shabbat out of concern that people would carry the shofar or *lulav* in the public domain (RH 29b). In the time of the Sages, there were no streets with 600,000 people passing through. If a place with fewer than that many people is not considered a *reshut ha-rabim*, no one could have been carrying in a *reshut ha-rabim* by Torah law. If this is the case, why did they make their decree? Third, if there is no such thing as a *reshut ha-rabim* by Torah law today, why did they decree (section 14 below) that women not go out with their jewelry, out of concern that they would carry it?

A possible answer is that the reason that the Sages decreed not to blow the shofar or go out with jewelry on Shabbat is that even according to the lenient position, intercity roads are considered *reshut ha-rabim* regardless of how many people use them, as explained in BHL 345:7 toward the end of s.v. "she-ein." In the time of the Sages, traveling on intercity roads was common since the cities were small. People would travel from city to city and from village to city on the same roads. The reason for the difference

9. IN PRACTICE

In practice, most observant Jews follow the lenient position and carry in cities, relying on an *eruv* of the *tzurat ha-petaḥ* type. This leads to an interesting question: given that half of the *poskim* are stringent, believing that an *eruv* of the *tzurat ha-petaḥ* type is not sufficient in cities with streets wider than sixteen *amot* (and that it is irrelevant how many people pass through), how is it that most observant Jews follow the lenient position? After all, it is a case of doubt pertaining to a Torah law, where we are normally stringent.

The simple answer is that in rare cases, when dealing with an issue in which it is very difficult to be stringent, sometimes the custom takes hold to rely on a lenient opinion even though there is a possible Torah violation at stake. Furthermore, it truly is difficult to follow the stringent position here, as that would mean that no one could go out on Shabbat with anything in his pockets, even tissues and the like, which are sometimes necessary. Additionally, families would not be able to visit one another, because one may not push a stroller in a *reshut ha-rabim*, and there would be no way to bring diapers, bottles, and so on. Since there is no alternative, and given that half of the *poskim* are lenient, we can rely on the lenient position in this case.

We should add that the *poskim* are not really evenly divided in this case. As we will see, some *poskim* ruled that there are additional requirements that must be met in order for an area to be considered a *reshut ha-rabim* by Torah law. If we take these requirements into account, it turns out that according to most *poskim*, today's streets would not qualify as a *reshut ha-rabim*. Therefore, an *eruv* of the *tzurat ha-petaḥ* type is sufficient. First, according to some *poskim*, an area is considered a *reshut ha-rabim* by

---

between intracity roads and intercity ones is that the roads outside a city belong to the entire world. Therefore, even if less than 600,000 people traverse an intercity road daily, it still belongs to the public and is considered a *reshut ha-rabim*. In contrast, a road within a city or adjacent to it belongs to the city residents and is not a *reshut ha-rabim* by Torah law. In such a case, only if 600,000 people traverse it daily is it considered a public road rather than belonging to the city's residents. Based on this, we can understand why the Sages said that if the gates of Jerusalem had not been locked at night, it would have been a *reshut ha-rabim* (*Eruvin* 6b), even though presumably fewer than 600,000 people passed through daily. Since Jerusalem served the entire Jewish people, its streets belonged to all the pilgrims, and thus were comparable to intercity roads. Therefore, had the city not been walled, and had the gates not been locked each night, it would have been deemed a *reshut ha-rabim*. See more in the next note.

Torah law only when the street bisects the entire city in a straight line. If it is slightly crooked, it is no longer a *reshut ha-rabim*. Most cities do not have a main street that is completely straight, and thus we may rely on an *eruv* of the *tzurat ha-petaḥ* type. Second, some *poskim* feel that since our streets are laid out such that every street is intersected by another street, all the streets are considered enclosed by a wall on three sides. Accordingly, they do not qualify as a *reshut ha-rabim* by Torah law, and an *eruv* of the *tzurat ha-petaḥ* type is sufficient (AHS and *Ḥazon Ish*). There are additional reasons to be lenient, as explained in the notes.

When we combine all these opinions, it turns out that according to the majority of *poskim*, today's streets are considered a *karmelit*, and carrying in them can be permitted with an *eruv* of the *tzurat ha-petaḥ* type.

Nevertheless, according to many, since a Torah prohibition may be at stake, *le-khatḥila* it is proper not to rely on an *eruv* of the *tzurat ha-petaḥ* type in a place where there are streets wider than sixteen *amot*.[9]

---

9. There are four, maybe five reasons that our streets are not considered *reshut ha-rabim* by Torah law.
   1. As we have seen, according to half the *poskim*, if 600,000 people do not traverse an area daily, it is not a public domain. Very few places meet this condition. Even though some maintain that even a street that occasionally has that many passersby is considered a *reshut ha-rabim* (AHS 345:26; *Beit Ephraim*, OḤ 26; *Hilkhot Eruvin*, p. 25 based on the Rishonim's expression "600,000 found there"), such a street is uncommon as well.
   2. According to Rashi and others, a street is only considered a *reshut ha-rabim* if it bisects the city in an absolutely straight line. Generally, this is not the case. (However, *Igrot Moshe*, OḤ 1:148 rejects this reasoning.)
   3. Some (*Beit Ephraim*, OḤ 26; AHS 345:19-22; *Ḥazon Ish*, OḤ 107:5-8) state that given the way our streets are laid out, where each street is intersected by another street, all the streets can be considered enclosed by a wall on three sides. For according to Torah law, a wall only needs to be mostly closed. Since buildings line most streets, closing off most of the area, a street is already enclosed by two walls. Since another street intersects it, and this second street also has buildings that are close enough together to be considered a wall, the intersecting street provides the third wall. It turns out that every city street is enclosed by three walls, and thus by Torah law is not deemed a *reshut ha-rabim*. It is only rabbinically that an enclosure requires four walls and that a wall must be completely closed. Since this is a doubt about a rabbinic law, we can be lenient.
   4. One can present a reasonable argument that it is the Sages who decided that an *eruv* of the *tzurat ha-petaḥ* type is not sufficient to permit carrying in a *reshut ha-rabim*; by the original Torah law, a *tzurat ha-petaḥ* is considered a true wall.

10. WEARING CLOTHES IS NOT CONSIDERED CARRYING

One may put on his clothes, shoes, and hat, and then enter a *reshut ha-rabim*, because clothes are secondary to one's body. As long as one is

---

Thus the entire debate is on the rabbinic level, and when there is a doubt about a rabbinic rule, we are lenient. (BHL presents this in 364:2 as the opinion of Rambam. Even though difficulties have been raised with it, *Or Le-Tziyon* 1:30 suggests that Rosh as well maintains that a *tzurat ha-petaḥ* is considered a wall by Torah law, in which case the debate is on the rabbinic level.)

5. Perhaps we may also say that since part of the State of Israel is surrounded by walls on three sides (albeit very distant ones), according to *Tosafot* they are considered legitimate walls by Torah law, so once again we are faced with a doubt about a rabbinic law (see *Harḥavot* 29:4:3).

Thus we see that the *poskim* are not truly evenly divided in this case. Rather, according to most *poskim*, our streets are not defined as a *reshut ha-rabim* by Torah law. Additionally, it is a *sfek sfeika* (in fact, there are four uncertainties). According to the rules of halakhic jurisprudence, in such a case the law follows the lenient position.

Some big cities contain streets where 600,000 people indeed pass through every day – not by foot but by car or bus. At first glance, it would seem that carrying in such cities cannot be permitted with an *eruv* of the *tzurat ha-petaḥ* type. Nevertheless, it seems reasonable to suggest that these intracity highways are not considered *reshut ha-rabim*. For since they are closed to pedestrians, they are not really open to the public. Besides, each car is considered a *reshut ha-yaḥid* (*Yeshu'ot Malko*, OḤ 26). Following this reasoning, all would agree that most streets today are not public domains according to Torah law, because once we disqualify the part of a street used by cars, the street is no longer sixteen *amot* wide. Some disagree with this approach (AHS 345:26; *Igrot Moshe*, OḤ 1:139).

Other objections have been raised to our *eruvin*. First, if a city contains non-Jews or Jews who desecrate Shabbat, the Sages decreed that they cannot be included in the halakhic partnership on which an *eruv* is based, and thus it cannot work. See below 29:7 for solutions to this problem. Second, there are often large gardens in cities, larger than *beit satayim* (see n. 1). These areas disqualify the *eruv* because they are not designed for walking in. However, in practice, if one may walk in these gardens and there are paths running through them, they do not disqualify the *eruv*. If the gardens are enclosed by a fence, they also do not disqualify the *eruv*. Third, Rambam maintains that an *eruv* of the *tzurat ha-petaḥ* type is not effective if the distance between the poles is greater than ten *amot* (4.56 m). However, since most *poskim* disagree with him, and the law is rabbinic, we do not take his position into account. (This is according to the anonymous position cited in SA 362:10.)

Even in an area enclosed by an *eruv*, some people try to avoid relying on it. For example, when they need to bring a baby or anything else from one house to another via the street, they walk nonstop until they reach their destination. Since there is no *hanaḥa* in the *reshut ha-rabim*, according to many this is not considered carrying by Torah law (as explained in n. 3). Doing this adds another rabbinic element to the equation, and it seems that one may thus be lenient even *le-khatḥila*.

wearing them, they do not have independent status but are viewed as part of his body. Thus, he is not viewed as carrying them.

Even clothes that are designed to be worn under specific conditions are considered secondary to the body. Therefore, one may wear a plastic raincoat over a coat or galoshes over shoes, since these are examples of normal rain gear. One may also wear two pairs of socks or two shirts, one on top of the other, since in the winter some people do this regularly. Therefore, if one wishes to bring his friend a shirt via a *reshut ha-rabim*, he can wear it over his own shirt and walk to his friend's home, even during the summer. However, if he just picks up the shirt or carries it over his shoulder and then enters a *reshut ha-rabim*, he violates Torah law.[10]

If a woman wants to carry a blanket or tablecloth through the public domain, she may wrap herself in it the way she would wrap herself in a shawl. Even though these items are not themselves clothes, as long as they are worn in the same fashion as clothes, one may enter a different domain with them. Similarly, one who is going to immerse in a *mikveh* can wrap himself in a towel and walk through a *reshut ha-rabim*, and one who wants to carry a kerchief may wrap it around his neck like a scarf, and go out (MB 301:133; SSK 18:48). The underlying principle is that one may wear any item in the normal manner of dressing (SA 301:35-36).

The Sages ordained that one should not enter a *reshut ha-rabim* wearing an item of clothing that is likely to fall off, out of concern that he will end up carrying it four *amot* in the *reshut ha-rabim*.[11] In contrast,

---

10. According to SA 301:36, any item of clothing may be worn outside, even if it is worn in an unusual way. For example, one may wear two belts, one on top of the other. Since each belt is put on in the normal way of dressing – it is permitted. However, Rema maintains that this is only considered the normal way of dressing if there are people who sometimes dress that way. Accordingly, one may wear two shirts, one on top of the other, or similarly layer two pairs of socks. In contrast, since no one wears two belts in the manner described above, one may not go outside dressed this way on Shabbat.

11. AHS 301:53 maintains that if there is an item of clothing that is technically permissible to wear in a *reshut ha-rabim* but was rabbinically prohibited (out of concern that one might carry it four *amot* if it were to fall off, if people were to make fun of it, or if he were to need to remove it to go to the bathroom), that prohibition is applicable only in a *reshut ha-rabim* by Torah law. The only type of item that the Sages prohibited one to wear even in a *karmelit* is women's jewelry (see section 14 below).

one may go outside wearing a yarmulke, even if it is not held very firmly in place. Even if it were to fall off, we are not concerned that he would carry it four *amot*, since a man may not walk four *amot* without a head-covering. Therefore, if it falls off, we can assume that immediately after picking it up he will replace it (SA 301:7; MB *ad loc.* 153).

Some maintain that one should not wear gloves in an area without an *eruv*. After all, if it becomes warm, he might take them off, put them in his pocket, and walk four *amot*, thus violating Torah law. *Le-khatḥila*, it is proper to be stringent, but the custom is to be lenient (SA 301:37; see BHL *ad loc.*).

The *poskim* disagree about the status of a plastic cover that is made to protect a man's hat from the rain. Some forbid wearing this cover, arguing that it is not worn in the same way as clothing, and its sole purpose is to protect the hat. Others permit wearing it, maintaining that it is indeed worn in the same way as clothing. One who wishes may be lenient.[12]

11. ITEMS DEEMED SECONDARY TO CLOTHING

Any items that are normally attached to clothing, such as buttons and pockets, are considered part of the clothing and secondary to the person's body. Thus there is no prohibition of carrying them. Even though carrying buttons or pouches would be a violation of *Hotza'ah*, the buttons and

12. *Igrot Moshe*, OḤ 1:108-110 prohibits going out wearing a plastic hat cover. This is based on SA 301:13-14, which states that items designed to protect clothing are not considered clothing, and thus one may not go out wearing them. Since plastic hat covers are meant to protect hats and not people's bodies, they are not clothing. They are also not decorative, so they may not be worn on Shabbat. This is also the opinion of *Minḥat Yitzḥak* 3:26. There is also a concern that once the rain stops, one might remove the hat cover and carry it four *amot*. However, according to R. Shlomo Zalman Auerbach, a plastic cover that was made especially for a hat and that is not removed when the rain stops can be considered an item of clothing, and one may walk in a *reshut ha-rabim* wearing it (SSK ch. 18 n. 46). This is also the position of *Tzitz Eliezer* 10:23 and *Yabi'a Omer* 5:24. This debate constitutes uncertainty about a rabbinic law, for even those who prohibit agree that it cannot be a Torah prohibition, as this is not the normal way to carry. This is also a *melakha she-eina tzerikha le-gufah*. Moreover, according to many *poskim*, nowadays there is no public domain as defined by Torah law. Accordingly, one may be lenient.

pockets that are normally attached to clothing are part of the garment and secondary to it. Manufacturer's tags are also considered part of the clothing and secondary to it. One may also wear a coat with a hood, even when the hood is not actually being worn but is hanging down behind the person; even though he has no intention of putting it on, the hood is still considered part of the coat. Items attached to clothing for decorative purposes, like buttons on the cuffs of a suit or feathers attached to a hat or another garment, are also considered part of the garment.

Sometimes, extra buttons are sewn into a garment in a hidden area, to be used as replacements in case one loses a button. These buttons are not used to fasten or decorate the garment. Some maintain that since these buttons are not in current use yet are significant, one may not go out with them to a *reshut ha-rabim* (*Ḥayei Adam* 56:3). According to most *poskim*, however, one may go out with them. Since it is standard for these buttons to be attached to an item of clothing, they are considered a part of it and secondary to it. The same debate pertains to a ripped hanging loop, which is sewn into a coat or jacket to allow it to be easily hung up. Normally, the loop is attached and functional like a regular button. However, if one side of the loop rips, it is not in current use. The strict position would say that that it remains significant, and thus one may not go out with such a coat to a *reshut ha-rabim*. The lenient position would respond that regardless whether one intends to fix the loop, it is not considered significant, and remains secondary to the coat. Thus, one may wear the coat in a *reshut ha-rabim*. Since the disagreement here relates to a rabbinic prohibition, the *halakha* follows the lenient position.[13]

13. The law of extra buttons is the same as that of a ripped belt loop or buttonhole. According to *Ḥayei Adam* 56:3, if one intends to fix and reattach it, he renders it significant. Since it currently cannot be used for the button or belt, wearing it outside is considered carrying it. The law would similarly apply to one wearing unfit *tzitzit* outside, which is a transgression (SA 301:30). This is also the status of a hanging loop that has ripped on one side. Since one can no longer hang the item of clothing from it, one may not wear it in a public domain. This is the position of MB 301:150, and SSK 18:33, 42, and 44 follows it as well. Some suggest that one should resolve not to fix the loop, but rather to throw it away and attach a new one. This way the torn loop is not significant for him, and reverts to being secondary to the clothing. Thus one may wear the clothing in a *reshut ha-rabim*. Many *poskim*, though, maintain that these

12. ITEMS THAT SERVE THE BODY – GLASSES AND BANDAGES

Just as one may walk in a *reshut ha-rabim* while wearing clothes because they are deemed secondary to his body, so too one may enter a *reshut ha-rabim* with other items that serve him, as they too are considered secondary to his body (SA 301:22). For example, one who is hard of hearing may enter a *reshut ha-rabim* wearing a hearing aid (above 17:3). Similarly, one who is nearsighted may go out wearing glasses, because the glasses are secondary to the body. However, one may not wear sunglasses in a *reshut ha-rabim,* because there is a concern that when he reaches a shady area he will take them off, put them in his pocket, and carry them. If one needs to wear sunglasses because his eyes are sensitive, and he does not remove them even in the shade, then he may wear them in a *reshut ha-rabim.* If one has clip-on sunglasses that can simply be flipped up when necessary without being removed from the glasses, he may wear them in a *reshut ha-rabim,* since there is no concern that one will end up removing and carrying them (see SSK 18:18; *Yalkut Yosef* 301:35).

If one is wearing an adhesive or cloth bandage to help heal or protect a cut, it is considered serving his body and may be worn in a *reshut ha-rabim.* Similarly, one with a wounded arm may go out wearing a sling. One whose ear hurts may go out with cotton in it. Bite plates and

---

loops are not significant and are always considered secondary to the clothing. They are only considered significant if they are made out of gold, and it would be forbidden to wear them outside if they are not functional. This is the position of SAH 301:47, AHS *ad loc.* 107, *Tehila Le-David* §32, and other *poskim* as quoted in *Menuḥat Ahava* 3:27:27. In any case, it would seem that even those who prohibit would concede that the prohibition is only rabbinic, since this is not the normal way of carrying, and it is a *melakha she-eina tzerikha le-gufah.* Thus, this constitutes an uncertainty about a rabbinic law. (However, further analysis is required before comparing our case to that of unfit *tzitzit,* which is discussed in SA 301:30. There, one can say that wearing *tzitzit* on clothing is the normal way to carry them. Furthermore, the act of carrying there is *le-tzorekh gufah;* it is for the sake of the *tzitzit* itself, as the mitzva requires the *tzitzit* to be attached to the clothing that one then wears outside. Even if the *tzitzit* are disqualified, the person wishes to bring them home in order to fix them, so he is carrying them in the normal fashion. All this is not true of our case, in which the person walks around in the clothing without giving a thought to the extra buttons or torn loop. Thus this is not *le-tzorekh gufah,* nor is anyone accustomed to carrying buttons or loops in this fashion.)

orthodontic retainers may also be worn. All of these serve the body and are secondary to it (SA 301:28; MB *ad loc.* 108; SSK 34:29).

13. CANES, SEEING-EYE DOGS, AND WHEELCHAIRS

If one is partially disabled and needs a cane to walk, he may walk in a *reshut ha-rabim* with a cane because the cane has the same status as his shoes – indispensable for walking. However, if he can walk without a cane, even if only with great difficulty, he may not enter a *reshut ha-rabim* with a cane (SA 301:17).

A blind person, who normally uses a white cane to help him get around, may not use it on Shabbat if he can manage without it; in such a case, the cane is considered a burden and may not be used where there is no *eruv* (SA 301:18). If he cannot manage without it, for example, if he needs to navigate an unfamiliar neighborhood, he may go out with his cane (AHS 301:72).[14]

A blind person may enter the public domain with a seeing-eye dog. Even though he is holding onto the harness attached to the dog, this is not prohibited. Since the harness is always attached to the dog, it is secondary to its body, and there is no problem of carrying (*Igrot Moshe*, OḤ 1:45; *Menuḥat Ahava* 3:27:49; see SSK ch. 18 n. 62 and above 20:2).

One who is wheelchair-bound and propels the wheelchair manually may go out in the public domain with the wheelchair, as the wheelchair is considered comparable to his shoes (SA 30:16-17; *Igrot Moshe*, OḤ 4:90). However, if the disabled person is unable to propel himself, he may not be pushed, just as a baby who cannot walk may not be carried in the public domain or a *karmelit* (MB 308:153). For the sake of a mitzva, though, a non-Jew may be asked to push someone in a wheelchair. This is classified as a *shvut di-shvut*, which is permissible for a great need and for the sake of a mitzva (above 9:11).[15]

---

14. Nowadays the blind are taught to use a white cane, and so they feel unable to manage without one even in familiar areas. Thus it may be permissible for them to enter a *reshut ha-rabim* with a cane even in a familiar area.

15. Some question the permissibility of a disabled person propelling himself in a wheelchair on Shabbat (*Har Tzvi*, OḤ 1:170; SSK 34:27). The concern is that even if the disabled person is able to propel the wheelchair himself, it might still not be

14. JEWELRY

As we have seen, the prohibition of *Hotza'ah* does not apply to items that are secondary to the body. Therefore, one may go out in a *reshut ha-rabim* wearing all types of clothing. Following this line of reasoning, it would seem that jewelry, which is used to beautify a person, should be considered secondary to the body as long as it is worn on the body or clothes, and should not present a problem of *Hotza'ah*.

Nevertheless, the Sages were concerned that a woman might want to show her friend her jewelry and thus remove it, hold it, forget about Shabbat, and walk four *amot* in the public domain, thus violating Torah law. Therefore, the Sages prohibited wearing all jewelry that one might want to show someone else. This includes earrings, bracelets, rings, necklaces, and headbands.

However, since the time of the Rishonim, women customarily go out wearing jewelry on Shabbat. The *poskim* disagree regarding why this has been the case. Some say that while it is true that technically it is rabbinically prohibited, the rabbis did not try to prevent the practice when it became widespread, because they came to the conclusion that even if they were to protest, the women would not change their ways. Therefore, the rabbis preferred not to publicize the prohibition, as it is better that people transgress unknowingly rather than knowingly.

---

considered secondary to him. However, the primary position is the lenient one. See *Yalkut Yosef* 301:56; *Piskei Teshuva* 301:9.

Many maintain that one may only ask a non-Jew to push a disabled person in a wheelchair in a *karmelit*, because, according to them, the chair is not secondary to the person, and thus pushing it is prohibited by Torah law. Thus in a *reshut ha-rabim* there is only one *shvut* involved (*Ḥelkat Yaakov* 1:66; *Minḥat Yitzhak* 2:114:6; *Nishmat Avraham* 301:16, n. 1). Nevertheless, there is room to say that a disabled person's wheelchair is secondary to him. Accordingly, since "a living being carries itself," moving him is only rabbinically prohibited. This case is comparable to that of a bedridden person, about whom the Talmud states that carrying him in a *reshut ha-rabim* is only rabbinically prohibited (*Shabbat* 93b). Thus, one may ask a non-Jew to push the disabled person even in a *reshut ha-rabim*. This is the position of Rabbi Peretz (*Otzar Piskei Eruvin* §38). It can also be argued that the status of the disabled is similar to that of the ill, for whom the Sages permitted transgressing the rabbinic prohibition of having *melakha* performed by a non-Jew.

Other *poskim* try to provide some justification for the practice, explaining that the reason for the rabbinic prohibition was the concern that people would end up carrying four *amot* in *reshut ha-rabim* and thus violate Torah law. Nowadays, however, when according to many there is virtually nowhere that meets the criteria of a *reshut ha-rabim* by Torah law, even if one does end up carrying jewelry, it will not be a Torah transgression. We do not extend the prohibition on going out with jewelry into areas considered *reshut ha-rabim* rabbinically, as there is a principle that we do not enact a rabbinic safeguard around a rabbinic safeguard.

Others say that since jewelry is more common now, we do not need to worry that a woman will remove her jewelry in the street to show her friends. Therefore, even in an area that is a *reshut ha-rabim* by Torah law, one may wear jewelry on Shabbat.

Since the entire issue is rabbinic, one may rely on the lenient opinions. Indeed, women customarily go out wearing jewelry even where there is no *eruv*.[16]

---

16. According to Rif and Rambam, in any area other than a *reshut ha-yaḥid*, a woman may not wear jewelry that she might remove. This is also the primary position cited in SA 103:18. Accordingly, there is no way to permit going out today wearing jewelry (Rosh and Ran). If so, the reason we do not object to this practice is because it is preferable that people transgress unknowingly rather than knowingly. Ramban and Rashba take this a step further and maintain that one should not wear jewelry even in a courtyard where there is an *eruv*, because one might forget and wear it in a *reshut ha-rabim*. In contrast, based on *Tosafot, Shabbat* 64b, *Sefer Ha-Teruma* maintains that nowadays, when there are no public domains that meet the Torah's criteria, there is no prohibition against wearing jewelry. (However, as I explained in n. 8, all would agree that intercity highways are *reshut ha-rabim* even today. Thus we must ask why those Rishonim were not concerned about this. It would seem that in the times of the Rishonim, women were not accustomed to travel between cities, while in the earlier times of the Sages they had been accustomed to do so. Therefore, the Sages decreed that women may not go out wearing jewelry, but later the Rishonim were less concerned.) R. Shimshon writes in the name of Rabbeinu Sar Shalom that since it has become much more common than it used to be for women to wear jewelry, women are no longer accustomed to removing jewelry to show one another in *reshut ha-rabim*; therefore a woman may go out nowadays wearing jewelry. This is the common practice. Nevertheless, some maintain that *le-khatḥila* it is still preferable to be stringent and not wear jewelry in an area without an *eruv*.

It should be noted that there were specific types of jewelry that the Sages prohibited wearing on Shabbat. This was because women customarily immersed in wells

15. WATCHES, KEYS, IDENTITY CARDS, AND MEDICATIONS

The *poskim* disagree about the status of a watch. Some maintain that only if it is decorative like jewelry may it be worn in the public domain. The test for whether it can be considered decorative is what the owner does if the watch stops. If he would take it off, it indicates that the watch is not jewelry and is used only to tell time. Since that use is not for the sake of his body, wearing the watch in the public domain is considered carrying and is prohibited on Shabbat. In contrast, if the owner leaves it on even when it has stopped because it is decorative (for example, if it is made of gold), then it is deemed jewelry and may be worn in the public domain.

Many *poskim* maintain that since a watch is worn on the body as is clothing – a person without a watch feels as if he is not fully dressed, and the normal use of a watch is while it is on the body – it follows that the watch is secondary to the body. Thus it is considered like an item of clothing or jewelry, which may be worn on Shabbat in a *reshut ha-rabim*. The primary opinion is the lenient one, but one who chooses to be stringent should be commended.[17]

A serious problem arises for people who live in or visit an area without an *eruv*. What can they do when they leave the house and need to take a key with them? The solution is to use the key as a belt buckle.

---

and streams to purify themselves after menstruation, and the Sages were concerned that prior to immersion they might remove their jewelry and carry it four *amot* to the immersion place. However, *Orḥot Ḥayim* points out (*Hilkhot Shabbat* §261) that nowadays immersion is done in a *mikveh*, which is in a *reshut ha-yaḥid*, so the concern no longer applies. This can justify the current practice of wearing jewelry on Shabbat (SSK ch. 18 n. 55).

17. SSK 18:27 follows the first opinion but adds that those who are lenient have grounds for their leniency. *Yaskil Avdi* 7:19 and *Le-horot Natan* 4:26 state similarly. It seems that *Minḥat Yitzḥak* 1:67 is stringent even when a watch is made of gold. In contrast, R. Shlomo Zalman Auerbach is lenient, as cited in SSK ch. 18 n. 113. Similarly, *Igrot Moshe* states that the primary ruling permits wearing a watch (OḤ 1:111). This is also the opinion of *Yeḥaveh Da'at* 3:23 and *Menuḥat Ahava* 3:27:33. In an area enclosed by an *eruv*, even those who are normally stringent and do not rely on an *eruv* of the *tzurat ha-petaḥ* type for streets wider than sixteen *amot* are lenient to allow wearing a watch there.

This means one should take a shoelace and thread it through the key, tie it with a bow knot, and put it on as a belt, so that the key will serve as a buckle. In this way one may wear the key in the public domain (SSK 18:49-50; see n. 10 above).

There are places where people must carry an identity card or passport on their person at all times. If someone there must go out on Shabbat for a great need or for the sake of a mitzva, he should carry the passport or identity card with a *shinui*. For example, he may place it under his hat, or inside his shirt where it is held up by his belt. In this way, one does *Hotza'ah* via a *shvut di-shvut*, which he may do for a great need or for the sake of a mitzva (above 9:11).

Similarly, if a doctor has ordered a patient not to leave the house without carrying a certain medication, the patient may go out for a great need or for the sake of a mitzva, as long as he carries the medicine with a *shinui*. One who must rely on this leniency should try not to come to a stop in the *reshut ha-rabim* until he reaches the *reshut ha-yaḥid* that is his final destination (SSK 40:7; n. 3 above).[18]

In a place without an *eruv*, if life-and-death security concerns demand that people carry a gun and a cell phone, these items may be taken along on normal Shabbat activities. The phone should be carried with a *shinui*, but the gun should be carried normally, as carrying it with a *shinui* could be dangerous. One may not go out on Shabbat with a gun or a walkie-talkie just for an outing. This rule will be explained in detail later on (27:17).

---

18. First, everyone agrees that the *shinui* renders the prohibition rabbinic in this case. Second, for those who maintain that there is no *reshut ha-rabim* today, this becomes a *shvut di-shvut*. Third, *Maharash Engel* 3:43 explains that this act of carrying is a *melakha she-eina tzerikha le-gufah*, because the person does not need the identity card for its own sake (*le-gufah*), but only to protect himself. However, it is difficult to claim that one who must carry medication does not need the medicine for its own sake (see *Tzitz Eliezer* 13:34). According to those who maintain that there are areas that qualify as *reshut ha-rabim* even nowadays, there is less room for leniency. Thus, it is proper when carrying medication to avoid stopping in *reshut ha-rabim*, as explained above in n. 3 (see *Nishmat Avraham* 301:2, n. 1). *Le-khatḥila*, one should not stop when carrying an identity card either.

Chapter Twenty-Two

The Spirit of Shabbat

1. THE MITZVA TO PRESERVE SHABBAT AS A DAY OF REST

The Torah commands us to refrain from *melakha* on Shabbat: "But the seventh day is Shabbat of the Lord your God; you shall not do any *melakha*" (Shemot 20:9), that is, any of the 39 types of *melakha* done while erecting the *Mishkan*, as explained to Moshe at Sinai (see above, 9:1-2). The Sages added safeguards ("fences") so that no one would do anything that might then lead to the violation of a Torah prohibition (see above, 9:3-4). There is an additional commandment in the Torah to rest on Shabbat: "Six days you shall do your work, but on the seventh day you shall cease" (Shemot 23:12). The point here is that in addition to avoiding *melakha* on Shabbat, we are also meant to cease and rest from toils and troubles. Thus one should not open his store or move heavy objects in preparation for the workweek. Even though these are not included in the 39 prohibited categories of *melakha*, nevertheless acting in these ways negates the mitzva of resting on Shabbat (Ramban, Vayikra 23:24; see MT 21:1 and the next section below).

Continuing with this line of thought, we find the prophets enjoining us to preserve the holy and sanctified atmosphere of Shabbat, a day on which one must avoid mundane activities. One who is careful to follow this merits great rewards, as Yeshayahu proclaims:

> If you refrain from trampling the Shabbat, from pursuing your affairs on My holy day; if you call Shabbat "delight," the Lord's holy [day] "honored," and if you honor it, and not go in your own way, nor look to your affairs, nor speak of them – then you will seek the Lord's delight. I will set you astride the heights of the earth, and let you enjoy the heritage of your father Yaakov – for the mouth of the Lord has spoken. (Yeshayahu 58:13-14)

The Sages derive many guidelines about Shabbat from this verse, and the common denominator is that one should not behave on Shabbat as one does during the week. The Gemara elaborates:

> "Honor it" – your Shabbat clothes should not be like your weekday clothes.... "Not go in your own way" – the way you walk on Shabbat should not be like the way you walk on weekdays. "Nor look to your affairs" – it is forbidden to look after your own affairs on Shabbat, but one may look after the affairs of heaven [i.e., religious matters]. "Nor speak of them" – your speech on Shabbat should not be like your speech on weekdays. Speaking [about mundane matters] is forbidden, but thinking about them is permitted. (*Shabbat* 113a).

These directives have a higher status than general rabbinic enactments since they are rooted in the Torah's commandment to rest and are elaborated upon by the prophets.

We have already explained the *mitzvot* connected to honoring and delighting in Shabbat (chs. 2, 4, 5, 7). Honor (*kavod*) is expressed by wearing special Shabbat clothes, showering, cleaning the house, and lighting candles. Delight (*oneg*) is expressed by making Shabbat enjoyable through meals, sleep, and Torah study. In this chapter, we will explain the *mitzvot* and the rabbinic safeguards meant to protect Shabbat's atmosphere as a holy day of rest. These *mitzvot* are at the root of everything that the Sages through the ages forbade as a weekday activity. Any activity that is unquestionably mundane is prohibited on Shabbat. This includes ball-playing for adults, swimming, working out, and bike-riding. To protect the spirit of Shabbat, the Sages also introduced the prohibition of *muktzeh* (as explained in the next chapter) and ordained that one may not play musical instruments (sections 17-19 below).

Even though the *mitzvot* to preserve Shabbat's spirit and avoid weekday activity (*uvdin de-ḥol*) are of a higher status than the safeguards of the Sages, nevertheless the *halakha* is stricter in demanding adherence to the safeguards, such as the prohibition to do *melakha* with a *shinui* or to ask a non-Jew to do a *melakha*, which are forbidden even for the sake of a mitzva (as explained above 9:3-4, 11), whereas the prohibitions connected to preserving the spirit of Shabbat may be disregarded in the service of a mitzva (as explained below). There are some prohibitions that are comprised of both of these elements: if prohibited solely to preserve the spirit of Shabbat, it might have been permitted for the sake of a mitzva, but since the Sages decreed that it is prohibited, it remains prohibited even for the sake of a mitzva.

2. BUSINESS

One may not engage in commerce on Shabbat. One who opens his store, buying and selling on Shabbat just as he does on weekdays, negates a Torah commandment. This prohibition applies even if he is careful to avoid transgressing any of the 39 *melakhot*. The Torah commands that Shabbat be a "*shabbaton*" (Shemot 31:15), a complete cessation. One who does business in his store is not resting (Ramban, Vayikra 23:24; Ritva; *Ḥatam Sofer*). Neḥemia faced this problem when he arrived in Jerusalem and found that people were holding a market day on Shabbat. He recounts:

> Tyrians (merchants) who lived there brought fish and all sorts of wares and sold them on Shabbat to the Judahites in Jerusalem. I censured the nobles of Judah, saying to them, "What evil thing is this that you are doing, profaning Shabbat day! This is just what your ancestors did, and for it God brought all this misfortune on this city; and now you give cause for further wrath against Israel by profaning Shabbat!" (Neḥemia 13:15-18)

As a result, the merchants began selling their goods outside the city walls on Shabbat. In response, Neḥemia ordered that the gates of the city be closed over Shabbat. "Once or twice the merchants and the vendors of all sorts of wares spent the night outside Jerusalem, but I warned them, saying, 'What do you mean by spending the night alongside the wall? If you do so again, I will lay hands upon you!' From then on, they did not come on Shabbat" (*ibid.* 19-21).

The Torah prohibition on commerce applies to one who regularly does business on Shabbat. However, one who buys or sells on Shabbat occasionally still transgresses the words of the prophets, as Yeshayahu said: "if you honor it, and not go in your own way, nor look to your affairs, nor speak of them" (58:13), and the Sages explained this to mean that one should not deal in mundane matters on Shabbat (*Shabbat* 113a).

It should be noted that those verses do not record a prohibition on buying and selling for the sake of a mitzva. Nevertheless, as a safeguard, the Sages prohibited all business dealings, even in service of a mitzva, out of concern lest one write (Rashi and *Tosafot, Beitza* 37a; MB 306:11). The only exception to this prohibition is the mitzva of settling the land of Israel, for which one may purchase land from a non-Jew on Shabbat. The non-Jew should write the contract and take the money on his own (SA 306:11; *Eliya Rabba ad loc.* 22; *Mor U-ketzi'a*; as opposed to MA *ad loc.* 19; see above 9:12).

Some are stringent and do not sell *aliyot* on Shabbat, because of the prohibition of doing business on Shabbat. However, many are customarily lenient, and they have grounds for their leniency. This is because, in this case, there is no acquisition (*kinyan*) or payment on Shabbat, and the assumption of the obligation to pay for the *aliyot* is deemed to be for the sake of a mitzva (MB 306:33; *Yeḥaveh Da'at* 2:41). However, if the synagogue's income from this practice is minimal, it is improper to be lenient and waste the congregation's time.

3. OBTAINING PRODUCTS FROM STORES

One who finds himself short of food on Shabbat for the Shabbat meals, whether on account of poor planning or the arrival of unexpected guests, may approach the owner of a store and ask him for food from his store, with the unspoken understanding that the customer will pay for the food after Shabbat. Payment is not mentioned explicitly. Rather, the customer should request the item from the owner in the same way that he would borrow the food from a neighbor. He should not use the words "buy," "sell," or "pay." He may assure the store owner that later, whether Saturday night or afterward, they will discuss what was taken and settle up. Even though the store owner understands from this assurance that the customer intends to pay him, as long as payment has not been explicitly mentioned (but only hinted at), this is not forbidden.

The store owner and customer should both be careful not to mention the price of a product, nor should they measure it or weigh it out as one would do during the week to determine its price. However, they may fill up a container (not a measuring cup) and agree that the container will be measured on Sunday, with the understanding that the price will be determined based on the amount it holds. One may use a measuring cup to transport food but not to measure out the exact amount to be poured into the customer's container, because then it is clear that the intention is to measure. For example, one may ask a store owner for five oranges or five bottles because that is the normal way to describe the required quantity. This terminology is not used exclusively for a sale. If this customer has received items from the store owner in the past, the owner may not refer to the accumulating tab nor calculate its updated amount (SA 323:1-4; MB *ad loc.* 20; SSK 29:18-25).

If the store owner does not trust the customer to remember to pay him after Shabbat, he may ask him to leave an article of clothing or an object, but he should not refer to it as "collateral," "security deposit," or the like (Rema 307:11).

One who takes food from a store on Shabbat should not carry it out in a large box, as one would normally do during the week, so that witnesses do not think that he is transporting the food for commercial purposes. Rather, he should hold the items in his hands or place them on his shoulders, as one would normally do when bringing food to a meal. Even if this means he will have to make multiple trips in order to bring all the necessary food, this extra walking is preferable to giving the appearance of doing business. However, if one's guests are waiting for the meal, then he should hurry and bring all the food at once, even if it means carrying the food as he would during the week. Additionally, if he is walking in a place where there is no chance that anyone will suspect him of doing business, he may carry the food in the normal way in order to minimize the walking ("*yesh omrim*" in SA 323:5; MB *ad loc.* 25; Rema 510:8).

If a store or hotel owner would like to make food available on Shabbat for his customers, before Shabbat he may sell different-colored cards or tickets that entitle their bearers to various items. For example, a yellow card presented to a waiter will entitle a guest to Friday night dinner; a green card to lunch on Shabbat day; a red card to a drink; a blue card to cake, etc. If there are not enough different colors for the different options, the names of the options may be written on the cards. However, the prices may not be written on the cards because this would make the cards the equivalent of monetary contracts, which may not be read on Shabbat (MB 307:50 and 323:20; SSK 29:26).

4. LENDING, BORROWING, AND GIVING GIFTS

Just as one may not buy and sell on Shabbat, one may not lend anything or repay a loan. Since these activities often involve writing contracts, there is a concern that engaging in them may lead one to write. Therefore, one who needs to borrow food, clothing, or chairs for Shabbat should formulate his request in a way that makes it clear that he is borrowing the objects as one would borrow from a friend, not as one would borrow money from a bank, as it is unusual keep a written record when borrowing from a friend. Since English does not distinguish between these two types of borrowing (unlike Hebrew, which has "*hashala*" to refer to borrowing objects and "*halva'ah*" to refer to monetary lending), one should simply say "Give me" or "Can I have." If the owner of the item is concerned that the borrower will forget to return it, he may request that the borrower leave something with him, but he should not refer to it as a deposit or collateral, as he would during the week (*Shabbat* 148a; Rema 307:11). If the borrower mistakenly asked for a loan, the owner may give it to him while clarifying that he may use it temporarily though one may not make a loan on Shabbat (*Shulḥan Shlomo* 307:15:2).

According to many *poskim*, one may not give or receive presents on Shabbat because by doing so one transfers ownership of the gift, which resembles commerce (MA 306:15; *Birkei Yosef ad loc.* 7; MB *ad loc.* 33). Others maintain that one may give a gift on Shabbat because nobody writes contracts for gifts (*Beit Meir* based on Rif and Rambam).

In practice, we are stringent *le-khatḥila* and avoid giving gifts on Shabbat, but if it is necessary to fulfill a mitzva, everyone agrees that one may give a gift (SA 658:3-4). Therefore, one may give a gift of utensils or food for a Shabbat meal (MB 306:33). One may also give prizes to children for participating in Torah study, as this is for the sake of a mitzva – to encourage the children to study Torah.

It is proper for one who wants to give a bar mitzva present on Shabbat to perform the act of acquisition (*kinyan*) before Shabbat. That is, he should request someone else to take the gift, lifting it up (*hagbaha*) in order to acquire it on behalf of the bar mitzva boy. Thus, the gift is transferred to the boy's ownership before Shabbat. On Shabbat it may be presented to him, as it already belonged to him prior to Shabbat. If *hagbaha* was not done, the gift can be left with the boy (who should have in mind not to acquire it) for the duration of Shabbat, and after Shabbat he may officially acquire it (SSK 29:31). Some are lenient and give gifts to a groom on Shabbat, as there is an element of mitzva involved in bringing him happiness (*Eliya Rabba*; *Ḥatam Sofer*). In a time of need, one may rely upon them (*Seridei Esh* 2:26).

One may not use a lottery or other random selection mechanism on Shabbat in order to decide who will receive each portion of food. Since everyone wants the biggest and tastiest portion, there is a concern that people will end up measuring and weighing the portions or speaking about their price. Moreover, it contains an element of gambling. Members of a household may use a lottery, but only as long as the portions are of equal value (*Shabbat* 148b-149a; SA 322:6; see below 22:8). One may draw lots to determine who will have the privilege of getting an *aliya* or saying *Kaddish*, because there is nothing to measure or calculate (MB 322:24).

5. COURT ACTIVITY, WEDDINGS, *TERUMA* AND *MA'ASER*

The Sages forbade rabbinical courts to sit in judgment or mete out punishment on Shabbat. Similarly, they prohibited betrothals, marriages, divorce, *yibum* (levirate marriage), or *ḥalitza* (levirate divorce) out of concern that people would end up writing (*Beitza* 37a). It is similarly prohibited to redeem a firstborn son on Shabbat, because the redemption (*pidyon ha-ben*) involves a transfer of money, which resembles commerce. If the 31st day after birth coincides with Shabbat, the redemption is done the following day, Sunday. It is also forbidden to vow, consecrate, or dedicate items or their value to the Temple on Shabbat, as this transfers ownership of the objects to God, as it were, and resembles commerce. However, one may pledge to give charity, because such a commitment involves no act of acquisition. If one did buy, sell, or perform any of these actions on Shabbat, the transaction is effective (*m. Beitza* 36b; SA 339:4).

Teruma, ma'aser and *ḥalla* may not be set aside on Shabbat, because setting them aside resembles dedicating them to God. Additionally, it looks like one is fixing or improving the produce (*Beitza* 36b; MT 23:14). If one made a mistake and unknowingly set them aside, the remaining produce may be eaten on Shabbat. In contrast, if he did this knowingly, although the action is effective and the remaining produce may be eaten, no Jew may eat it until after Shabbat (*m. Terumot* 2:3; MB 339:25).

One who is concerned that he will not have time to separate *teruma* and *ma'aser* before Shabbat may recite the formula for the separation before Shabbat (but without the *berakha*). By doing so, he has begun the process of separation. Then, after Shabbat begins, he may tithe in the normal fashion and recite the *berakha*. This procedure may also be followed if one is concerned that he will not have time to set aside *ḥalla*.

Only the owner of the produce may separate *teruma* and *ma'aser* on Shabbat by means of the procedure described in the previous paragraph; it is not effective for anyone else. If a guest is concerned that his host may forget to tithe, he may ask the host before Shabbat to appoint him a *shali'aḥ* (proxy) to tithe on his behalf. The guest may then recite the formulation before Shabbat and perform the actual tithing on Shabbat (*m. Demai* 7:1, 5; MT, Laws of Tithes 9:7-9).[1]

---

1. When I wrote above that only the owner of the produce or his *shali'aḥ* may tithe on Shabbat by means of this procedure, this applies to cases where the produce definitely has not been tithed yet (*tevel*). However, if it is uncertain whether the produce was tithed (*demai*), someone else can tithe this way as well (*Orḥot Shabbat* 22:65-70). The formula recited before Shabbat is the usual one, but all the words should be changed to the future tense, e.g., "What I will tithe" (*Ḥazon Ish, Demai,* 9:13:15 as quoted in *Orḥot Shabbat* 22:62 and n. 86). *Be-di'avad,* if one simply says, "Whatever I separate tomorrow should be considered *teruma* and *ma'aser*," he has fulfilled his obligation, as he has begun the process of separation before Shabbat (see SSK 11:23). After the tithes are actually set aside, he may not move them, as they are *muktzeh*.

6. IMMERSING AND MEASURING ON SHABBAT

As is well known, a Jew who bought or received an eating utensil or receptacle from a non-Jew may not use it for food until it has been immersed in a *mikveh*. If one did not immerse it before Shabbat, some maintain that doing so on Shabbat is forbidden because it looks like one is fixing the implement (*tikun kli*). After all, before its immersion, one may not use it, while afterward, one may (Rosh). Others maintain that if one needs to eat from it, he may immerse it on Shabbat with a *berakha*. Accordingly, immersion is not considered fixing, because if *be-di'avad* the *kli* was used for food without having been immersed, the food retains its kosher status (Rif). If there is a trustworthy non-Jew in the vicinity, it is proper to give the *kli* to him as a gift, and then request his permission to use it. In this way, a Jew may use the *kli* for food even though it has not been immersed (SA 323:7). After Shabbat, it is proper to ask the non-Jew to give it back to him as a gift; he should then immerse it with a *berakha*.[2]

All agree that one may immerse on Shabbat to purify himself from *tum'a*. Even those who maintain that *kelim* may not be immersed because it resembles fixing them agree that when it comes to people, since one may bathe, and since the immersion will not necessarily be seen as an act of purification, one may also immerse to purify himself (see above 14:9). In contrast, one converting to Judaism may not immerse on Shabbat as part of the conversion process because his immersion is transformative; he becomes a new person, a process that certainly qualifies as a *tikun*. Additionally, immersion for conversion requires the presence of a rabbinic court; just as a court does not meet on Shabbat for judgment, it also does

2. According to *Beit Yosef*, in a time of need one may immerse *kelim* on Shabbat. Rambam too is lenient, following Rif; and SA 323:7 implies this as well. Maharam ibn Ḥabib writes in *Responsa Kol Gadol* §15 that the immersion should be done with a *berakha* (*Livyat Ḥen* §§72, 75). Others (*Zivḥei Tzedek*, AHS) maintain that we see from SA YD 120:16 that R. Yosef Karo retracted, and the only solution is to have a non-Jew acquire the *kli* (so that it is not owned by a Jew). Rema in *Darkhei Moshe* is stringent, as is *Sha'agat Aryeh* §56. *Be-di'avad*, if a *kli* was immersed on Shabbat, it may be used (MA; MB 323:33). BHL has a thorough analysis of this issue. If the *kli* still belongs to a non-Jew but is in the possession of a Jew, it should be immersed without a *berakha*. Therefore, it is proper to ask the non-Jew to return the item to him as a gift so he may immerse it with a *berakha* (*Taz*; MB 323:35).

not meet to supervise immersion (*Yevamot* 46b). If a court transgressed and did supervise an immersion on Shabbat, the immersion is valid, and the person is Jewish (SA YD 268:4).

One may not measure anything on Shabbat, because measuring is a weekday activity (SA 306:7; MB *ad loc.* 34). Therefore, one may not weigh himself or measure his height on Shabbat (SSK 14:42). Similarly, one may not measure the dimensions of furniture or a room.

One may measure and weigh for the sake of a mitzva. Therefore, one may check whether a *mikveh* has sufficient water (forty *se'ah*). One may also measure out medicine for sick people and take their temperature (SA 306:7; SSK 40:2). Since a baby has the same halakhic status as a sick person, when necessary one may measure out the amount of food that a baby needs. Similarly, when necessary one may measure if a baby has gained weight after eating (using a non-electric scale; SSK 37:5).

7. WALKING, RUNNING, AND JUMPING

The world we live in is full of shortcomings. To perfect it, we rush around all week long, working and exerting ourselves in a variety of ways. However, on Shabbat, which is like the World to Come, we are commanded to cease all work and act as if everything has already been perfected, with no further need to rush around. We are meant simply to delight in the holiness of Shabbat and take a faith-filled look at the perfect inner essence of the world as God created it. There is a mitzva to express this spiritual perspective by walking at a leisurely pace on Shabbat. Thus the Sages expound: "'Not go in your own way' – the way you walk on Shabbat should not be like the way you walk on weekdays" (*Shabbat* 113a).

Therefore, running is prohibited on Shabbat, as is striding. This prohibition applies to one who is going somewhere for his own sake, in which case he should walk at a leisurely pace to honor Shabbat. However, if one is going to attend a Torah class or to pray, it is a mitzva for him to run (*Berakhot* 6b; SA 301:1), because running for the sake of a mitzva does not detract from the honor due Shabbat. On the contrary, it expresses the spirit of Shabbat, which allows us to rest from the troubles of this world. This peacefulness in turn encourages us to serve God.

One may run and jump if one benefits greatly from it. For example, one may run in order to get out of the rain, and one may jump over a puddle to avoid dirtying his shoes. One may also run in order to watch something enjoyable (*Shabbat* 113b; SA 301:2-3). Children and teens who enjoy running may participate in games that involve running, since this type of running is pleasurable rather than burdensome (SA 301:2). Also, adults may jump for pleasure as part of playing with small children.

8. WORKING OUT AND RIDING A BICYCLE

One may not run for exercise on Shabbat, because it is burdensome rather than pleasurable. Even though people who work out enjoy it, this enjoyment derives from their awareness that they are taking care of their health and physical fitness, not from the exercise itself. Even one who is very fit, runs every day, and enjoys it may not run on Shabbat, because it is a weekday activity. It will appear to others that he is belittling Shabbat and treating it like a weekday. However, one who enjoys exercise may jump or work out for pleasure inside his home on condition that he does not overexert himself, does not follow a regimen, and does not use special equipment, any of which would be deemed a weekday activity. One may not play ball for the same reason; even children may not play with a ball that adults use for sports, because it is a weekday activity.[3]

One may walk on Shabbat for one's health, on condition that he walks regularly and not more briskly or more intensively than usual.

---

3. According to *Or Le-Tziyon* 2:36:12, exercise is forbidden only when undertaken in order to sweat to improve health, but one may run for callisthenic exercise just as youths may run for pleasure (based on Rambam, and as opposed to Rashi; see BHL 328:42). However, in practice, it would seem that exercise is, in some way, a weekday activity, as we can see from *t. Shabbat* 17:16, which states: "One may not run on Shabbat for exercise; but walking in the usual fashion, even all day long, is no problem." Even though youths who enjoy running may run, this is because they enjoy the running itself; but when the pleasure is derived from improving one's health, it is prohibited. This is made explicit in SA 301:1-2; *Taz ad loc.* 1; AHS *ad loc.* 44. It is also the position of *Tzitz Eliezer* 6:4 and SSK 34:22. One who enjoys the exercise itself may exercise (*Melamed Le-ho'il*, OḤ 53; R. Shlomo Zalman Auerbach in SSK ch. 16 n. 106) on condition that he does not do so in an organized and professional way, which would qualify it as a weekday activity. It would also seem that an adult who enjoys running may not run outside, because it seems to belittle Shabbat and is consequently deemed a weekday activity. See *Harḥavot*.

Although one may not address medical needs on Shabbat, since it is not discernible that his walking has a medical purpose, and many people take walks, he may walk for health and fitness on Shabbat (MB 301:7). One may also do gentle stretches in order to loosen up.

The later *poskim* agree that one may not ride a bicycle on Shabbat. Some maintain that the reason for this prohibition is a concern that one will travel outside the *teḥum*, while others say that the concern is that the bicycle will break and he will end up fixing it. In fact, the main reason is that it is a weekday activity, since people ride bicycles primarily to travel to work or to exercise.[4]

9. WALKING FOR NON-SHABBAT PURPOSES

Even when one takes a relaxed walk, he may not walk to his fields or factory in order to plan out his workweek. Doing so is included in the category of "your affairs," which may not be addressed on Shabbat, as it is stated: "if you honor it, and not go in your own way, nor look to your affairs" (Yeshayahu 58:13). However, if it is not obvious that his intention is to plan his work, there is no prohibition. Therefore, one may take a Shabbat walk as long as onlookers cannot tell that he is looking over his fields. It is pious to avoid thinking about business on Shabbat altogether (see SA 306:8).

---

4. However, *Ben Ish Ḥai* permits riding a bicycle. It explains that we need not be concerned that people will mistakenly conclude that one may ride in vehicles drawn by humans or animals. Furthermore, we do not have the right to enact new decrees (*Responsa Rav Pe'alim* 1:25). Nevertheless, almost all *poskim* are stringent, for the reasons mentioned above (*Ketzot Ha-shulḥan* §110, *Badei Ha-shulḥan* §16; *Yaskil Avdi* 3:19; *Tzitz Eliezer* 7:30; *She'elat Yaakov* §45; *Kaf Ha-ḥayim* 404:8, SSK 16:18). *Or Le-Tziyon* 2:42:1 adds that though it is technically possible to permit, since the widespread practice is to forbid bike riding, it is forbidden.

Those who maintain that riding a bicycle is a weekday activity can find support in *Beitza* 25b: "The Rabbis taught: The blind do not go out [on Yom Tov] with their canes, nor do we go out with a chair." Rashi explains that since canes were considered weekday items, going out with them would belittle Yom Tov. He adds that the chair in question is a sedan chair (litter) carried by people. The Gemara specifies that the prohibition on carrying the chair applies when people lift it up on their shoulders (as opposed to holding it lower down). Rashi explains that when a chair is carried on the shoulders it looks like a weekday activity, it is more public, and it indicates that the chair is being carried further.

Similarly, one who is building a house should not check the progress on Shabbat, because it is obvious that he is planning his work, and one who intends to renovate or expand his home may not examine other projects if it is clear that he is planning the renovations. So too, one considering buying an apartment may not check out apartments for sale on Shabbat. In contrast, one considering buying an apartment may walk to a street where new apartments are being built even though his intention is to look them over, as long as it looks like he is just out for a walk and he does not stop and scrutinize them; this way, he does not look like he is planning his purchase. If one is planning to buy an electrical appliance, he may window-shop at appliance stores while walking on the street. However, he should not look at prices (SSK 29:10). In addition, it is pious to avoid thinking about these matters at all on Shabbat.

Toward the end of Shabbat, one may not walk to the edge of the *teḥum* in order to hire workers as soon after Shabbat as possible. Similarly, one may not go to his field, store, or factory at that time so that he can begin work immediately after Shabbat. Since it is clear that he is going there on Shabbat in order to work afterward, in effect he is dealing with his weekday affairs on Shabbat. However, if it is not clear that this is the reason he is going there, as is the case, for example, if many people take walks there, then he may walk there on Shabbat even if he intends to hire workers or begin his work immediately afterward. This is because the prohibition only applies when it is clear that he is going for a mundane purpose (SA 306:1; MB *ad loc.* 1; BHL s.v. "she-me'ayen; SA 307:9; MB *ad loc.* 40).[5]

---

5. The prohibition on walking to the edge of the *teḥum* on Shabbat applies when going to do something that cannot be done permissibly on Shabbat. However, if his objective is to collect already-picked fruits that are outside the *teḥum*, or to visit relatives who live outside the *teḥum*, the walking is permitted, as there is no essential prohibition involved (after all, if there were an *eruv*, he would be permitted to undertake these activities even on Shabbat). In contrast, one may not walk to the edge of the *teḥum* on Shabbat with the goal of picking fruits or collecting *muktzeh* fruits after Shabbat, because the act is fundamentally prohibited (there is no way to undertake these activities permissibly on Shabbat). A similar principle governs the prohibition of speech, as described in the next section. One may speak about an activity if it can be done on Shabbat in a permissible way, such as if there were an *eruv*. So, one may speak on Shabbat of plans to visit an area the next day in order to collect fruit from there (*Shabbat* 150b; SA 307:8; MB *ad loc.* 35. SAH, *ad loc.* 16 explains the basis of the permission. *Orḥot Shabbat* ch. 22 n. 7 suggests additional reasons for it).

10. TALKING ABOUT WORK AND BUSINESS

It is a mitzva to honor Shabbat in the way one speaks, as it is written: "and if you honor it, and not go in your own way, nor look to your affairs, nor speak of them" (Yeshayahu 58:13). The Sages elaborate: "'Nor speak of them' – your speech on Shabbat should not be like your speech on weekdays" (*Shabbat* 113a). This means that one should not speak on Shabbat about things that one may not do on Shabbat. Therefore, one should not say, "Tomorrow I will travel by car," "I will write a letter," or "I will buy an item." Clearly, then, it is also prohibited for one to ask someone else to travel the next day on his behalf, write a letter for him, or buy something for him (SA 307:1). This prohibition applies to things that one intends to do in the future. However, one may speak about what he has already done, as long as he does not intend to provide useful information to the listener on how best to perform the *melakha*.

The prohibition applies to talking about actions prohibited on Shabbat. In contrast, one may think about them. Thus the Sages expound: "Speaking [about mundane matters] is forbidden, but thinking about them is permitted" (*Shabbat* 113a). Speech that merely alludes to a *melakha* is considered "thinking" and is thus permitted. For example, while one may not say, "Tomorrow I will phone so-and-so," one may say, "Tomorrow I will speak with so-and-so," even though it is clear that he will do so by phone. Similarly, one may not say, "Tomorrow I will drive to Jerusalem," since traveling by motor vehicle is prohibited on Shabbat, but one may say, "Tomorrow I will go to Jerusalem," since one can "go" by walking, and even though Jerusalem is outside the *teḥum*, theoretically one could build an *eruv* to Jerusalem and it would be permitted to walk there on Shabbat. Since walking to Jerusalem is not fundamentally prohibited, one may talk about "going" there. Even if the listener realizes that the speaker means that he is planning to travel by car or bus and that the listener may join him if he wishes, the statement is still considered only a hint and is permitted.

Similarly, if one plans to travel by cab after Shabbat, on Shabbat he may ask his friend who is a cabdriver, "Do you think you will be able to come over after Shabbat?" Since he has not asked his friend to come with his cab in order to drive him, then even though his friend understands that this is what is meant, it is not prohibited. However, he may not say to his cabdriver friend, "Come over after Shabbat, please," because an allusion in the imperative form is prohibited. Following the same principle, one who wishes to hire a worker on Sunday may say to him on Shabbat, "I hope to see you on Sunday," but he may not say, "Please come on Sunday" (*Shabbat* 150a; SA 307:7).

One may not speak about monetary transactions that have business implications, while one may talk about them if they have no practical import. Therefore, one may not speak about wages owed to workers, but one may speak about wages already paid. Similarly, one may not tell another how much a house sold for if the listener is interested in buying a similar house, while one may pass on this information to someone who is not interested in buying a home. Likewise, one may report on how much yield a field produced the previous year, what the government's budget is, and the like. This is because the people involved in these conversations have no plans to act on these discussions during the week (SA 307:6).[6]

It is preferable to minimize trivial conversations on Shabbat. One who enjoys such conversations may engage in them a bit more than usual, as they are part of his physical enjoyment of Shabbat. However, he should not indulge himself excessively, just as he should not eat or sleep excessively, as these indulgences will take away from the time he needs to set aside for Torah study on Shabbat. We have already seen that a minimum of six hours must be dedicated to Torah study on Shabbat (SA and Rema 307:1; MB *ad loc.* 4; see above 5:1).

11. WALKING AND TALKING FOR THE SAKE OF A MITZVA

One may speak about activities that are prohibited on Shabbat if it is for the sake of a mitzva. In such a case, one may also examine sites where *melakha* must be done or make financial calculations for the sake of a mitzva. It is written: "and if you honor it, and not go in your own way,

6. If there is a great need to speak on Shabbat about business matters (for example, if one encounters a person with whom he will not be able to meet on a weekday, and if he does not speak with him he will suffer a great loss), he may talk about business matters as long as he uses a *shinui* when choosing his words. For example, he should speak of a hundred challahs rather than a hundred dollars (*Eshel Avraham* [Buczacz] §307). As with any rabbinic prohibition on Shabbat, using a *shinui* reduces it to a *shvut di-shvut*, and is permitted in order to prevent a great loss (*She'arim Metzuyanim Ba-halakha* 90:3 and *Kuntres Aḥaron*).

nor look to your affairs, nor speak of them" (Yeshayahu 58:13), and the Sages expound: "'Nor look to your affairs' – it is forbidden to look after your own affairs on Shabbat, but one may look after the affairs of heaven ('*ḥeftzei shamayim*,' i.e., religious matters)" (*Shabbat* 113a). Therefore, if necessary, one may walk to inspect a synagogue construction site. If something is needed for an upcoming wedding or funeral, one may walk to the edge of the *teḥum* so that one can deal with these matters immediately after Shabbat. Near the end of Shabbat, one may also start walking to a location from which people will be picked up after Shabbat in order to comfort mourners (*Shabbat* 151a; SA 306:3; SSK 29:13).

Similarly, in cases of necessity, one may speak about mundane matters that relate to mitzva needs. This includes calculating the costs of a wedding meal or a *brit mila*, as each of these is a *se'udat mitzva* (a festive meal associated with a mitzva). One may plan the hiring of a band for a wedding or deal with the bride's dress. However, one may not actually close a deal, because business deals are prohibited even for the sake of a mitzva. It is altogether prohibited to discuss hiring a photographer for a wedding, or the purchase of wedding outfits for family members of the bride and groom, since these do not qualify as mitzva needs.

One may take up a collection in which everybody pledges to give a certain amount of money to charity or to a synagogue. Parents may calculate the sum needed for their children's education, whether religious, secular, or vocational. Those involved in education may discuss school or class budgets. A principal may offer a job to a teacher and mention a salary figure, though it is forbidden to reach an agreement on wages. One may discuss communal needs such as paving roads or levying taxes, as the needs of the community are deemed mitzva needs (*Shabbat* 150a; SA 306:6). In all these cases, it is proper to be lenient only when there is a specific need. If the matter will be addressed in any case, it is proper not to speak of mundane matters or walk in order to inspect them, even for the sake of a mitzva (MB 307:1).

If necessary, one may announce that an object has been found on Shabbat, even if the item in question is *muktzeh* (such as a purse), in order to facilitate the fulfillment (after Shabbat) of the mitzva of returning a lost item (SA 306:12). In an area where it is difficult to locate matza for Pesaḥ or a *lulav* and *etrog* for Sukkot, one may announce on Shabbat where they are available for sale (MB 306:55).

12. PERMITTED AND FORBIDDEN READING MATERIAL

One may not read contracts and financial documents on Shabbat, such as loan and purchase contracts, bank statements, phone and electric bills, and prices on flyers or in shop windows. Reading them is considered dealing with mundane affairs (*ḥeftzei ḥol*), which is forbidden on Shabbat (Rosh). Furthermore, there is a concern that as a result of reading them one will end up writing or erasing (Rambam).

According to Rambam, one may read only sacred words on Shabbat; all other reading material is forbidden, even to study the sciences, so that Shabbat is not treated as a weekday and situations that might lead to writing are avoided. However, in practice, we follow the majority of *poskim* (Rashi, Ri, Rosh), who limit the prohibition to reading financial and business material. In order to ensure that no one will end up reading these materials, the Sages also prohibited reading secular material that has no value. In contrast, secular material that has value may be read on Shabbat. This includes material on physical fitness, proper nutrition, and ingredient lists on food packaging. One may also study the sciences and other branches of knowledge.

One may not read run-of-the-mill secular material and stories if they have no value. However, one who enjoys reading them may do so occasionally, as the Sages did not forbid reading for pleasure on Shabbat. In contrast, one should not read gripping novels that cause sadness or anxiety on Shabbat (MB 306:38 and 307:3). It would seem that one may read depressing stories from Jewish history and rabbinic biographies, since they are valuable as Torah and are morally edifying. Nevertheless, it is preferable to study pleasant things, which are more appropriate for Shabbat.

In principle, one may read the newspaper for informative content. One who enjoys reading news, stories, and analysis may do so, but one may not read sad and worrying content on Shabbat. One may read general financial articles as long as they do not give practical advice, but one may not read articles that give practical business and investment advice. It is also forbidden to read advertisements for products that one may wish to buy in the future.

Even though technically one may read parts of the newspaper, many maintain that it is proper to avoid reading it on Shabbat because it is full of advertisements and disturbing news, and it is difficult to distinguish between what one may and may not read. Additionally, reading a newspaper negates the main purpose of Shabbat, which is Torah study. Therefore, one may read its informative content and non-disturbing news, but only while in the bathroom.[7]

One may read (and place) ads in leaflets distributed in synagogues, as long as they are advertising products that fulfill mitzva needs, such as Torah books or homes in Israel (to potential customers from abroad). If these products are being sold cheaply and advertising might encourage readers to fulfill the mitzva, one may even publish the price (see MB 306:55, 307:1, and 323:20).

One may not read a guest list or menu of a Shabbat meal as it resembles reading a contract. In addition, there is a concern that the host may wish to correct the list by writing or erasing (*Shabbat* 149:1; SA 307:12-13). In contrast, for the sake of a mitzva, such as the meal accompanying a *brit mila*, or in order to avoid greatly insulting someone, a waiter may read the list, as there is no concern that he will change it. However, the host or head waiter may not read the list, because they might end up correcting it (MB 307:47; SHT *ad loc.* 54).

The *gabbai* may read the notebook or cards that contain the list of people to be called up to the Torah, since this is for the sake of a mitzva. We are not worried that he will end up writing or erasing, since he is standing

7. According to Rambam, only Torah material may be read on Shabbat. All other reading materials are forbidden out of concern that people will end up writing. In contrast, Rashi, Ri, Rosh, Ramban, and Rashba maintain that the original prohibition was limited to reading material dealing with business or other things that are forbidden on Shabbat. The Sages extended this prohibition to include stories or material with no value, to make it less likely that people will read the previously prohibited material. The majority of *poskim* follow this lenient approach (*Baḥ* 307:5; SAH 307:21-22; MB 307:52; SSK 29:48-49). The Gemara forbids reading captions under pictures, and this includes mundane stories as well (*Shabbat* 149a; SA 307:15). According to *Ma'amar Mordechai* and SAH, even one who enjoys them may not read them, but according to MA 301:4, *Birkei Yosef*, *Pri Megadim*, and Maharsham, he may read occasionally. Disturbing material, no matter how gripping, should not be read (see MB 307:3).

She'elat Ya'avetz 1:162 states that while technically one may read newspapers, in practice it is proper to forbid it lest people end up reading prohibited material. MB 307:63 states similarly, while *Shvut Yaakov* 3:13 is permissive. See SSK 29:48 and *Harḥavot*.

in the middle of a group of people. If he forgets and wants to write, others will remind him that it is Shabbat. The *gabbai* may also call people to the Torah from a list he has been given by a family that is celebrating a special occasion in the synagogue. If they wish to change the list, the *gabbai* should not review it without at least one other person reviewing it with him who can remind him that it is Shabbat, lest he forget.

13. GAMES ON SHABBAT

Poskim disagree whether one may play games on Shabbat. Some say that since Shabbat is meant for Torah study, one may not play games, as that would be wasting time that could be used to study Torah. Accordingly, one may not play checkers, chess, backgammon, billiards, or any ball game, whether the games are played inside on the floor or outside on a paved area. And since one may not play these games, they are considered *muktzeh* as well (R. Aharon Sasson, cited in *Birkei Yosef* 338:1; *Petaḥ Ha-devir ad loc.* 4).

Others maintain that there is no prohibition on playing games on Shabbat, as long as nobody is playing for money (Rema 338:5; *Ma'amar Mordechai*). Indeed, some rabbis would play chess on Shabbat, as it is a game that requires thought and sharpens the mind (*Shiltei Giborim*).[8]

In practice, it is appropriate for adults to be stringent and not play ball games, chess, and the like, both because it is prohibited according

8. Ḥida is inclined to forbid playing chess (*Birkei Yosef* 338:1). He suggests that the rabbis who played chess on Shabbat were suffering from depression. In order to take their minds off their worries, they played chess, after which they were able to return to their Torah study. However, barring this situation, one should not play on Shabbat. The Sages tell us that there was a place named Tur Shimon that was destroyed even though the people there respected Shabbat. Some say the reason was that they played ball there on Shabbat (*y. Ta'anit* 4:5). R. Elazar of Worms explains that by playing games they were wasting time during which they would have been learning Torah (*Roke'aḥ* §55). Based on this, some conclude that one may not play ball on Shabbat, and that therefore balls are *muktzeh* (*Shibolei Ha-leket, Beit Yosef,* and SA 308:45). Others are permissive and maintain that one may play ball in a paved yard (*Tosafot,* Rema). Nevertheless, one may not play on an unpaved surface, out of concern that people will end up leveling the ground (above 15:2). As for the punishment of Tur Shimon, that was because they were playing ball in the public domain (Vilna Gaon), or because they were taking away too much time from their Torah study.

to some *poskim* and because one should not to get used to neglecting Torah study on Shabbat. Those who wish to be lenient have an opinion on which to rely (see SA 308:45; MA 338:5; MB *ad loc.* 21; *Kaf Ha-ḥayim ad loc.* 39). Children should also be trained to study Torah on Shabbat, but almost all *poskim* agree that one should not prevent them from playing games on Shabbat (as explained below in 24:7).

In contrast, sports that are a big deal, like soccer, basketball, baseball, and football, may not be played on Shabbat, because of the prohibition on weekday activities. It goes without saying that one may not play them on the court or field designated for them. Children may not play these sports either, because it is a weekday activity (below 24:9).

14. PAYMENT FOR WORK DONE ON SHABBAT (*SEKHAR SHABBAT*)

The Sages prohibited accepting payment for work done on Shabbat, because this is included in the prohibition on commerce. Even if the "work" is intrinsically permissible on Shabbat (such as guard duty or waiting tables), one may not accept payment for it on Shabbat (BM 58a; SA 306:4). It is also forbidden to accept rent money for anything, whether real estate or objects, that had been rented out on Shabbat (MB 246:3). Even *be-di'avad,* one may not benefit from money paid for any service rendered on Shabbat (SA 245:6; MB 243:16).

In contrast, payment for work done on Shabbat may be subsumed within weekday payment. For example, an agreement may stipulate that a worker will do guard duty or wait tables for a few hours after Shabbat as well as on Shabbat itself. Even though, in reality, most of the hours were on Shabbat and the payment is primarily for those hours, as long as an agreement was reached before the work started that the employee would also work on Saturday night, the compensation covers the hours worked during the week as well as those on Shabbat. Thus, the Shabbat payment is subsumed within the weekday payment. However, if an agreement was not reached before the work started, then even if the employee did work after Shabbat as well, each workday stands on its own, the payment for Shabbat work cannot be subsumed within the payment for weekday work, and the worker thus may not accept the payment (*Ḥayei Adam* 60:8; MB 306:21; SSK 28:64-68).

Along the same lines, one may rent out a room for Shabbat, as long as the rental period includes time either on Friday before Shabbat begins or on Saturday night after Shabbat ends. A cab driver can rent out his cab to a non-Jew for Shabbat, as long as the rental period either begins before Shabbat or extends after Shabbat, so that the Shabbat payment can be subsumed within the weekday payment. One may also collect interest on one's bank account, since the calculations are based on the calendar day and not the times that Shabbat starts and ends. Accordingly, whatever is earned over Shabbat can be seen as subsumed within the weekday earnings of Friday morning and afternoon and Saturday night.

One who immerses in a *mikveh* on Shabbat may pay the *mikveh* fee after Shabbat. There are two reasons for this. First, it is for the sake of a mitzva, and second, the payment is not for the immersion itself, but for the cleaning and heating of the *mikveh*, which started before Shabbat.[9]

---

9. If Shabbat is followed by Yom Tov or vice versa, there is an entire calendar day that is sanctified, and yet one is receiving interest then. At first glance this would seem to be forbidden (*Minḥat Yitzḥak* 9:59; *Be-tzel Ha-ḥokhma* 3:38). Nevertheless, this too is permissible because interest is not actually paid daily, but rather all the days are calculated together. Accordingly, the interest in this case can be subsumed within the times before and after the holy days (see *Menuḥat Ahava* 1:10:30 with n. 69, and *Yalkut Yosef* vol. 2, p. 133). Similarly, MB 306:20 cites an opinion that payment for Shabbat work is subsumed within payment for weekday work even if an agreement was not reached before the work started if it is likely that the work under the agreement will continue during the week.

A waiter may not work on Shabbat with the understanding that his employer will in turn work for him in a different capacity, because working for someone is considered payment. However, one may do guard duty on Shabbat for a friend and arrange for this friend to cover his assigned guard duty elsewhere, because guard duty that prevents loss is not considered payment (SA 307:10). Similarly, one may babysit a family on Shabbat with the understanding that the second person will babysit for the first person's family at some point in the future (SSK 28:59). If it is one's turn to set up the dining hall and serve the food on Shabbat, he may switch his Shabbat slot for a different slot. Since there is no monetary compensation involved, swapping is not considered payment (SSK 28:61).

As written above, one who immerses in a *mikveh* on Shabbat may pay after Shabbat because the payment is for the cleaning and heating done before Shabbat begins (*Noda Bi-Yehuda, Mahadura Tinyana*, OḤ 26; SSK 28:72). One can also be lenient and rent an apartment for Shabbat only, since it can be argued that the rent also covers the cleaning that takes place before Shabbat (SSK 28:70). It is important to

One may give a gift on Saturday night to someone who worked voluntarily over Shabbat. Examples include one who set up the synagogue and one who served as a waiter at a Shabbat meal. Since there is no obligation to compensate him at all, whatever is given is not considered payment (*Pri Megadim*; MB 306:15).

The *poskim* disagree about whether one may accept payment for serving as a *ḥazan* or for other mitzva-related jobs undertaken on Shabbat. Some say that even when a job involves a mitzva, one may not accept payment for it. If this is correct, a *ḥazan* may not be paid for leading the services on Shabbat. Others maintain that one may be paid for a mitzva-related job on Shabbat, but that nothing good will come of this income. In practice, it is proper to stipulate that any payment will also include work performed during the week. For example, a *ḥazan* will be paid for practicing before he leads the Shabbat services, or for an additional prayer service that he will lead during the week. This way the Shabbat payment can be subsumed within the weekday payment (SA and Rema 306:5).

A doctor who is on call to provide medical care during Shabbat is entitled to demand payment after Shabbat. The reason is that if he cannot assume that he will be paid, he might refuse to provide care in the future (MB 306:24; *Minḥat Shabbat* 90:19; SSK 28:75).

15. PREPARING ON SHABBAT FOR WEEKDAYS, AND CLEANING UP THE HOUSE AND TABLE

Shabbat is meant to bring holiness and rest into our lives. Making efforts on Shabbat to prepare for the week belittles its honor, and therefore the Sages forbade doing so.

Thus, one may not make the beds on Shabbat in preparation for going to sleep on Saturday night. However, one may make the beds on Shabbat so that the bedroom will look nice on Shabbat. Similarly, one may clear off a table so that one's home will look nice on Shabbat. For the same reason, if *se'uda shlishit* is finished well before the end of Shabbat, one may clear the table and put the dishes in the sink. However, if *se'uda shlishit* finishes only a few minutes before the end of Shabbat,

---

know that in a time of need, when a large loss is at stake, one may accept payment for work done on Shabbat (Rema 244:6; BHL s.v. "de-bimkom").

or if people are not planning to remain in the room where it was served, so that clearing off the table is not for Shabbat's sake but for the week's sake, one may not clear off the table. One who does so is expending effort on Shabbat to prepare for afterward (*m. Shabbat* 113a; MB 302:19).

One may wash dishes if they will be used again at some point on Shabbat. If many dishes were used, and only one cup is needed for later Shabbat use but there are no more clean cups, one may wash all the cups, since he could use any of them. Similarly, if he needs one plate but none are clean, he may wash all the plates and use one of them. However, if he does not intend to use any of them during Shabbat, he may not wash any of them (*Shabbat* 118a; SA 323:6; MB 323:26).

One who never leaves dirty dishes in the sink even during the week, and who feels that a pile of dirty dishes left in the sink for hours belittles the honor of Shabbat, may wash the dishes even if they will not be used again during Shabbat, so that his home will be clean in honor of Shabbat. However, even in this case, he may not wash the pots, since they are *muktzeh* and require burdensome work (*Responsa Maharshag,* OḤ 1:61; *Tzitz Eliezer* 14:37). (We have already seen in 13:4-5 how to clean off a table that water or juice spilled on, and in 15:9 how to clean the floor.)

One may not fold a *talit* so that it will be unwrinkled for next Shabbat. However, one may fold it so that it will not be left out on Shabbat in a disrespectful way (see above 13:9).

One may not prepare on Shabbat for weekdays even when a mitzva is involved. For example, one may not roll a Torah scroll to the passage that will be read during the upcoming week or the next Shabbat (MB 667:5). If necessary, one may roll the Torah scroll to the next reading and then study a few verses from it, so that the rolling will serve a purpose on Shabbat as well (AHS 667:2). One may bring a book to the synagogue if it is needed after Shabbat, as long as one studies a bit from it on Shabbat as well.

On Shabbat one may study for a test in a Torah subject that is scheduled for the upcoming week, since studying these topics is itself a mitzva. However, it is proper not to study on Shabbat for tests in secular subjects. First, Shabbat must be dedicated to Torah study. Second, the student's primary goal in studying is to succeed on his test, not to become more knowledgeable. In a time of need one may be lenient, since there is intrinsic value to secular studies. In contrast, one may not study a foreign language on Shabbat, because such study has no intrinsic value. It is also prohibited to study for a test in a subject that normally involves writing exercises, because (as we saw) one may read on Shabbat only when there is no concern that one might end up writing or erasing.

One should not say on Shabbat, "I will go to sleep now, so that I will have energy after Shabbat." This belittles Shabbat, since he is using it to prepare for weekdays. However, if he does not verbalize this but only thinks it, it is not forbidden, since sleeping on Shabbat is a pleasure (*Sefer Ḥasidim*; MB 290:4; see above 5:3).

When Yom Tov follows Shabbat, one may not prepare on Shabbat for Yom Tov. *Be-di'avad*, if one prepared something on Shabbat for afterward, he may benefit from his actions.

16. WHEN PREPARATION ON SHABBAT FOR THE WEEKDAY IS PERMITTED

The prohibition of preparing on Shabbat for the weekday is limited to activities that require effort. However, easy, effortless activities that people routinely undertake are permitted. This is true even if the activities are useful for the weekday, as doing them does not belittle Shabbat. For example, after shaking the *lulav* on the first day of Sukkot, one may put it back in water, even though this is done to keep it fresh for the next day (*Sukka* 42a; SA 654:1). One who is studying Torah may insert a bookmark, even though this will not be helpful until he continues his studies during the week. One who took a *siddur* to the synagogue may bring it home (where there is an *eruv*), even if he will not be using it again on that Shabbat.

Similarly, one may put leftover food in the refrigerator as usual. Dishes may be left soaking in water as usual to prevent food remnants getting stuck to them. One leaving the house on Shabbat afternoon may take a key and sweater with him for use after Shabbat, though he should not state explicitly that he is doing so for after Shabbat (see SA 416:2; SSK 28:89).

In a time of need, in order to avoid serious inconvenience, one may do simple things on Shabbat in preparation for the weekday even if they are not part of the normal routine, but only on condition that it is not obvious that he is doing them for the weekday, so as not to belittle Shabbat. For example, if one is going to a place where it is difficult to find wine for *havdala*, he may bring wine with him on Shabbat, on condition that he brings it while there is still plenty of daylight left, so that it will not be obvious that he is bringing the wine for after Shabbat. If he drinks some of the wine at *se'uda shlishit*, he may even bring wine *le-khatḥila* (see *Ḥayei Adam* 153:6; MB 667:5).

In a time of need, in order to prevent a loss, the Sages permitted doing things on Shabbat even when it is obvious that they are for the weekday. Examples include bringing in items from outside and that would likely be damaged by rain, and putting food into the freezer if it would likely spoil if left out (SA 308:4; MB 321:21).[10]

17. PLAYING MUSICAL INSTRUMENTS AND PRODUCING SOUND

The Sages prohibited playing instruments on Shabbat and Yom Tov, lest the instrument break and the player fix it, thus violating Torah law (MT 23:4). In contrast, in the Temple, rabbinic Shabbat prohibitions (*shvut*) did not apply; therefore, even on Shabbat and holidays, the Levi'im would accompany offerings with flutes, harps, lyres, trumpets, and cymbals (*Beitza* 11b).

Included in the prohibition of playing musical instruments is the prohibition of blowing a shofar. Even on Rosh Ha-shana, once the mitzva of shofar has been fulfilled in the optimal and most beautiful fashion, we do not blow further. Children under the age of bar mitzva may blow the shofar all day on Rosh Ha-shana so that they can learn how to do it (Rema 596:1; MB 3-5).

One may produce sound that is not musical in nature. Thus, one may clap his hands to wake someone up, knock on a door with his hands or an instrument so that the people inside will hear and open up, or tap

10. If slaughtered meat is left unsalted for three days, it can no longer be rendered kosher through salting. However, if the meat is soaked in water before the three days end, the window for salting is extended. According to MA 321:7, one may not soak unsalted meat whose time is running out and soak it on Shabbat to make sure that it will be permissible to cook after Shabbat, because it is forbidden to deal with something on Shabbat in order to prevent loss after Shabbat. However, MB 321:21 adds that under pressing circumstances, one may rely on *Eliya Rabba* and *Noda Bi-Yehuda*, which permit it. This is also the opinion of SSK 28:91 and *Yalkut Yosef* vol. 2, p. 218.

a glass or bottle with a spoon to quiet a crowd. One may also snap in order to wake someone up or to make a baby laugh (SA 338:1).

The *poskim* disagree whether one may use a door knocker or mechanical bell. Some forbid it on the grounds that it resembles a musical instrument too closely (Rema). Others permit it since one is not trying to make music (SA 338:1). If during the week an electric doorbell is used, then on Shabbat a mechanical doorbell or knocker may be used (MB 338:7).[11]

One may place a decorative crown with bells on a Torah scroll even though the bells produce sound. Since they are decorative and honor the Torah, it is for the sake of a mitzva, and since the person carrying the Torah does not intend to make noise, it is not forbidden (*Shakh* and MA, as opposed to *Taz*).

---

11. *Eruvin* 104a records a disagreement about this issue. According to Ula, one may not produce sound on Shabbat even without intent to make music. Therefore, one may not knock on the door so that the people inside will hear him. Rava maintains that only producing sound with the goal of creating music is prohibited. The Yerushalmi tells the story of R. Ila'i, who returned home on Friday night and called out to the members of his household to let him in. They did not hear him. Since he was personally stringent not to knock, he slept outside (*y. Beitza* 5:2). Indeed, Rabbeinu Ḥananel and the Vilna Gaon rule in accordance with Ula's strict approach. In any case, even according to them, knocking with a *shinui* is permitted (BHL 338:1 s.v. "aval"). However, based on the subsequent discussion in the Gemara, Rif and Rambam (MT 23:4) conclude that the law is in accordance with the lenient approach of Rava. Rosh is inclined to follow this as well. Almost all the *poskim* follow the lenient approach, including SA 338:1, MB *ad loc.* 2-3, and SSK 28:41. However, regarding a door knocker, an instrument designed to produce sound, Maharil is stringent. *Beit Yosef* suggests that Maharil's stringency is due to the concern that the person knocking may in fact intend to produce music. Rema 338:1 is stringent, following Maharil. According to BHL 338:1 s.v. "ho'il," this is the position of SA as well. However, *Livyat Ḥen* §110 and *Or Le-Tziyon* 2:39:1 argue that according to SA, one may use a door knocker. If the knocker is meant to be used only on Shabbat, then Rema permits it as well (MB 338:7; *Shevet Ha-Levi* 9:76). Therefore, one may use a mechanical doorbell on Shabbat if an electric one is used during the week (SSK 23:55 with n. 159).

A *ḥazan* may not use a tuning fork to help him determine the pitch for his singing, because it is included in the prohibition on musical instruments (MB 338:4). While some are permissive, since a tuning fork produces a sound that is uniform and relatively quiet, and it is being used for the sake of a mitzva, it is proper to be stringent, because that is the opinion of almost all the *poskim*. If one wishes to rely on those who are lenient, it is not necessary to object (AHS 338:8; see *Yabi'a Omer* 3:22).

Some forbid opening a door that has bells or chimes attached to it, since they are considered musical instruments (*Taz* and *Eliya Rabba*). Others permit it, because those entering do not intend to make noise, they just want to open the door (MA). *Le-khatḥila,* it is proper for homeowners to remove bells from the door before Shabbat; if they did not do so, the door may still be used (see MB 338:6).

One may whistle on Shabbat because it is considered a type of music made with the mouth, not with an instrument. Some even permit using one's fingers to improve the whistle (AHS 338:7; see below in 24:7 about toys that make noise).

18. CLAPPING AND DANCING

The Sages' prohibition of playing instruments includes dancing, clapping, and slapping one's thigh with one's hands to accompany singing out of concern lest one play an instrument and fix it (*Beitza* 36b). However, one may clap with a *shinui,* such as using the back of one's hand; by using a *shinui,* he is reminded that it is Shabbat and will not end up fixing an instrument (*y. Beitza* 5:2). It would seem that very muted dancing, in which one's feet never leave the ground at the same time, is not included in the prohibited dancing (*ibid.*).

The prohibition applies specifically while singing, because there is a concern then that it will lead to playing instruments. In contrast, if there is no singing, one may jump a bit for his enjoyment. Similarly, one may clap or to bang on a table in order to wake someone up.

In practice, many observant Jews dance, clap, and bang on a table when they sing on Shabbat. The *poskim* disagree about the legitimacy of this practice, as follows.

One approach, that of many *poskim,* is that this practice is mistaken. The only reason that the Sages did not object is that the prohibition is not stated explicitly in the Torah, so it is better that people transgress unknowingly rather than knowingly (*Beitza* 30a). However, if there is any possibility that people can be convinced to accept the proper *halakha,* we must teach them not to clap or dance on Shabbat, in accordance with the rabbinic enactment (Rif; Rambam; Rema 339:3). Nevertheless, on Simḥat Torah, when there is a special mitzva to rejoice and honor the Torah, even those who are normally stringent dance and clap (Maharik in the name of R. Hai Gaon). However, for other celebrations with a mitzva component, such as weddings, they are not lenient (MB 339:8).

A second approach defends the leniency. After all, the reason behind the prohibition is a concern that people will end up fixing a musical instrument. Nowadays, when those who play an instrument do not know how to fix it, the enactment no longer applies, and one may dance and clap on Shabbat (*Tosafot*, *Beitza* 30a, s.v. "tenan"). Some do not accept this, maintaining that all the players know how to tune their instrument (tightening guitar strings, harp strings, or the top of a drum), which is considered fixing an instrument. However, there is a different reason to be lenient. Some maintain that the rabbinic enactment was specifically relevant to the times of the Sages, when people would take out instruments whenever there was dancing and clapping. Nowadays, when many people sing, dance, and clap without instruments, the enactment no longer applies (AHS 339:9).

A third approach notes that the great Ḥasidic masters of recent centuries focused on the value of music and dance to awaken people's hearts to cling to God joyfully. Such dancing and clapping are considered true mitzva needs. Accordingly, just as there is a leniency for Simḥat Torah, there should be a leniency for every Shabbat (*Devar Yehoshua* 2:42:4).

It would seem that even those who are lenient should not drum on the table on Shabbat. Such drumming is very similar to that of an actual drum, which all agree is forbidden, even for the sake of a mitzva. Furthermore, the concern that people will take out a drum is a serious one today, when many are used to bringing drums, darbukas, and the like when they sing. In contrast, when people are singing during prayer, a leader may drum with his hand on the *bima*. One leading the songs at the Shabbat table may also be lenient.[12]

---

12. As we said above, on Simḥat Torah all customarily clap and dance based on the opinion of R. Hai Gaon as cited by Maharik and *Beit Yosef* 339:3. However, the *poskim* do not apply this leniency to other mitzva situations (SA 339:3). Rema is inclined to follow this as well, commenting that the reason we do not object to those who clap and dance on Shabbat is that it is better that people transgress unknowingly rather than knowingly. However, Rema cites as an alternative the lenient approach of *Tosafot*, namely, that nowadays there is no reason to be concerned that people

19. MUSIC AND FILMS ON ELECTRONIC DEVICES

There is a clear consensus among *poskim* that one may not listen to the radio or watch television on Shabbat. Even if the radio or television is turned on before Shabbat so that no *melakha* is performed on Shabbat, it is forbidden, and for several reasons. First, if there are Jews who work at the station, one may not derive enjoyment from Shabbat desecration.

Second, even if all the station's workers are non-Jewish, one may not listen to or watch broadcasts because it belittles and detracts from the honor of Shabbat. We already saw (2:9) that some maintain that one may not leave a flour mill running before Shabbat if it will continue to run on Shabbat, because the noise of the grinding detracts from the honor of Shabbat. Listening to the radio and watching television are much more serious. While the mill makes noise that no one wants to

---

will end up fixing a musical instrument. *Yam Shel Shlomo* (*Beitza* 5:6) seems to state that technically one may rely on *Tosafot* when it is in the service of a mitzva. This opinion is quoted in *Eliya Rabba* 339:1 and MB *ad loc.* 10. (See SHT 339:6-7.) Based on the logic of this approach, Ḥasidim are customarily lenient (*Devar Yehoshua* 2:42:4; *Minḥat Elazar* 1:29). Sephardim may rely on this reasoning as well for the sake of a mitzva (see *Or Le-Tziyon* 2:43:9 and *Harḥavot*.) However, the leniency pertains to dancing and clapping – both of which are done with the body – and not to drumming on something else (*Eliya Rabba* 339:1; MB *ad loc.* 10; *Avnei Yashfe* 2:35:1). The reasoning is straightforward. Drumming on a table is similar to playing a drum, which is a musical instrument. Nevertheless, when it comes to a *gabbai* leading the congregation in song, there are two reasons to be lenient and allow him to drum with his hand on the *bima*. First, this is more clearly for the sake of a mitzva, and we already saw that R. Hai Gaon and Maharik are lenient for the sake of Simḥat Torah (see SHT 339:7). Second, since the *gabbai* is in the middle of the congregation, we are not worried that he might bring instruments that will need to be fixed. Perhaps this is also one of the reasons for the leniency on Simḥat Torah. The logic is similar to that of the permission for two people to read by candlelight (*Shabbat* 12b), or for even one person to read by candlelight as long as his friend is there to make sure he will not unknowingly do anything that would affect the flame (SA 275:3). This also explains why *Sha'arei De'a* (YD 282) allows putting a crown with bells on a Torah scroll (as opposed to *Taz*; see *Yabi'a Omer* 3:22). Perhaps we can extend the leniency to leading the singing at the Shabbat table, and allow one to drum with his hand on the table. Nevertheless, it is not proper for the rest of the participants to drum. Besides, their drumming is not always for the sake of the mitzva, as often these additional drummers actually make it harder to sing because they are out of sync with the song.

hear, one who turns on the radio or television before Shabbat indeed wishes to listen or watch on the holy Shabbat. All would agree that this infringes upon Shabbat's honor.

Third, it is a weekday activity. Just as the prophets and Sages forbade many things that are reminiscent of weekdays, so that our behavior on Shabbat would be different from that of the workweek, so too we should prohibit listening to the radio and watching television on Shabbat.

Fourth, there is a concern that the radio or television might malfunction, and the listeners or viewers might try to fix it on Shabbat. One might want to raise or lower the volume or adjust the device in some other way (see above 17:2). A similar concern led to the ban on using musical instruments, and the same ban should apply.

For all these reasons, one may not listen to radio or watch television on Shabbat, even when they are turned on before Shabbat. For the same reasons, it is also forbidden to set a timer to turn on a recording device or video or audio player (see *Yesodei Yeshurun* vol. 3, pp. 50-55; *Tzitz Eliezer* 3:16; SSK 42:43; *Yabi'a Omer* 1:20; *Yalkut Yosef* 318:34-38).

Chapter Twenty-Three

Muktzeh

1. THE BASIS OF THE PROHIBITION

The Sages prohibited moving things that are not fitting for Shabbat and that one puts out of his mind (*maktzeh mi-da'ato*). There are two fundamental reasons for this prohibition: 1) to preserve the atmosphere of Shabbat as a day of holiness and rest. The idea of rest applies to one's hands as well; they should not move objects or be involved with activities that are not connected to Shabbat; 2) to set up a safeguard so that one will not come to do *melakha* on Shabbat. We will begin by explaining the first reason.

In addition to the *melakhot* that are prohibited on Shabbat, the Torah commands us to rest and relax on Shabbat, as it states: "but on the seventh day you shall cease, so that your ox and your donkey may rest, and the son of your maidservant and the stranger may be refreshed" (Shemot 23:12). Similarly, we read: "Six days shall work be done, but on the seventh day there shall be a Shabbat of complete rest, holy to the Lord" (Shemot 31:15). In order to fulfill the Torah commandment to rest and relax on Shabbat, the Sages established several ordinances meant to protect the spirit of Shabbat as a day of sanctity and rest. One of them is the prohibition of *muktzeh*.

If moving items unnecessary for Shabbat were permitted, people might well spend all of Shabbat cleaning and arranging their homes and belongings, thus negating the mitzva to rest. Additionally, the prophets instructed the people that the atmosphere of Shabbat should be different from that of the weekday – one should walk and talk differently. Following this line of thought, the Sages decreed that people should not handle objects and implements on Shabbat in the same way as during the week. This way Shabbat is truly felt by all, including those whose weekday activities do not normally involve any forbidden *melakhot*. We see that the prohibition of *muktzeh* is rooted in the words of the Torah and the prophets, while its precise parameters and details are rabbinic (AHS 308:4-5; above, 22:1).

As we said, the second reason is so that one will not end up doing *melakha* on Shabbat. As with all *mitzvot*, the Sages instituted safeguards in order to distance people from sin. The prohibition of *muktzeh* makes it less likely that people will carry objects in the public domain or use *muktzeh* items to perform *melakha* (Rambam and Raavad, MT 24:12-13).[1]

---

1. AHS 308:4-5 suggests that the prohibitions of *muktzeh* date back to the time of our teacher Moshe. Additionally, the Gemara mentions that in the days of Kings David and Shlomo, the prohibition of *muktzeh maḥmat gufo* was already in effect (*Shabbat* 30b). During the time of Neḥemia, the Sages saw that Shabbat desecration was widespread, and they decreed that all implements (*kelim*) would be considered *muktzeh*. There were only three *kelim*, considered necessary for eating, exempted from the prohibition. When the situation improved and people were once again careful about Shabbat laws, the Sages once again permitted the movement of most *kelim*, though a small number remained banned (*Shabbat* 123b; SAH 308:17; sections 7-9 below). Rashi and *She'iltot* maintain that the prohibition of *muktzeh* is by Torah law, since Rabba's statement that one must prepare before Shabbat what he needs for Shabbat is based on the verse: "But on the sixth day, they shall prepare what they have brought in" (Shemot 16:5). The implication of the verse is that anything that has not been prepared is *muktzeh* (*Pesaḥim* 47b; *Beitza* 2b). However, almost all Rishonim maintain that Rabba changed his mind and would agree that the prohibition of *muktzeh* is rabbinic. This is the opinion of *Tosafot*, Rambam, Ramban, and Rashba. One interpretation of Rashi is that only the most serious types of *muktzeh* are prohibited by Torah law, while the rest are rabbinic (*Pnei Yehoshu'a*, *Beitza* 2b). Alternatively, Ḥatam Sofer explains that Rashi means that *muktzeh* is prohibited by Torah law only in the case of food items, as we are commanded to prepare food for Shabbat; in contrast, all other *muktzeh* prohibitions are rabbinic (OḤ 79). In any case, as we wrote in 22:1 based on Ramban, all the laws connected to the spirit of Shabbat are rooted in the Torah, while the Sages established the details of their observance. This is also implied by Rambam. See *Harḥavot* there.

The prohibition of *muktzeh* synchronizes the mind and the hands. Any item that one knows is not fit for use on Shabbat will not be touched by his hands either.

2. PRINCIPLES OF *MUKTZEH*

As a rule, the Sages forbade moving things on Shabbat that are not fitting for use on Shabbat and that one puts out of his mind (section 10 below). There are several types of *muktzeh*:

1. *Muktzeh maḥmat gufo* (inherently *muktzeh*) – items that are not fitting for any use on Shabbat, such as rocks, trees, sand, animals, and inedible food (as explained below, section 3).
2. *Muktzeh maḥmat ḥesron kis* (*muktzeh* because of monetary loss) – valuable objects that one takes care not to handle except for their sole designated use, out of concern that they will be ruined. Since they have no use on Shabbat, one puts them out of his mind (section 4 below).
3. *Basis le-davar ha-asur* (a base for a forbidden object) – refers to a case where one places a *muktzeh* item on an object that is not itself *muktzeh*; since he intends for it to remain there on Shabbat, he puts the "base" out of his mind as well, and it too becomes *muktzeh* (sections 5-6 below).
4. *Kelim she-melakhtam le-isur* (implements whose usage is forbidden) – have a special status. Since they are designed to perform forbidden activities, one puts them out of his mind. On the other hand, sometimes they are used for permitted purposes. Therefore, one may not move them for their own sake (e.g., to protect them, *le-tzorekh atzmam*), but one may move them to use them permissibly (*le-tzorekh gufam*) or because one needs the space they occupy (*le-tzorekh mekomam*) (sections 7-9 below).

If a *muktzeh* item is painfully unpleasant, like a chamber pot (*graf shel re'i*), the Sages permitted removing it (section 12 below).

The prohibition is to move a *muktzeh* object manually, but one may touch a *muktzeh* item without moving it. Therefore, one may spread a cover over a computer, telephone, or other *muktzeh* items on Shabbat. One may also move *muktzeh* "from the side" (*min ha-tzad*). For example, if one needs to pick up an object or food, and in so doing a *muktzeh* item that is next to the object or food will be moved indirectly, as long as he does not touch the *muktzeh* item with his hands, it is not prohibited. However, if the *muktzeh* item needs to be moved for its own protection, one may not move it even *min ha-tzad*. As long as he is using his hands, even if they have no direct contact with the *muktzeh* item (for example, if he is using a broom), it is prohibited. However, one may use any other part of the body (*be-gufo*); for example, one may move an object that is *muktzeh* using his foot or elbow (section 14 below).

Sometimes it is unclear whether or not a particular item is *muktzeh* because we lack facts about the situation. For example, if one found fruit under a tree and it is uncertain whether they fell before Shabbat (and are permitted) or on Shabbat (and are *muktzeh*), we are stringent and consider it *muktzeh* (*Beitza* 24b; SA 325:5). In contrast, if there is a halakhic disagreement about whether an item is *muktzeh*, the law follows the lenient position (*Beit Yosef* 279:4; SHT 309:24).

3. *MUKTZEH MAḤMAT GUFO*

Any item that is unfit for any use on Shabbat is *muktzeh maḥmat gufo*. This means that it is inherently *muktzeh*; because it is of no use on Shabbat, it is put out of one's mind, *muktzeh*. This category includes rocks, animals, coins, straw, dust, trees, leaves, all types of waste, and corpses.

This type of *muktzeh* may not be moved even if one wants to use the item for a permissible purpose. For example, one may not pick up a rock to use as a door stopper or nutcracker. If one wants to prevent the rock from becoming *muktzeh*, he must either mentally designate it for the desired purpose before Shabbat or use it for that purpose at least once during the week (SA 308:20, 22).

Sand is *muktzeh* and may not be used to cover up something disgusting. If the sand has been put in a particular place specifically for this purpose, it is not *muktzeh* (SA 308:38). Similarly, sand in a sandbox for children is not *muktzeh* (above, 15:2).

Food that may not currently be eaten, but that one intends to make permissible after Shabbat – such as food from which *teruma* and *ma'aser* or *ḥalla* have not yet been separated – are *muktzeh* on Shabbat (MT 25:19). However, non-kosher meat that one intends to give to a non-Jew or feed to a dog is not *muktzeh* (SA 324:7).

Foods that can be eaten under pressing circumstances are not *muktzeh*. However, if they are not edible at all without being cooked or baked – such as flour, potatoes, beans, raw meat, and raw fish – they are *muktzeh*. Even though animals can eat them, they are still *muktzeh*, since normally animals are not given food meant for people.

In pressing circumstances, such as if a freezer has stopped working and the meat and fish inside are likely to spoil, we rely on the opinion that since a dog would eat these foods raw, they are not *muktzeh*. Accordingly, one may move them into a working freezer.[2]

Animals are *muktzeh* since they serve no purpose on Shabbat. In a time of need, one may take hold of them and drag them in order to feed or protect them, but one may not pick them up (above 20:3). House pets, which are normally played with and picked up, are not *muktzeh* (above 20:5).

Food scraps that dogs or cats can eat are not *muktzeh*. Even if one does not own a cat or dog, there are cats and dogs in town that would be happy to have them. Similarly, bones are not *muktzeh*, since dogs and cats eat them. However, food scraps that neither man nor animal will eat – such as the nutshells, husks, and fish bones – are *muktzeh*. Additionally, if food scraps would be eaten by some animals but not by any found locally, they are *muktzeh* (SA 308:29). Apricot pits that

2. SA 308:31-32 explains that raw meat is not *muktzeh* since some people eat meat that way. In contrast, raw fish that people generally do not eat is *muktzeh*. According to MA and others, raw meat that is soft (such as chicken) is not *muktzeh*, but raw meat that is hard and inedible is *muktzeh*. According to *Taz* (*ad loc.* 20), if fish is edible by dogs, then even if in practice we do not feed such fish to dogs, it is not *muktzeh*. See MB and BHL, which incline toward the position of SA. It would seem that nowadays, when there are people who feed dogs meat and fish that people would eat as well, under pressing circumstances one may rely on *Taz*. This is the opinion of *Yalkut Yosef* vol. 2, p. 359 and *Orḥot Shabbat* 19:108.

children play with and that were extracted on Shabbat are not *muktzeh* (see SSK ch. 16 n. 33).

4. *MUKTZEH MAḤMAT ḤESRON KIS*

Valuable items that have no use on Shabbat and that people always take care not to move except for the specific purpose for which they are designed (to ensure the items do not get damaged or lost) are *muktzeh maḥmat ḥesron kis*. For example, knives designed for ritual slaughter or for leatherworking are *muktzeh*. Even if one wants to cut his food with them, he may not pick them up (*Shabbat* 123b, 157a; SA 308:1).

Included in this category of *muktzeh* are: musical instruments, smartphones, radios, tape recorders, expensive or fragile music players, cameras, and mixers. These may not be used even for a permissible purpose, for example, as a paperweight. Similarly, one may not wrap himself in an expensive piece of fabric that has been set aside for sewing. In contrast, a valuable or fragile item that is frequently used on Shabbat, such as a gold watch, eyeglasses, or a magnifying glass for reading, is not *muktzeh*.

Other examples of *muktzeh maḥmat ḥesron kis* are paper money, important business documents, identity cards, credit cards, stamps, bus tickets, parchment to be used by a scribe, and stationery paper that is not used for any other purpose (SSK 20:20).

Wall clocks and valuable pictures, which people are careful not to move so as to avoid possible damage, are included in this category of *muktzeh* (MB 308:168). Also included are large free-standing closets that people are careful not to move without a good reason, for fear that they will fall apart (MB 308:8). The prohibition here is limited to moving the entire closet; one may open its doors and drawers, as they are meant to be used regularly.

Cups, plates, and clothes that are meant to be sold are *muktzeh maḥmat ḥesron kis*, since sellers usually insist that no one use them. If a seller does not insist upon this, his wares are not *muktzeh*. People who sell food generally do not insist that no one eat from their merchandise, and therefore the food in stores and warehouses is not *muktzeh* (*Beit Yosef* and Rema 308:1; MB *ad loc.* 6-7; SA 310:2; MB *ad loc.* 4).

5. *BASIS LE-DAVAR HA-ASUR* AND CONSCIOUS PLACEMENT

If a *muktzeh* item was placed atop a non-*muktzeh* item with the intention that it stay there all of Shabbat, then the permitted item becomes *muktzeh*, as it serves as a *basis* (base) for a forbidden object. For example, if one placed money on a table, then even though the table is not in itself *muktzeh*, since he placed *muktzeh* money on it, the table becomes *muktzeh* because it is now a *basis le-davar ha-asur*. In other words, the decision to place money on the table implies consent not to use the table on Shabbat, making the table *muktzeh* just like the money on it. Even if the money were to fall off during Shabbat, it would not matter; since the table was *muktzeh* during *bein ha-shmashot*, it remains *muktzeh* all of Shabbat (SA 310:7).

In contrast, if one did not intend for the money to stay on the table over Shabbat but simply left it there by mistake, then the table does not become *muktzeh*, since he did not decide to make it a *basis* for something *muktzeh*. Nevertheless, *le-khatḥila* one should still not move the table while the *muktzeh* item is on it. Rather, he should tilt the table so that the money falls off and then move the table wherever he wants. However, if the *muktzeh* item would be damaged if it slid off upon falling to the floor, then one may move the table along with the *muktzeh* item to a place where the latter can safely be slid off without being damaged. For example, if the *muktzeh* item is a smartphone, which would likely break if dropped, one may move the table elsewhere. Similarly, if the *muktzeh* item is a stone, and next to the table are fragile glass items that would likely break if the stone were to fall on them, one may move the table elsewhere (*Shabbat* 142b; SA 309:4; SA 277:3; section 14 below).

The same applies to a laptop left on top of a book, valuable candlesticks left on a tray, valuable knives left in a case, raw potatoes left in a drawer, or a *tzedaka* box left on the *bima*. If these items were intentionally placed there, then whatever they are resting upon becomes a *basis le-davar ha-asur* and is *muktzeh*. If they were forgotten there, the base does not become *muktzeh*.

Sometimes, during the week, one wishes to place something *muktzeh* in a closet, but because there is no space he puts it on top of clothing in the closet. There is a disagreement whether such a placement renders the clothing *muktzeh*. Some say that since ultimately the *muktzeh* was consciously placed atop the clothing, the clothing becomes a *basis* (*Taz*). Others maintain that since the person did not intend for the *muktzeh* to be there specifically, but it simply ended up there, the item of clothing does not become a *basis* (MA). In practice, when necessary one may be lenient (MB 309:18).[3]

If one finds money or other *muktzeh* items in his pocket, he may assume they were forgotten there, so his clothes do not become a *basis*. However, in order that he not continue to carry around *muktzeh* in his pocket, he should try to shake it out. If he is embarrassed to do so in public, or if he is worried that the *muktzeh* item will get lost, he may continue to wear this item of clothing until he reaches a place where he can shake out the *muktzeh* without fear of losing it or embarrassing himself.[4]

---

3. If one intended to place the *muktzeh* item on a permitted item for only part of Shabbat, according to Rabbeinu Tam it does not become a *basis*, while according to Rashi it does. SA 309:4 is inclined to be stringent, but in times of necessity one may be lenient (MB *ad loc.* 21). There is a similar disagreement about the law if the *muktzeh* item was placed atop an item in the middle of Shabbat (by the owner or with his consent). According to *Tosafot*, as long as the *muktzeh* item is there, the base is *muktzeh*; according to *Or Zaru'a*, however, it is not *muktzeh*. According to Rashba and Ran, if one's intention is that the *muktzeh* remain there until Shabbat is over, then as long as the *muktzeh* item is there, the base is *muktzeh* as well. MB 266:26 follows those who are lenient. See BHL 310:7 s.v. "mateh."

   The base becomes a prohibited *basis* only when it serves the *muktzeh* upon it; but when the *muktzeh* item serves the base, it does not become prohibited. Therefore, if one places a rock on a barrel to weigh down its cover and prevent it from opening, or if he places pieces of *muktzeh* wool on a pot to keep it warm, the barrel or pot does not become *muktzeh* (SA 259:1; MB *ad loc.* 9).
4. If one intended to leave money in his pocket but decided on Shabbat that he would like to wear the clothing, what is the status of the clothing? If the garment itself is one of the sides of the pocket, as is generally the case with a shirt pocket, then the garment becomes a *basis* and may not be moved. In contrast, if the pocket is part of a separate lining sewn onto the clothing, as is the case with most pants pockets, the clothing does not become a *basis*, because the pocket is secondary to the whole garment. Thus, the pants may be moved. However, when possible, one should first shake the *muktzeh* item out of the pocket, taking care not to put one's hand in the pocket or touch it from outside in order to shake the *muktzeh* item out. This is because the pocket itself is *muktzeh* (Rema 310:7; MB *ad loc.* 29-30; see SSK ch. 20 n. 275). If a money pouch is tied to an item of clothing, since the pouch is not sewn on, it is not secondary to the clothing, and thus the clothing becomes a *basis*.

6. MORE ON *BASIS LE-DAVAR HA-ASUR*

If an assortment of items have been placed on a tray or table, some *muktzeh* and some not, the *muktzeh* status of the tray depends upon which items one considers to be more important. If the *muktzeh* items are more important, then the tray becomes a *basis*. If the non-*muktzeh* items are more important, the tray does not become a *basis* and is not *muktzeh* (SA 310:8). For example, let us say the Shabbat candles and the challahs are on the table. If the candlesticks are made of clay, the challahs are more important, and the table may be moved. However, if the candlesticks are silver (which makes them *muktzeh maḥmat ḥesron kis*), they are more important than the challahs; the table becomes a *basis* and may not be moved.[5]

If one left a *muktzeh* item on top of something belonging to his friend, he has not rendered it a *basis*; as a general rule, one cannot render someone else's possession forbidden without permission. However, if he acted at his friend's behest or he knows that his friend wished it to be done, then he has rendered it a *basis* (Rema 309:4; MB *ad loc.* 27).

Even when the *basis* is much more expensive than the *muktzeh* item placed upon it, it still takes on its *muktzeh* status, since it serves as

---

5. Some are lenient even if the candlesticks are silver because, in their opinion, candlesticks are merely *kelim she-melakhtam le-isur* (R. Akiva Eger). One should not rely on this opinion, because silver candlesticks are very expensive and therefore are *muktzeh maḥmat ḥesron kis* (*Ḥazon Ish* 44:13; *Yalkut Yosef* vol. 2, p. 334; *Piskei Teshuvot* 279:1). Also see SSK 20:61 with n. 242.

There is a dispute about the status of the *basis* of a *kli she-melakhto le-isur*. Some maintain that the base of a *kli she-melakhto le-isur* assumes the same status as the *kli* itself. Therefore, one may move it *le-tzorekh gufo* or *le-tzorekh mekomo* (*Tehila Le-David* 308:1). Others maintain that since a *kli she-melakhto le-isur* is not completely *muktzeh*, it does not render the base supporting it a *basis* at all (*Yeshu'ot Yaakov*; see SSK 20:50). Since *muktzeh* is a rabbinic law, the *halakha* follows the more lenient position.

If a desk or table has a drawer that contains *muktzeh* items of significance, then if the drawer can be completely removed from the table, the desk becomes a *basis* for the drawer and may not be moved (similar to the case in the previous note of a money pouch tied to clothing). If the drawer cannot be removed from the desk, then it is secondary to it (as a pants pocket is secondary to the pants), and the *muktzeh* items in the drawer do not render the desk *muktzeh*. In any case, the drawer itself is *muktzeh* because it is a *basis* (MB 310:31).

its base. However, when the *muktzeh* item is of no importance compared to the *basis* on which it was placed, the *basis* does not become *muktzeh*. Therefore, if one left small change on a table or bones on a plate, since the *muktzeh* item is negligible vis-à-vis the table or plate, they do not become a *basis*. Similarly, if the main function of the *basis* is not to be a *basis* – for example, if the door of a closet or refrigerator is attached to drawers that contain *muktzeh* objects – since the main function of the door is to open the closet or refrigerator and not to be a *basis* for what is in the drawers, the door does not become a *basis* (MB 310:31, 277:7; SSK 20:77).

A table that has become a *basis* may not be moved, but it may be used for eating or studying, as long as it is not moved. One may also expand the table or shorten it, as long as he does not use his hands to move the part of the table that has the *muktzeh* item on it. If the table has drawers, they may be used as well, as long as the table itself is not moved (*Tehila Le-David* 310:7; SSK 20:61).

7. *KELIM SHE-MELAKHTAM LE-ISUR*

Kelim she-melakhtam le-isur are objects normally used for activities that are prohibited on Shabbat. Some examples are hammers, scissors, needles, pliers, and phone books. Since they are designed for things that are prohibited on Shabbat, they are *muktzeh*. Nevertheless, since they can be used for permissible activities as well, one does not put them out of his mind completely over Shabbat. Therefore, the Sages established an intermediate category for such items. On the one hand, they are *muktzeh*, and one may not move them even if they were left in a place where they are likely to be damaged or stolen. On the other hand, one may move them in two cases: *le-tzorekh gufam* or *le-tzorekh mekomam* (SA 308:3).

Le-tzorekh gufo (pl. "*gufam*") means using the *kli she-melakhto le-isur* to do something permissible, like using a hammer to crack nuts, scissors to open a milk bag, a needle to remove a thorn, pliers to open and shut a faucet whose handle is missing, and a telephone book to look up an address. If the same goal can be attained without using a *kli she-melakhto le-isur*, it should not be used (MB 308:12).

Le-tzorekh mekomo (pl. "*mekomam*") means moving the *kli she-melakhto le-isur* to use the space it occupies. Thus, if such an object was left on the table one wishes to eat at, the bed he wishes to lie in, or a chair he wishes to sit upon, he may move it. Similarly, if such an item was left on the floor in a spot where people will likely trip over it, one may move it. If the door of a washing machine was left open and is getting in the way, it may be closed. If a *kli she-melakhto le-isur* makes it difficult to open or close a window, it may be moved.

Once the *kli she-melakhto le-isur* has been picked up, whether *le-tzorekh gufo* or *le-tzorekh mekomo*, one may move it to where it will be safe (SA 308:3; section 15 below).[6]

Other examples of *kelim she-melakhtam le-isur* are: pens, pencils, pencil sharpeners, paintbrushes, lined paper, accounting forms, sandpaper, carbon paper, candles, matches, nails, and cigarettes.[7]

Some *kelim she-melakhtam le-isur,* such as an artist's knives or a diamond cutter's tools, are considered *muktzeh maḥmat ḥesron kis,* since their owners are careful not to use them for other purposes. The laws pertaining to them are stricter – they may not be moved even *le-tzorekh gufam* or *le-tzorekh mekomam* (see section 4 above).

Electrical appliances such as fans, washing machines, refrigerators, and other appliances with no incandescent filament are considered *kelim she-melakhtam le-isur*. Electrical appliances with a heating element or incandescent filament, such as light bulbs, heaters, radiators, and warming trays (*platas*) that were on during *bein ha-shmashot* on Friday (when Shabbat started) are considered *muktzeh maḥmat gufam* and may not be moved during Shabbat even *le-tzorekh gufam* or *le-tzorekh*

6. Even though one may not move a *kli she-melakhto le-isur* to prevent it from being damaged or stolen, one may use a halakhic loophole (*ha'arama*) to accomplish this goal indirectly. In other words, one may pick up the *kli* initially *le-tzorekh gufo* or *le-tzorekh mekomo* and then put it down where it is protected from the elements and from theft (MB 308:16; *Yalkut Yosef* vol. 2, p. 412).
7. In contrast, any item that is not a *kli* but is used for an activity prohibited on Shabbat, such as firewood, kerosene, bar soap, thick liquid soap, laundry detergent, and shoe polish – is considered *muktzeh maḥmat gufo,* and thus may not be moved even *le-tzorekh gufo* or *le-tzorekh mekomo* (MB 308:34; *Orḥot Shabbat* 19:7).

mekomam. In contrast, if they were off throughout *bein ha-shmashot*, they are considered *kelim she-melakhtam le-isur* and may be moved *le-tzorekh gufam* or *le-tzorekh mekomam*.[8]

8. *KELIM* WITH BOTH PERMITTED AND PROHIBITED USES

The status of *kelim* used for both permissible and forbidden activities is determined by the majority of their use (*Pri Megadim*; MB 308:10). Therefore, a pocket knife with scissors is not *muktzeh*, because most of its blades can be used as cutlery for eating and are not *muktzeh*, and it is only the scissors that are used primarily for a forbidden activity. Similarly, a wristwatch with a built-in calculator is not *muktzeh*, because its primary use – telling time – is permitted on Shabbat. In contrast, a cell phone (that is not a smart phone) that displays the time is a *keli she-melakhto le-isur*, since its main use – as a telephone – is prohibited on Shabbat. Therefore, it may not be moved for its own sake, but it may be moved *le-tzorekh gufo* – in order to see what time it is (however, he should not carry it around in his pocket for that purpose). It may also be moved *le-tzorekh mekomo*. Thus, if one wants to use the place where the phone is resting, it may be moved. Similarly, if the phone's alarm goes off, and the owner wants to move it so the ringing will not disturb his rest, he may do so.

A pot is a *kli she-melakhto le-isur*, since its primary purpose is for cooking. Nevertheless, when there is food in it, the pot is secondary to the food, and therefore may be moved. Once the food has been removed from the pot, one may remove the pot from the table, even if one does

8. An incandescent filament that was on throughout *bein ha-shmashot* has the same status as a flame that was lit throughout *bein ha-shmashot* – it is absolutely *muktzeh*, as explained in SA 279:1. However, some maintain that an incandescent filament differs from a flame, because flames are not normally moved, whereas devices with incandescent filaments are normally moved. Therefore, according to them, the status of the appliance is that of a *kli she-melakhto le-isur* (*Ḥazon Ish* 41:16; *Igrot Moshe*, OḤ 3:50). Nevertheless, according to most *poskim* an incandescent filament has the same status as a flame, and the entire appliance is considered secondary and a *basis* to the filament and thus completely *muktzeh* (SSK 20:15*; *Minḥat Yitzḥak* 3:43; *Yalkut Yosef* vol. 2, pp. 425-426; *Orḥot Shabbat* 19:181-184). See *Harḥavot*.

not need the space it is occupying. The reason is that the food waste at the bottom of the pot renders it disgusting, and a disgusting item (*graf shel re'i*) may be moved (MB 308:20; BHL s.v. "kli"; see section 12 below).

Even if an oven is used to store baking pans and baked goods, since its primary purpose is baking, it is a *kli she-melakhto le-isur*. Nevertheless, one may open its door to remove food, since this is moving it *le-tzorekh mekomo*. If one wishes to put food in the oven and keep it there on Shabbat, he may open the door and close it, because this is *le-tzorekh gufo* (SSK 20:79).

Tefilin are considered a *kli she-melakhto le-isur*, since one may not wear them on Shabbat and Yom Tov (SA 31:1). Therefore, they may be moved only *le-tzorekh gufam* or *le-tzorekh mekomam*. *Le-tzorekh gufam* would apply if one wishes to put the *tefilin* on, in the hope that they will protect him from danger. *Le-tzorekh mekomam* would apply if they are sitting in their bag together with a *talit*, and one wishes to remove the *tefilin* in order to get to the *talit* on Shabbat (*Taz*; MA). Under pressing circumstances, if the *tefilin* are in danger of being damaged, they may be moved (MB 31:2; BHL *ad loc.*).

A flower pot is a *kli she-melakhto le-isur*, since it is associated with several *melakhot* – planting, watering, and picking. Thus, it may be moved *le-tzorekh gufo* – to decorate the table – or *le-tzorekh mekomo* – to use the place where the flower pot is sitting (see above 19:10).

9. *KELIM SHE-MELAKHTAM LE-HETER*, FOOD, AND BOOKS

Kelim that are used for permitted purposes (*kelim she-melakhtam le-heter*), a category that includes tables, chairs, beds, pillows, thermoses, clocks, and brooms, may be moved for any reason, though one may not move them for no reason at all. In Neḥemia's time, when people failed to observe Shabbat, the Sages decreed that no *kelim* should be moved at all. When meticulous observance was restored, they permitted moving *kelim she-melakhtam le-heter* but left the decree in place for moving them for no reason. The idea was for people to pay attention to what they do with their hands on Shabbat. Making sure not to move *kelim* without a reason keeps people aware of Shabbat and makes it more likely that they will not end up transgressing any Shabbat prohibitions. Furthermore, on

Shabbat one aspires to inner peace and restfulness. This includes one's hands as well – they should be at rest, not busy moving and carrying things unnecessarily.

In contrast, no decree ever limited the movement of food, books, clothes, or jewelry. Because they make Shabbat enjoyable, one may move them even without a reason.

The *poskim* disagree regarding *kelim* that are used very frequently, such as cutlery, plates, and cups. According to some, these *kelim* possess the same halakhic status as food and may thus be moved for no reason. Others maintain that they have the same status as *kelim she-melakhtam le-heter*, which may not be moved without a reason. Since *muktzeh* is itself a rabbinic law, the lenient position is the primary one. *Le-khatḥila*, though, since many *poskim* are inclined to be stringent, it is preferable to take their opinion into account and to avoid moving cutlery and dishes for no reason.[9]

---

9. According to a *beraita* in *Shabbat* 123b, in the time of Neḥemia, when many failed to keep Shabbat, the Sages decreed that all *kelim* are considered *muktzeh* (except for three; see below). Once the people returned to meticulous observance, the Sages again permitted moving *kelim* in a three-step process. Rava explains that the Sages permitted moving a *kli she-melakhto le-isur* only *le-tzorekh gufo* and *le-tzorekh mekomo*, but *kelim she-melakhtam le-heter* could be moved even in order to prevent their being damaged. According to most Rishonim, this permission to move *kelim* used for permissible things is limited to situations where there is a reason to move them (such as "from the sun to the shade" to protect them), but one may not move them unnecessarily. This is the opinion of Ran and *Magid Mishneh* (which derives this position from Rambam), and Rashba is inclined to be stringent as well. *Tur* and SA 308:4 rule accordingly. However, according to Ra'ah and Ritva, when the Sages permitted moving *kelim* from the sun to the shade, they also permitted moving them for no reason at all. Aḥaronim recommend being stringent here, following SA.

In contrast, all agree that food and books were never decreed *muktzeh* at all and may be moved even for no reason. This is also the case regarding clothing and jewelry (*Ketzot Ha-shulḥan* §105, *Badei Ha-shulḥan* §7 as cited in SSK 20:83).

There is a disagreement about *kelim* that are regularly used during meals. The first position is that of Rambam (MT 25:1-3), *Shlah*, *Ḥayei Adam* 66:3, and *Ben Ish Ḥai*, Year 2, Miketz 1. According to them, as stated in the Mishna (*Shabbat* 123b), three *kelim* were not included in the decree of *muktzeh* because they were necessary for eating. These three are: a tool for cutting pressed-fig cakes, a spoon to remove scum from the surface of soup, and a small knife left on the table to cut bread and meat. However, other *kelim* used for eating may not be moved without a reason. The second

10. AN ITEM THAT WAS *MUKTZEH* THROUGHOUT *BEIN HA-SHMASHOT*

If an item was *muktzeh* throughout *bein ha-shmashot* on Friday, it remains *muktzeh* throughout Shabbat, even if the reason it was considered *muktzeh* no longer applies. Therefore, if one left money on a table before Shabbat, the table becomes *muktzeh* as a *basis le-davar ha-asur*. Even if the money falls off the table at some point on Shabbat, the table remains *muktzeh*, since it was *muktzeh* during *bein ha-shmashot* (SA 310:7; section 5 above). Similarly, if an oil lamp or a candle was lit before Shabbat, it may not be moved on Shabbat even after it has burned out, and its leftover oil or wax may not be used. Since it was *muktzeh* during *bein ha-shmashot*, it is *muktzeh* for the whole day (SA 279:1; MB *ad loc.* 1). So too, if a valuable item that was *muktzeh maḥmat ḥesron kis* broke into usable pieces during Shabbat, the pieces remain *muktzeh*, since the item was *muktzeh* during *bein ha-shmashot* (MB 308:35 following MA 308:19).

Nothing is *muktzeh* unless it meets two conditions:

1. The object was not fit for use during *bein ha-shmashot* on Friday.
2. One has put the idea of using it out of his mind.

The Talmud's classic example is figs and grapes that were left to dry on the *muktzeh* (an open space in a back yard). During the drying process, they are inedible because they are fermenting, so one puts them out of his mind. Even if the drying process is completed on Shabbat and they become edible, since they were *muktzeh* at *bein ha-shmashot*, they remain *muktzeh* for all of Shabbat.

---

approach is that of *Tosafot* (*Shabbat* 123b, s.v. "miktzo'a"), Rosh, *Shiltei Giborim*, *Tehila Le-David* 308:4, *Ḥesed La-alafim*, and MB 308:23. According to them, the three *kelim* mentioned in the *mishna* are only examples of *kelim* used frequently at meals. In fact, all tableware – cutlery, cups, and plates – have the same status and are not *muktzeh* at all. R. Ovadia Yosef rules stringently, even forbidding a nervous person from fidgeting with such items in order to calm his nerves (*Yalkut Yosef* vol. 2, pp. 452-457). Some who are generally stringent about *kelim* are lenient in this last case. This is the implication of AHS 308:15. SSK 20:83 agrees: "It is permitted for one to move an item if he finds pleasure in occupying himself with it, even if there is no practical purpose." *Orḥot Shabbat* ch. 19 n. 108 records a similar ruling in the name of *Ḥazon Ish*.

However, if only one of these conditions is met, the item is not *muktzeh* for all of Shabbat. For example, one may have left wheat on the ground to take root, and has put it out of his mind. Since in fact the wheat was still edible during *bein ha-shmashot,* it does not become *muktzeh,* and may be picked up on Shabbat and eaten (SA 310:2).

Similarly, if one knows that an item that was unusable during *bein ha-shmashot* will become usable on Shabbat, he does not truly put it out of his mind. Therefore, it does not become *muktzeh*. For example, if a pot is on the *plata* when Shabbat starts, even if the food is inedible at that point, nevertheless since one knows that it will be ready to eat later, he does not put it out of his mind. Similarly, if damp clothes were hung out to dry before Shabbat, even though they are not wearable during *bein ha-shmashot,* as long as the climate is such that they will definitely dry over the course of Shabbat, one does not put them out of his mind. Therefore, one may move them once they are dry (*Levushei Serad;* SSK 22:11).[10]

---

10. Why are a cooking pot and a burning lamp treated differently? A pot does not become *muktzeh,* because one does not especially want the food to cook during *bein ha-shmashot.* He would be happy if it had finished cooking beforehand. In contrast, a lamp remains *muktzeh* throughout Shabbat because one does want it to give off light during *bein ha-shmashot.* Since he puts the lamp out of his mind during that time, it stays *muktzeh* all of Shabbat (SA 279:1). Interestingly, if one has in mind to use the leftover oil after the lamp burns out, then since it is clear that the candle will go out, the remaining oil is not *muktzeh* (SA 279:4). However, according to Rema, once the lamp became *muktzeh* during *bein ha-shmashot,* it may not be moved all day, and one's intentions are irrelevant.

MB 308:63 states that clothes that were wet during *bein ha-shmashot* are *muktzeh* for all of Shabbat. Many explain that he is referring to a case where it is not certain that they will dry over the course of Shabbat. In contrast, if it is clear that they will dry, MB would agree that they are not *muktzeh* (*Minḥat Shlomo* 1:10:2, n. 4; *Minḥat Yitzḥak* 1:81). Alternatively, some explain that the clothes remain *muktzeh* because there is a concern that people will end up wringing out the clothes to dry them, which is prohibited on Shabbat (*Az Nidberu* 1:5). In any case, in practice if it is clear that the clothes will dry on Shabbat, they may be moved (*Livyat Ḥen* §37; *Orḥot Shabbat* ch. 19 n. 563 in the name of *Ḥazon Ish*). See *Harḥavot.*

If pieces of fruit were still attached to their tree during *bein ha-shmashot,* and then fell off during Shabbat, they are *muktzeh* for all of Shabbat because they were not fit for use during *bein ha-shmashot.* It is assumed that one puts them out of his mind; had he wanted to use them on Shabbat, he would have picked them before Shabbat

11. MAKING AN ITEM UNSUITABLE FOR ITS NORMAL USAGE ON SHABBAT

One may not cause an object to become unsuitable for its normal usage (*levatel kli me-heikhano*) on Shabbat. Doing so is akin to demolishing something (*Soter*) on Shabbat. Therefore, if oil is dripping from a lamp, one may not put a container underneath it to collect the oil. Since the lamp and its oil are *muktzeh*, the container will become forbidden to move, and thus it will no longer be fit for normal use on Shabbat. If one wants to ensure that the dripping oil does not make a mess, he should put something under it before Shabbat. Similarly, one may not put a container under a chicken in which it can lay its eggs. Since an egg laid on Shabbat is *muktzeh*, the container with an egg in it will become forbidden to move (*Shabbat* 42b; SA 310:6, 265:3).

However, there is a way around this problem. Before placing the receptacle beneath the lamp or the chicken, one may place an item that is more important than the oil or egg. One may then move the container for the sake of that non-*muktzeh* item (MB 265:6).

If one is worried about sparks flying from a lamp, he may put a *kli* underneath it to collect the sparks. Because sparks are insubstantial and go out almost immediately, the *kli* may subsequently be moved. It is not rendered unsuitable for its normal use. However, he should not put water into the *kli*, because that will extinguish the sparks more quickly (*Shabbat* 47b; SA 265:4).

Making pillows and blankets wet is forbidden, because doing so makes them unsuitable for their normal use (SA 305:19). It is also

---

began (SA 322:3; MB *ad loc.* 7). Additionally, the Sages made a special decree against eating fruits that fall off on Shabbat, to ensure that no one would end up picking them on Shabbat (*Beitza* 3a; MB 325:22). Therefore, even if it is known before Shabbat that a non-Jew is planning to pick the fruit on Shabbat, in which case they are not *muktzeh*, they nevertheless may not be eaten because of this decree (SHT *ad loc.* 26).

In contrast, if a kosher animal was alive during *bein ha-shmashot*, and was slaughtered on Shabbat to feed a dangerously sick person, a healthy person may eat from the fresh meat. We do not say that it was *muktzeh* during *bein ha-shmashot*, as we do with the fruit. The difference is that while anyone can pick fruit (and would have done so before Shabbat if they were interested), not everyone knows how to slaughter. Thus, even though the owner did not slaughter the animal, that does not mean he put it out of his mind (SA 318:2; MB *ad loc.* 8).

forbidden to make an item of clothing so dirty that it is no longer wearable without washing. If liquid spilled on the floor, one may not use clothing to mop it up; by doing so, one is making the clothing unfit to wear. However, one may use a rag to mop up the spill, since this is the intended use of the rag. It is also permissible for many people to dry their hands on a towel, even if it will eventually become too wet to use any longer. This is because they are not making it unusable; rather, they are using it for its intended purpose. Similarly, one may put a garbage bag into a garbage can on Shabbat and put garbage in it, even though doing so gives the bag the *muktzeh* status of the garbage inside it. This is not considered rendering it unusable, as holding garbage is the purpose of the garbage bag (*Levush* 265:3; *Shulḥan Shlomo* 308:17:7; *Yalkut Yosef* vol. 2, p. 480; *Orḥot Shabbat* 2:19:329).

One may place a box in front of chicks as a step stool so that they can go back and forth from their coop. Even though animals are *muktzeh*, this is not considered making the box unusable, since he can shoo the chicks away from it whenever he wants. However, while they are on the box, he may not move it (*Shabbat* 128b; SA 308:39).

12. THE PERMISSIBILITY OF REMOVING FILTHY ITEMS – "*GRAF SHEL RE'I*"

Even though a truly disgusting item – such as a *graf shel re'i* (a receptacle that contains excrement), a dead mouse, or food scraps – is *muktzeh maḥmat gufo*, the Sages permitted removing it for the sake of human dignity. They did not encumber this removal by requiring that it be done with a *shinui* or *min ha-tzad*. Rather, one may remove it directly. This is all on condition that the item is in a place where it is disturbing people. However, if it is in a place where it is not bothering anyone, it may not be moved (*Beitza* 36b; *Shabbat* 121b; SA 308:34).

The details of this law depend on how disgusting the item is and where it is located. Inside one's home, even if an item is only slightly dirty – such as a pot with food remnants, a cup with a little wine left over, or an oil lamp covered in soot – as long as it causes discomfort, it is considered a *graf shel re'i* and may be removed. This is also the case in a yard if people are sitting nearby. However, if there are no people nearby, one may not remove it. If there is excrement in the street or in a yard where people walk, since it is truly repulsive, it may be removed even if no one is sitting nearby. However, if it is in a backyard that almost no one walks through, removing it is forbidden. If there is a dead animal giving off a horrible stench, then even if no one walks by it may be removed (MB 308:131; BHL 308:4 s.v. "keli"; Rema 279:2; MB *ad loc.* 5).

Even though shells and pits are *muktzeh,* one may clear them from the table with one's hands and throw them in the garbage. This may even be done in two steps: first piling them on the side of the table, then collecting them to deposit in the trash (some say that this is the basis for permission to sweep on Shabbat; see n. 14 below).

One who is cracking seeds with his mouth may remove each shell from his mouth by hand and either throw it away or pile it on a plate and then dispose of it later. However, he should not keep them in his hands in order to throw them out later (SSK 20:26). Similarly, one may empty out the refuse that accumulates in a sink strainer.

A garbage can that has garbage in it is *muktzeh.* However, if it is unpleasant to have a full garbage can, it may be taken out (on condition that there is an *eruv*). If one lives somewhere that has a dumpster (as opposed to private garbage cans), the garbage pail may be emptied into the dumpster and then brought back inside (SSK 22:48).[11]

---

11. One may not turn something into a *graf shel re'i* in order to make it permissible to move. If he did so, however, *be-di'avad* it may be moved. For a great need or to prevent loss, one may to turn something into a *graf shel re'i* in order to be permitted to move it (SA 308:36-37). Therefore, if a roof is leaking dirty water (which is *muktzeh* as it is unusable even for washing), or if an air conditioner is dripping clean water (which is *muktzeh* as it is *nolad,* a new creation), one may not set out a bucket to collect the water. Doing so would make the bucket unusable, since one may not move an item that contains a *muktzeh* item within it. While it is true that one may remove the dirty water because it is a *graf shel re'i,* as we said, *le-khatḥila* we do not turn something into a *graf shel re'i* to make an item disgusting for this purpose (Rambam; SA 338:8; MA *ad loc.* 12). Nevertheless, in a case of great need, in order to prevent dirtiness or damage, one may rely on those who permit placing a bucket to collect the water. Since the water is leaking in any case, and since one may dump the water out of the bucket because of *graf shel re'i,* the bucket has not become unusable. Therefore, one may pour the water out of the bucket before it fills up, in order to avoid dirtying the floor (*Tur* §338, *Taz ad loc.* 4; *Ḥayei Adam;* BHL *ad loc.,* s.v. "asur").

13. BROKEN *KELIM* AND WORN-OUT CLOTHING

As we have seen (section 3), any item that is not suitable for Shabbat use is *muktzeh maḥmat gufo*. We must now clarify at what point an item is considered unusable and therefore *muktzeh*. As a rule, there are two factors that affect the status of such an object: its objective state, and the owner's subjective attitude toward it. We will now explain.

If one threw out perfectly good clothes or *kelim* before Shabbat, they do not become *muktzeh* even though he is their owner. Since his personal attitude differs from that of most people, it is disregarded by *halakha*. Nevertheless, if before Shabbat he threw out used clothing and *kelim*, they become *muktzeh* even if some people would use such items. Since the owner threw them out, and they are used, they become *muktzeh* (SA 308:12; MB *ad loc.* 51; Rema 308:7). But if he threw them out on Shabbat, they do not become *muktzeh*. Since they were not *muktzeh* when Shabbat began (as they were still somewhat fit for use), they do not lose their status over the course of Shabbat (MB 308:32).

If a *kli* breaks on Shabbat and the broken parts are still usable, the parts are not *muktzeh*. The broken pieces are only *muktzeh* if there is no possibility of using them. Nevertheless, if there is a danger that people may be hurt by the broken pieces, one may even use his hands to clear them away. If a *kli* broke before Shabbat and the owner threw away the broken pieces, then even if they could be used on Shabbat, they are *muktzeh* (SA 308:6-7; MB *ad loc.* 48; SSK 20:42).

If one part of a *kli* fell off (whether on Shabbat or before Shabbat) but it can be reattached, then even though it is not usable over Shabbat, it is not *muktzeh*. Just as one may move the *kli*, one may move the part that broke off, because it is still considered part of the *kli*. Therefore, if a beaded necklace broke, since one intends to restring the beads, they are not *muktzeh* (on condition that there is no concern that a knot will be tied on Shabbat to hold the necklace together). Similarly, false teeth or crowns that fall out are not *muktzeh*, since one intends to put them back. A button that falls off an item of clothing is not *muktzeh* either, since it will be replaced. Even though a new button is *muktzeh* since there is no use for it on Shabbat, in this case the button is not *muktzeh,* since it has already been part of the item of clothing.[12]

In contrast, if an item was attached to the ground and then broke on Shabbat, it is *muktzeh* because nobody plans to move something attached to the ground. Therefore, if a door in a house falls off on Shabbat, one may not move it (*Shabbat* 122b; SA 308:8-10; MB *ad loc.* 35).[13]

If disposable dishes have been used but could still be reused, they are not *muktzeh.* However, once they have been thrown into a filthy garbage can, they are *muktzeh.* Even if they have not been thrown away, they are *muktzeh* if they are so dirty that they would generally not be

12. This is the approach of *Minḥat Shabbat* 88:2; *Az Nidberu* 7:46; *Menuḥat Ahava* 1:12:40; and *Orḥot Shabbat* 19:167. SSK 15:72 and *Yalkut Yosef* vol. 2, p. 394, agree, but conclude that it is good to be stringent and avoid carrying a button that fell off because there are Rishonim (Me'iri, R. Yonatan of Lunel) who maintain that the only reason that one may move the detached door of a *kli* is that it can still be used (to cover something), not that it retains its status of part of the *kli.* If so, a button that cannot be used at all on Shabbat is *muktzeh.*

We should add that if there is a concern that one might end up taking the part of the *kli* that fell off on Shabbat and reattaching it in a permanent way, thus transgressing *Boneh,* the Sages forbade moving the broken part. For example, if the leg of a bench fell off, one may not move the broken bench on Shabbat in order to rest it on a different bench, because he may end up fixing it. However, if it would be difficult to fix the *kli,* or if it has already been used in its broken state before Shabbat, we are not concerned that anyone will forget and fix it on Shabbat, so one may move it, as explained in SA 313:8 and Rema 308:16; above, 15:6.

13. Other similar examples include a door handle, a faucet handle, or a toilet seat that fell off. In each of these cases, the item may only be used on Shabbat if two conditions are fulfilled: first, it must be possible to replace the broken part in a clearly temporary way, so that it can still be used for its designated purpose; and second, there must be no reason to be concerned that one will reattach it properly on Shabbat. Some further details about a door handle are explained in 15:3 above. See also *Ḥut Shani,* 2:36:4:7, 9.

Another example is if the door of a cabinet or closet fell off. If the cabinet is small (its volume is less than forty *se'ah,* which is an *ama* by an *ama* by three *amot*), then if the door will eventually be reattached, it is not *muktzeh* (Rema 314:1; SSK 20:45 and n. 164). However, if the cabinet or closet is larger than forty *se'ah,* its door is considered the same as the door of a house, and it is *muktzeh. Orḥot Shabbat* ch. 19 n. 236 suggests that if a piece of furniture is larger than forty *se'ah* but is occasionally moved (like the *bima* on which the Torah scroll is read), when it comes to *muktzeh* it is considered a *kli* (rather than a house).

reused. However, if they are in a place where their filthiness disturbs people, they may be cleared away, as they are considered a *graf shel re'i* (as explained in section 12; SSK 20:42).

If one dried his hands with paper towels and then put them into the paper recycling bin, they are still not *muktzeh* if people sometimes reuse them to wipe up spills. However, if the paper towels were deposited in a regular dirty garbage can, from which people generally would not retrieve them, they are *muktzeh*.

14. THE PERMISSIBILITY OF MOVING *MUKTZEH* INDIRECTLY OR WITH THE BODY

The main prohibition of *muktzeh* consists of taking a *muktzeh* item in one's hand, the way it is normally moved. The more one deviates from the normal manner of taking an object, the more lenient the law becomes. There are two types of change (*shinui*) that can be used: *min ha-tzad* (indirectly, literally "from the side") and *be-gufo* (using a part of the body besides the hand. One may move a *muktzeh* item indirectly, but only for a permitted activity. One may move a *muktzeh* item with his body even for the sake of the *muktzeh* item or a prohibited activity. We will now explain:

Min ha-tzad is accomplished by hand, but indirectly. For example, one may pick up fruit covered in straw or dirt in a way that causes them to move. Since the *muktzeh* items are moved indirectly, through the permitted action of moving the fruit, and the purpose is a permitted activity – eating the fruit – there is no prohibition (*Shabbat* 123a; SA 311:8-9). Similarly, if one wants to study Torah from a book that has a pen lying on it (assuming the pen was forgotten there, so the book is not a *basis*; see section 5 above), he may pick up the book even though the pen will then fall off. Likewise, if one accidentally left coins on a pillow and he now wants to sleep on it, he may lift up the pillow so that the coins will fall off. If one accidentally left a rock on top of a barrel and now wants wine from the barrel, he may tip the barrel and cause the rock to fall off. If the barrel was packed tightly among other barrels so that it cannot be tipped over, or if tipping it would break the barrel next to it, he may lift up the barrel while the rock is on top of it and move it to where he can slide the rock off without causing damage (*Shabbat* 142b; SA 309:4).

One may pick up a broom and use it to sweep up dust or leaves, which are *muktzeh*. This is because one is doing it indirectly, not with his hands but with a broom, for a permitted purpose – so that the place will be clean. Similarly, if one wants to use a table, he may use a knife to move away shells (that do not have the status of *graf she re'i*) that have been left on the table (*Taz* 308:18; MB *ad loc.* 115).[14]

If one wants to move the *muktzeh* item for its own sake, to protect it, one may not move it even indirectly. For example, if money was left on a chair and one is concerned that the money will be stolen, he may not tip the chair so that the money will fall off and become hidden.

In contrast, one may use part of his body to move the money and conceal it. For the entire prohibition of moving *muktzeh* on Shabbat is to do so in the normal manner, with one's hand. The Sages did not prohibit moving *muktzeh* with the body. This includes moving with one's foot, his arm, his breath, or any other limb other than the hand (SA 311:8; Rema 308:3). Therefore, if money is lying on the ground, one may move it with his foot to conceal it. Similarly, if an item is lying on

---

14. It is true that some are stringent, maintaining that since a broom is taken in order to move *muktzeh* objects, moving with a broom is considered direct, not *min ha-tzad* (SAH 308:60; *Ḥayei Adam* §67 and *Nishmat Adam ad loc.* 6; *Ḥazon Ish* 47:14). Nevertheless, since *muktzeh* is a rabbinic law, the lenient ruling is primary. This is the approach of SSK 22:37-38 and *Yalkut Yosef* vol. 2, pp. 326-327. Besides, there are additional reasons to justify leniency in the case of sweeping – e.g., because what is being swept is considered a *graf shel re'i* or because it is insignificant. See *Harḥavot*.

The Aḥaronim disagree whether one may indirectly move something *muktzeh* in order to use the *muktzeh* object itself for a permitted activity. For example, may one move a tray with a burning lamp on it in order to benefit from the lamplight (assuming that the tray also has a non-*muktzeh* item on it that is more important than the lamp, and thus the tray is not a *basis*, as we explained in section 6)? *Beit Meir* 276:3 and *Pri Megadim* (*Mishbetzot Zahav* 308:18) are lenient; it is indirect movement for a permitted activity. However, SAH 376:10 is stringent; since the primary purpose of moving the tray is to use the lamp, the activity is not permitted, as it constitutes moving *min ha-tzad* for the purpose of something forbidden. SSK ch. 20 n. 194 states that one who wishes to be lenient has an opinion on which to rely.

One may move part of a *muktzeh* item for a permitted activity. For example, one may adjust the vents of an air conditioner or the dials on a wall clock, even though the clock is *muktzeh maḥmat ḥesron kis*, according to SSK 28:26, n. 55. *Orḥot Shabbat* ch. 19 n. 466, disagrees and prohibits doing so.

the ground and is at risk of being stepped on and broken, he may use his foot to move it out of harm's way. So, too, if a drawer has become a *basis* but has an item in it which one needs, he may open the drawer with part of his body and remove the necessary item. One may sit on a stone or on the wood of a construction site even though sitting down causes it to move (MB 308:82). Similarly, one may lean on a car, on condition that doing so will not set off the alarm.

15. IF ONE PICKED UP *MUKTZEH* PERMISSIBLY OR MISTAKENLY, AND THE STATUS OF A MINOR

As we have seen, one may move a *kli she-melakhto le-isur* for a permitted purpose (*le-tzorekh gufo*) or for its space (*le-tzorekh mekomo*). Thus, one may take a hammer to crack nuts. After use, one is not required to drop it. Rather, he may return the hammer to its proper place. If there were scissors on the table where one now wants to eat, he need not drop them as close to the table as possible, but may put them away. Since he picked them up in a permitted fashion, he may carry them to their proper place.

Similarly, if one finished eating fruit and is left holding peels or pits that are *muktzeh maḥmat gufo*, he does not need to drop them. Since they reached his hand permissibly, he may take them where he wants.

In contrast, once one has already put down a *muktzeh* item that he had been permitted to hold, it resumes its *muktzeh* status. At that point, even if it is not in its proper place, he may no longer move it (SA 308:3; MB 506:29). Similarly, if one forgot that an item is *muktzeh* and picked it up, he must put it down immediately (MB 308:13).

If one is carrying a *muktzeh* item that he had been permitted to hold, *le-khatḥila* he should not shift the object from one hand to the other. This is because some maintain that moving the item to his other hand is like putting it down, in which case he may no longer move it. *Be-di'avad*, if he did shift the *muktzeh* item to his other hand, he may continue going to the place where he wants to put it down.[15]

15. Those who prohibit continuing to carry after shifting a *muktzeh* object from one hand to the other include *Tosefet Shabbat*, introduction to §308; *Ben Ish Ḥai*, Year 2, Miketz 3; *Kaf Ha-ḥayim* 308:27; *Az Nidberu* 9:33; *Menuḥat Ahava* 1:13:2. Those who permit include *Pri Megadim, Mishbetzot Zahav* 446:2; *Torat Shabbat* 308:4; SSK ch. 20 n. 27 is inclined this way as well.

If a child is younger than the age of *ḥinukh* (see ch. 24), one may hold his hand and walk with him, even if he is holding something *muktzeh* in his other hand. As long as the adult is not carrying the child, the adult is not considered carrying the *muktzeh* item. However, one may not pick up a child who is holding something *muktzeh*. Rather, the adult should first shake the *muktzeh* item out of the child's hand, and then pick him up. This shaking is permitted, because it is *min ha-tzad* for a permitted purpose, i.e., to pick up the child. If the child is crying hysterically and will not calm down unless someone picks him up along with the *muktzeh* item he is holding, one may pick him up. As we will see (24:6), the Sages permitted transgressing rabbinic enactments for the sake of a sick child, and a child who is crying hysterically is liable to become weak like a sick person. However, if the object the child is holding is valuable, one may not pick him up, because we are concerned that if the object falls, the adult will end up picking it up and carrying it (*Shabbat* 141b; SA 309:1).[16]

According to MA 308:7, if one mistakenly picked up a *kli she-melakhto le-isur*, he may put it down wherever he wants. According to most *poskim*, though, the status of a *kli she-melakhto le-isur* is the same as that of other types of *muktzeh* – he should put it down immediately, wherever he is (*Bi'ur Ha-Gra* 266:12; MB *ad loc.* 13; SSK 22:34).

16. Some say that one may not even hold the hand of a child and walk with him if the child is carrying an expensive *muktzeh* item in his other hand. Others maintain that as long as one does not carry the child, it is permitted (Ramban). Under pressing circumstances, one may be lenient (BHL 309:1).

Chapter Twenty-Four

Children

1. THE MITZVA OF *ḤINUKH*, EDUCATING ONE'S CHILDREN

It is a Torah commandment to teach Torah to children. Thus we read: "Teach them to your children" (Devarim 11:19). The primary objective of this teaching is to ensure that the children observe all the Torah's instructions: "Study them and be careful to do them" (Devarim 5:1). Therefore, the Sages stated that alongside the mitzva to teach children Torah is the obligation to educate them toward mitzva observance. For how can they be taught the *mitzvot* without getting used to keeping them in practice? Thus, there is a Torah commandment both to teach children Torah and to accustom them to keeping the *mitzvot* in general. Nevertheless, the actual observance of specific *mitzvot* by the child is a rabbinic obligation.

A child should be educated to keep the positive commandments from the time that he can understand what the mitzva involves, and can properly observe it. Thus, the appropriate age for each mitzva varies in accordance with its complexity and the difficulty of its observance. For example, a boy should be educated about *tzitzit* once he knows how to put them on, can make sure that there are two sets of strings in back and two in front, and can recite the *berakha*. However, since one may only put on *tefilin* if he is able to maintain a clean body and utter concentration, a boy should only be educated about this mitzva shortly before his bar mitzva (*Sukka* 42a; MB 343:3).

The age at which we begin to educate children about *mitzvot* is about six or seven because that is when children start to study Torah in earnest and thus can begin to keep most *mitzvot* properly. This applies to *berakhot* and prayers as well. The age of *ḥinukh* is six or seven, as that is when most children can begin to do them properly. Nevertheless, we begin habituating them to recite *berakhot* and prayers from around the age of three, just as they start learning Torah at that age (BB 21a; *Sukka* 42a; SA YD 245:5).

The same principle applies to *kiddush* and *havdala*; from the age of three we begin to encourage the children come and listen. When the child understands the idea of Shabbat and can listen properly to *kiddush* and *havdala*, we make sure that he does so. If he is not present when *kiddush* or *havdala* is made, he should recite it himself.

2. EDUCATING CHILDREN ABOUT NEGATIVE COMMANDMENTS

It is a mitzva to train children to avoid prohibited activities from the time they begin to understand that certain things are permitted and certain things are prohibited. In other words, it is not enough that a child understands that he must stop what he is doing when he is told "no"; rather, he must understand that what he is doing is never allowed. Most children begin to understand this at approximately age three. From then on, if one sees his child engaged in a prohibited activity, such as eating non-kosher food or turning on a light on Shabbat, one must stop him from doing so (MB 343:3). Once the child reaches the age of *ḥinukh* – when we start teaching him Torah at about age six or seven – one should begin to explain more about the principles behind the prohibitions, so that he will know how to observe them properly.

There is no mitzva to teach one's child who is younger than three to avoid prohibitions. Therefore, if such a child finds prohibited food and wants to eat it, or if he wants to turn a light on or off on Shabbat, one does not need to stop him from doing so. Similarly, if one's small child is a Kohen, and he goes to a place of ritual impurity (such as a cemetery), one does not need to stop him, since he does not understand the prohibition.

All of this refers to situations in which the small child is acting autonomously. In contrast, if an adult causes a child, even a day-old baby, to do something prohibited, the adult violates a Torah prohibition, for the Torah commands us not to cause a child to violate prohibitions. Thus one may not feed a child blood or insects or bring a young Kohen into contact with ritual impurity (*Yevamot* 114a; MB 343:4). An adult may not even feed a child rabbinically prohibited food (SA 343:1).

However, it is not prohibited to give a small child an item that he might use in an impermissible fashion. For example, one may give paper to a small child on Shabbat even though it is likely that he will tear it and destroy letters that are written upon it, as giving him paper is not considered the same as instructing him to tear paper. However, one who puts non-kosher food into a small child's hand, though, is considered feeding him, as this is the normal way to feed a child (MA; MB 340:14).

On Shabbat, there is an additional prohibition, for we are commanded not to have children undertake *melakha* on our behalf: "But the seventh day is a Shabbat of the Lord your God; you shall not do any *melakha* – you, your son or daughter" (Shemot 20:10). This means that if a child turns on a light because he thinks this is what his parents want, and his parents know and do not object, then in addition to neglecting the rabbinic mitzva of *ḥinukh,* they are also transgressing a Torah prohibition by having their child do *melakha* for them. If a child turns on the light for another Jew (other than a parent), who sees him doing so and does not object, that Jew transgresses rabbinically (SHT 334:54).

Even though we have seen that one may not feed a minor forbidden food, if a child is hungry or thirsty before *kiddush* or *havdala* or during a fast, then even after he has reached the age of *ḥinukh,* the adult may give him food and drink. It is only forbidden to feed a child food that is intrinsically non-kosher. If the food is kosher but rendered unfit by the time, a child who is hungry or thirsty may be fed (MB 269:1; above 6:9).

3. WHO IS OBLIGATED TO EDUCATE AND OBJECT?

According to some, the obligation of *ḥinukh* devolves equally upon the father and mother (*Terumat Ha-deshen*). However, most *poskim* maintain that only the father is obligated to train children to do *mitzvot,* that is, objecting when they transgress negative commandments and requiring them to perform positive commandments. This is an extension of the obligation to teach them Torah, which also devolves upon the father.

Despite this, it is clear that the mother has a general mitzva to educate her children about Torah and *mitzvot*; the general commandment to love one's fellow and the demand for truth obligate every mother to educate her children to cling to the holy Torah and observe its commandments. What is incumbent upon the father alone is the responsibility to meticulously educate about Torah and *mitzvot* (Ri; Maharam; *Hagahot Maimoniyot*). If no father is present, whether due to death or absence, then the mother is obligated to teach her children meticulously about the Torah and mitzva observance (*Eliya Rabba* 640:4; *Kaf Ha-ḥayim* 343:9).

Thus, if a child who has reached the age of *ḥinukh* (about six or seven) is involved in a game and does not want to come to hear *kiddush* or *havdala* or recite *Birkat Ha-mazon*, the father must insist, so as to educate him properly. However, the mother may occasionally ignore such breaches in order to maintain a pleasant atmosphere in the home. If the father has passed away or is absent, the mother must take his place and insist that her children become habituated to keeping the *mitzvot*.[1]

1. All agree that a mother must educate her children about Torah and *mitzvot*. Part of the mitzva of "Love your fellow as yourself (*Ve-ahavta le-re'akha kamokha*)" (Vayikra 19:18) is enabling one's child to benefit from engaging in Torah and *mitzvot*. The mother is also obligated on account of "Reprove your friend (*Hokhe'aḥ tokhi'aḥ et amitekha*)" (*ibid.* v. 17). Elaborating on this, the Sages tell us: "If one is able to object to the members of his household sinning but does not do so, he is held responsible for their sin" (*Shabbat* 54b). Nevertheless, the Torah tasked the father with the specific obligation to teach children Torah. If he does not wish to do so, the rabbinic courts can force him to pay for the education of his sons (SA YD 245:4). If he has no money to do so, he must sell his clothing or seek charity. The mother has no such obligation. Since the father is obligated to teach the children Torah, he is also obligated to make sure that they observe the *mitzvot* with precision. Thus, the father has a more demanding role – educating toward exacting mitzva observance – while the mother has a more general job – establishing a positive relationship between the children and Torah and *mitzvot*. This is the meaning of the verse: "My son, heed the discipline of your father, and do not forsake the instruction of your mother" (Mishlei 1:8). The Vilna Gaon (on Mishlei 20:20) writes similarly: "The son is taught Torah by his father. His mother guides him to do *mitzvot* and walk a straight path" (see *Berakhot* 17a). However, if the father is not present, the mother must take his place, dealing with *ḥinukh* in order to fulfill *Ve-ahavta le-re'akha kamokha*, *tzedaka*, and *Hokhe'aḥ tokhi'aḥ et amitekha*. (See *Eliya Rabba* 640:4; *Kaf ha-ḥayim* 343:9.) In some families, it is easier for the mother to be the demanding parent, while it is more difficult for the father. In such cases, it is a mitzva for the mother to take over the role of educating toward exacting mitzva observance.

When parents neglect to educate their children and do not stop them from violating Torah law, the local *beit din* or public representatives who are responsible for local education must admonish the father. However, if the parents are negligent in educating their children about rabbinic obligations, there is no need to admonish the father.

The *poskim* disagree regarding what an adult must do if he sees someone else's child of educable age (six or seven) desecrate Shabbat or eat forbidden foods. Some maintain that the obligation to educate children is the sole responsibility of the father, and nobody else is obligated to prevent them from sinning (Rambam; SA 343:1). Others maintain that all Jews are obligated to prevent children of educable age from transgressing (*Tosafot*; Rosh; Rema). Practically speaking, several Aḥaronim rule that if an adult sees any child transgressing a Torah prohibition – such as turning on a light or washing his clothes on Shabbat, or eating foods prohibited by Torah law – he must stop him. However, if one sees a child transgressing a rabbinic prohibition – such as eating chicken with milk, or playing with *muktzeh* items on Shabbat – he does not need to stop him (*Ḥayei Adam*; MB 343:7). It would seem that if a minor repeatedly transgresses the same prohibition, even if it is rabbinic, it is proper to inform his parents.

If a minor is in danger of harming someone or damaging property, one must stop him in order to prevent the harm or damage. This law is derived from the mitzva to return a lost object to its owner: "If you see your fellow's ox or sheep gone astray, do not ignore it ... restore it to him" (Devarim 22:2). If there is a mitzva to return another's lost item, there is certainly a mitzva to prevent damage to his property. Similarly, we are told: "Do not stand idly by the blood of your neighbor" (Vayikra 19:16). According to the Sages, the mitzva of saving someone's property is included in this mitzva (*Sifra*).

We must stress that the mitzva of *ḥinukh* must be done in such a way that the child will be receptive. Therefore, one should not force a child to begin keeping all the *mitzvot* and saying all the prayers properly at the age of six or seven. A child's early years are meant to allow him to get used to praying and keeping *mitzvot*. This way, by the time children reach halakhic maturity at the age of bar or bat mitzva, they will be capable of keeping all the *mitzvot* properly.

4. THE PROHIBITION FOR A CHILD TO TURN LIGHTS ON AND OFF

If the lights went off in a home, and a child understands that his parents would be pleased if he would turn them back on, the parents must tell him not to do so. As we have already learned, parents have an obligation to educate their children to keep the *mitzvot*, and this includes preventing them from transgressing prohibitions. Even if a child is not yet three years old, which is generally the age at which we begin teaching children to avoid prohibited activities, the law is more stringent for Shabbat. As long as the child understands that turning on the lights would be helpful to his parents, it is as if he is doing it for them, and they must prevent him from doing it, based on the verse we cited above: "But the seventh day is a Shabbat of the Lord your God; you shall not do any *melakha* – you, your son or daughter" (Shemot 20:10). This means that we are commanded to make sure that children do not perform *melakha* on our behalf. Even if the lights went off in a neighbor's home and one's child goes over to turn on the lights for them, the neighbor must not allow him to do *melakha* for them.

Similarly, if a fire breaks out on Shabbat and a child attempts to put it out, whether at his parents' home or at someone else's house, he must be stopped from extinguishing it. Since the child understands that the adults want the fire to be extinguished, he is essentially doing the *melakha* for them, and thus they are obligated to tell him not to do so (*Shabbat* 121a; SA 334:25; MB *ad loc.* 66). Certainly, then, one may not tell a child explicitly to turn on a light or extinguish a fire; as we already learned, an adult may not cause a child to do anything prohibited (*Yevamot* 114a).[2]

2. If an adult tells a child to do a *melakha* on Shabbat or to violate any other Torah prohibition, the adult violates Torah law, since the Torah forbids causing a child to sin. If the adult tells the child to transgress on the rabbinic level, the adult is transgressing rabbinically (*Yevamot* 114a; SA 343:1). There is an additional stringency that applies to Shabbat. If a child is about to engage in a prohibited activity on Shabbat in order to help an adult, then even if the adult did not ask the child to do so, the adult must object. If he does not, he is transgressing. If the adult is the child's father, he is violating Torah law; otherwise, he is transgressing rabbinically (SHT 334:54). Therefore, when it is permissible to ask a child to perform a rabbinic prohibition, it is preferable to avoid asking one's own child, as will be explained in the next note.

Of course, if a child mistakenly turned off a light, it is important that no one yell at him in a way that will cause him to try to "correct" his mistake by turning the light back on. Even if no one yelled at him, but he simply wants to correct his mistake and turn it back on, he must be told not to do so.

If a child mistakenly performed a *melakha* on Shabbat (such as turning on the light), others may not benefit from it if he did it for the sake of an adult, but if he did it for his own sake, others may benefit from the light (BHL 325:10, s.v. "eino yehudi").

5. PERMISSIVE RULINGS UNDER PRESSING CIRCUMSTANCES

Sometimes, under pressing circumstances, one may tell a minor to transgress a rabbinic prohibition, but one may never tell a minor to violate Torah law. First, as we saw regarding *ḥinukh* in general, the Torah forbids causing a child to transgress. Second, as noted, there is an explicit injunction against children doing *melakha* on Shabbat: "But the seventh day is a Shabbat of the Lord your God; you shall not do any *melakha* – you, your son or daughter" (Shemot 20:10). We will now explain when one may ask a minor to transgress a rabbinic injunction.

According to Rashba and Ran, one may tell a child to transgress a rabbinic prohibition if it is for his own sake. Even though this is forbidden according to most Rishonim (Rambam; *Tosafot*; SA 343:1), under pressing circumstances we rely on those who are permissive (R. Akiva Eger; BHL 343:1, s.v. "mi-divrei"). Therefore, if the light in a child's room was accidentally left on or turned on, and he finds it difficult to sleep, one may tell him to turn off the light, as this action is rabbinically prohibited. It is preferable that a child under the age of six do it. If the child is older than six, it is preferable that he turn it off with a *shinui*.

Under pressing circumstances, one may tell a child to transgress a rabbinic prohibition, even if he does not stand to gain from the transgression personally. As we have seen (9:11), the Sages permitted transgressing a *shvut di-shvut* for the sake of a mitzva or under pressing circumstances. The entire obligation of a child to keep Shabbat is rabbinic, so if he transgresses a rabbinic prohibition, it is by definition a *shvut di-shvut*. As long as one is lenient in this respect only occasionally, there is no concern that the child will become accustomed to belittle Shabbat (*Mordechai; Taz* 346:6; SAH 343:6; *Livyat Ḥen* §124).[3]

If the light went out on Shabbat in a place where it is needed, a baby who is not old enough to understand that his parents want him to turn on the light (about a year old) and who will play with a switch without understanding whether he is doing something helpful or harmful may be held in front of the switch with the hope that he will play with it and turn it on and removed from there as soon as he turns it on. Since he does not understand the implications of flipping the switch on and off, his action is not significant for the purposes of transgression. Rather, he is considered *mitasek* (performing a *melakha* obliviously; see below, 26:3) (Rashba, *Yevamot* 114a; *Orḥot Shabbat* 24:7-8).

6. A CHILD IS COMPARABLE TO A SICK PERSON

The Sages forbade a Jew to ask a non-Jew to do *melakha* for him on Shabbat. In contrast, if a child needs something very badly, his status is akin to that of one who is ill, for whom one may ask a non-Jew to do *melakha*. For example, if a child has no food and is hungry, one may ask a non-Jew to cook for him. If he desperately needs light, one may ask a non-Jew to turn on a light for him (Rema 276:1; MB *ad loc.* 6; see below 28:2). In general there is greater need to be lenient on behalf of babies, but one may be lenient even with very needy older children just as he would be lenient with a sick person.[4]

---

3. In cases where it is permissible to ask a child to perform a rabbinically prohibited *melakha*, it is preferable that the act not be done by the child of the person who needs it done. As we saw in the previous note, there is a Torah commandment not to have *melakha* performed by one's children, so even though for the child the prohibition is a *shvut di-shvut*, for the parent there is only one *shvut* involved. If one of the parents needs to ask the child to perform a *melakha*, it is somewhat preferable that the mother ask rather than the father, since the primary responsibility for *ḥinukh* is the father's. See *Pri Megadim* cited in BHL 266:5.

4. Some maintain that the comparison of children to the sick applies only until the age of two or three (*Melamed Le-ho'il* citing *Sha'agat Aryeh*; *Ḥazon Ish* 59:3). Others maintain that it extends until age six (*Tzitz Eliezer* 8:15:12:7, based on *Mor U-ketzi'a*). Still others say age nine or ten (SSK 37:2), while the most lenient say it extends until the age of bar or bat mitzva (*Or Le-Tziyon* 2:36:4). It would seem that everything depends on the specific details of the situation. Thus MB 276:6 states that if a child is "very needy," he has the status of a sick person. The younger the child is, the needier he is. A similar point is made by *Nishmat Avraham* 328:57 and *Orḥot Shabbat* ch. 20 n. 162.

A child who is not feeling well may take medicine even if the pain is mild. Just as the enactment prohibiting the use of medication on Shabbat does not apply to a sick person, so too it does not apply to a child. Thus, if necessary, one may put cream on a baby's skin, on condition that one does not spread it. Rather, one should simply place the cream on the skin. If the baby's diaper then causes the cream to spread, one does not violate any prohibition, since the cream was not applied in order to smooth the skin (see 14:5 above and 28:8 below).

7. PERMITTED AND PROHIBITED GAMES ON SHABBAT

It is a mitzva to educate children to study a great deal of Torah on Shabbat. It is thus proper to teach them to minimize game playing so that they will not get used to wasting the precious and holy time of Shabbat on mundane activities. The closer they get to the age of bar or bat mitzva, the more they should be encouraged to study Torah more and play games less. It is good for the parents themselves to learn with their children, thus fulfilling the mitzva of "Teach them to your children" (Devarim 11:19). It is proper for each community to offer many Torah classes for children on Shabbat.

Nevertheless, children may play on Shabbat. Therefore, the laws detailed in the following paragraphs apply to all children who are under bar or bat mitzva age. However, for adults the laws are different. First of all, *le-khatḥila* it is preferable to follow the opinion that adults may not play any games on Shabbat (22:13 above). Second, even according to those who allow adults to play games on Shabbat, some games are problematic. For children, who are obligated to keep Shabbat only as training for adulthood, we are lenient; for adults, who are required to keep Shabbat by Torah law, we are stringent. Below we will explain the laws for minors. When adults need to be stringent even according to the lenient position that allows them to play games, we will say so explicitly.

One may play checkers, chess, and memory games on Shabbat. One may also play with dice and spinning tops. However, one may not play any game in which the winner is awarded money or food. It is also forbidden to play games that normally involve writing (SA 338:5, 322:6; *Ḥayei Adam* 38:11). Some maintain that it is preferable not to play Monopoly or other games in which people win money and property, even though it is not real money. Children who wish to be lenient about this may (SSK 16:33), but adults should be stringent.

All games that involve writing, pasting, cutting, or weaving are forbidden on Shabbat. However, minors may put together a jigsaw puzzle or form words by joining letters on a board. Even though adults must be stringent in these two cases, children may rely on those who are lenient. According to this opinion, there is no violation of *Kotev* since all the writing was already there, and the letters and puzzle pieces are simply being moved together temporarily (18:4 above).

One may not build model planes or boats out of plastic parts if they require a great deal of precision and are meant to last for a long time.

Children may play with interlocking blocks, build with them, and take apart what they have built. Children may also make paper planes or boats. However, it is proper for adults to be stringent. (See above 15:7 and *Harḥavot.*)

The Sages forbade making a temporary tent on Shabbat, but this is permissible if it is erected in a different order from usual. Therefore, children may not drape a blanket over chairs in order to create a tent to play in. However, this is permissible if they hold the blanket horizontally in the air, and afterward place chairs underneath. It is also forbidden to use interlocking blocks to build a house or garage whose inside area is a square *tefaḥ* or more, but if they start by holding the roof up and then attach the walls from underneath, it is permitted (above 15:5).

One may use a kit to make jewelry that is not made to last, on condition that the end of the thread is not tied with a regular knot but rather with a bow knot (SSK 16:22).

One may not sort playing pieces or cards of two games that got mixed up together, as it constitutes *Borer*. However, if people want to play one of the games, they may remove the pieces they need from the mix. This sorting is not considered *derekh melakha* but rather *derekh misḥak* (the normal way to play), because one normally begins such a game by taking out its pieces (above 11:16).

One may not make shapes out of Play-Doh or modeling clay, as it constitutes *Memare'aḥ* (SA 314:11). If one makes shapes that have meaning, it also constitutes *Kotev* (*Ḥayei Adam, Yom Tov,* 92:3). Therefore, Play-Doh and modeling clay are *muktzeh.*

8. ADDITIONAL GAMES AND PLAYING IN THE YARD

One may compress a spring on a toy car so that the car will move forward, as long as the car does not make noise and no lights light up. One may not play with any battery-operated toy (17:2 above).

One may not blow up a balloon because a knot is usually tied at the end. However, if the balloon is sealed with a valve instead of a knot, and it has previously been inflated, it may be inflated on Shabbat (above 15:8).

Children may not play with toy musical instruments such as trumpets, pianos, guitars, bells, and noisemakers on Shabbat. Such toys are *muktzeh*. However, one may give a baby a toy that makes noise when it is shaken or a button is pushed. However, the adult himself may not cause the toy to make noise (MB 338:1; BHL s.v. "aval"; SSK 16:2-3 and n. 10; *Harḥavot*).

Sand is *muktzeh* unless it was set aside before Shabbat for children to play with (23:3 above). In that case, they may play with the sand as long as it is fine and dry enough that it cannot be used to fashion shapes. However, if the sand is wet enough that one can scoop out holes or fill them up, one may not play with it on account of the *melakha* of *Boneh*. One may not make sand wet, because of the *melakha* of *Lash* (15:2 above).

One may not play with marbles on the ground, because one may level the ground to make sure that the marbles roll smoothly. Similarly, one may not play any game on the ground that requires that the ground be flat, because one may end up leveling it. Even if the ground is paved, one may not play there, as there is a concern that one might then end up playing on unpaved ground. However, one may play on the floor inside; since all homes today have flooring, we are not worried that playing there will lead anyone to play outside on unpaved ground (15:2 above).

It is permissible to play with apricot pits, which children commonly play with; since they are set aside for this purpose by the children, they are not *muktzeh* like other pits. Even pits removed from apricots on Shabbat are not *muktzeh*, since many children play with them (see SSK ch. 16 n. 33).

One may swing on a swing, but if it hangs from a tree, even if only on one side, it is prohibited. If the swing hangs from a peg that was driven into the tree, it is permitted (19:7 above).

9. BALL GAMES AND RUNNING

Children may not play soccer, football, baseball, or basketball on Shabbat. Since adults make a big deal out of these games and they have intricate rules and procedures, they are prohibited, as they are considered a prohibited weekday activity. Besides, sometimes these games involve additional prohibited activities, such as preparing the field for a game, driving to the field, registering for the game, and buying and selling tickets or team merchandise. It is also prohibited to watch a soccer or basketball game on Shabbat, because this is a weekday activity. It is even prohibited to play with the balls associated with these sports at home or in a yard, because they are *muktzeh* and because it is a weekday activity. For the same reasons, all of the above applies to tennis as well.[5]

Children may play and run around for their enjoyment but may not participate in exercise classes (see above 22:8).

Children may play with balls designed for young children, on condition that they play indoors or in a paved yard. However, they may not play on grass or on a dirt yard, out of concern that they will level

5. Some prohibit playing soccer and basketball on Shabbat out of concern that people will end up leveling the ground, similar to what appears in SA 338:5 and MB 308:155. Others forbid these games out of concern that the players will end up fixing the ball or inflating it (*Ketzot Ha-shulḥan*). In any case, the rabbinic consensus is that one may not play soccer or basketball on Shabbat. It would seem that the primary reason is that it is a weekday activity (which is also the reason behind the prohibition to ride bicycles). This prohibition should not be taken lightly, as it is rooted in the Torah. Any activity that is burdensome and taxing serves to destroy the peace and rest of Shabbat, and is prohibited by Torah law (Ramban on Vayikra 23:24). The book of Yeshayahu elaborates upon this: "If you refrain from trampling the Shabbat, from pursuing your affairs on My holy day; if you call Shabbat 'delight,' the Lord's holy [day] 'honored'; and if you honor it, and not go in your own way, nor look to your affairs, nor speak of them" (Yeshayahu 58:13). The Sages elaborated further: "'Not go in your own way' – the way you walk on Shabbat should not be like the way you walk on weekdays.... 'Nor speak of them' – your speech on Shabbat should not be like your speech on weekdays. Speaking [about mundane matters] is forbidden, but thinking about them is permitted" (*Shabbat* 113a). Since soccer games and basketball games involve a big production, have intricate rules and regulations, and are taken very seriously by many people (some even make their living playing these sports), they are the ultimate weekday activity. The leniency for children to run for enjoyment is limited to running around freely, not in the organized framework of a sport or exercise. Rav Kook presents this approach in *Oraḥ Mishpat* §152.

the ground. They may play table tennis for fun, since that is generally played indoors. There is no need to worry that by allowing children to play with balls at a young age, they will get used to it and will continue doing so as adults, since the permission is limited to balls designed for children, which in any case adults do not play with.

One may not recover a ball from a tree using one's hand or a stick, as it might lead to breaking a branch. If the ball fell out on its own, one may play with it (19:7 above; SSK 16:8).

10. BICYCLES, SCOOTERS, AND SKATES

One may not ride a regular two-wheeler bicycle, because this is a weekday activity (22:8 above). Even if a bicycle has training wheels, one may not ride it. However, small children may ride tricycles, because tricycles are only used by small children, and there is a significant difference between tricycles and bicycles. Therefore, riding them is not considered a weekday activity (above, 22:8 and n. 4).

Some allow children to ride scooters and wear skates on Shabbat. According to them, just as children may run on Shabbat, they may use scooters and skates. Opposing them are those who feel that while children may run on Shabbat, that permission is limited to unassisted movement. In contrast, using equipment that makes one move faster and more effectively is considered a weekday activity.

Even though those who are lenient here have an opinion on which to rely *be-di'avad*, it is proper to be stringent, since the stringent opinion seems more compelling. Just as the widespread practice is to refrain from riding bicycles because this is a weekday activity that clashes with the spirit of Shabbat, it is similarly inappropriate to use scooters or skates on Shabbat. Additionally, by our limiting small children to simpler games, older children will learn to dedicate Shabbat to Torah and to rest.

Chapter Twenty-Five

Melakha Performed by a Non-Jew

1. ASKING A NON-JEW TO DO *MELAKHA* ON SHABBAT

Shabbat belongs to Jews alone, as the Torah states: "For it is a sign between Me and you throughout the ages, that you may know that I the Lord have consecrated you" (Shemot 31:13). In addition, the Sages go so far as to say that "A non-Jew who observes Shabbat is liable for the death penalty" (*San.* 58b). In other words, if a non-Jew were to invent his own religion and establish a "Shabbat" for himself, during which he would refrain from engaging in *melakha* and in developing the world, he would be liable for death at the hands of heaven (see Rashi *ad loc.* and MT, Laws of Kings 10:9).

Although a non-Jew may do *melakha* on Shabbat, the Sages forbade a Jew to ask a non-Jew to do *melakha* for him on Shabbat. This includes even rabbinically prohibited activities. The Sages found support for this from the wording of the verse: "No *melakha* shall be done on them" (Shemot 12:16). The verse does not use the active "Do not do *melakha*," but rather the passive "No *melakha* shall be done." Thus we see that it is proper that no *melakha* is done for a Jew on Shabbat or Yom Tov. As the Midrash elaborates: "'No *melakha* shall be done' – neither by you, nor by your friend, nor by a non-Jew" (*Mekhilta ad loc.*).[1]

If the *melakha* will be done with a Jew's property, one may not ask a non-Jew to do a *melakha* even for the non-Jew's benefit. For example, one may not tell a visiting non-Jew: "Turn on the light for yourself." Similarly, one may not say to a non-Jew: "Cook my food for yourself." However, if the meat belongs to the non-Jew, one may tell him to cook it for himself. Since the non-Jew is performing the *melakha* with his own possessions for his own benefit, the Sages did not forbid such speech (SA 307:21; MB *ad loc.* 73).

The Sages decreed that a Jew may not benefit from a *melakha* performed by a non-Jew for the Jew's benefit. For example, if the lights in one's home went out, and a non-Jewish neighbor came and turned the lights on, neither the Jews living in that home nor any other Jews may benefit from these lights, since they were turned on for a Jew on Shabbat (SA 276:1). If the *melakha* undertaken by the non-Jew is time-consuming, a Jew may not benefit from it immediately after Shabbat either. Rather, he must wait until enough time has passed so that the *melakha* could have been done after Shabbat. For example, if a non-Jew picked fruit or fished for a Jew on Shabbat, the fruit or fish may not be

---

1. *Smag, Lo Ta'aseh* §75, indicates that this *Mekhilta* means that the prohibition of asking a non-Jew to do *melakha* is a Torah law. *Beit Yosef* §244 quotes this. However, the overwhelming majority of *poskim* maintain that the prohibition is rabbinic, and the verse is not the law's source but merely a support for it. This is stated by Rambam (MT 6:1); Ramban, Shemot 12:16; SAH 243:1; and SHT 243:7. There are two reasons presented for this prohibition. Rashi (*Shabbat* 153a) writes that if one requests that a non-Jew perform *melakha* for him, it is as if the non-Jew is acting as the Jew's proxy. Alternatively, Rambam suggests that if one asks a non-Jew to do *melakha* for him, he will take Shabbat less seriously and thus may come to do *melakha* himself (MT 6:1). Either way, the rabbinic prohibition is an extension of the Torah's command that servants rest on Shabbat, as explained above in 9:10.

   One may not even ask a non-Jew on Shabbat to do *melakha* for a Jew after Shabbat (MB 307:9) or ask him before Shabbat to do *melakha* for a Jew on Shabbat. However, one may hint to a non-Jew to do *melakha* in the future. For example, one may say: "Why didn't you turn off the extra light in my house last Shabbat?" The non-Jew will realize that the Jew would like him to turn out the light the next Shabbat (SA 307:2).

eaten after Shabbat until enough time has passed that they could have been picked or caught then (SA 325:5-6).[2]

If the *melakha* performed by the non-Jew for the Jew is only prohibited rabbinically, then only the Jew for whom the *melakha* was performed may not benefit from it on Shabbat. Other Jews may benefit from the *melakha* even on Shabbat. Once Shabbat is over and enough time has passed so that the *melakha* could have been done after Shabbat, even the Jew for whom the *melakha* was performed may benefit from it (SA 325:8; MB *ad loc.* 41).

2. BENEFITING FROM A *MELAKHA* THAT A NON-JEW PERFORMED FOR HIMSELF

The prohibition on benefiting from a *melakha* done by a non-Jew on Shabbat is limited to a case where the non-Jew undertook the *melakha* for the benefit of a Jew. However, if he did the *melakha* for himself or for another non-Jew, then a Jew may benefit from it. For example, if a non-Jew turned on a light because he wanted to read a book, a Jew may benefit from this light (SA 276:2). Moreover, even if the non-Jew intended to turn on the light for both himself and a Jew, the Jew may benefit from it since in any case the non-Jew needed to turn on the light for himself (*Ḥayei Adam*; AHS 276:8; BHL 276:2 s.v. "ve-im" is inclined this way as well, in contrast to MA).

Therefore, if the lights went out in a Jew's home, he may not ask a non-Jewish neighbor to turn on the light, but he may arrange things so that the non-Jew will turn on the light for himself, after which the Jew may benefit from the light. For example, he can invite the non-Jew to come over and eat something. When the non-Jew arrives and sees that the house is dark, he will realize that he should turn on the light. Since the

2. The prohibition on benefiting from *melakha* done by a non-Jew on Shabbat is explained in *Shabbat* 122a, while the need to wait after Shabbat is explained in *Beitza* 24b. According to Rashi and Ran, the reason for the first prohibition is so that one will not benefit from *melakha* done on Shabbat; while according to *Tosafot* and Ramban, it is so that a Jew will not desecrate Shabbat by asking a non-Jew to do *melakha* for him (MB 325:29). If the *melakha* is undertaken publicly so that everyone knows that it was done for a particular Jew, that Jew may never benefit from it (SA 325:14; MB *ad loc.* 73).

non-Jew is turning the light on for himself, so that he can see the food that is being served, the Jew may benefit from the light as well (AHS 276:9).

Similarly, if a Jew has non-Jewish household help, one may send him to wash dishes in the kitchen even if it is dark there. Upon entering the kitchen, the non-Jew will turn on the light for himself, after which the Jew may benefit from the light. The Jew may even request that the non-Jew leave the light on after finishing his work (MB 276:27; SSK 30:57). However, if a Jew needs to walk somewhere in the dark, he may not ask his non-Jewish domestic worker to come along so that he will turn on a flashlight for himself. In this case, it is clear that the non-Jew is actually doing the *melakha* for the Jew (SA 276:3).

If a non-Jew heated water for himself on Shabbat and some extra water remained, a Jew may not use it, since the non-Jew may have heated the extra water with him in mind. Even if this was not the case, if the non-Jew sees the Jew using the remaining water, he may decide to add extra water for the Jew on future occasions. However, if the non-Jew does not know the Jew, then the Jew may use the extra water, because there is no concern that the non-Jew added the water for him or will add water for him in the future (SA 325:11; MB *ad loc.* 66). If a non-Jew picked fruit, caught fish, or milked cows on Shabbat for his own use, a Jew may not eat or drink the products on Shabbat, even if the non-Jew is a stranger. Since these food items were not edible when Shabbat began, they are *muktzeh* (SA 325:5).[3]

3. However, after Shabbat a Jew may benefit from these products immediately, since the non-Jew picked, caught, or milked them for his own use (SA 325:5). According to some, a Jew may not benefit from bread that was baked by a non-Jew on Shabbat, for two reasons. First, it is *muktzeh*. Second, there is a concern that the Jew will end up requesting that the non-Jew bake for him on Shabbat in the future. Others permit benefiting from the bread, maintaining that since a non-Jew may bake on Shabbat, the bread is not *muktzeh*. One may rely upon this opinion under pressing circumstances or for the sake of a mitzva (SA 325:4).

In 17:9 above, we explain that if one forgot to remove the light bulb in the refrigerator, he may suggest to a non-Jew to take some food for himself from the refrigerator. Even though the light will turn on when the non-Jew opens the refrigerator, the request is permitted because he is not telling the non-Jew explicitly to perform a *melakha*. Afterward, one may ask the non-Jew to remove the light bulb. Since turning off a light is only rabbinically prohibited, removing the bulb is a *shvut di-shvut* for the sake of a mitzva, as explained below in section 5.

3. MAKING USE OF A *MELAKHA* PERFORMED ON SHABBAT FOR A JEW

If a Jewish home was dimly lit – enough to allow the household members to eat, clean up, and wash the dishes, but not enough to allow them to read – and a non-Jew came and turned on an additional light for them, a Jew may use its light to eat, clean up, and wash the dishes, but not read. They may only do what they could have done without the additional light, but activities that were impossible to do without the additional light may not be done (SA 276:4; MB *ad loc.* 32).

If a non-Jew turned off a light to help a Jew sleep, the Jew may sleep in that room. Even though the non-Jew turned off the light on his behalf, and had he not done so the Jew would not have been able to sleep, the Jew is not benefiting from anything substantive created by the non-Jew's *melakha* but from the absence of light.

Even though a Jew may benefit in the above situations from the light or darkness that a non-Jew contributed to a room, a Jew may not ask a non-Jew to turn the lights on or off. However, he may hint at such a request. He must be careful with his formulation, though. It may not include anything that might be taken as a command. For example, if there is not enough light, one may not say to a non-Jew: "Do me a favor – there is not enough light in the room." Pointing to the light is also forbidden, because this is considered a hint that resembles a command (*Ḥayei Adam* 62:2). Similarly, if the light is on and is keeping one from sleeping, he may not say to a non-Jew: "Do what needs to be done" or "Do me a favor – I cannot sleep here," nor may he point to the light.

In contrast, one may hint by way of description. Thus if one needs more light, he may say to a non-Jew: "It is difficult for me to clean the house or to read when the light is so dim," or "The house is not well lit because only one light is on." These descriptions do not comprise a request that the non-Jew act; he is simply reporting the facts. The non-Jew then decides on his own to help the Jew by turning on an additional light. Similarly, if light is keeping a Jew from sleeping, he may say: "It is hard for me to sleep with the light on." The non-Jew will then figure out on his own that if he wants to help the Jew, he should turn off the light.

If no toilet paper was cut before Shabbat, this also may be reported to a non-Jew in descriptive form: "I have no toilet paper." The non-Jew will then cut toilet paper for him. This is not considered benefiting from a *melakha* that a non-Jew performed, because it is possible in a pinch to use toilet paper even when it has not been cut. However, he may not formulate his statement as a command, such as "Do me a favor – I have no toilet paper." Similarly, if the oven was left on accidentally, one may say to a non-Jew: "What a shame that so much electricity is being wasted." The non-Jew will understand the hint on his own and turn it off. However, one may not include a command in the hint, such as: "Whoever turns it off will not lose [i.e., will be rewarded]."[4]

In short, one may benefit from the actions of a non-Jew on Shabbat as long as he is careful to avoid two rabbinic prohibitions. First, he may not tell the non-Jew to perform a *melakha*, but must hint at it by reporting the facts. Second, one may not benefit from *melakha* performed by a non-Jew if it makes it possible for him to do something that he could not have done otherwise. Thus one may hint one's request to a non-Jew by means of a description, and one may benefit from light that a non-Jew added where there was already enough light to manage in a pinch. In addition, one may benefit from a non-Jew's act of turning off a light or an oven, since this does not involve direct benefit from the *melakha* he performed.[5]

All the methods presented here are permitted *le-khatḥila*. When none of these methods are sufficient, then for a great need or for the sake of a mitzva, the Sages permitted asking a non-Jew to perform a rabbinically forbidden *melakha*. Sometimes one may even ask him to perform a *melakha* that is prohibited by Torah law, as will be explained in the upcoming sections.

---

4. In a case where there is a possibility of major financial loss, such as a fire, the Sages permitted saying to a non-Jew: "Whoever puts it out will not lose" (SA 334:26). This is because in such a case, it would likely be ineffective to say: "Too bad about the house," because the non-Jew cannot be expected to expend effort to put out the fire if he does not expect to be rewarded. If the Jew hints that a reward is involved, this will motivate the non-Jew to expend major effort to help the Jew. Therefore, the Sages permitted hinting that the non-Jew will profit, even though this is the type of hint that is generally not permitted because it encourages the non-Jew to take action and is thus considered a kind of command.
5. If one sinned by explicitly asking a non-Jew to turn on a light in a room where there was already some light, then even though the Jew has transgressed, since there was some light was there prior to his request, a Jew may benefit from the additional light (MB 276:20).

4. FOR THE SAKE OF A MITZVA OR FOR A GREAT NEED

The Sages permitted asking a non-Jew to do a rabbinically forbidden *melakha* in cases of great need, such as to prevent suffering or loss, or for the sake of a mitzva. Such cases are a *shvut di-shvut,* a combination of two rabbinic prohibitions: the action itself is prohibited rabbinically, and the entire prohibition of asking a non-Jew to perform *melakha* on Shabbat is rabbinic.

In contrast, one may not ask a non-Jew to perform a *melakha* that is prohibited by Torah law, even for the sake of a mitzva. One may do so only for the sake of settling Eretz Yisrael or when there is a pressing communal mitzva need. Additionally, if not doing the *melakha* would entail suffering a very large financial loss, the Sages permit asking a non-Jew to do it. This is because they were afraid that if they were to prohibit this, the person suffering the loss would end up desecrating Shabbat himself on account of his great anguish. These laws are detailed above (9:11-12; 16:5 and n. 1).

Let us illustrate this principle. One may ask a non-Jew to remove a shofar from a tree in order to use it on Rosh Ha-shana, since the prohibition of using a tree is rabbinic (SA 307:7; above, 19:7). Similarly, one may ask a non-Jew to bring wine for *kiddush* or *siddurim* for the synagogue through a *karmelit,* as carrying there is rabbinically prohibited (MB 325:60; 21:3 above). One may also ask a non-Jew to bring food that is essential to the Shabbat meals through a *karmelit,* as this food enables people to fulfill the mitzva of *oneg Shabbat.* However, one may not ask a non-Jew to carry food that is not essential to the meal (MB 325:62).

One may ask a non-Jew to move *muktzeh* items in order to prevent a loss. For example, one may ask a non-Jew to collect scattered money, so that it will not get lost or stolen. One may also ask a non-Jew to bring bags of cement from the yard into the house so that they are not ruined in the rain (SA 307:19; see MB *ad loc.* 69).

If a door is squeaking so loudly that it is difficult to sleep, one may ask a non-Jew to oil the hinges. The relevant prohibition is rabbinic, since the door can be used even if the hinges are not oiled (*Melakhim Omnayikh* 6:1 and n. 1). Additionally, if mosquitoes are buzzing around in a room and disturbing one's sleep, one may ask a non-Jew to spray and kill them. Since mosquitoes are not being killed to use their bodies, the prohibition is rabbinic (20:8 above).

If it is uncertain whether a particular action is prohibited rabbinically or by Torah law, one may ask a non-Jew to undertake the action for the sake of a mitzva or a great need. The prohibition of asking a non-Jew to perform *melakha* is rabbinic, and in general when there is uncertainty pertaining to a rabbinic rule, we are lenient.

If the lights went out in a synagogue or in a *beit midrash,* one may ask a non-Jew to turn them on using a *shinui,* since doing so is only prohibited rabbinically. If using a *shinui* is not feasible, as long as there is a pressing need that relates to a communal mitzva, one may ask a non-Jew to turn on the light even without a *shinui.* If possible, it is preferable to give him something to eat there, so that he will be turning the light on for himself, which is permissible even if it is not for the sake of a mitzva.

5. A NON-JEW'S *MELAKHA* FOR SOMEONE SICK OR SUFFERING (AND AIR CONDITIONERS)

Under normal circumstances, one may not ask a non-Jew to perform *melakha* on Shabbat. However, for the sake of a sick person, one may ask a non-Jew to perform *melakhot,* even those that are prohibited by Torah law. These leniencies apply even to one who is not dangerously ill. If one is dangerously ill, then even a Jew must desecrate Shabbat in order to help him, as saving a life overrides Shabbat (SA 328:17). The laws pertaining to sick people will be explained below in chapters 27 and 28.

A child who needs something very badly has the same status as a sick person, and one may ask a non-Jew to do even *melakhot* that are prohibited by Torah law on his behalf. Therefore, one may ask a non-Jew to cook for a child who has nothing to eat or to turn on a light in the home of children who are very scared of the dark (Rema 276:1; MB *ad loc.* 6; Rema 328:17; 24:6 above).

In the cold areas of northern Europe, keeping homes warm on Shabbat was an ongoing struggle. Since homes were generally heated by coal- or wood-burning stoves, by Shabbat morning the fuel supply would be depleted and the fire in the stove would go out. Since all people are considered ill when it comes to extreme cold, the rabbis permitted asking a non-Jew to come and light the stove on Shabbat morning (SA 276:5).

The non-Jew who did this was known as the "Shabbos goy." Nowadays, however, when heaters are powered by electricity or gas and do not run out during Shabbat, there is no justification for using a "Shabbos goy" on a regular basis. Only if, by chance, the heater went off and it is extremely cold, may one ask a non-Jew to turn on the heat. One may do this even if there are no small children. In a home with children who truly need the heat, one may ask a non-Jew to turn on a heater even if it is not extremely cold (SSK 23:28; see n. 87 *ad loc.*).

Permission to ask a non-Jew to do *melakhot* that are prohibited by Torah law is limited to the needs of the ill. For one who is suffering but not ill, one may ask a non-Jew to perform a rabbinically prohibited *melakha* but not one that is prohibited by Torah law. Based on this, some maintain that on a hot day one may ask a non-Jew to turn on an air conditioner, claiming that turning on an air conditioner is only rabbinically prohibited. Accordingly, for the sake of the mitzva of *oneg Shabbat,* and in order to alleviate great suffering, one may ask a non-Jew to turn on an air conditioner. However, since others maintain that turning on an air conditioner is prohibited by Torah law (17:2 above), it is proper to ask the non-Jew to turn it on using a *shinui* (for example, using a teaspoon to depress the air conditioner's on button), which renders the action a *shvut di-shvut.*

If the air conditioner is running and has gotten too cold, one may ask a non-Jew to turn it off. Preferably, one should simply tell him that it is too cold, and allow him to figure out on his own that he should turn off the air conditioner. If he does not take the hint, one may tell him directly.[6]

---

6. According to *y. Sanhedrin* 10:5 and *Tosafot* (*Ketubot* 30a, s.v. "ha-kol"), heat causes more suffering than cold but does not cause as much illness as the cold. Therefore, the Sages permitted asking a non-Jew to do a rabbinically prohibited activity in order to avoid the heat, but not one that is prohibited by Torah law. For those who say that turning on an electrical appliance without a heating element is only rabbinically prohibited, asking a non-Jew to do so is a *shvut di-shvut*; accordingly, one may alleviate great suffering, and even more so when the mitzva of *oneg Shabbat* is involved as well. Many rule accordingly (SSK 13:39; *Minḥat Yitzḥak* 3:23-24; *She'arim Metzuyanim Ba-halakha* 90:20). In contrast, according to those who maintain that using electricity is prohibited by Torah law (17:2 above), asking a non-Jew to turn on the air conditioner is only a single *shvut*. Therefore, one should ask the non-Jew to turn it on using a *shinui*. Then all would agree that the case is a *shvut di-shvut*.

6. EMPLOYEES, SHARECROPPERS, AND RENTERS IN FIELDS AND FACTORIES

A Jew may not hire workers to do work for him on Shabbat, as a Jew may not ask a non-Jew to do anything for him on Shabbat that he may not do himself. Therefore, a Jew may not hire a non-Jew to work in his field, factory, or store. However, one may hire a non-Jewish worker to help serve food or wash dishes on Shabbat. Since a Jew may do these activities on Shabbat, he may hire a non-Jew to do them. In this case, it is not necessary for the Shabbat payment to be subsumed within a weekday payment (*Tehila Le-David* 243:1; SSK 28:63; and above 22:14).

If a non-Jew did some work for a Jew on Shabbat, the Jew may not benefit from it on Shabbat. After Shabbat he may benefit from it, but only once enough time has elapsed so that the *melakha* could have been performed after Shabbat. If the *melakha* that the non-Jew did for him was done publicly on Shabbat, such as building a home, the Sages decreed that he may never live in the house. However, he may sell it to another Jew. Under pressing circumstances, the first Jew may live in the house the non-Jew built for him (SA 244:3-4 and MB *ad loc.* 19-20; SA 325:14 and MB *ad loc.* 73).

All of the above applies to a wage earner. In contrast, a non-Jewish sharecropper or tenant farmer in a Jew's field may work on Shabbat. Since he shares in the profits, he is working for his own benefit.

Therefore, a Jewish factory owner or store owner may allow a non-Jew to run his business over Shabbat if the non-Jew receives a percentage of the earnings. Even though the Jew is profiting from the work of the non-Jew on Shabbat, since the non-Jew is working to earn money for

---

If it cannot be turned on using a *shinui*, one may ask the non-Jew to turn it on normally rely on the opinion that turning on an air conditioner is only rabbinically prohibited when asking a non-Jew to do a *melakha*, which itself is only rabbinically prohibited. Furthermore, we can take into account the opinion of *Itur* that one may ask a non-Jew to do even a *melakha* that is prohibited by Torah law for the sake of a mitzva, as explained in 9:11 above. As for turning off an air conditioner, all *poskim* agree that it is only rabbinically prohibited, so one may ask a non-Jew to do this for the sake of the mitzva of *oneg Shabbat* or in order to alleviate great suffering, since such a case is a *shvut di-shvut*. Thus *Igrot Moshe*, OḤ 3:42 permits asking a non-Jew to turn off the air conditioner in the synagogue, so that the congregants can remain there.

himself, he is not viewed as working on behalf of the Jew. The Jew may profit from a percentage of this work.[7]

Similarly, a Jew in Israel who owns a field, factory, or store abroad may rent them to a non-Jew in return for a set fee. The non-Jew may then keep the establishment open on Shabbat. Since the Jew gets his rent money in any case, the non-Jew who works on Shabbat is viewed as working for himself. This is on condition that the non-Jew is not only renting on Shabbat, because then it would be clear that the Jew wants the non-Jew to work on Shabbat. Rather, he should rent out the store on a weekly, monthly, or yearly basis, so Shabbat is subsumed within the total.

7. *MARIT AYIN* AND CAUSING A JEW TO SIN

Every case where we have learned that a Jew may rent his store or factory to a non-Jew or give his field to a non-Jewish sharecropper applies only where there is no *marit ayin* ("appearance" of transgression). However, if the site is known to be Jewish-owned, and those who see it operating on Shabbat are liable to suspect the owner of hiring non-Jews to work for him on Shabbat, such rental or profit-sharing arrangements are prohibited.

This is what the Sages meant when they forbade a Jew to contract his bathhouse to a non-Jew to operate on Shabbat. Since generally bathhouses were run by day laborers, people who saw the bathhouse open on Shabbat would suspect that a Jew had desecrated Shabbat by hiring non-Jews. This could breach the boundaries of Shabbat, as others might begin hiring non-Jews to work for them on Shabbat. However, if it was publicly announced that the Jew rented the bathhouse to a non-Jew, it is permitted. So too, if the widespread local custom is to operate

---

7. *Noda Bi-Yehuda* 1:29 is permissive even if the non-Jew is an employee with a regular salary, as long as he also gets a small commission for each sale. In this case too, the non-Jew is viewed as working for himself. This is a possible solution for owners of factories and telemarketing firms. If their employees receive a commission for each sale, they can be viewed as working for their own benefit. Ḥatam Sofer requires that this commission be a significant amount. If it is minimal, then an employee's primary motivation remains his regular salary paid by the Jewish owner (OḤ 59).

bathhouses under profit-sharing arrangements, the custom may be followed (SA 243:1-2).[8]

The same applies to a store. If it is known that a store is Jewish-owned, one may not rent it out to a non-Jew who will open it on Shabbat, because of *marit ayin*. However, if it has been publicly announced that the store has been rented to a non-Jew, it is not prohibited.

Even if there is a possibility that Jews who do not observe Shabbat will enter this store and shop there on Shabbat, the Jew is not viewed as aiding their transgression, since they could buy what they need in a different store. However, if most prospective customers are Jews, and keeping the store open breaches the boundaries of Shabbat, then the arrangement is prohibited (see *Tzitz Eliezer* 13:39).[9]

---

8. The Sages distinguished between different cases: If a *melakha* is performed outside the *teḥum*, one need not be concerned about *marit ayin* (SA 244:1). It is important to be aware that big businesses stand to lose large amounts of money if they do not operate on Shabbat. In such cases, even if the business is known to belong to a Jew, a profit-sharing arrangement can be made with a non-Jew. The Jew may even buy the business *le-khatḥila* with such an arrangement in mind (SA 244:6). One may be lenient to prevent a large potential profit from being forfeited (*Igrot Moshe*, OḤ 4:53). One may rent a business to a non-Jew for all *Shabbatot* (Rema, *ad loc.*). It is preferable to rent it for a few hours on Friday as well, so that the Shabbat rent can be subsumed within the weekday (see BHL *ad loc.* s.v. "de-vimkom" and MB 243:16). Additionally, when dealing with big businesses, there is less concern about *marit ayin*, because whatever the companies do is generally public knowledge.

   At first glance, it seems problematic to forbid certain arrangements because of *marit ayin*, as doing so would seem to violate the principle that we do not make a protective fence around a protective fence ("*gezeira li-gezeira*"). After all, the prohibition of asking a non-Jew to do *melakha* is already rabbinic. So why disallow these arrangements? *Pri Megadim* (*Mishbetzot Zahav* 244:1) explains that the prohibition of asking a non-Jew to do *melakha* is supported by a verse and therefore treated more stringently than regular rabbinic rules.

9. *Binyan Tziyon* §15 and *Meshiv Davar* 2:31 permit a Jew to assign work to a non-Jewish contractor who has Jewish employees who might work on Shabbat, because even without him they would desecrate Shabbat; thus, the Jew does not transgress *lifnei iver* ("Do not put a stumbling block in front of the blind" – Vayikra 19:14). If he were to assign them the work on Shabbat, he would be viewed as aiding (*mesayei'a*) their violation. However, when it is assigned before Shabbat, there is no prohibition. This point is made in the book *Amira Le-nokhri* 77:16. Along the same lines, Maharsham 2:184 permits renting one's home to Shabbat desecrators. However, if most customers of a rented store will be Jews, R. Eliezer Waldenberg forbids the rental (*Tzitz Eliezer* 13:39). It seems correct to be stringent when such an arrangement will breach the boundaries of Shabbat.

8. NON-JEWISH CONTRACTORS

The prohibition on hiring non-Jews to work on Shabbat applies to wage-earners but not to contractors. For these purposes, "contract work" means that the worker agrees to complete a job by a specified date for an agreed-upon amount of money. It makes no difference which days the contractor works. As long as he finishes the work by the agreed-upon date, he receives payment in full. Since the non-Jew can complete the work without working on Shabbat, even if he works on Shabbat it is for his own benefit, to complete the job he contracted, and is permitted even though the Jew benefits from the swift completion of the work.

For example, a Jew may make an agreement with a non-Jew to sew clothes or make shoes for him for a certain sum. The non-Jew's choice to work on Shabbat does not make it prohibited. However, a Jew may not ask a non-Jew on Friday to sew clothes or make shoes for him by the time Shabbat ends, since in order to do so the non-Jew would have to work on Shabbat. This is the equivalent of a Jew asking a non-Jew to work for him on Shabbat.

Similarly, a Jew may bring his car to a non-Jew's garage on Friday, even though he knows that the non-Jewish mechanic might fix it on Shabbat. Since the non-Jew is being paid contractually, at the going rate for the job, and the Jew did not ask him to work specifically on Shabbat, he is not viewed as working for the Jew on Shabbat. Even if he informs the Jew immediately after Shabbat that he finished working on the car, the Jew may retrieve the car and use it. However, one may not arrange with the mechanic to finish the job by a time that would require him to work on Shabbat. In such a case, the non-Jew is working for the Jew on Shabbat (SA 244:1; MB *ad loc.* 2).[10]

---

10. This is the opinion of MA 307:4; *Taz ad loc.* 3; SAH 252:4; MB 247:4 and 252:15; and *Orḥot Shabbat* 23:173. However, according to *Beit Yosef* (307:3), as long as one did not explicitly tell the non-Jewish contractor to work on Shabbat, even if it would be impossible for him to finish the job by the time specified without working on Shabbat, it is permitted. *Minḥat Kohen* 1:4, *Beit Yehuda* 1:44, *Rav Pe'alim* 2:43, and *Yeḥaveh Da'at* 3:17 concur. In a time of need, such as if one needs the car urgently on Sunday, one may rely on them.

Sometimes it is impossible to agree upon a price for the work in advance, as for example when one brings a car to a garage without knowing what the problem is. In such a case, if an agreement was reached that the going rate for the job would be

A non-Jew may only do contract work for a Jew on Shabbat if it is not apparent that the work is being done on a Jew's behalf. If it is apparent, as is the case if the work is being done in the Jew's home, it is forbidden to contract the work to a non-Jew because of *marit ayin*. Therefore, the Sages instructed that one should not allow a non-Jewish contractor who is hired to build a home to work on Shabbat, since if people see the contractor working they will think that the homeowner has desecrated Shabbat by hiring a non-Jew to work on Shabbat (SA 244:1). Today, when the norm is to hire a contractor to build one's home, it would seem that it should be permissible to be lenient. Observers will generally assume that the non-Jewish workers are working for a non-Jewish contractor, and there will be no issue of *marit ayin*. However, in practice, the custom is to be stringent and follow the opinion that even today people will likely suspect the homeowner of building his house using wage-earners (Ran). Furthermore, there is a concern that the homeowner, who knows that his house is being built on Shabbat, will end up supervising the construction and desecrating Shabbat. However, under pressing circumstances, for a great need, where there is a concern that if the non-Jews do not work on Shabbat the construction will not be completed, one may be lenient at the instruction of a halakhic authority.[11]

---

paid, or that a price for the job would be worked out, then since the non-Jew knows he will receive reasonable payment for his work, he is considered a contractor. But if the non-Jew is uncertain that he will receive the going rate, even if he knows he will receive some payment, he is viewed as working for the Jew, and a Jew may not arrange for him to work on Shabbat on the Jew's behalf (SA 247:2; BHL 252:2, s.v. "im katzatz"). If the non-Jew volunteers to do the work for free, since he hopes to be rewarded, it is considered contract work. If the Jew requests that he work for free, and the non-Jew agrees, according to SA 247:4 this is also considered contract work and is permitted, while according to Rema it is preferable to be stringent.

11. According to Rambam, Rosh, Ramban, and others, if a non-Jew accepted contract work from a Jew, he may be allowed to work on Shabbat. Only if this type of work is generally done by wage-earners is it prohibited on account of *marit ayin*, so that no one will think that they are wage-earners working for a Jew on Shabbat (SA 243:1; see BHL, s.v. "she-ken"). In contrast, Ran and those who follow him maintain that even when it is common practice for a field to be contracted out, it is still prohibited to let a non-Jew work there on Shabbat. Since the non-Jew does not receive a share of the produce the way a sharecropper does, he resembles a wage-earner and it will lead people to hire day laborers. Thus, according to Ran, one may not contract the

9. PARTNERSHIPS, STOCKS, AND BANKS

If a Jew and a non-Jew have joint ownership of a store or factory, they must agree when they enter into the partnership that the non-Jew will be responsible for the store on Shabbat and all of that day's earnings will be his, while the Jew will be responsible for the store on a designated weekday and all of that day's earnings will be his. For the remainder of the week, they may split the earnings evenly. This assumes that the owners keep track of the store's daily earnings so that these calculations can be made. If each day's profit is roughly similar or cannot be determined, they may split all the profits evenly. Then it is assumed that each partner collects the earnings of the day when the store is his sole responsibility (SA 245:1; SAH *ad loc.* 5; MB *ad loc.* 5-6; *Igrot Moshe,* OḤ 2:65).[12]

---

construction of a house. Although other Rishonim agree with Ran, the *halakha* follows the lenient position. This is the ruling of SA and Rema 244:1 as well as *Noda Bi-Yehuda* and R. Akiva Eger. (Additionally, there are Rishonim who maintain that even in a place where many regularly hire wage-earners one may still contract a field to a non-Jew, since people will think that he is a sharecropper. Rabbeinu Tam even considers permitting contract work indoors.) While in practice we do take the opinion of Ran into account, and the common practice is not to rely on those who are lenient to use a contractor to build a house, nevertheless one may be lenient under pressing circumstances at the instruction of a halakhic authority. Thus MB 244:13 states that if a synagogue is being built where there is a possibility that unless building continues on Shabbat it may not get built at all, a non-Jewish contractor may build it on Shabbat. Following this reasoning, in times of need the practice is to be lenient and allow a non-Jewish contractor to build homes in Judea and Samaria, if there is a chance that building there will be halted. See BHL 244:1, s.v. "o liktzor" and *Igrot Moshe,* OḤ 3:35. According to *Yalkut Yosef* 244:1, if an agreement was reached with a contractor to remove construction waste within a few days, and the non-Jew shows up on Shabbat, one need not object. Since this type of job is generally done by a contractor, there is no problem of *marit ayin*.

12. What if they did not initially make this agreement? When they come to divide the profits, the Jew may not say to the non-Jew, "You take the profits from Shabbat, and I will take the profits from one of the weekdays." The non-Jew would then be considered the Jew's *shali'aḥ* on Shabbat, because the Jew would receive the profits from the given weekday as a direct result of the non-Jew's Shabbat work. If they wish to split the profits equally, without stating explicitly that the Jew has worked on a weekday to make up for the non-Jew having worked on Shabbat, they may not do so according to Rambam and SA 245:1, but according to Rosh it is permitted. Rema permits as well if one would otherwise incur a major financial loss.

This is all, of course, on condition that it is known that they are partners, so there is no concern that observers will think that the non-Jew is working for the Jew. Alternatively, the partnership is permissible if it is common to have profit-sharing arrangements in this type of business.[13]

One may purchase stock in a company that is managed by non-Jews and does business on Shabbat, because the non-Jews running the company on Shabbat are doing so for their own profit. The Jew's profit is a byproduct (SA 245:4). Even when it is likely that the company employs Jews who desecrate Shabbat as part of their work, a stockholder is not responsible for this. Those Jews are desecrating Shabbat in any case, so buying stock does not directly abet their Shabbat desecration (see above, n. 9). However, if the company is run by Jews, or if the majority of its work is done by Jews who are desecrating Shabbat, a stockholder would become a partner in Shabbat desecration. Thus, one may not purchase stock in such a company.[14]

All of this is relevant to a business in which the two partners do not generally both work at the same time and thus the non-Jew's work on Shabbat is in addition to the evenly-divided work during the week. In such a case, the non-Jew is considered the *shali'aḥ* of the Jew, which is prohibited. However, if it is a business in which they do generally work at the same time, and the non-Jew wants to work alone on Shabbat, the Jew may split the profits with the non-Jew, as the non-Jew is considered like a sharecropper in this case. Since he is working for his half of the profits, he is not viewed as the Jew's *shali'aḥ* (Rema 245:1; MB *ad loc.* 9-11).

If the store's sales on Shabbat are double the volume on weekdays, the partners should agree from the outset that Shabbat profits will belong to the non-Jew, while the profits from two of the weekdays will go to the Jew.

13. If it is impossible to publicize the fact that the non-Jew is a contractor or sharecropper, then as long as the non-Jew is a minor partner in addition to being a contractor or sharecropper, *marit ayin* is not a problem (*Responsa Maharam Schick*, OḤ 97). This is also quoted as the ruling of R. Yosef Shalom Elyashiv in *Orḥot Shabbat* ch. 23 n. 376. However, *Orḥot Shabbat* qualifies this, explaining that it works only when the business does not need the non-Jew to work on Shabbat. Nevertheless, as we saw in n. 10, many disagree with this and are lenient. In a time of need, one may rely upon them. When a major financial loss is involved, all would allow leniency, as explained in n. 8.

14. See *Minḥat Yitzhak* 3:1, 3:31:2, and *Amira Le-nokhri* ch. 67. *Yalkut Yosef* vol. 2, p. 130 permits the purchase of stock in a Jewish company that does business on Shabbat, on condition that the stocks are bought after they have already been traded, i.e., from a previous shareholder. Since the company is open on Shabbat in any case, buying its stock did not cause it to do any additional work. In contrast, buying initial shares is

If a bank is under Jewish ownership and has non-Jewish clients, it may enter into an agreement with a bank under non-Jewish ownership specifying that on Shabbat the non-Jewish bank will take care of all necessary transactions for the Jewish bank's non-Jewish clients. The non-Jewish bank is not viewed as working for Jews on Shabbat; since it profits from each transaction, it is viewed as working for its own profit (*Melamed Le-ho'il* 1:33).[15]

---

forbidden. Even though the company will work on Shabbat in any case, this purchase aids in the commission of a transgression. In my humble opinion, one should be stringent even about buying shares from a shareholder, as shareholders are in some sense partners in the company. Accordingly, if the company is Jewish, the shareholder is a partner in Shabbat desecration. In any case, under pressing circumstances, the lenient opinions may be used in combination with others.

One may place a limit order (an order to buy or sell stocks when they reach a certain price), even though non-Jewish brokers might end up buying or selling the stocks on Shabbat. Since the stocks could hit the threshold at any time, he has not specified that the non-Jews work for him on Shabbat. Therefore, the brokers are making the purchase in order to earn their percentages. See *Amira Le-nokhri* 67:6, which rules stringently in this case.

15. One may receive daily interest on money that is held in a Jewish-owned bank (assuming the bank uses a *heter iska* – a method of restructuring a loan as an investment). Even though one's account receives interest on Shabbat, this is not considered earning money on Shabbat. Since the bank considers a day to start in the afternoon, the interest accrued on Shabbat is subsumed within the interest accrued from Friday and Saturday night (see above, 22:14 and n. 9.) If one signs a standing direct deposit or direct withdrawal order at a non-Jewish bank in which the money will be transferred according to secular dates and occasionally on Shabbat, it is preferable that he let the bank workers know that he does not need the transaction to take place on the exact date, and that from his perspective it is acceptable if they do it a day earlier or later. Then, even if they execute the transaction on Shabbat, they are doing so for their own convenience (*Ḥeshev Ha-efod* 3:51).

Chapter Twenty-Six

Ma'aseh Shabbat and *Lifnei Iver*

1. PRINCIPLES BEHIND THE PROHIBITION OF BENEFITING FROM *MELAKHA* DONE ON SHABBAT

The Torah commands us to refrain from *melakha* on Shabbat. The Sages added a protective fence by prohibiting deriving benefit from *melakha* done on Shabbat (*ma'aseh Shabbat*), as it is improper to benefit on Shabbat from Shabbat desecration. Whether the *melakha* was done knowingly (*be-mezid*) or unknowingly (*be-shogeg*), it is forbidden for any Jew to benefit from the *melakha* for the rest of that Shabbat. Some maintain that if the *melakha* was done *be-shogeg*, one may benefit from it. Some rely on this opinion under pressing circumstances (as explained in the next section). For our purposes, *shogeg* means that one was aware of his actions but forgot that it was Shabbat or was unaware that this act is a forbidden *melakha* on Shabbat; we have translated it, here and elsewhere, as "unknowing."

After Shabbat, anyone may benefit from a *melakha* that was done on Shabbat except for the perpetrator, if he did it *be-mezid*, who may never benefit from it (SA 318:1, as explained in section 7 below).

If a small child performed a *melakha* on Shabbat on behalf of an adult, during Shabbat no one may benefit from it. On Saturday night, anyone may benefit once enough time has passed that the *melakha* could have been completed after Shabbat. If the child did the *melakha* for his own sake, an adult may benefit from it on Shabbat (above, 24:4).

If a non-Jew did *melakha* on Shabbat for a Jew, no Jew may benefit from it until enough time has elapsed after Shabbat for the *melakha* to have been completed, so that no one benefits from *melakha* done on Shabbat and no one profits from work done by a non-Jew on Shabbat (above, ch. 25 n. 2). If a non-Jew did a *melakha* for himself, a Jew may benefit from it on Shabbat (above, 25:2). In some cases, one may hint to a non-Jew to do *melakha* on Shabbat (above 25:3). For the sake of a mitzva, or to avoid great loss or suffering, one may ask a non-Jew to do a rabbinically prohibited *melakha* (25:4).

2. THE PROHIBITION OF BENEFITING FROM A *MELAKHA* PERFORMED ON SHABBAT

As we have seen, if a Jew knowingly performs a *melakha* on Shabbat, neither he nor any other Jew may benefit from it during Shabbat. Even if he did the *melakha* unknowingly, according to most *poskim* no one may benefit from it, because the Sages did not want any Jew to benefit from *melakha* done on Shabbat (SA 318:1). Others maintain that only if the *melakha* was done knowingly is it forbidden to benefit from it on Shabbat; in contrast, if the *melakha* was done unknowingly, one may benefit from it. Some allow one to rely on this opinion when necessary (MB 318:7). A non-observant Jew who is aware that it is Shabbat and that the action he is taking may be prohibited is considered to be transgressing knowingly. Even those who are lenient maintain that one may not benefit from his *melakha* on Shabbat.[1]

1. According to R. Meir, one who cooks on Shabbat unknowingly may eat the food on Shabbat, while one who cooks knowingly may eat the food only after Shabbat. According to R. Yehuda, if one cooked food on Shabbat, whether knowingly or unknowingly, no one may eat from the food on Shabbat. After Shabbat, others may always eat the food. The one who cooked the food may eat it after Shabbat only if he cooked it unknowingly, while if he did so knowingly he may never eat it (*Ḥullin* 15a). Since there is an accepted principle that in a disagreement between R. Meir and R. Yehuda we follow R. Yehuda, most Rishonim rule that one may not benefit

Therefore, if a Jew turned on a light on Shabbat, neither he nor any other Jew may benefit from the light. As we have already seen, some maintain that under pressing circumstances, as long as the light was turned on unknowingly, one may benefit from it. Under normal circumstances, though, or if the light was turned on knowingly, one may not benefit from it.

Nevertheless, if one could have engaged in a certain activity with difficulty even without the light, one may also engage in this activity after the light is turned on. For example, if a light in a stairwell was turned on on Shabbat, as long as one could have ascended the stairs in the dark, one may do so in the light. However, one should not run up the stairs, as this would constitute taking advantage of the light. If a bathroom light was turned on on Shabbat, one may still use the bathroom, since one could have done so without light as well. However, if one could not have arranged certain items in one's home without the light, one may not arrange them using the light. If there was originally enough light to read, even with difficulty, and then an additional light was turned on, one may continue reading even though it has become easier.

If a light in a room was on and one knowingly turned it off, one may sleep in the room. Even though it is now easier to sleep there, it is permitted, since there is no direct benefit from the *melakha*; it simply removed an impediment to sleep.

If a Jew turned on a radio or music player on Shabbat, one may not benefit by listening to it. However, if it would be inconvenient to leave the room, he need not do so, since the sound was turned on against his wishes, and he does not want to benefit from it. Even if a non-Jew turned on such a device, one still may not benefit from it, both because

---

on Shabbat from *melakha* that was done unknowingly. This is the opinion of Rif, Rambam, Ramban, and many others. This is also the ruling of SA 318:1. Nevertheless, according to a minority of *poskim* (*Tosafot, Ḥullin* 15a; *Sefer Ha-Teruma*; Ritva; Vilna Gaon), in this case the *halakha* follows R. Meir, since the Talmud goes on to say that Rav taught his students R. Meir's opinion on the topic. MB states that in a time of need, one may benefit from an unknowing violation on Shabbat (318:7). However, if one picked fruit unknowingly on Shabbat, even those who are lenient concede that one may not benefit from it, since it is *muktzeh*.

it is a weekday activity and because it detracts from the honor due Shabbat (above 22:19).

One is not obligated to stay out of his room because his roommate sinned by turning on the heat in their shared room. However, *le-khatḥila* he should try to prevent his roommate from transgressing. If he was unsuccessful, he should have in mind not to benefit from the prohibited action. He should not move toward the heater in order to warm up. Rather, he should remain in his usual place. If he benefits against his will, he is not transgressing. If he can open a window in order to avoid benefiting from the heat, this is preferable (based on Rema 276:1; AHS *ad loc.* 4; MB *ad loc.* 11-13).[2]

Some maintain that one must not even fulfill a mitzva through a *melakha* that was performed on Shabbat. Others maintain that since *mitzvot* were not given for our benefit, doing a mitzva cannot be considered deriving benefit from a *melakha*. In their opinion, if a light was turned on during Shabbat, one may study Torah or pray by its light. One who wishes to follow this leniency has an opinion to rely on. However, if food was cooked on Shabbat, all agree that one may not eat it. Even though eating it would fulfill the mitzva of *oneg Shabbat*, since the way one fulfills this mitzva is by experiencing pleasure, it would violate the Sages' decree forbidding benefit from a *melakha* done on Shabbat. Similarly, if a light was turned on during Shabbat, one may not eat by its light.[3]

2. This is the ruling in *Ha-tzava Ka-halakha* 34:1-2 and *Yalkut Yosef* 318:36. It would also seem to be the opinion of *Har Tzvi*, OḤ 1:185. However, the one who turned on the light, the heat, or the radio knowingly, as well as the person who told him to do so, technically must leave the room in order to avoid benefiting from the *melakha* (MB 276:13; *Yalkut Yosef* 318:14, n. 20).

3. See *Sdei Ḥemed* (*Kuntres Ha-klalim, Ma'arekhet Mem, Klal* 95), which quotes dissenting opinions. These are also cited in *Ha-tzava Ka-halakha* 33:7 and *Yalkut Yosef* 318:18-20. When dealing with a physical pleasure such as eating, one should be stringent, as it is not clear that any authority would be lenient. See *Ḥayei Adam* 62:6 and *Igrot Moshe*, OḤ 1:126. When there is no physical pleasure involved, then since it is a rabbinic dispute, one who wishes to be lenient has an opinion to rely on. This applies even more so if the *melakha* was done unknowingly, as then one can take into account the authorities who follow R. Meir and permit benefiting from it.

3. CASES IN WHICH DERIVING BENEFIT IS PERMITTED

The prohibition on deriving benefit on Shabbat from the unknowing performance of a *melakha* applies only to a case of a *melakha* that is prohibited by Torah law. In contrast, if a rabbinically prohibited action was done unknowingly, one may benefit from it on Shabbat. Nevertheless, if it was done knowingly, it has the same status as a Torah prohibition: one may benefit from it only after Shabbat (MB 318:3 and BHL *ad loc.*; *Yalkut Yosef* 318:3). For example, the Sages prohibited separating *teruma, ma'aser,* and *ḥalla* on Shabbat, because it resembles *tikun* (fixing or improving) of the produce. If one unknowingly performed the separation on Shabbat, the "improved" produce may be eaten on Shabbat, but if he did this knowingly, it may not be eaten until after Shabbat (MB 339:25; above 22:5).

If one unknowingly turned on an electrical appliance without a heating element (e.g., a fan, air conditioner, or refrigerator), since some maintain that this action is not prohibited by Torah law, one who wishes to be lenient and benefit from the appliance has an opinion on which to rely. However, if one turned on a heater with metal heating coils or a light bulb with an incandescent filament, he has definitely transgressed a Torah prohibition. Thus, even if it was done unknowingly, he may not benefit from the results of his action on Shabbat. In the case of the heater, he should open the window or leave the room to avoid benefiting from the *melakha*.[4]

If one performed a *melakha* obliviously (*mitasek*), there is no prohibition on deriving benefit from it, since the *melakha* had no intent. This is true even if the *melakha* is prohibited by Torah law. For example, if one absentmindedly brushed his hand or leaned against a light switch and turned it on, one may derive benefit from it.

4. As we have seen above (17:2 and n. 1), according to many contemporary authorities, turning on an electric appliance with no incandescent filament or heating element is only rabbinically prohibited. Even though in practice we tend to be stringent and treat turning on electricity as a Torah prohibition, here we may also take into account the opinion of those who follow R. Meir. According to him, even if one transgresses a Torah prohibition, as long as it was unknowing, one may derive benefit from it. This is the approach of *Yalkut Yosef* 318:56.

There is a difference between *shogeg* and *mitasek*. As noted, *shogeg* means that one was aware of his actions but forgot that it was Shabbat or was unaware that this act is a forbidden *melakha* on Shabbat. When the Temple stood, one who did a *melakha be-shogeg* was obligated to bring a sin offering. In contrast, *mitasek* means that one did a *melakha* obliviously, without being aware of his actions. Such an act did not obligate its perpetrator to bring an offering. Since *mitasek* is less severe than *shogeg*, there is no prohibition to benefit from what was done obliviously.[5]

However, if one absentmindedly turned on a light out of habit, as he does all week long when entering a room, he is considered *shogeg*. Even though he was not thinking explicitly about what he was doing, nevertheless since the intent of his action was to turn on the light, he is considered *shogeg* and one may not derive benefit from his *melakha*.

4. BENEFITING FROM AN ACTION THAT DID NOT ALTER AN ITEM

Some say that if a *melakha* did not physically alter an object, like if it was transported from a public domain to a private domain, the item does not become prohibited, and one may benefit from it on Shabbat in the private domain (Rabbeinu Yona and Ritva). The same would apply to food that was transported via motor vehicle on Shabbat; since the food itself underwent no change, it would not be prohibited. However, others maintain that there is no difference between types of *melakhot* (*Tosafot*, Ramban, and Rashba). Even if the *melakha* did not alter the food at all, one may not benefit from it on Shabbat if it was transported

5. Among those who say *mitasek* does not constitute a transgression are *Leḥem Mishneh* (1:5) and *Eretz Tzvi* §76. Some are stringent and maintain that even *mitasek* constitutes a transgression, and therefore one may not derive benefit from a *melakha* done *be-mitasek* (*Oneg Yom Tov*; *Minḥat Barukh*). According to R. Akiva Eger, in some cases *mitaskek* has the same status as *shogeg*. Nevertheless, in practice, one may be lenient in all cases of *mitasek*. First, the prohibition on benefiting from *melakha* done on Shabbat is rabbinic, so in cases of uncertainty we are lenient. Second, the *poskim* who follow R. Meir are permissive even in the case of *shogeg*. This is also the opinion of *Az Nidberu* 6:17 and *Yalkut Yosef* 318:23. See *Orḥot Shabbat* 25:4.

in a prohibited fashion. In practice, *le-khatḥila* it is proper to be stringent, but under pressing circumstances one may rely on those who are lenient, particularly if the *melakha* was done unknowingly.[6]

If a *melakha* that was performed on Shabbat enables an additional, permissible action to occur, one may benefit from the permissible action. For example, if a hammer was fixed on Shabbat, it may not be used, even for permitted purposes like cracking nuts. However, if one violated this prohibition and cracked nuts with the hammer, he may benefit from the nuts, since the act of cracking the nuts is not intrinsically forbidden.

If a locked door was unlocked in a forbidden fashion, such as with the use of an electronic key card, some say that one may not enter the room through that opening, since the door was unlocked in a prohibited fashion. Others maintain that one may enter, since unlocking the door

6. According to Rabbeinu Yona and Ritva, if the object was not physically altered, the prohibition of *ma'aseh Shabbat* does not apply to it. This is also the opinion of *Korban Netanel*. In contrast, *Tosafot*, Ramban, and Rashba as well as *Har Tzvi* maintain that this is not grounds for leniency. In practice, if the *melakha* was done unknowingly, in times of need one may be lenient. (This is the implication of *Ḥayei Adam* 9:11; MB 318:7; and BHL 318:1 s.v. "aḥat.") Under pressing circumstances, one may be lenient even if the *melakha* was done knowingly, since the prohibition of *ma'aseh Shabbat* is rabbinic. See *Yabi'a Omer*, 10:25. This applies when soldiers have been brought food by a vehicle on Shabbat: under pressing circumstances, they may eat the food. However, if their consumption of the food will cause additional Shabbat desecration in future, they should not eat it (*Ha-tzava Ka-halakha* 35:10). All agree that if fruit was knowingly brought from outside the *teḥum* (at a height of under ten *tefaḥim*), one may not benefit from it, as explained in *Eruvin* 41b and SA 405:9. According to Rabbeinu Yona, the reason for this is that the Sages reinforced their own safeguards.

Regarding *melakha* performed by a non-Jew, all agree that *Hotza'ah* is just as severe as other *melakhot*. For example, if a non-Jew delivered something to a Jew via an action that is prohibited on Shabbat by Torah law, the Jew may not benefit from it until enough time has elapsed after Shabbat that the item could have been brought after Shabbat. This is to make sure that Jews do not ask non-Jews to do *melakha* for them on Shabbat. If a non-Jew performed a rabbinically prohibited *melakha*, then the Jew for whom the *melakha* was performed may not benefit from it until enough time has elapsed after Shabbat that the *melakha* could have been done. Other Jews may benefit from it even on Shabbat (SA 325:10), as explained in 25:1 above.

did not create anything new; it simply removed an impediment to entering. *Be-di'avad*, in a time of need, one may be lenient. If a refrigerator door was opened and the refrigerator light went on, one may remove food from the refrigerator (see above, 17:9).

If a Jew who does not observe Shabbat approached an automatic door and thus caused it to open, one may not enter through it. Only under pressing circumstances may one be lenient. If another Jew passed by and unintentionally caused the door to open, one may enter through it (see above, 17:11).[7]

---

7. According to *Mor U-ketzi'a*, *Ma'amar Mordechai*, and *Nehar Shalom*, if a fire was lit on Yom Tov (which is prohibited) and then used to cook food, one may benefit from the food since cooking is not prohibited on Yom Tov (in opposition to *Taz* 502:1, which forbids). This indicates that one may benefit from a consequence of *ma'aseh Shabbat*. A key that was transported via a public domain is subject, as we saw in the previous note, to a disagreement about whether one may benefit from a *melakha* that did not physically alter an object. Under pressing circumstances, one may be lenient. In any case, if the door has already been unlocked with that key, entering through the doorway does not constitute benefiting from the transgression itself, but rather from a consequence. As we said, in such a case one may benefit. This is the opinion of R. Shlomo Zalman Auerbach and R. Yosef Shalom Elyashiv (however, *Igrot Moshe*, OḤ 2:77 prohibits; see 2:71 as well).

In contrast, if a door was unlocked in a prohibited fashion, such as with an electronic key card, then it would seem that one may not benefit by entering, since the very act of unlocking was done in a prohibited manner. (As we saw, according to *Tosafot*, Ramban, and Rashba, *ma'aseh Shabbat* applies to *Hotza'ah* even though the item is not changed.) This is certainly the position of *Igrot Moshe*, and it seems to be that of R. Shlomo Zalman Auerbach as well. Nevertheless, according to R. Yosef Shalom Elyashiv (cited in *Melakhim Omnayikh*, p. 525), it is permissible because opening the door is simply removing an impediment, and this kind of benefit is not prohibited. Furthermore, even without this explanation, we saw above in n. 6 that under pressing circumstances one may rely upon the opinion of Rabbeinu Yona. If a refrigerator door was opened and the refrigerator light went on, even R. Shlomo Zalman Auerbach allows removing food from the refrigerator, since the light was turned on only incidentally (SSK 10:16 and n. 47). For further discussion of all these cases, see *Orḥot Shabbat* 25:29-32 and §14 in the *Birurim* section.

If a non-observant Jew opened an electric door by approaching it, one should be stringent and avoid taking advantage of his transgression, as doing so is a desecration of God's name. However, under pressing circumstances, where there is no choice, one may rely on Rabbeinu Yona (as mentioned above in 17:11 and n. 11).

5. IF ONE DID AN ACTION OF DISPUTED PERMISSIBILITY

The prohibition on benefiting from a *melakha* done on Shabbat only applies when the action is clearly prohibited. However, if the action is the subject of dispute, even if general practice follows the stricter opinion, one may benefit *be-di'avad* from the *melakha*. This is because the entire foundation of the prohibition on benefiting from work done on Shabbat is rabbinic, and since we are lenient whenever there is a uncertainty pertaining to a rabbinic rule, we follow the lenient position in the dispute over whether this act is prohibited (*Pri Megadim*; MB 318:2).

For example, if one cooks raw meat, it is clear that he has transgressed, and the food may not be eaten on Shabbat. However, if one took partially-cooked food that is edible under pressing circumstances and placed it on a fire until it cooked fully, it may be eaten on Shabbat. Even though the *halakha* follows the opinion that doing so is prohibited by Torah law (SA 318:4), since there is an opinion that if the food was already edible, cooking it further is not prohibited (above, ch. 10 n. 1), if one transgressed and cooked such food on Shabbat, it may be eaten.

Similarly, if one took cold soup that had been cooked before Shabbat and heated it on a *plata* on Shabbat, although many maintain that he has violated Torah law (SA 318:4), it may be eaten, because Rambam allows doing this (above, 10:5-6).

Let us say one took a tea bag, put it in a glass, and poured boiling water over it directly from an urn, which is a *kli rishon*. Doing so is prohibited because, according to most *poskim*, pouring boiling water from a *kli rishon* cooks the outer layer of the food (above, 10:7-8). Nevertheless, *be-di'avad* one may drink the tea, because some maintain that one does not violate *Bishul* by pouring hot water over a tea bag, only by placing the tea bag directly into a *kli rishon* (Rashbam, Ramban, Rashba).

6. POWER OUTAGES

If there is a power outage, whether local or citywide, Jewish technicians may do what is necessary to restore power to all the area's residents. This is because many areas have sick people whose lives would be at risk without the electric equipment they need. Because of the possibility of loss of life, the area's electricity supply must be restored. Moreover, since the restoration is permissible, all residents of the neighborhood may benefit from it (above, 17:5). If there was food on the *plata* that cooled down while the electricity was off and then warmed up again when the electricity was restored, it may be eaten even if the food was not fully cooked beforehand, and only finished cooking after the electricity was restored, since it was cooked in a permissible manner.

If a small area lost electricity and it is clear that there is no risk to life involved, one may not restore the electricity. If the electricity was nevertheless restored, and as a result a light came on, one may not benefit from it. This means that anything that could not have been done without the light may not be done using the light (as explained in section 2 above). If food warmed up as a result of the electricity that was restored impermissibly, one must wait until it cools off before eating it. If food finished cooking as a result of this transgression, one may not eat it (R. Shlomo Zalman Auerbach cited in SSK ch. 32 n. 182; see above, 10:3).

7. BENEFITING AFTER SHABBAT FROM A *MELAKHA* PERFORMED ON SHABBAT

As we have learned, one who performs a *melakha* on Shabbat *be-shogeg* may benefit from it immediately after Shabbat, as may other Jews. If he transgressed *be-mezid,* he may never benefit from it, though others may benefit from it after Shabbat. For example, if one knowingly cooked food on Shabbat, he may never eat it. Others, including those he cooked for, may eat the food after Shabbat (MB 318:5). Similarly, if one built a house on Shabbat, others may benefit from it after Shabbat, but he may never use it. However, he may sell the house to others (MB 318:4).

One who knowingly laundered his clothes on Shabbat may not wear them even after Shabbat, because one may never benefit from a *melakha* that he performed knowingly on Shabbat. A solution in such a case is to wash the clothes again during the week, after which he may wear them (*Ben Ish Ḥai,* Year 2, Vayeḥi 19).

If a non-observant Jew regularly performs *melakha* on Shabbat for other Jews, they may not benefit from this *melakha* even after Shabbat. Only when a *melakha* is done occasionally may those on whose behalf the *melakha* was done benefit from it after Shabbat, as there is no concern that they will ask him to desecrate Shabbat again so that they can benefit after Shabbat. However, if he does this *melakha* regularly, they may never benefit from it. For example, one may not buy bread from one who regularly bakes it on Shabbat in order to sell it after Shabbat, even if all the ingredients are kosher. Eating it encourages him to continue desecrating Shabbat, and they would take part in his transgression. Similarly, no Jew may eat at a restaurant where a Jewish chef cooks on Shabbat for customers who will come after Shabbat.

One may not watch sports games or other televised events after Shabbat if these events were filmed by Jews on Shabbat. Since the filming involved intentional Shabbat desecration on the part of the videographers for the sake of their viewers after Shabbat, the viewers may not benefit from this Shabbat desecration. The same applies to fruits and vegetables brought to market on Sunday. If it is known for certain that they were picked by Jews on Shabbat, no Jew may eat them.[8]

8. If a Jew knowingly cooked on Shabbat for his friend, after Shabbat only the cook may not enjoy the food; the friend may do so immediately after Shabbat, as explained in *Beit Yosef* and MB 318:5. However, *Responsa Ketav Sofer*, OḤ 50 limits this law to a case in which the cook is an observant Jew; in contrast, if the cook is a *mumar*, a Jew who regularly commits this transgression, then the people for whom he undertook the *melakha* may never benefit, because that would encourage him to continue desecrating Shabbat. *Responsa Har Tzvi*, OḤ 180 is lenient and allows the people for whom the *melakha* was done to benefit after Shabbat, as long as the desecration was not done in accordance with their wishes. Nevertheless, many Aḥaronim maintain that one should be stringent (*Or Le-Tziyon* 2:30:1; *Yalkut Yosef* 318:6 and 318:71-76; *Orḥot Shabbat* 25:8).

A pot in which a non-observant Jew knowingly cooked kosher food on Shabbat, according to MA (following Rashba), has the same status as the food he cooked and is therefore prohibited until he performs *hagala*. *Pri Megadim* and MB 318:4 state this as well. Others maintain that only the food is forbidden, not the pot. This is the lenient position of Ra'ah and Rosh, who are not discussing *ma'aseh Shabbat* but rather *bishul akum*, the general prohibition for Jews to eat food cooked by a non-Jew. The laws of *ma'aseh Shabbat* are not as strict as those of *bishul akum*. For example, in the case of *bishul akum* no Jew may ever eat the food, while with *ma'aseh Shabbat* the food is forever forbidden only to the person who cooked it (and according to R. Meir, even the cook may eat it if he cooked the food unknowingly). Accordingly, the lenient position of Ra'ah and Rosh in a case of *bishul akum* should certainly apply to *ma'aseh Shabbat* as well (*Erekh Ha-shulḥan* 318:1; *Livyat Ḥen* §42). In any case, according to all opinions, a pot that was used to cook food on Shabbat may be used by anyone besides the cook, the same way that they may eat the food itself after Shabbat.

Technically, one may buy dairy products from a dairy farm that desecrates Shabbat when milking the cows (see above 20:4), because the milk produced on Shabbat is mixed with the milk produced on other days. Thus, for any bag of milk that one buys, it is uncertain whether it was milked on Shabbat. Since the prohibition of benefiting from *melakha* done on Shabbat is rabbinic, in cases of uncertainty we may be lenient. This also applies to a factory that produces paper all week long, including Shabbat. Technically, one may buy its paper. Nevertheless, it is always preferable to buy products from factories and companies that observe Shabbat. If all Shabbat observers were to unite in order to strengthen Shabbat observance, it would be possible as a temporary measure to forbid any benefit from the products of factories that desecrate Shabbat (see *Yalkut Yosef* 318:72, 74-5; *Orḥot Shabbat* 25:57-61).

8. AFTER SHABBAT

Starting half an hour after Shabbat ends, one may listen to news broadcasts produced by Jews, since sufficient time has elapsed for the producers to have collected the material and write the stories after Shabbat. However, one who listens to the news immediately after Shabbat transgresses the prohibition on benefiting from *melakha* done on Shabbat. Starting fifteen minutes after Shabbat, one may listen to other types of programs, because in that amount of time a news program can be prepared for broadcast. Even if the technicians and newscasters live far from the studio and desecrated Shabbat to travel to the studio, since the listeners gain nothing from this desecration, it is not forbidden to listen to the broadcast.

When Shabbat is over in Israel, one may not listen to broadcasts by Jews in America, since Shabbat there ends between seven and ten hours later than in Israel. Thus, one who listens in Israel would be benefiting from the Shabbat desecration of American Jews. For the same reason, one who is in Israel must wait approximately two hours after Shabbat ends before listening to Jewish broadcasts from Western Europe. In contrast, one may listen to broadcasts produced by non-Jews immediately after Shabbat in Israel ends.

One may travel by bus starting half an hour after Shabbat, as that is a reasonable amount of time for the bus driver to reach one's stop without having desecrated Shabbat. If the bus route is so long that it is clear that the driver started the route when it was still Shabbat, some forbid riding the bus (*Minḥat Yitzḥak* 9:39; *Orḥot Shabbat* 25:62), and others permit (*Mishneh Halakhot* 7:50). Many maintain that there is technically no prohibition because one who boards the bus half an hour after Shabbat does not benefit from the fact that the bus traveled on Shabbat; nevertheless, they continue, it is proper to be stringent as a protective measure (*Tzitz Eliezer* 13:48; SSK 59:9; *Yalkut Yosef* 318:76).

9. INTERACTING WITH NON-OBSERVANT JEWS AND *LIFNEI IVER*

The Torah commands: "Do not put a stumbling block before the blind" (Vayikra 19:14), meaning that one may not cause another person to transgress (MT, Laws of a Murderer 12:14). This commandment is known as "*lifnei iver*" ("before the blind"). If the other person would have transgressed even without his aid, many maintain that the accessory has not transgressed the Torah prohibition on causing others to sin. However, he has transgressed the rabbinic prohibition of aiding (*mesayei'a*) a transgressor. Therefore, one may not allow a non-observant Jew to borrow his car or radio on Shabbat.

Similarly, one may not give directions to a Jew who is driving on Shabbat and stops to ask for directions, even if the driver may actually end up spending more time driving without directions. There are two reasons for this. First, one may not aid a transgressor. Second, one may not speak on Shabbat about things that are prohibited on Shabbat (above 22:9). It is proper to apologize to the driver and explain that giving him directions is forbidden on Shabbat.[9]

9. R. Avigdor Nebenzahl reports in the name of R. Shlomo Zalman Auerbach (in the journal *Kotlenu* vol. 14, pp. 254-255) that it is preferable to give the driver directions so as to minimize his driving on Shabbat. Nevertheless, *Tzitz Eliezer* 15:18 and *Yalkut Yosef* vol. 2, p. 180 prohibit doing so. See *Re'akha Kamokha*, pp. 152-156. There is a dispute regarding the nature of the prohibition of aiding a Jew to transgress in a situation where he can transgress even without that aid. Some say that the prohibition is rabbinic (*Tosafot*; Rema, YD 151:4); according to others, Rabbeinu Ḥananel and Rambam maintain that it is prohibited by Torah law (*Melumdei Milḥama*, p. 33f); still others maintain that if the transgressor is a *mumar* and sins knowingly, there is no prohibition at all (*Shakh*, YD 151:6). It is generally assumed that the prohibition is rabbinic.

An observant soldier may leave the light on in the bathroom before Shabbat, even though he knows that at some point a non-observant soldier will turn it off. One does not need to waive his right to leave the light on just so that his non-observant friend does not transgress by extinguishing the light. Additionally, it is reasonable to assume that his non-observant friend would turn the light on and off in any case (R. Shlomo Zalman Auerbach cited in *Ha-tzava Ka-halakha* 31:5).

One may invite a non-observant Jew for an entire Shabbat, even if he knows that after Friday night dinner his friend will drive home. This is as long as one honestly offers him a place to stay, such that the invitation does not necessitate Shabbat desecration. Although some forbid this, one may be lenient when one's intent is to spread love among Jews, bringing people closer to Torah and to each other. However, sometimes it is proper to be stringent for educational reasons.

Some are stringent and forbid a synagogue to host the celebration of a bar mitzva from a non-observant family when it is clear that some of the guests will drive to the synagogue. They maintain that the synagogue's agreement to host the bar mitzva is like accepting and aiding Shabbat desecration. Others permit it on the grounds that these guests would be desecrating Shabbat in any case. Furthermore, the synagogue members did not ask anyone to drive, and in fact they would prefer that people come on foot. In practice, as long as the non-observant guests are respectful of the synagogue and are careful not to desecrate Shabbat inside it, the synagogue may host the bar mitzva. Nevertheless, according to many, it is still preferable to advise the family to have the boy called up to the Torah on a Monday or Thursday during *Minḥa* instead of on Shabbat.

There is a similar disagreement about hosting a *brit mila* on Shabbat when it is clear that many family members will desecrate Shabbat by driving to the *brit*. In practice, a *mohel* may perform the *brit* on Shabbat in this situation.[10]

10. According to *Igrot Moshe* (OḤ 1:98-99 and 4:71), one may not invite a non-observant Jew to a Shabbat event if it is clear that he will drive, but if necessary, he may notify the non-observant acquaintance of the event. *Shevet Ha-Levi* 8:256 states this as well. *Shevet Ha-Levi* 1:205 and 4:135 forbid holding a *brit* on Shabbat if this will lead

10. KEEPING WEBSITES AND VENDING MACHINES OPEN ON SHABBAT

If a Jew owns a vending machine, and most of its users are Jewish, he must disable it for Shabbat in order to avoid aiding their desecration of Shabbat. If most of the customers are non-Jews, he need not disable it (see SSK 29:28-29 and n. 75). The money that the non-Jews put in the vending machine is not considered payment for work done on Shabbat, since they are paying primarily for the product and not to operate the machine itself.

Some maintain that websites designed for a Jewish audience must be disabled on Shabbat so that they do not aid transgression. Since this is difficult practically, the site owner is not obligated to take them down; after all, the site visitors can easily desecrate Shabbat by visiting other sites, and as long as the site owner has done nothing to promote his site on Shabbat, there is no prohibition. However, if the site is primarily commercial, and most prospective customers are Jews, it means that the owner of the site benefits from the Shabbat activity, so he must make efforts to disable it for Shabbat. If this is very difficult, it is not obligatory. Since those who access the site are already desecrating Shabbat knowingly and regularly, some maintain that the prohibition

---

people to desecrate Shabbat by driving to the *brit* and taking pictures. In contrast, R. Shlomo Zalman Auerbach says that one may invite a non-observant Jew for Shabbat as long as the guest is given the opportunity to stay without desecrating Shabbat. This opinion is cited in *Rivevot Ephraim* 7:402 and *Sho'alin Ve-dorshin* vol. 2, pp. 18-19. *Tzitz Eliezer* 6:3 states that one may hold a *brit* on Shabbat even when this may lead to Shabbat desecration. See *Re'akha Kamokha*, pp. 157-163. In the text above, I am lenient, since non-observant Jews will desecrate Shabbat in any case. Besides, while they are in the synagogue they will not desecrate Shabbat, so one is not aiding them in their transgression by inviting them but in fact minimizing it. Nevertheless, to ensure that a bar mitzva celebration is free of transgression, it is preferable to celebrate by having the boy called up to the Torah on a Monday or Thursday at *Minḥa*. The guests may form a *minyan* for this purpose. Since some of the participants will not have heard the Torah reading that normally takes place every Monday and Thursday morning, they may read the Torah with the *berakhot* as part of *Minḥa* (*Peninei Halakha: Prayer* 22:9). This way, there is no problem with traveling or taking pictures of the event. In contrast, performing a *brit mila* on the baby's eighth day is mandated by the Torah; if the eighth day is Shabbat, the *brit* should take place on Shabbat.

of aiding someone's transgression does not apply. In contrast, if most of the customers are non-Jews, it is not necessary to disable the website for Shabbat. The purchases made on Shabbat are not considered payment for work done on Shabbat since the work to set up the site was done during the week.[11]

11. See also *Orḥot Shabbat* 22:41. In n. 55, it states that a commercial website has the same status as a vending machine. It is true that some are stringent, as discussed in *Kedushat Ha-Shabbat* vol. 2, p. 15f. Nevertheless, what I wrote in the main text seems most reasonable. This is also the conclusion of *Responsa Be-mar'eh Ha-bazak* 5:37-40. I will now explain the underlying principles. According to *Responsa Maharil Diskin* (*Kuntres Aḥaron* §145), one is not obligated to spend money to avoid violating *lifnei iver*, even though it is a Torah prohibition. According to *Atzei Ḥayim* (YD 5), one need not spend money to avoid *mesayei'a*, as it is only a rabbinic prohibition (though one would need to spend to avoid *lifnei iver*). In any case, leaving a website up is certainly no more than *mesayei'a*, as there are always alternative websites. According to *Shakh*, there is no prohibition at all of aiding a *mumar*'s violation of *halakha*. Therefore, if it is difficult for one to take down his website for Shabbat, he is not obligated to do so. Furthermore, the owner of the website is not transgressing the prohibition of buying and selling on Shabbat, since he is not doing anything. Rather, what takes place on the site is a commitment to complete the transaction. The money is not collected from the customer's account until after Shabbat. If a site earns money based on page views or subscriptions, we can say that the payment is for setting up the site and publishing content, which is how we permit paying rent or for use of a *mikveh* on Shabbat. It is assumed that the payment is for the cleaning and heating of the premises, which takes place before Shabbat (*Noda Bi-Yehuda*, OḤ 2:26; see above, 22:14 and n. 9). We may also take into account the position of BHL 244:6, which permits accepting money for work done on Shabbat if one would otherwise sustain a major financial loss. One need not worry about *marit ayin*, since everyone understands that no Shabbat desecration on the part of any Jew is necessary in order to keep a website open on Shabbat.

Chapter Twenty-Seven

Sick People and Saving Lives

1. THE PRINCIPLES OF *PIKU'AḤ NEFESH* (SAVING A LIFE)

Saving a life overrides Shabbat, as the Torah states: "Keep My decrees and laws, which a person shall do and live by; I am the Lord" (Vayikra 18:5). The Sages expound: "'live by' – and not die by" (*Yoma* 85b); the *mitzvot* of the Torah were given so that people may live by them, not die to fulfill them.[1]

We desecrate Shabbat to attempt a rescue, even if the chances of its success are slim. Thus, we desecrate Shabbat to bring someone medication, even if it works in only a small percentage of cases, and even if it is an experimental drug that might not be effective. However, we do not desecrate Shabbat to acquire a drug if there is no substantive reason to think that it might help (MA 328:1; Rema, YD 155:3; *Orḥot Shabbat* 20:7).

1. Saving a life overrides all *mitzvot*, with the exception of the three cardinal sins: idolatry, murder, and sexual transgressions. Concerning these three, the rule is "One should be killed and not transgress" (*San.* 74a; MT, Laws of Torah Principles 5:1-2). The punishment that the Torah prescribes for Shabbat desecration is stoning, the most severe punishment in the Torah and the same punishment specified for idol worship. Nevertheless, when it comes to lifesaving activities, performing *melakha* on Shabbat is not considered a transgression. In contrast, the three cardinal sins are considered transgressions no matter how dire the situation. This is because if one transgresses one of them, his life loses all meaning, and he brings death and destruction to the world.

In a case of uncertainty, we still desecrate Shabbat. For example, if a building collapses, and we do not know whether anyone was inside, and even if someone was inside, we do not know whether he is still alive, we clear away the rubble on Shabbat despite the uncertainty (SA 329:2-5). The act of clearing rubble ("***mefakhin** et ha-gal*") lends its name to the general category of ***piku'aḥ** nefesh*, which overrides Shabbat.

Even if a rescue attempt fails, God rewards all who made an effort. Similarly, if several people drove to different places to obtain a certain medicine that someone needed, they all receive divine reward, even though some of them traveled for naught (*Menaḥot* 64a; SA 328:15).

Even though one may desecrate Shabbat to save a sick person, one who knows that he will need to care for a dangerously sick person on Shabbat should prepare as much as possible beforehand to minimize the *melakhot* he will perform on Shabbat, since one must prepare for Shabbat before Shabbat (MB 344:11). If it is uncertain whether one will need to care for a sick person on Shabbat, it is good for him to prepare before Shabbat, though it is not obligatory (MB 330:1). For instance, if one sometimes is called upon to care for the wounded, he should preferably prepare adhesive and cloth bandages before Shabbat so that he will not have to cut them on Shabbat.

It is good for a woman who is due to give birth to prepare her hospital bag before Shabbat. If the expectant couple is planning to drive to the hospital in their car, they should preferably remove unnecessary items from the car before Shabbat. However, the expectant mother does not need to spend the *Shabbatot* near her due date close to the hospital, as that is an excessive burden that one is not required to undertake on Friday. If she has to travel to the hospital on Shabbat, she may do so, since saving a life overrides Shabbat (SSK 32:34 and 36:6-7).

2. DETERMINING DANGER

Any illness that doctors normally consider dangerous or from which regular people would hasten to save a suffering patient is deemed dangerous halakhically, even if only a small minority of people die from it, and therefore justifies desecrating Shabbat. Thus, one may drive a woman in labor to the hospital, even though in a clear majority of cases she can safely give birth at home (*Magid Mishneh* 2:11). However, one may not desecrate Shabbat on account of illnesses and risks that are generally not considered dangerous (*Shevet Mi-Yehuda* 1:19:2; SSK ch. 32 nn. 2 and 23).

The Sages defined certain conditions as dangerous. These include internal injuries (severe pains or wounds or internal bleeding); injuries on the back of the hand and foot (that is, infections and dangerous cuts); very high fevers; scorpion or snake bites; and eye afflictions (SA 328:3-9). The Sages determined all of these cases based on experience, and today's doctors agree in principle, though they use different terminology to describe the conditions. This is not the place to expand on the definition of a life-threatening condition, but there is a general principle: If those present think that the ill or injured party might be in mortal danger, they immediately do whatever is necessary to help him. If they need to call a doctor, they should do so; if they need to drive him to the hospital, they should do so.

When the people nearby do not know whether the patient might be in danger, they should ask a doctor, nurse, or medic in the vicinity, or they should call a doctor. If the doctor thinks that the patient might be in mortal danger, even if the patient claims that his condition is not dangerous, they must heed the doctor (SA 328:10 and 618:1, 5).

If the patient maintains that he is in danger, then even if the doctor thinks he is not, we must desecrate Shabbat and take him to the hospital to be examined. This is because "The heart knows its own bitterness" (Mishlei 14:10), meaning that sometimes only the patient can assess his own condition. Similarly, if a sick person demands a certain medicine or treatment that, based on his experience, could save his life, we heed him (SA 618:1). We only rely on the patient's intuition on condition that it makes some sense. However, if his illness is known and he demands a treatment that the doctors believe is ineffective, we heed the doctors (BHL 328:10, s.v. "ve-rofe"). Similarly, if the sick person is known to be hypochondriac or excessively fearful, and a medically knowledgeable person is certain that he is not in any danger, we do not desecrate Shabbat on his account.

If, in an effort to be pious, one asks a rabbi whether to desecrate Shabbat in order to help someone in mortal danger, he is a killer, for while he is asking, the patient's situation may deteriorate, and the Torah commands us: "Do not stand idly by the blood of your neighbor" (Vayikra 19:16). Furthermore, the rabbi whose students ask such questions is reprehensible, as he should have taught them that saving a life overrides Shabbat (*y. Yoma* 8:5; MB 328:6).

3. FOR WHOM DO WE DESECRATE SHABBAT?

The Sages offered a rationale for desecrating Shabbat to save someone's life: "Desecrate one Shabbat so that he will observe many *Shabbatot*" (*Yoma* 85b). However, in practice, even when it is clear that the person being saved will not observe Shabbat, one is commanded to desecrate Shabbat to save him because the Torah strives to increase life. Therefore, we desecrate Shabbat to save a mentally impaired person (*shoteh*), who is exempt from observing the *mitzvot*. Similarly, we desecrate Shabbat for someone who is unconscious and about to die, in order to prolong his life for a short while (BHL 329:4, s.v. "ela").

We desecrate Shabbat in order to save an unborn fetus, even if forty days have not yet passed since conception (*Behag*; Ritva; BHL 330:7, end of s.v. "o"). Similarly, we desecrate Shabbat to save a premature baby. Although in the past it was forbidden to desecrate Shabbat to save a baby born in the eighth month, whose nails and hair had not yet grown in, as it was certain that it would not survive, nowadays, with the improvement of medicine and the invention of the incubator, whenever doctors assess that the baby has a chance of long-term survival, we desecrate Shabbat to save him. (See SA 330:7-8; SSK 36:12 and n. 26.)

Technically, a Jew may not desecrate Shabbat to save a non-Jew, since one may only desecrate Shabbat for the sake of someone who is himself commanded to keep Shabbat. However, in practice, this rule only applies when another non-Jew is present to save his fellow non-Jew. If no other non-Jew is present, one must treat the non-Jew, even if this requires desecrating Shabbat. Since we want non-Jews to save Jews, we must save them as well. Thus, saving a non-Jew's life is included in the category of *piku'aḥ nefesh*.[2]

---

2. The basis of this permissive ruling, namely, that it ultimately prevents danger to Jews, is articulated in *Ḥatam Sofer*, YD 131 and *Divrei Ḥayim*, OḤ 2:25. Similar rulings appear in *Igrot Moshe*, OḤ 4:79; R. Shlomo Zalman Auerbach, cited in SSK ch. 40 n. 47; *Tzitz Eliezer* 8:15:6 and 9:17:1; and *Yabi'a Omer* 8:38. Additionally, according to Ramban (*Hasagot Le-sefer Ha-mitzvot, Hosafot Le-mitzvot Aseh* 15), we desecrate Shabbat to save a *ger toshav* (a "resident alien," a non-Jew who has accepted the seven Noaḥide laws

4. USING A NON-JEW OR CHILD TO MINIMIZE SHABBAT DESECRATION

As we have seen (above, 25:1), a Jew who performs *melakha* on Shabbat violates Torah law, whereas a Jew who asks a non-Jew to perform *melakha* for him violates rabbinic law. Similarly, a minor who performs *melakha* on Shabbat only transgresses rabbinically (above, 24:1). Consequently, it would seem, at first glance, that when it is necessary to do *melakha* in order to save a sick person, it is preferable to ask a non-Jew or a child to do it, thereby minimizing Shabbat desecration. However, the Sages stated: "These things should not be done by non-Jews or children, but rather by adult Jews" (*Yoma* 84b; SA 328:12). This means that even if a non-Jew or a child is present, one should not ask him to do the *melakha*. Only an adult Jew should do it. Rishonim offer two possible explanations for this rule. First, it is possible that a non-Jew or a child will hesitate and not act aggressively enough to help the sick person (*Tosafot*). Second, even when it is clear that they will act aggressively enough, we are concerned that those present might incorrectly conclude that an adult Jew may not desecrate Shabbat in order to help someone who is dangerously ill. Then, if faced with a similar situation sometime in the future, they might delay helping in order to look for a non-Jew or a child. In the meantime, the sick person might die (Ran).

Therefore, the Rishonim write that if many people are available to help the sick person, it is a mitzva for the most respected person present to do so, thus making it clear to everyone that saving a life overrides

---

before a *beit din*). This is also the opinion of Rashbatz. Others maintain that even if a non-Jew did not accept the Noahide laws before a *beit din*, if he observes these laws in practice, he is considered a *ger toshav* (Maharatz Chajes; R. Meir Dan Plotzky). This is also the opinion of R. Naḥum Rabinovitch in *Melumdei Milḥama*, p. 143. Many others maintain that we do not desecrate Shabbat for a *ger toshav*, and that this category does not even exist nowadays. However, according to all opinions, in practice we desecrate Shabbat to save the life of any person, as explained above. In a hospital that operates in accordance with *halakha*, it is preferable to have non-Jewish doctors and nurses on duty during Shabbat. If non-Jewish patients arrive, the non-Jewish medical staff can care for them. If a Jewish doctor has the most expertise on an illness afflicting a non-Jewish patient, and during the week such a case would normally be referred to him, the Jewish doctor treats the non-Jewish patient, even if this will involve performing *melakhot* that under normal circumstances are prohibited by Torah law.

Shabbat and that there is no need to seek ways to minimize the *melakha* (Ri'az; Tashbetz; MB 328:34).

If the situation is less pressured, and it is easy to find a non-Jew or a child to do the necessary *melakhot,* and doing so will not cause any delay, then even though *le-khatḥila* an adult Jew may do whatever *melakha* is necessary to save a life, it is a greater enhancement to minimize Shabbat desecration by having a non-Jew or a child perform the *melakhot* (SSK 38:2). However, if there is even the slightest, tiniest shadow of a doubt that using a non-Jew or a child will delay the provision of lifesaving treatment, either now or in the future, it is better for an adult Jew to do the *melakha.*[3]

5. USING A *SHINUI* TO MINIMIZE SHABBAT DESECRATION

When dealing with saving lives on Shabbat, a serious dilemma arises. On the one hand, it would seem to be preferable to use a *shinui* when

3. According to Rashba and Ran, Shabbat is superseded (*deḥuya*) by danger to life; in contrast, according to Maharam of Rothenburg, danger to life effectively suspends Shabbat and causes all *melakha* to become completely permitted (*hutra*). It would seem that according to those who feel that Shabbat is simply superseded, Shabbat desecration should be minimized whenever possible. Those *melakhot* that are necessary should be done using a *shinui* or by a non-Jew or minor. In contrast, according to those who maintain that Shabbat is suspended, everything may be done in the normal way and all is permitted *le-khatḥila*. In truth, there is little practical difference between these approaches, since even according to those who maintain that Shabbat is merely superseded, it is still preferable for a Jew to engage in lifesaving activity rather than a non-Jew (SAH 328:13), as stated in *Yoma* 84b. Rishonim there explain that if one asks a non-Jew to help, he might not act aggressively enough (*Tosafot*), or Jews who witness this might hesitate and not act aggressively enough in future cases (Ran). Therefore, even though Rema writes in 328:12 that it is preferable to use a non-Jew, a minor, or a *shinui*, almost all Aḥaronim follow SA's opinion that it is preferable for a Jew to be the one to desecrate Shabbat to save a life (*Taz; Eliya Rabba; Tosefet Shabbat;* MB *ad loc.* 37; SSK 32:6). Nevertheless, when there is no concern about hesitation, either in the present or in the future, it is preferable to minimize Shabbat desecration and ask a non-Jew to do the *melakha*. After all, when *Shabbat* 128b discusses the case of a woman in labor who is not in a state of panic, it states that one should use a *shinui* if possible, in order to minimize Shabbat desecration. SSK 38:2 states this as well. The order of preference is: a non-Jew, a minor, a Jew using a *shinui*, and two Jews working together.

doing whatever *melakhot* are necessary. After all, when a *melakha* is done in the normal way, one violates Torah law, while when it is done with a *shinui*, one transgresses only rabbinically (above 9:3). On the other hand, when it comes to saving a life on Shabbat, the Sages proclaimed that "One who acts quickly is to be praised" (*Yoma* 84b; SA 328:2). If so, it would seem preferable to refrain from placing constraints upon one who is attempting to save a life. Rather, he should act as he would on a weekday, as efforts such as minimizing Shabbat desecration or attempting to do the *melakhot* with a *shinui* are likely to slow him down. This is especially true if he thinks it is necessary to consult with a rabbi about how to act when a person's life is in danger.

In practice, the basic principle is that rescue efforts must be undertaken in the best and fastest way possible. If trying to do *melakhot* with a *shinui* is likely to delay treatment, it is preferable to do them in the normal fashion, without any *shinui*. This is because according to *halakha*, the rescuer may do *melakhot* in the normal way, since saving a life overrides Shabbat. Nevertheless, when it is clear that a *shinui* will not hamper the rescue in any way, it is preferable *le-khatḥila* to make use of a *shinui*. Therefore, it is advisable for doctors, nurses, and emergency medical workers to learn how to minimize Shabbat desecration while saving a person's life.

There is a similar dilemma regarding treatments normally administered to a gravely ill patient during the week, some of which are not necessary to prevent his death. Since the caregivers do not know which treatments are truly necessary and which are not, they must treat the patient just as they would treat him during the week. However, one who understands medicine and knows for certain that a specific *melakha* is not necessary to save the patient, or that the treatment can be postponed until after Shabbat, he should avoid doing the *melakha* on Shabbat (SA 328:4). Palliative treatments are administered on Shabbat even when it is clear that they do not treat the disease, because when the patient's pain is reduced, he will have more strength to overcome his illness.[4]

4. At first glance, according to those who maintain that Shabbat is suspended (*hutra*) by danger to life, all treatments normally administered to the patient are permitted, and there is no need to use a *shinui* or to minimize prohibitions. Indeed, this is implied in

6. TRAVELING TO THE HOSPITAL

When rushing a patient to the hospital, one drives normally, as he would during the week. He should not try to drive with a *shinui*, as this may cause delay or be dangerous. One may travel to the hospital in a private vehicle or call an ambulance. All items necessary for the patient or woman in labor – vital medications, medical documents, and proper identification – may be carried from the house to the car, even in an area without an *eruv*. Even items that are not vital to saving lives but are important to the patient or his chaperone – including changes of clothing, food, and books – may be taken to the hospital. If there is no *eruv*, such items should be carried with a *shinui*. In addition, the person carrying

---

SA 328:4: "We do everything for him [on Shabbat] that we do for him during the week." However, BHL, s.v. "kol" states that since the vast majority of Rishonim maintain that Shabbat is merely superseded (*deḥuya*) by danger to life, one should not do *melakhot* that are prohibited by Torah law unless they are necessary to save a life. Additionally, Rema writes in 328:12 that when possible, it is proper to employ a *shinui* when doing a *melakha*. Nevertheless, it seems that in practice there is almost no disagreement. Even according to MB, we must do anything that effectively minimizes the patient's pain or strengthens him, because this can indirectly affect his ability to heal (SSK 32:22, 57). On the other hand, when it is possible to do the *melakha* with a *shinui* without causing any delay or hesitation, it is preferable to do so, as in the case of a woman in labor (SA 330:1). This is also the opinion of *Ben Ish Ḥai*, Year 2, Tetzaveh 15. Indeed, although some maintain that a woman in labor is an exceptional case, and that for any other sick person one should not do anything differently from what would be done during the week (*Or Le-Tziyon* 2:36:2-3; *Halikhot Olam* vol. 4, Tetzaveh 1:4), it nevertheless seems, as I wrote in the main text, that when there is no concern that using a *shinui* will delay treatment, it is preferable to use a *shinui* and minimize Shabbat desecration. This can be seen in *Menaḥot* 64a and SA 328:16, which state (in the context of cutting figs for the needs of a gravely ill person) that one should minimize Shabbat desecration. At the same time, in order to make sure that people will not hesitate to take care of sick people, the basic instruction is that on Shabbat we do for the sick person "everything that we do for him during the week" (SA 328:4). Anyone who acts accordingly, even if he could have incorporated a *shinui*, has acted properly, as saving a life overrides Shabbat. In my humble opinion, it seems that all *poskim* would agree with this delineation. Even if those who maintain that Shabbat is suspended would say that it is unnecessary to use a *shinui*, one should *le-khatḥila* follow the majority opinion, that Shabbat is superseded, when possible (see *Harḥavot*). Hospital administrators should examine their Shabbat procedures, including the arrangements for operations, tests, changing sheets, and food preparation, in order to minimize transgressing as much as possible without harming the standard of care. It is also proper to use non-Jews for Shabbat shifts whenever possible.

them should walk directly from the house to the car without stopping, so that the act of carrying will qualify as a *shvut di-shvut*, which is permitted in a case of great necessity. *Muktzeh* items may not be brought, but if they were packed in the hospital bag together with necessary items, one may bring the bag. *Muktzeh* items that will be greatly needed after Shabbat – such as money and a cellphone – may be placed in the bag on Shabbat using a *shinui* and brought to the hospital along with the bag.[5]

After arriving at the hospital and parking in a place that does not interfere with the arrival of other vehicles, it is, at first glance, forbidden to turn off the car. After all, thus far all travel was for the patient's sake; in contrast, one turns off the car for the sake of the car itself – to lock it and to make sure that the batteries do not die. Therefore, when possible, one should ask a non-Jew to turn off the car's motor and headlights and then to lock the car.

If no non-Jew is available, or if searching for one is likely to delay attending to the patient, one may turn off the car and headlights with a *shinui*, so that the prohibition is only rabbinic. For example, he may grasp the key or press the button that operates the headlights with the back of his fingers. He should also lock the car with a *shinui*, for example, by pushing the remote control with the back of his fingers. Then, even though the headlights will go on as a result, it will have been done with a *shinui*. The reason all this is permitted is that the Sages allowed one to take such steps at the end of a rescue effort to ensure that people are willing to do what needs to be done at the beginning. After all, if a driver knows that

---

5. Many maintain that one may carry vital items if one simply walks from the house to the car without stopping (as our streets are considered a *karmelit* according to many, and if he walks without stopping there is no Torah prohibition according to most *poskim*; see 21 n. 3). Under pressing circumstances, if one cannot figure out how to incorporate a *shinui*, one may rely upon these authorities. However, *le-khatḥila* it is proper to carry items with a *shinui*, thus meeting the requirements of all the *poskim*.

Many *halakha* books have lengthy discussions about how to drive with a *shinui*. However, concerning oneself with this is likely to make it more difficult to save lives, and sometimes could even endanger the driver and passenger. Therefore, the rule is that one should drive without a *shinui*. Only one who knows how to incorporate a *shinui* without endangering anyone's life should do so. *Nishmat Avraham* (278:4, n. 37) presents this approach in the name of R. Shlomo Zalman Auerbach. Regarding *muktzeh* items, see *Harḥavot*. A soldier who is called up on Shabbat may take his *tefilin* with him, because under pressing circumstances we rely on those who maintain that *tefilin* are not *muktzeh* (above, 23:8).

he will not be able to turn off and lock his car upon arrival at the hospital, the next time he might avoid taking the patient to the hospital altogether. Therefore, the Sages permitted transgressing any rabbinic prohibitions to make it easier for those individuals helping to save lives.[6]

7. CHOOSING A HOSPITAL AND DOCTOR

When one must drive a gravely ill person or a woman in labor to the hospital, he should drive to the nearest hospital, in order to avoid additional Shabbat desecration. Even if there are better hospitals available, for routine matters, like births and treatment of injuries and common diseases, there is no significant difference between hospitals, so one drives to the closest one. Even if the patient or woman in labor prefers a more distant hospital because it is cheaper, has nicer rooms, or is more conveniently located for relatives who will wish to visit, since these are not medical considerations, one may not drive farther on Shabbat for any of these reasons. Similarly, if a woman is away from home for Shabbat and goes into labor, she should go to a local hospital.

When a case is more complicated and there is a medical reason to prefer a more distant hospital, one may drive there on Shabbat. For example, if the more distant hospital specializes in the treatment of the patient's illness, or if the illness is complex, and the more distant hospital is already familiar with the patient and will therefore be able to provide the appropriate treatment more quickly, one may drive the patient there. So too, if a woman's pregnancy is considered high-risk, and the distant hospital has a protocol in place for her needs, one may drive her there on Shabbat. Everything should be done in accordance with accepted medical recommendations. The more complicated and difficult the case,

---

6. See SSK 40:72, nn. 146, 153; *Nishmat Avraham* 278:4, nn. 24, 28; *Yalkut Yosef* 330:8. Whenever a *shinui* is used to turn off a car, it is a *shvut di-shvut*, and is permitted in order to prevent loss (above, 9:11). However, when one uses a *shinui* and the headlights are turned on, there is only one *shvut* involved. Nevertheless, it is permitted because the Sages allowed desecrating Shabbat at the end of a rescue effort in order to ensure that there is no hesitation at the beginning. Perhaps there is another possible reason for leniency: the act of locking the car, which causes the headlights to turn on, might be merely rabbinic, as it is a *psik reisha de-lo niḥa lei* (since one is not interested in activating the headlights).

the farther one may travel to ensure the best care. Thus, if there is only a slight medical advantage, one may travel only slightly farther to gain that advantage. After all, during the week, sick people and women in labor are not advised to travel long distances to the best hospitals for every minor medical issue. So too on Shabbat, they may not travel farther to reach the best hospitals, since accepted medical recommendations do not demand it.

If a woman in labor claims that she will receive better medical care at a more distant hospital, even if her claim has no realistic basis, one may drive a bit farther in order to ease her mind, but not a lot farther. Even when one may extend the drive for a medical reason, it must remain within reason.

In general, it is preferable to go to a hospital that operates in accordance with *halakha*. On Shabbat, one may travel slightly farther in order to reach such a hospital. This way there will be less Shabbat desecration in the hospital, and the patient will feel more comfortable. However, one should not travel much farther for this purpose.[7]

---

7. If the more distant hospital has a medical approach that is more compatible with the patient's or pregnant woman's outlook (for example, a preference for natural childbirth over Caesarean sections), one may travel farther to get there. However, since this is not a clear advantage, and in most cases this difference in outlook does not come into play, one should not travel much farther to reach the preferred hospital for this reason.

According to R. Eliezer Waldenberg, if there is no medical reason to prefer a more distant doctor, but the patient believes that the distant doctor is better, one must listen to the patient and call the preferred doctor, even when it involves additional Shabbat desecration (*Tzitz Eliezer* 13:55-56). As the Yerushalmi states: "A person does not merit to be healed by just anyone" (*y. Nedarim* 4:2). He also infers this from AZ 55a, which speaks of suffering resulting from the treatment of a particular doctor. Therefore, one must listen to a patient who demands a specific doctor. SSK 32:38 states similarly, as does R. Yitzḥak Zilberstein (*Torat Ha-yoledet* 7:2), who adds that if a woman in labor feels that the standard of medical care is better in the more distant hospital, one may travel there. He cites R. Scheinberg (n. 4) as saying that under normal circumstances, one should rely on the nearest hospital since we do not allow additional Shabbat desecration in order to put the patient's mind at rest unless it is a situation where the Sages tell us that if we do not ease his mind, he will be in danger.

In my opinion, if there is no substantive medical reason to prefer the more distant hospital, but nevertheless the patient feels that the distant hospital is medically superior, one may travel a little farther, but not much farther. The reason for this is that for a dangerously sick person, we do everything on Shabbat that we would do during the week (Rambam; SA 328:3). However, going beyond this is overly indulgent. During the

8. ACCOMPANYING A SICK PERSON OR WOMAN IN LABOR TO THE HOSPITAL

A patient who is rushed to the hospital generally needs a chaperone, to offer support and to ensure that he is given proper care by the medical staff. Unfortunately, due to heavy volume of patients at a hospital, patients who are alone are sometimes overlooked. Therefore, if a family finds out that a relative has been hospitalized with a serious injury or illness and is alone in the hospital, one of the family members must travel there, even on Shabbat.

---

week, medical opinion is that it is proper to travel a little farther to ease the mind of a gravely ill person or a woman in labor, but that there is no need to travel much farther. A possible support for this position appears in another area of Shabbat law: during the course of a circumcision, one may cut away bits of skin that do not invalidate the circumcision, even though cutting them off on Shabbat would otherwise be prohibited by Torah law (*Shabbat* 133b; SA 331:2). This is because once circumcision overrides Shabbat, everything that is part of the circumcision process overrides it as well (Rashi). Thus, arguably, once one may travel on Shabbat, one may extend the trip a little to get to the hospital that the patient thinks is medically superior. However, to extend the trip greatly would mean that the patient would no longer view the extra travel as an addition to the basic trip but rather a separate trip – which may be undertaken only if it may save a life. In contrast, if the patient concedes that the more distant hospital is not medically superior, but he just has a better feeling about it, the trip should not be extended at all. See *Torat Ha-yoledet* ch. 7, end of n. 4. We should add that in the case of a complex illness, there can sometimes be a medical advantage if the patient is personally acquainted with a member of the medical staff.

R. Zilberstein points out that one should not increase travel time in order to reach a hospital just because it has higher *kashrut* standards. However, if the more distant hospital will make a point of minimizing Shabbat desecration, it may be that it is preferable to travel to it, because of the principle (*Menaḥot* 63b, 72a) that it is better to transgress one *melakha* many times than several *melakhot* a few times each (*Torat Ha-yoledet* 7:3-4). We should add that it also may be that the sick person has more confidence in the medical staff at the religious hospital, in which case one may travel a little farther to reach it.

If a woman in labor tells an ambulance driver that she prefers the more distant hospital because she feels that it is medically superior, but the real reason for her preference is so that her family will be able to visit her, the resulting Shabbat desecration is her responsibility, since the driver has no way to know that she is lying. From his perspective, this may be a case of saving a life, on account of which one desecrates Shabbat.

Similarly, a woman in labor must be accompanied to the hospital. Even if she does not request, someone – her husband, mother, or doula – should travel with her. If the woman in labor or the patient arrives at the hospital without a chaperone, it is permitted to call someone to travel to the hospital. Even though caring for a woman in labor is straightforward and familiar, there is still a concern that she will panic and endanger herself. Therefore, one may desecrate Shabbat on her behalf and do whatever he may do for a dangerously sick person (SA 330:1; MB *ad loc.* 3; BHL s.v. "u-madlikin").

Recently, some women request the presence of both their husbands and their mothers at the hospital. Some also ask their doulas to attend. Since this is not a lifesaving medical necessity, only one chaperone may travel along – her husband, her mother, or her doula. Only in an unusual circumstance, such as when a woman becomes hysterical and insists that both her husband and her mother must accompany her, may they both do so. Similarly, if she experiences anxiety and demands that they call her doula, the doula may be called. Nevertheless, one may not plan for more than one person to accompany her on Shabbat.

Others disagree and maintain that one should do whatever the woman in labor wants, even if she is not hysterical. If she wants her husband, mother, and doula to come with her, they all travel along, to put her mind at ease. According to this approach, one may even make a detour in order to pick them up or call them to request that they make their own way to the hospital. However, this would seem to be excessive, and it does not legitimate driving on Shabbat. The widespread custom is that one person accompanies a woman in labor. However, if the drive is long and the husband is driving, the mother or doula may come along as well, since sometimes another person is needed to help the woman during the drive.

If the woman in labor has small children at home, one must prearrange for neighbors to care for the children in the event that the parents must travel on Shabbat. However, if they live in a remote location, or if the neighbors are bad or untrustworthy people, with whom it is dangerous to leave children, and leaving the children home alone would also be dangerous, the children may travel with the parents to the hospital. One may also make a slight detour in order to drop them off with a family that can take care of them.[8]

9. DRIVING HOME ON SHABBAT

If the patient is released after it is determined that he is not in danger, he and his chaperones may not desecrate Shabbat to return home. If necessary – for example, if the patient needs rest – he may be transported home by a non-Jewish driver. However, the chaperone may not ride along unless the patient needs help en route (see below, 28:2).

Similarly, if a woman is rushed to the hospital to give birth and then released after an examination reveals that she is not yet ready to

8. One may violate Torah prohibitions in order to accompany a sick person or a woman in labor, just as one may light a fire for a woman in labor even when it is not truly necessary (SA 330:1; MB *ad loc.* 3; BHL s.v. "u-madlikin"). This is even more relevant today, when the generally accepted wisdom is that the patient needs someone to accompany him in the hospital in order to ensure that he receives proper care (*Nishmat Avraham*, OḤ 278:4 with n. 29, and 330:6 citing R. Yehoshua Neuwirth; R. Yoel Katan in *Assia* 9). If a non-Jew is available to drive the children to family or friends, one may ask him to do so, even if the neighbors can watch the children in a pinch. If it is not necessary to take a detour or make an extra trip to pick up the mother or the doula, then even if the woman in labor is not completely hysterical, if she demands that they travel with her even on Shabbat, they may be picked up in a pinch. However, one may not plan for them to travel with her, because in fact there is no need for more than one person to escort her.

A woman in labor who wants to rely on the lenient opinion and have two people accompany her must be honest with herself regarding how much she truly needs the extra person. She should imagine that, for example, she went into labor on a Shabbat that her mother or doula happened to be hosting large numbers of guests for a son's *aufruf*, when traveling to the hospital would mean deserting her guests until after Shabbat and missing her son being called up to the Torah. If, under such circumstances, the woman in labor would still demand that her mother or doula accompany her in addition to her husband, and they would still agree to go, this indicates that they really do consider their role in her childbirth potentially lifesaving, and they may accompany her according to the lenient opinion. However, if under such circumstances the woman in labor would forgo their presence, it indicates that she does not consider their role to be life-saving. Accordingly, even on a regular Shabbat, she should suffice with one chaperone. The ambulance driver does not count as a chaperone, as he will not stay in the hospital with the patient or woman in labor (see *Igrot Moshe*, OḤ 1:132; *Or Le-Tziyon* 2:36:23; BHL 330:1, s.v. "u-madlikin"; *Yalkut Yosef* 330:9). It is proper not to rely on the lenient opinion at all, because adding another chaperone has no lifesaving value; the merit of keeping Shabbat is more effective.

give birth, she may not desecrate Shabbat to return home. In a time of need, if she is still considered sick – for example, if she needs to lie down – she may be driven home by a non-Jew, but her chaperone may not ride along.

A Jewish ambulance driver from an outlying community, which needs an ambulance for emergencies, may return to his community after transporting a patient to the hospital. However, he may not drive home the patient or his chaperone, as transporting them entails transgressing Torah prohibitions, since their added weight causes the engine to burn more fuel. Even if the prohibition were merely rabbinic, it would still be forbidden for them to ride home with a Jewish driver.[9]

If a Jewish ambulance driver in a city drives to treat a patient, he may not drive back to the EMT station afterwards on Shabbat. Since ambulances contain two-way radios, the driver can be contacted at his present location if he is needed for another emergency. However, if there is a real need to drive back – for example, if he expects that he will need an additional medic or more medical equipment for his next trip, or if resting at the station will enable him to treat people more effectively later – he may return to the station.

If an ambulance was summoned to treat someone in grave danger, but before the ambulance arrives another way to rush him to the hospital was found, someone must call and cancel the request for an

9. As explained in the next section and in n. 12, the Sages' permissive ruling that "the end is permitted because of the beginning" applies primarily to doctors, nurses, and emergency medical volunteers, who often need to travel on Shabbat. If we would not make it easy for them to return home, there is a real concern that in the future they will avoid setting out in the first place. In contrast, the Sages were not lenient for the patients themselves and their chaperones because there is no concern that they will hesitate to come in the future. After all, a person will always be concerned about his own health. Moreover, the incidents are infrequent and would not regularly disrupt the patient's Shabbat rest. However, in a time of need a patient may return home with a non-Jewish driver because one may instruct a non-Jew to perform *melakhot* that are prohibited by Torah law on behalf of a sick person, even if there is no danger to life (SA 328:17; MB *ad loc.* 47; below, 28:2). However, there are no grounds for leniency for a chaperone, as his added weight would cause the engine to burn more fuel (*Nishmat Avraham* 278:4 and n. 47; 330:9). But if the patient requires a chaperone on the trip back, the chaperone may travel with the patient and the non-Jewish driver.

ambulance, as it may be needed for a patient elsewhere while it continues to a destination where it is no longer needed. Additionally, there is a concern that medical personnel will not take things seriously when they are alerted on Shabbat in the future, thinking that their help might no longer be necessary but that no one has notified them because they do not want to make a phone call on Shabbat.

If a Jewish driver is transporting a woman in labor to the hospital, and during the drive she says that her contractions have stopped (to the point that, if she were at home, she would not consider going to the hospital), he may not continue driving. He must stop and park in a safe place until Shabbat is over (R. Shlomo Zalman Auerbach). If the ambulance must be returned to the station for reasons of *piku'aḥ nefesh*, the driver returns to the station, and the woman and her chaperone may remain in the ambulance and return with him.

A Jewish doctor who is summoned to treat a gravely ill patient may drive to the patient without ascertaining the details, since even the possibility of saving a life overrides Shabbat. Nevertheless, it is preferable that he call to clarify the patient's state, since it is possible that the clarification will lead the doctor to decide that the trip is unnecessary, and it is preferable to minimize the Shabbat desecration. Even when it is clear that the patient is gravely ill and requires the doctor, the phone conversation is still useful. First, it is possible that the doctor will be able to give specific instructions for how to care for the patient until he arrives. Additionally, it may become clear to the doctor that he needs to bring additional equipment with him.[10]

---

10. The Talmud states in *Eruvin* 32b that it is preferable for a learned person to transgress a minor prohibition in order to save an unlearned person from unknowingly transgressing a severe prohibition. This is the ruling of SA 306:14 and MB *ad loc.* 56, which state that one should desecrate Shabbat to save a Jew from apostasy. Based on this, when an ambulance was summoned but an alternative arrangement was made after the request was issued, one should call and cancel the request. Compared to driving on Shabbat, which involves multiple violations of *Mav'ir*, making a phone call is a less severe transgression. However, R. Shlomo Zalman Auerbach opposes this approach, presenting a strong argument: there is no transgression involved in traveling to save lives, so calling to cancel does not minimize Shabbat desecration (cited in *Ha-tzava Ka-halakha* 32:1, n. 3). *Torat Ha-yoledet* ch. 21 n. 2 makes the same point in the name of R. Yosef Shalom Elyashiv. Nevertheless, R. Chaim Pinchas Scheinberg comments there that even those who are undertaking

10. DOCTORS AND NURSES DRIVING TO WORK AND BACK HOME ON SHABBAT

If a doctor has a shift on Shabbat morning and lives too far away from the hospital to reach it on foot, he must drive to the hospital before Shabbat so he will not have to desecrate Shabbat. *Be-di'avad,* if he did not drive to the hospital beforehand, he may drive there on Shabbat, since saving a life overrides Shabbat. Nevertheless, if he knows before Shabbat that he will have a shift on Shabbat, he must arrange to spend Shabbat in the hospital or nearby (*Igrot Moshe,* OḤ 1:131).

The best solution for doctors and nurses in such a situation is to hire a non-Jewish driver to drive them from their homes to the hospital. This way, these doctors and nurses can enjoy Shabbat in their homes, and then when they need to go to the hospital, they can get there with the help of a non-Jew. Even though the Sages prohibited benefiting from *melakha* performed by a non-Jew on Shabbat (above, 25:1), they permitted this for the sake of a sick person.[11]

---

lifesaving work should minimize Shabbat desecration, as MB states in 328:35. It would seem, though, that someone must cancel the request for an ambulance for a different reason: to potentially save another life. There may be someone elsewhere who is gravely ill, and the ambulance will not be available to help him if it is making this unnecessary trip. In addition, a false alarm is likely to cause the emergency medical workers to hesitate in the future, especially if they know that on Shabbat people will not call to cancel the request for a doctor or an ambulance.

If a Jewish ambulance driver is in the process of driving a woman in labor to the hospital and her contractions stop, he may not continue traveling (R. Shlomo Zalman Auerbach, *Minḥat Shlomo* 1:91:21; *Nishmat Avraham* 330:25 and n. 7). However, if he is from an outlying community and must return there with the ambulance, he need not stop to drop off the passengers before he returns to the station. Doing so would require additional violations of *Mav'ir* with respect to the lights and the engine. Since the passengers are already in the vehicle, they may return with him.

11. In a place where using a non-Jewish driver is not possible, R. Shlomo Zalman Auerbach says (in opposition to *Igrot Moshe*) that a doctor may stay at home until he needs to go to the hospital for his shift. When the time comes for him to leave, since it is for a lifesaving endeavor, he may drive to the hospital. Even though it is true as a rule that one should prepare before Shabbat to obviate the need for Shabbat desecration, there is no need to take the very difficult step of spending all of Shabbat away from home, thus harming both his *oneg Shabbat* and his family time. However, R. Shlomo Zalman Auerbach emphasizes that one should be lenient in this case only if the hospital administration makes serious efforts to prevent unnecessary Shabbat desecration.

Doctors and nurses who finish their shifts on Shabbat morning may return home with the help of a non-Jewish driver. The Sages ruled that those involved with saving lives on Shabbat may transgress rabbinic prohibitions in order to return home, so that they will not be tempted in the future to refuse to go in the first place. If they are forced to stay in the hospital until after Shabbat, it will be very upsetting for them and their families, and we are concerned that as a result they will quit their jobs or avoid working shifts on Shabbat.[12]

Therefore, in his opinion, one should not in fact be lenient in this situation nowadays, as it is possible to arrange for a non-Jewish driver. With a non-Jewish driver, one may also be lenient and travel farther than twelve *mil*, which some say is the *teḥum* by Torah law (SSK ch. 32 n. 106; ch. 40 n. 71; see the end of the next note).

12. The Mishna in *Eruvin* 44b states that those who set out on a rescue mission outside of the *teḥum* may travel 2,000 *amot* in any direction, the same as anyone else at their destination. *Tosafot* (s.v. "kol") comment that this is an example of the rationale of "the end is permitted because of the beginning," where certain actions at the end of an undertaking are permitted in order to ensure that people will be willing to do what needs to be done at the beginning. For instance, if we do not allow the rescuers 2,000 *amot* of movement, they will hesitate to undertake the rescue mission in the first place. Similarly in RH 23b, the Talmud states that a midwife who traveled beyond the *teḥum* on Shabbat may then travel 2,000 *amot* as well. This is the ruling of SA 329:9 and §407. See below, 30:11. Most *poskim* limit this rationale to rabbinic transgressions (MA 497:18; *Tzitz Eliezer* 11:39), and they do not always permit these either (*Har Tzvi*, OḤ 2:10; *Minḥat Shlomo* 1:8). However, *Minḥat Shlomo, Mahadura Tinyana* 60:11 permits returning with the help of a non-Jewish driver if it is within twelve *mil*. Some maintain that when necessary, this principle overrides even Torah prohibitions, to ensure that people will not hesitate before setting out on future lifesaving trips (see *Ḥatam Sofer*, OḤ 203; *Igrot Moshe*, OḤ 4:80; *Amud Ha-yemini* §17). See *Ha-tzava Ka-halakha* 24 n. 18; *Orḥot Shabbat* 20:59-61 and Essay 5 at the end of the work; SSK 40:81, 83; *Nishmat Avraham* 278:4 and n. 47.

In practice, since it is possible to arrange for a non-Jewish driver to take doctors and nurses back to their homes, under no circumstances should one be lenient and drive home on Shabbat with a Jewish driver. If no non-Jewish driver is available, there is no concern that in the future they will hesitate to go to the hospital in the first place because of this one instance. With a non-Jewish driver, one may be lenient and drive even beyond twelve *mil*, since according to most Rishonim even this distance is only a rabbinic prohibition (Rosh and Rashba; see below 30:1). In addition, when people are inside a vehicle, the road is a *karmelit* and the Jewish passenger is not actively doing anything, so there is a strong case to say that even those who are stringent regarding twelve *mil* would not maintain that any Torah prohibition is involved (see *Assia* 7, pp. 241-249).

11. SCHEDULING SURGERIES AND CIRCUMCISIONS ON THE DAYS PRECEDING SHABBAT

Sometimes, one may need to schedule a surgical procedure that will then require follow-up care involving the performance of various *melakhot*. Similarly, some procedures, such as the extraction of a wisdom tooth, cause pain for several days, which may impair one's ability to enjoy Shabbat. If the surgery is not urgent, it is proper *le-khatḥila* to schedule it for the first three days of the week. However, if the best surgeon is only available during the second half of the week, the operation may be scheduled for then, even if it is possible to get an appointment at the beginning of the week with a less expert surgeon (see above, 2:10-11).

If a woman is due to give birth and her doctors decide that labor should be induced, it may be done on Friday, even though it is reasonable to assume that this will cause her to give birth on Shabbat (SSK 32:33 and the notes).

If an operation is urgent, it should not be postponed, even if it is possible to postpone it until the beginning of the week. This is because sometimes problems arise, and the surgery may be delayed beyond the time that is medically desirable.

If a baby boy was sick and his circumcision was delayed, *poskim* disagree whether the circumcision may be held on a Thursday or Friday. Some argue that since it has already been postponed beyond the Torah-mandated eighth day, the baby should not be circumcised on Thursday or Friday, because in the days following the circumcision he might require care that would involve Shabbat desecration. This is the custom in many Sephardic communities (*Tashbetz* 1:21; *Rav Pe'alim*, YD 4:28; *Yabi'a Omer*, YD 5:23). Others maintain that the likelihood of needing to desecrate Shabbat following the circumcision is not high, and since there is a mitzva to perform the circumcision as soon as possible, one should do so even on Thursday or Friday (*Shakh*, YD 266:18; MA 331:9). This is the widespread custom among Ashkenazic and Yemenite Jews, as well as some Sephardim.

12. FIGHTING WARS ON SHABBAT

It is a mitzva to wage a defensive war against Israel's enemies. This mitzva is even greater than the mitzva of saving human life, as one is not required to risk his own life in order to save the life of another, or even multiple lives. In contrast, it is a mitzva – incumbent upon every individual – to risk one's life to save the Jewish people from their enemies (*Mishpat Kohen* §143; *Tzitz Eliezer* 13:100; see *Peninei Halakha: Collected Essays* II 11:3).

Therefore, if enemies attack Israel, it is a mitzva to wage war against them even if this will endanger lives and require Shabbat desecration. Indeed, Rambam rules: "There is a mitzva incumbent upon all capable Jews to come to the aid of their brothers who are under siege, and to save them from non-Jews on Shabbat; they may not delay until after Shabbat..." (MT 2:23). Similarly, if it is known that enemies or terrorists are planning to attack Jews, it is a mitzva to attack them in order to deter them. If there is a strategic objective served by attacking them on Shabbat, we attack on Shabbat (*Heikhal Yitzḥak*, OḤ 37:3; *Amud Ha-yemini* §16; see Rema 329:6).

Furthermore, it is also a mitzva to wage war to prevent future danger, even though doing so will put lives at risk and require Shabbat desecration. This is in accordance with the statement of the Sages that if enemies come to pillage border towns, even if they are taking only straw and hay, "we attack them with weapons and desecrate Shabbat on their account" (*Eruvin* 45a). We do this because if our enemies know that they can steal without repercussions, they will ultimately end up attacking people. This is also the ruling of *Shulḥan Arukh* (329:6). Accordingly, it is a mitzva to perform ongoing security operations on Shabbat, to protect our borders from our enemies. Nowadays, the entire country of Israel has the status of border towns with respect to preventing terror attacks (R. Shlomo Goren). Therefore, throughout Israel, it is a mitzva to perform ongoing security operations on Shabbat, to protect life and property.

If Jews who do not observe Shabbat go on a hike on Shabbat in an area where it is necessary to travel with an armed escort, and there is no way to prevent them from hiking in the first place, it is a mitzva for soldiers to protect them, even if this entails Shabbat desecration. Even though it is the hikers' Shabbat desecration that creates the need for security, nevertheless, since they are in fact in a dangerous place, they must be protected from the enemy (R. Goren, *Meshiv Milḥama* 1:7 and 2:110; see *Ha-tzava Ka-halakha* ch. 21). However, soldiers may not help them desecrate Shabbat. Thus, soldiers may not open checkpoints for them so that they can pass through, give them travel permits, or board their bus to enable them to set out. Only after the group is already underway may soldiers provide security for them.

Bodies of fallen soldiers may be retrieved from the battlefield on Shabbat to ensure that they do not fall into enemy hands. Even though technically one may not desecrate Shabbat in order to save corpses, since abandoning bodies harms the morale of soldiers, and since Israeli society is willing to free terrorists in order to retrieve bodies captured by the enemy, retrieving them from the battlefield prevents danger to life. After the bodies are recovered, one may not desecrate Shabbat any further to care for the bodies (*Meshiv Milḥama* vol. 1, p. 61 and 2:117; *Ha-tzava Ka-halakha* ch. 20).

The war to conquer the Eretz Yisrael is considered a *milḥemet mitzva* (obligatory war). Accordingly, when there is a tactical advantage, one may initiate an attack even on Shabbat, as our ancestors did in the days of Yehoshua when they conquered Yeriḥo on Shabbat (*y. Shabbat* 1:8; *Tur*, OḤ 249:1).[13]

---

13. A *milḥemet reshut* (discretionary war) should not be started on Shabbat, nor on the last three days of the week. However, if a war continues until Shabbat, even if it seems as if it will not hurt the war effort to stop fighting on Shabbat, we do not stop. As the Torah states: "You may cut [trees] down for constructing siege works against the city that is waging war on you, until it has been reduced" (Devarim 20:20). The Sages tell us: "We do not begin a siege against a non-Jewish town in the last three days of the week; but if it was begun, we do not stop. Shammai used to say that 'until it has been reduced' means even on Shabbat." A *milḥemet reshut* is a war that is meant to extend the boundaries of Israel and increase its power. Such a war is undertaken only by a Jewish king and with the consent of the *Sanhedrin* (MT, Laws of Kings 5:1-2). It should be noted that in the past, when all monarchies would launch discretionary wars, the monarchy of Israel had to initiate such wars as well, in order to solidify its position. Had it not done so, it would have endangered its long-term survival.

In contrast, a war undertaken to conquer Eretz Yisrael is a *milḥemet mitzva*, as Ramban writes (*Hasagot Le-sefer Ha-mitzvot, Hosafot Le-mitzvot Aseh* 4). A great many authorities agree with him (see *Li-netivot Yisrael* vol. 1 ch. 23: "Le-mitzvot Ha-aretz"). At first glance, it seems Rambam believes that conquering Eretz Yisrael is not included in the definition of *milḥemet mitzva*. However, he too concedes that if an enemy attacks, it is a mitzva to mount a defensive war, both because of the mitzva to settle the land (*Devar Yehoshua*, OḤ 2:48), and because of the danger to life (*Melumdei Milḥama* §1). See *Ha-tzava Ka-halakha*, pp. 7-10.

In *Meshiv Milḥama* 1:2, R. Goren analyzes the Gemara's dictum, "'until it has been reduced' means even on Shabbat." He extrapolates that permission to violate

13. A COMMANDING OFFICER'S AUTHORITY DURING WARTIME AND NORMAL TIMES

During a war, one must do everything possible for the sake of victory, on Shabbat as well. One may not delay matters by referring questions to rabbis, nor should he bother commanding officers by asking them what is or is not necessary. Rather, anything required must be done as quickly as possible.

In contrast, in normal times, when routine and ongoing security operations and intelligence-gathering are being carried out, Shabbat desecration should be minimized. Only activities meant to prevent life-threatening situations should be undertaken. When possible, it is preferable to use a *shinui* or another method that renders these actions prohibited on the rabbinic level only. To that end, the military rabbinate of the Israel Defense Forces (IDF) must establish special Shabbat procedures that enable each soldier to carry out his security operations while minimizing Shabbat desecration. Normally, one may not conduct training exercises on Shabbat. Only when forces are on high alert and there is a security need may soldiers be trained for an upcoming operation in which they will participate.[14]

Shabbat for war is even more sweeping than permission to violate Shabbat to save a life. Specifically, a *milḥemet mitzva* completely suspends (*hutra*) Shabbat, whereas saving a life only supersedes (*doḥeh*) Shabbat. When Rambam limits starting a siege to the beginning of the week, he is referring to local battles, but an all-out war has no Shabbat limitations. It is as if Shabbat has been canceled entirely. However, many view the legitimacy of fighting on Shabbat as an expanded form of saving a life, since the soldiers are engaged in saving many lives. Others, based on MT 30:13, maintain that even for a *milḥemet mitzva*, we do not begin a siege at the end of the week. This is the opinion of Radbaz 4:77. *Tur*, OḤ 249, states that it is a *milḥemet reshut* that we do not start in the days preceding Shabbat, but we may start a *milḥemet mitzva* even on Shabbat itself. The entire disagreement is limited to a case in which there is no tactical advantage to beginning the war on Shabbat; but if starting the war on Shabbat is likely to save lives, then all agree that we may start the war on Shabbat. See *Ha-tzava Ka-halakha* 25:13, pp. 250-251.

14. See the previous note. In an all-out war, R. Goren maintains that Shabbat is suspended. Even according to those who disagree and argue that Shabbat is only superseded, we must avoid doing anything that might prolong the war. As we saw above in sections 4-5, a *shinui* should not be used if it may delay victory, either now or in the future. In contrast, in normal times, when one can wait patiently to undertake an activity, he

When things function properly, one may rely on a commanding officer's familiarity with both security needs and *halakha*, in accordance with the directives of the military rabbinate. Then, if he gives an order that entails Shabbat desecration, the implication is that it is necessary for security needs and must be obeyed. However, when there is reason to distrust the officer – whether because he does not take the rabbinate's directives seriously, because the rabbinate is not fulfilling its responsibilities, or because the order is illogical – the soldier must clarify with his commanding officer whether the action requested is necessary for security. If, despite what the officer says, it is clear to the soldier that the order involves Shabbat desecration that is not necessary to maintain security, he may not obey the order, as one may not desecrate Shabbat except to save a life. If the soldier is uncertain, he must follow the order, because even the possibility of saving a life overrides Shabbat. However, after Shabbat he must clarify with the army rabbinate, and if necessary with his own rabbis, whether the order was legitimate or not. If it was not, he must file a complaint against his commanding officer and object to his actions, using all avenues available to him.

The primary way to determine if the purpose of an army operation is connected to *piku'aḥ nefesh* is to see how the army actually relates to the operation. If all week long it is taken seriously and viewed as indispensable to security, and it is carried out even if it involves missing rest time or canceling an entertainment program, then it may be done on Shabbat. However, if all week long it is not taken seriously, and the operation is sometimes canceled for the sake of convenience, then there is no license to desecrate Shabbat in order to do it.[15]

---

should minimize Shabbat desecration as much as possible. For example, one should begin with the least severe prohibition, similar to how a sick person should eat on Yom Kippur (SA 619:7-8). Rema YD 155:3 and *Bi'ur Ha-Gra ad loc.* 24 extend this principle to medical treatments in general. See above in 18:2, where we discuss when writing is necessary on Shabbat and how to minimize the prohibitions involved. See also *Ha-tzava Ka-halakha* 16:26 with n. 51, and 17:8.

15. It is difficult to define what level of danger justifies desecration of Shabbat, since there are endless dangers. Even routine life is full of danger – on the roads, while going for a walk, and even while climbing a ladder at home. Even the flu can become life-threatening on rare occasions. Nevertheless, we do not hospitalize everyone who contracts the flu. The rule is that if something is generally considered dangerous,

14. COMMON ARMY QUESTIONS

Soldiers who are patrolling in a vehicle on Shabbat may not deviate from the established route in order to eat in a more convenient outpost or to meet up with friends, because driving is permitted to them only for the sake of security. However, if there is no specific patrol route, the soldiers may plan the route to suit their convenience. If they have a half-hour break to eat and rest, they may plan for that break to be at a place of their convenience. If they are expected to patrol inside settlements to make the army presence felt and to deter terrorists, they may park near a synagogue or somewhere convenient for eating.[16]

Soldiers who know that they will be commencing a military operation on Shabbat must spend Shabbat on their base, since if they travel home before Shabbat, they would have to desecrate Shabbat to return to the base (see MB 344:11). Even if the commanding officer is married and will greatly upset his family members by remaining on base, if the operation will definitely take place on Shabbat, he may not go home, since that would force him to travel back on Shabbat. However, if there is a chance that the operation will be canceled, he may go home for Shabbat. As long as it is not certain that the operation will be executed on Shabbat, he may try to preserve his and his family's *oneg Shabbat*. The officer should be sure to explain to his family that since it

---

and people take serious, directed action to avoid it, it is considered a danger for which one desecrates Shabbat. This is the position of R. Isser Yehuda Unterman in *Shevet Mi-Yehuda* 1:19:2, as quoted in SSK ch. 32 n. 2. R. Shlomo Zalman Auerbach and R. Eliezer Waldenberg (*Tzitz Eliezer* 9:17:8:22) agree with this position. Thus we can generally establish the *halakha* based on how people relate to the danger all week. See *Ha-tzava Ka-halakha* 16:8, 13, 14, 16-19.

16. The Talmud states in *Yoma* 84b that one may engage in actions that are aimed at saving lives even when the actions serve a secondary purpose as well. For example, one may use a net to retrieve a child who fell into a river, even if some fish will be caught as well. Similarly, one may build steps to rescue a child from a pit, even if these steps will be useful later on as well. This is the ruling of SA 328:13. All this is on condition that no additional *melakha* is done to achieve the secondary purpose. Rishonim disagree about whether one may intend to achieve the secondary purpose; this is discussed in SHT *ad loc.* 17. However, in the case of patrolling soldiers, even if they intend to eat at a convenient place, it would seem that all would permit this. After all, there is a slight tactical advantage in doing so, as they will be more refreshed as a result. See *Ha-tzava Ka-halakha* 17:6, pp. 172-3.

is uncertain whether or not he will be called, he may remain at home. This way they will not belittle Shabbat observance. If he finds out on Shabbat that the operation is taking place, he may drive to the base. If it can be arranged for a non-Jew to drive him to the base on Shabbat, then even if he is certain that the operation will take place on Shabbat, he may go home for Shabbat and then have the non-Jew drive him to the base. After the operation, if a non-Jew is available to drive him home, he may travel with him. If no non-Jewish driver is available, he may not return home.[17]

If soldiers are summoned to deal with an incident, but before they arrive it becomes clear that they are not needed, they should be called and told not to come, in order to minimize Shabbat desecration. An additional justification for this is that if it later becomes clear to soldiers that they were not informed of the cancelation because people did not want to use the phone on Shabbat, there is a concern that if they are summoned again on Shabbat, they will hesitate to come (see above, n. 10).

If an observant soldier is assigned guard duty or patrol duty on Shabbat, it is good if he swaps his Shabbat assignment with a non-observant soldier's weekday assignment as long as the non-observant soldier is

17. See section 10 and n. 11 above regarding a doctor who has a shift on Shabbat. It emerges from there that when it is certain that a military operation will begin on Shabbat, the officers and soldiers must spend Shabbat on the base. According to R. Shlomo Zalman Auerbach, they may spend Shabbat at home and then drive to the base on Shabbat, but the accepted ruling is to be stringent. Even if one could be lenient on a one-time basis, one may not rely on this leniency regularly (see section 2 and n. 7 above). Furthermore, R. Shlomo Zalman Auerbach himself did not rule this way in practice. He only said that one is not obligated to object if someone else is lenient (*Ha-tzava Ka-halakha* 26:19 and n. 41). Therefore, in practice, an officer who knows that he will need to lead an operation on Shabbat should remain on base. However, if there is a chance that the operation will be canceled, it would seem that a career officer may spend Shabbat at home. If he is called up, then he travels to the base. We must take into account that if we are too stringent and demand that he remains on base, the pressure from his family to leave the army will increase. Even though we do not use this reasoning to allow him to return home after an operation if Torah prohibitions are involved (as explained above in n. 12), nevertheless, before the operation, when there is some doubt about whether it will be carried out, he may be lenient. See further above, 2:10-11. If a non-Jewish driver is available, the officer may travel both ways with him just as doctors and nurses do, as explained above in section 10 and n. 12.

willing and there is no concern that switching the assignments will cause the guard duty to be taken lightly. Thus, the observant soldier will be able to pray and enjoy Shabbat, and the non-observant soldier will accrue merit for enabling this. Additionally, while the non-observant soldier is guarding, he is doing a mitzva and not desecrating Shabbat. Nevertheless, the observant soldier need not initiate such a swap, because defending the country is a mitzva, and there is no need to seek ways to get out of it on Shabbat (see *Ha-tzava Ka-halakha* ch. 27).

15. WHAT MUST ONE GIVE UP TO MINIMIZE SHABBAT DESECRATION?

One need not forgo his Shabbat rest or anything else that is dear to him in order to minimize the Shabbat desecration of another person who is involved in lifesaving activities. In addition, there is a concern that if one is forced to forgo something dear to him, he will hesitate to do what is needed to remove a hazard. For example, if one sees fallen electrical wires that are exposed and deadly, he could theoretically stand there for all of Shabbat in order to warn passersby not to touch the wires. Nevertheless, if this is difficult for him – e.g., if Shabbat will not be over for hours – he may alert the electric company, which will send repairmen to fix the wires on Shabbat (R. Shlomo Zalman Auerbach, cited in SSK 41:21; *Tzitz Eliezer* 8:15:11:7).

If a gravely ill person's home is so cold that it endangers his life, a neighbor whose home is heated need not be asked to inconvenience himself by taking in the sick person. Rather, the heat may be turned on in the sick person's home, as saving a life overrides Shabbat. Even if the neighbor is asked to take in the sick person, he is not required to do so (based on the ruling of R. Shlomo Zalman Auerbach in SSK ch. 32 n. 174; he derives this from the rule that one need not forgo his property and may confront a burglar even if the results may be lethal).

Similarly, a soldier on guard duty need not volunteer to do an extra shift in order to prevent his replacement from traveling on Shabbat. Since one may travel on Shabbat in order to perform guard duty, the first guard does not have to forfeit his rest in order to prevent this travel.

If soldiers need to travel in tanks for a security mission but will destroy the *eruv* if they take the shortest possible route, they should take a longer route, unless all of the *eruv*'s beneficiaries agree to let it be destroyed. This is because the *eruv*'s beneficiaries do not have to forfeit their benefit just so that the tank driver can minimize driving on Shabbat. Similarly, one who is driving a patient to the hospital should not barrel through private or public gardens, even when that is the shortest route to the hospital. Rather, the driver must go around, because neither the individual nor the community is obligated to forfeit its gardens so that someone involved in life-saving travel can minimize his Shabbat desecration (R. Shlomo Zalman Auerbach, as cited in *Ha-tzava Ka-halakha* 26:4-7; see there for the dissenting opinion as well).

16. POLICE ACTIVITY ON SHABBAT

All agree that police officers must desecrate Shabbat to save lives. Thus, if a suspicious object is found, or if dangerous people are seen engaging in suspicious activities, one must call the police. If a serious fight breaks out that could turn lethal, one must call the police. If robbers break into a home and might harm the residents, one must call the police. However, according to some *poskim*, in a situation where there is no danger to life, a police officer may not perform *melakhot* that are prohibited by Torah law. For example, if thieves robbed a home and left, since there is no longer any danger to human life, one may not call the police. Even if the thieves are still in the home, but the residents are not home, since there is no danger to life, one may not call the police. Similarly, if one witnesses thieves breaking into a closed store or bank, one may not call the police. In addition, a police officer may not write up reports about a theft, fingerprint an apprehended thief, or transport a thief to the police station on Shabbat (SSK 41:24-25; *Yalkut Yosef* 329:20-27).

However, several leading rabbinic authorities maintain that one may call the police in order to prevent theft or property damage, and a police officer may respond by driving to the scene of the crime, because if property damage or theft is not dealt with on Shabbat, the crime rate will skyrocket, and ultimately people's lives will be endangered. Within this opinion, there is debate about whether police officers may drive back to the station after an incident and whether they may perform regular patrols on Shabbat. Some are inclined to permit this when the drivers are not Jewish (*Heikhal Yitzḥak*, OḤ 32; *Yaskil Avdi*, OḤ 5:44; *Tzitz Eliezer* 4:4).

Our master and teacher R. Shaul Yisraeli (*Amud Ha-yemini* §17) allows Jewish police officers to drive on patrol, to drive back to the station after an incident, and to transport suspects. He argues that if we go easy on criminals or make it difficult for the police to do their jobs on Shabbat, police officers might quit or become hesitant in doing their jobs, and the crime rate will rise to the point that lives are endangered. Therefore, we may do whatever is necessary to prevent criminal activity on Shabbat. Furthermore, as we have seen, the Sages allow those involved with saving lives to return home, even though they will be carrying their weapons through a public domain. If we do not let them return, they might hesitate to go out to help people in the future (above, section 10).

Another factor supports this approach. As we have seen, the Sages stated that if a gravely ill person needs someone to take care of him, then even if a non-Jew is available, it is preferable for a Jew to undertake whatever *melakhot* are necessary to help him. If a non-Jew is asked to take care of him, it may happen that if someone is dangerously ill in the future and no non-Jew is available, people will be hesitant to desecrate Shabbat in order to help him (above, section 4). The same logic applies regarding police activity. If we restrict the ability of the police to catch thieves and prevent crime on Shabbat, ultimately this will lead to loss of life. We should add that nowadays some criminal activity in Israel is connected with terrorist activity. Therefore, the struggle against thieves is, to a large extent, also a struggle against terrorists, and thus directly involves saving lives.

According to all opinions, one may not call the police on Shabbat in order to fill out reports that are strictly financial, such as for the purpose of making an insurance claim or the like. Additionally, one may not call the police on Friday night to complain about noisy neighbors.

The police force should commission rabbis to review the entire array of police operations and determine, together with the police chiefs, what is vital and must be done on Shabbat and what is not. Similarly, they should establish special Shabbat protocols to minimize Shabbat desecration; for example, the officers can use a *shinui* whenever possible. They should also establish a procedure ensuring that if a non-Jewish police officer is on duty, he will be the one to drive and to write reports. All Jewish police officers should also be provided with a Shabbat pen, so that their writing will only be rabbinically prohibited (above, 18:2; see *Harḥavot*).

17. MOBILE PHONES AND WEAPONS NECESSARY FOR HEALTH AND SECURITY

In an area enclosed by an *eruv*, emergency medical professionals and volunteers who always carry beepers or cell phones may carry these devices on Shabbat. Similarly, one who always carries a pistol or rifle may carry it on Shabbat. *Muktzeh* is not an issue, because many maintain that a pistol is a *kli she-melakhto le-heter*, since its purpose is defense and deterrence. Similarly, since a two-way radio is designed to help save lives, it is also a *kli she-melakhto le-heter*. A cell phone is used primarily for calls that are unrelated to saving lives, so it is a *kli she-melakhto le-isur*. Nevertheless, one may carry such an object to use it *le-tzorekh gufo*, and therefore it may be carried to save lives.

However, in an area without an *eruv*, one should not carry these items. When there are life-saving reasons for people to remain close to weapons and communication devices in case of emergency, they may carry these items to places where one normally goes on Shabbat, such as to prayers and celebrations. If we do not allow this, no one will volunteer to undertake security and rescue efforts. In general, this consideration is used to permit rabbinic transgressions. Only under very pressing circumstances is it permitted for one to transgress Torah prohibitions (see above, n. 12). Therefore, one should carry the two-way radio with a *shinui* (for example, under one's shirt), which makes the transgression rabbinic. However, one should carry the gun normally, because it would be dangerous to carry it with a *shinui*. Additionally, some maintain that for security personnel, a weapon is not considered something that is carried, but an article of clothing that is worn.[18]

---

18. R. Goren writes that a gun is a *kli she-melakhto le-heter*, because it is meant to save lives (*Meshiv Milḥama* 2:61). This is also the opinion of R. Shlomo Zalman Auerbach, who maintains that guns, beepers, and hand-held computers (containing medical information that a doctor needs) are not *muktzeh* (*Shulḥan Shlomo* 2:308:16; *Nishmat Avraham* 301:19 and n. 6). A mobile phone, which is used primarily for everyday purposes, is a *kli she-melakhto le-isur* (above, 23:8). However, one may carry it to use it *le-tzorekh gufo*, like calling for help if necessary.

According to the Sages in the Mishna (*Shabbat* 63a), a sword and a bow are not considered ornamental, but rather they are considered shameful, because in the prophesied future, "no one will study war" (Yeshayahu 2:4). Therefore one may not bear them on Shabbat. R. Eliezer disagrees, saying they are considered ornamental,

However, one may not carry a gun or a two-way radio on Shabbat for the sake of a leisurely stroll to a place with no *eruv*. Thus, one should not take a walk outside the *eruv* in an area where he must be armed for security reasons, as this will require people to carry weapons needlessly.

If a soldier wants to leave his base in order to participate in prayer services taking place in a nearby community, and he will need to pass through an area with no *eruv* to get there, after he leaves the base he should rest his gun and two-way radio on a *mekom petur*. He should then carry the items from there to the community. He should do this on his way back as well, as explained above in 21:7.

Regarding putting out a dangerous fire, see 16:6-7 above. Regarding alarm systems, see 17:15 above.

---

and one may go out carrying them on Shabbat. SA 301:7 rules in accordance with the Sages. However, AHS 301:7 makes the innovative claim that soldiers may go with weapons on their bodies because the weapon is part of their clothing. R. Goren writes that one may rely upon this rationale if there is a great need to do so (*Meshiv Milḥama* 2:61). Therefore, when there is a need for some people to have weapons close at hand, but people will hesitate to volunteer to bear weapons unless we permit them to attend the synagogue and celebrations, it is preferable that they bear weapons in their belt as they normally do at all times, so that according to AHS, it is completely acceptable. However, if we ask people to carry weapons with a *shinui*, then not only is this dangerous, it also entails violating a rabbinic prohibition according to all opinions. In contrast, a beeper or cell phone should be carried with a *shinui*, so that it will only be rabbinically prohibited. If the *melakha* in question is walking in a *karmelit* in order to get to a synagogue, this would become a *shvut di-shvut* for the sake of a mitzva. Even if it is a *reshut ha-rabim* by Torah law, we can argue that this is a case in which "the end is permitted because of the beginning." According to *Igrot Moshe*, OḤ 4:81, it is considered dignified to carry a two-way radio, and therefore the radio is considered ornamental (see *Be-mareh Ha-bazak* 4:45). Nevertheless, since it is commonplace nowadays, carrying a two-way radio is no longer a source of pride, but simply a normal type of carrying (*Nishmat Avraham* 301:3 and n. 1). Therefore, it is proper to carry it with a *shinui*.

Chapter Twenty-Eight

Illness That Is Not Life-Threatening

1. PRINCIPLES OF THE *HALAKHOT* OF SICK PEOPLE

There are three categories of sick people according to *halakha*:

1. a gravely ill person – one whose life is in danger;
2. a "regular" sick person – one whose whole body is ill but whose life is not in danger;
3. a "mildly" sick person – one who is ailing in part of his body or who experiences pain from a bodily ailment.

When caring for a dangerously sick person, one does everything on Shabbat that he would do during the week. All Shabbat prohibitions are overridden in order to save a life, as we saw in the previous chapter.

When caring for a regular sick person – one who is sick enough that he is forced to lie down, but whose life is not in danger – one may disregard rabbinic prohibitions, but Torah prohibitions remain in force (as will be explained in the next section).[1]

---

1. According to most Rishonim, one may not violate a Torah prohibition for a person who is in danger of losing a limb (Rosh, Ran, Rashba, and seemingly Rambam). Others maintain that one may indeed desecrate Shabbat to save a limb (*Tosafot,*

A mildly sick person or one who is bothered by ailments – that is, one who can walk around as though healthy, but experiences discomfort from a mild ailment – is subject to all rabbinic laws, and one may not even violate *shvut di-shvut* on his behalf. However, if he is in pain, one may do certain things for him even though they are categorized as *shvut di-shvut*. Specifically, one may ask a non-Jew to transgress a rabbinic prohibition for him, or a Jew may make use of a *shinui* to do so (SA 307:5; MB 328:3; above 9:11).

There is a specific rabbinic enactment forbidding a mildly sick person to take medicine. The *poskim* disagree whether this prohibition pertains to today's medications, which are factory-made (the laws pertaining to one bothered by a mild ailment will be explained in sections 3-5).

The main idea of Shabbat is that on this day we calmly and tranquilly accept reality as it is. If we have no clean clothes, we wear dirty ones. If we forgot to cook a certain dish, we content ourselves with the food we have, or we ask a neighbor for help. If we forgot to turn on the heat, we put on a coat. If we forgot to turn on the air conditioning, we suffer a bit from the heat. Even though Shabbat laws sometimes cause suffering, they liberate us from the burden and tension of having to pay constant attention and ensure that every little detail of our lives is properly addressed. Therefore, Shabbat is a valuable gift. The feeling of faith, tranquility, and rest that results from accepting reality on Shabbat is enjoyable and uplifting.

The Sages continue this trend through their enactments, one of which is to refrain from using medicine on Shabbat. If we experience some discomfort, even if it is irritating and unpleasant, we bear it calmly, as this too is part of Shabbat rest. However, if the discomfort causes pain and negates *oneg Shabbat*, the Sages permitted transgressing minor rabbinic prohibitions (*shvut di-shvut*) to relieve the suffering.

Rabbeinu Tam, *Sefer Ha-aguda*, and Me'iri). In practice, SA rules that one may not violate a Torah prohibition in such a case (328:17). However, according to current medical opinion, in practice, when a person's limb is in danger, it is almost always life-threatening, as there is always the possibility of infection setting in (*Nishmat Avraham* 328:49). This may be the rationale of the Rishonim who are lenient in a case of danger to a limb. *Melamed Le-ho'il* 2:32 presents similar reasoning, as detailed in *Harḥavot*.

And when it comes to caring for one who is actually sick, the Sages allow us to transgress all rabbinic prohibitions, as taking care of one's health is a mitzva.

2. A REGULAR SICK PERSON

As is well known, there are two types of Shabbat prohibitions: Torah prohibitions and rabbinic prohibitions (the latter type is also called *shvut*). There is a principle that one desecrates Shabbat and performs even *melakhot* prohibited by Torah law on behalf of a gravely ill person, someone whose life is in danger. In contrast, when caring for someone who is ill but whose life is not in danger, one may not violate Torah prohibitions. However, the Sages permitted the violation of prohibitions that they themselves enacted to treat someone who is sick.

One who is bedridden due to his illness is considered a regular sick person. Even if, for some reason, he is not actually lying down, he is considered sick as long as this is the type of illness that generally causes people to lie down. Similarly, if one is suffering from pain that weakens his entire body (for example, a migraine), he is considered a sick person, even if he has not actually gone to lie down (SA 328:17). Furthermore, even if one is walking around and looks well, if it is clear that without a particular treatment he will need to lie down, one may transgress rabbinic prohibitions to prevent this from happening (SSK 33:1). If a child needs something very badly, he is considered a sick person, even if he has not gone to lie down (Rema 328:17; MB 276:6; above 24:6).

The easiest and most accepted way of taking care of a sick person is with the help of a non-Jew. As we have seen (above 25:1), under normal circumstances the Sages prohibited asking a non-Jew to undertake *melakha* on behalf of a Jew on Shabbat, but they permitted doing so for the sake of a sick person (*Shabbat* 129a). Therefore, one may ask a non-Jew to turn a light on or off for a sick person, to turn a heater on for him, to cook food for him, to travel in order to bring him medication, to press elevator buttons for him, and to administer X-rays for him. Similarly, one may ask a non-Jewish dentist to treat a patient whose toothache is causing him pain that extends throughout his body. One may ask a non-Jewish doctor to write a prescription for a sick person. One may ask a non-Jew to drive a sick person to the doctor or to the hospital. In such a case, a Jew may accompany the patient, on condition that neither he nor the sick person performs any *melakha* themselves.

A regular sick person may take whatever medications he needs, since the rabbinic prohibition against taking medicine applies only to a mildly sick person (Rema 328:37; see BHL *ad loc.*).

If no non-Jew is available, according to Ran, a Jew may not transgress rabbinic prohibitions for a sick person. According to Rashba, however, he may, and we follow this position in practice. However, *le-khatḥila*, if possible, it is still preferable to arrange for a non-Jew to do whatever is necessary, or for a Jew to use a *shinui*, so that the prohibition will be reduced to a *shvut di-shvut* (above, 9:11). If there is no choice, and the sick person desperately needs care, a Jew may do rabbinically prohibited *melakhot* on his behalf. For example, if he needs a light turned on or off, one should do this with a *shinui* such as using one's arm or leg, so that the prohibition is only rabbinic (above, 9:3). Similarly, if the sick person needs a heater or air conditioner turned on or off, one may do this with a *shinui*.[2]

2. According to Ran, the Sages' dispensation for a sick person was limited to requesting things of a non-Jew, as stated in *Shabbat* 129a. In contrast, according to Rashba (and Rambam as well, according to *Magid Mishneh* and *Tur*) one may transgress all rabbinic prohibitions for a sick person. This is borne out by the law recorded in the Gemara that a sick person may nurse from an animal on Shabbat; while this is a prohibited form of milking the animal, the *shinui* renders the prohibition rabbinic (*Ketubot* 60a). Ramban agrees that all rabbinic prohibitions are suspended if there is danger to a limb. But, he continues, if there is no danger to a limb, one may only ask a non-Jew to help; a Jew may not transgress even rabbinic prohibitions in such a case. That is permitted only if a *shinui* is used, in which case the action is reduced to a *shvut di-shvut*. SA 328:17 states that Ramban's position seems correct. The Vilna Gaon follows it as well, as do MB *ad loc.* 57 and SHT 396:9. In contrast, *Ḥayei Adam* 69:12 states that when it is impossible to use a *shinui* to do what is necessary, one may do it without a *shinui* (even though he thus transgresses a *shvut* rather than a *shvut di-shvut*). MB 328:102 concurs. Going even further, some Aḥaronim maintain that a Jew may even perform a *melakha* that is prohibited by Torah law with a *shinui* if no non-Jew is available. This is based on Rashba and his followers. (Some maintain that Ramban would agree as well, and that this can be inferred from his book *Torat Ha-adam*.) This is the approach of SAH 328:19; *Eglei Tal, Toḥen* 18; and *Tehila Le-David* 328:22. Since this is a rabbinic disagreement, the law follows the lenient opinion. Recent *poskim* who agree include: R. Shlomo Zalman Auerbach, as cited in SSK 33:18; *Or Le-Tziyon* 2:36, n. 4; and R. Ovadia Yosef, as cited in *Yalkut Yosef* 328:11. See too *Orḥot Shabbat* ch. 20 nn. 148-149.

3. A MILDLY SICK PERSON AND ONE EXPERIENCING DISCOMFORT

If one walks around and seems to be healthy, but in fact is mildly sick or experiencing discomfort, his status is the same as that of anyone else. He must observe all the Shabbat prohibitions, including the rabbinic ones. The permission to transgress rabbinic prohibitions (as explained in the previous section) is for a regular sick person, but this permission does not extend to one who is bothered by a mild illness or ailment. Therefore, if the light is bothering him, one may not ask a non-Jew to turn it off; if he needs light, heat, or air conditioning, one may not ask a non-Jew to turn them on. Even asking a non-Jew to do these things with a *shinui* – which would reduce the prohibition to a *shvut di-shvut* – is prohibited, because all rabbinic prohibitions still apply to him (SA 328:1).

All of this applies in a case where the illness is merely irritating and uncomfortable. However, if the illness or ailment causes pain, one may relieve it by performing a *shvut di-shvut*. If the person suffering has a great need for light, heat, or air conditioning, one may ask a non-Jew to turn them on using a *shinui*, such as with his arm. However, a Jew may not do so even with a *shinui*, because there would still be a standard rabbinic prohibition (*shvut*), which applies even when there is some pain (SA 307:5; 328:25; above 9:11-12; *Harḥavot*).

All agree that one may not turn off a light so a sick person can sleep (*Shabbat* 30a). At first glance, since this is a *melakha she-eina tzerikha le-gufah*, which according to many *poskim* is only rabbinically prohibited (above, 9:6), Rashba and those who follow him should permit it for a sick person even without a *shinui*. Nevertheless, since turning off the light is more severe than other rabbinic prohibitions, the Sages forbade doing it even for a sick person (MB 278:3). Turning off a light to allow a sick person to sleep is permitted if one does so with a *shinui*, for example by using his arm.

Eating rabbinically prohibited food is more severe than transgressing a *shvut*, and a regular sick person thus may not do this (Rema, YD 155:3). However, he may eat food that was cooked by a non-Jew (SA 328:19), and he should make the regular *berakhot* over the food (MB *ad loc.* 63). One may move a *muktzeh* item for a sick person without using a *shinui*. Some are stringent and maintain that *le-khatḥila* one should still use a *shinui* (MB 328:58). Some argue that the enactment against taking medicine (out of concern that people will end up grinding ingredients) applies to a regular sick person. (See BHL 328:37, s.v. "ve-khen.") However, in practice, we rule that the enactment applies only to a mildly sick person or to one experiencing discomfort, as described in the next section (*Beit Yosef* and Rema 328:37).

If one's fingernail has been torn off most of the way and is bothersome, this is considered an ailment, and one may not remove the nail even via a *shvut di-shvut*. However, if the torn nail is painful, one may remove it using a *shinui*, such as with one's hand or teeth. Since most of the nail has already been torn off, it is viewed as if it has already fallen off, so the prohibition to tear it off completely is only rabbinic. For this reason, the Sages permitted removing a nail with a *shinui* if it is causing pain (*Shabbat* 94b; SA 328:31; above, 14:2). If the nail was not torn off most of the way but is painful, one may ask a non-Jew to remove it with a *shinui*, since doing so reduces the prohibition to a *shvut di-shvut*.

Similarly, if a splinter becomes embedded in a person's skin and it is clear that removing it will cause bleeding, one may not remove it if it is merely irritating. However, if it is painful, one may remove it, since the prohibition of causing bleeding in this way is only a *shvut di-shvut*, as one does not intend to cause bleeding, and the bleeding is effected via a *shinui*, as a side effect of removing the thorn (see MB 328:88; above, ch. 9 n. 3 and 14:2).

4. THE ENACTMENT AGAINST MEDICINE – GRINDING INGREDIENTS

The Sages further enacted that one who is bothered by an ailment or mild illness may not obtain medical treatment on Shabbat. That is, he may not ingest medicine, apply a medicinal ointment, or take any actions designed for the purpose of healing. The concern is that one who is preoccupied with alleviating the ailment will pulverize herbal ingredients to prepare a medication and thereby violate the Torah prohibition of *Toḥen* (*Shabbat* 54b and Rashi).

Thus, the Sages forbade someone with an eye ailment to drip wine or another medication to his eye (SA 328:20). Similarly, one may not apply ointment to a wound to heal it (SA 328:22). If one has a sore throat, he may not gargle with oil for therapeutic purposes. One who has a toothache may not rinse his teeth and gums with vinegar, salt water, or alcohol for therapeutic purposes. However, he may drink an alcoholic beverage in order to relieve the pain, on condition that he does not retain the liquid in his mouth longer than usual (SA 328:32).

If the ailment causes pain, one may ask a non-Jew to drip wine to his eye or apply alcohol to his painful tooth. This reduces the prohibition to the level of *shvut di-shvut*, which the Sages permitted if one is in pain (SA 307:5; 328:25; above, 9:11-12 and *Harḥavot*; according to Radbaz and R. Mordechai Benet, a Jew in pain may take medicine by himself; see n. 3 below).

The enactment prohibiting taking medicine also includes eating or drinking items that only sick people eat or drink. However, a sick person may eat or drink items that healthy people eat or drink as well, even if his intention is to use these items as medicine (*Shabbat* 109b; SA 328:37). Therefore, one who has a sore throat may not suck on throat lozenges, but he may suck on ordinary hard candies (SSK 34:4). Similarly, one may not drink water with flaxseed to ease constipation, but prune juice is permitted, as healthy people sometimes drink it as well.

One who experiences discomfort may do things that healthy people normally do, even if his intention is to relieve the discomfort. For example, one who has itchy skin may apply oil that healthy people apply as well (SA 327:1). One may also apply oil to one's hands and lips, since nowadays people do so even when their skin is not chapped – to soften them or for pleasure.

If one has medicine that helps relieve his minor aches and pains, he may mix it into a drink before Shabbat, as long as no one can tell that it contains medicine. He may then drink the medicinal liquid on Shabbat (R. Shlomo Zalman Auerbach, cited in SSK 34:5).

5. MODERN MEDICATIONS

Some maintain that one may take modern, mass-produced medications on Shabbat for any type of ache or pain, as there is no real concern that anyone will grind anything in order to produce the medicine. However, most *poskim* maintain that even nowadays one who is only mildly ill or bothered by an ailment may not take medicine on Shabbat. There are two reasons for this. First, according to many, no rabbinic enactment may be nullified except by a larger and more prominent *beit din* than the one that passed the enactment. Second, some people still prepare household remedies, so there are cases where the reason for the enactment still applies.

In practice, as long as the ailment is merely irritating but not painful, it is proper to be stringent and avoid taking mass-produced medications. However, if the ailment causes pain, one may take medication, because some maintain that the Sages never prohibited taking medication when pain is involved. Even though many maintain that the Sages' enactment applies even when pain is involved, in the case of mass-produced medication, where there is no concern that a private individual would try to prepare it himself, it is proper to be lenient. It is worth noting that when the technical law allows leniency, it is proper to act accordingly so as to fulfill the mitzva of *oneg Shabbat*.

Therefore, if one is bothered by an ailment of the eyes or ears, he should not use drops. However, if the ailment causes him pain, he should use the drops. The same applies to a runny nose: if it is merely irritating, one should not use nose drops, but if it causes pain, he should. Similarly, one may take sleeping pills to relieve insomnia, since without them he will suffer pain. Perhaps we can suggest that if one is pained to the point that he would be willing to walk a kilometer in order to get medicine, it indicates that he is truly suffering and may thus take mass-produced medications. However, if he thinks it is unnecessary to go to that much trouble, it indicates that he has a mere ailment, and he should thus refrain from taking medicine.[3]

---

3. *Ketzot Ha-shulḥan* (§134, *Badei Ha-shulḥan* 7) states the argument for leniency based on the fact that nowadays people do not prepare medicine by themselves. However, for the two reasons I presented above, it is inclined to be stringent. *Tzitz Eliezer* 8:15:15 states that it depends on the rationale for the enactment against medicine. If the concern is specific – that in order to prepare the medicine, people will end up grinding the ingredients – then there is room for leniency. In contrast, if the concern is more general – that as part of dealing with medical issues, people will end up violating various transgressions – then the prohibition stands even nowadays. *Tzitz Eliezer* concludes by inclining toward leniency. *She'arim Metzuyanim Ba-halakha* 91:2 also inclines toward leniency. Many oppose them and prohibit taking mass-produced medicine on Shabbat, including SSK 34:3; *Igrot Moshe*, OḤ 3:53; R. Ovadia Yosef, *Halikhot Olam* vol. 4, Tetzaveh §19; and *Or Le-Tziyon* 2:36:9. Nevertheless, when great pain is involved, R. Ovadia is lenient, even if the sick person is not bedridden. SSK 34:3 rules stringently, stating in n. 7 in the name of R. Shlomo Zalman Auerbach that the entire enactment is relevant only when there is pain, because that is when one would end up grinding medication. Nevertheless, SSK 33:16 permits taking sleeping pills in order to relieve great pain.

6. MEDICATIONS TAKEN IN REGULAR DOSES

If one began taking a medication during the week, and it must be taken for several days consecutively so that skipping the Shabbat dose will harm its effectiveness, he may continue taking the medicine on Shabbat. This is because some maintain that the rabbinic enactment does not apply to dosing that began before Shabbat (R. Shlomo Kluger). When dealing with mass-produced medicine, one may rely on this opinion even *le-khatḥila*, and one may take such medicine even when he is not in pain.

Similarly, a woman who is taking birth control pills or medication to help her maintain a pregnancy may continue taking this medication on Shabbat as well.[4]

Some are lenient concerning all medicine, even for regular pain. This is the opinion of R. Mordechai Benet, who argues that sometimes the Sages were permissive when one is in pain, even in a case resembling a *melakha she-eina tzerikha le-gufah* (SA 328:28; above, 14:2); certainly, then, they would permit taking medicine in a case of pain. *Minḥat Shabbat* 91:1 and *She'arim Metzuyanim Ba-halakha* 91:3 take this position as well. Radbaz 3:540, appearing earlier than any of them, states that the prohibition on taking medicine is even less severe than a *shvut di-shvut*. Therefore, when any pain is involved, one may be lenient.

Thus there are two disagreements here: 1) Does the enactment apply to mass-produced medicine? 2) Does it apply to people who are in pain? It is true that in each of these disagreements, most *poskim* feel that one should be stringent. Nevertheless, since these disagreements concern a rabbinic prohibition, one who is lenient has an opinion to rely upon. Furthermore, in a situation where there are two reasons to be lenient, such as if the medicine is mass-produced and the person is in pain, then it is a twofold doubt that affects *oneg Shabbat*. Accordingly, one may be lenient even *le-khatḥila*. (We should add that when the medication simply relieves pain but does not cure the illness, some *poskim* maintain that it is not considered medication for purposes of the rabbinic enactment. See *Tzitz Eliezer* 8:15:15:21 as well as 14:50, and *Yalkut Yosef* 328:52.)

4. Some permit anyone who has started taking a medication before Shabbat to continue taking it on Shabbat, as they maintain that the Sages' enactment was not meant for such a case. Since he has already started taking the medicine on Friday, he has enough time to prepare whatever amount he needs for Shabbat, and there is no concern that he will need to grind anything (R. Shlomo Kluger, *Sefer Ha-ḥayim* 328:25). Some are lenient only when a medication must be taken every day for at least a week, and skipping a day could be harmful (R. Shlomo Zalman Auerbach). See SSK ch. 34 n. 77 and *Orḥot Shabbat* 20:124. Even if the medication is not mass-produced, there is room for leniency, since the disagreement concerns a rabbinic law; certainly, then, one may be lenient when the medication is mass-produced.

If one takes daily vitamin supplements or weight loss pills to improve his health, he may continue on Shabbat as well.

7. INJECTIONS, INTRAVENOUS INFUSION, AND NURSING

Sometimes, a regular sick person needs an injection or intravenous (IV) infusion on Shabbat. Since a subcutaneous injection does not necessarily cause bleeding, *halakha* views it no differently from other types of medicine: it is permitted for a sick person. If one is not sick but is in pain, he may ask a non-Jew to administer the injection.

However, a Jew may not administer an intravenous injection or infusion on Shabbat, because doing so causes bleeding, which some maintain is prohibited by Torah law. Thus, as long as the person is not dangerously ill, one should defer to this stringent opinion. If a port was installed beneath the skin (with a catheter surgically inserted into a vein) before Shabbat, one may attach an IV bag to it on Shabbat, even when there is no danger to life (see SSK 33:7). A non-Jew may administer an intravenous injection or infusion to a regular sick person.

If a wound or a needle needs to be disinfected with iodine or peroxide, one may not apply the disinfectant using cotton wool or a bandage, because squeezing liquid out of them is prohibited on account of *Seḥita*. Rather, one should pour the iodine or peroxide directly onto the surface that needs to be disinfected. Alternatively, one may apply it with a tongue depressor or synthetic, non-absorbent material.

If one knows before Shabbat that he will have to administer an injection on Shabbat, it is preferable that he prepare and disinfect the

---

SA 328:37 rules that a healthy person may eat food that sick people eat to help them get better. According to this, a healthy person may take vitamins and diet pills on Shabbat. However, according to MA and MB *ad loc.* 120, a healthy person may not do this in order to improve his health. *Igrot Moshe*, OḤ 3:54 takes this stringent opinion into account for a weak person, but permits a healthy person to take vitamins prophylactically. This is also the opinion of R. Ovadia Yosef, *Halikhot Olam* vol. 4, Tetzaveh §41. Nevertheless, if a sick person wishes to be lenient, he may rely on *Tzitz Eliezer* (cited in the previous note), which rules leniently because people do not grind medicine themselves anymore. Certainly, then, one may be lenient if he takes the vitamins daily, as we explained above.

syringe and needle before Shabbat. If he forgot to prepare in advance, or if it was medically inadvisable to do so, he may prepare the shot on Shabbat, as this does not involve a Torah prohibition (see SSK 33:8-10).

A nursing woman whose breasts are engorged may express or pump her excess milk on Shabbat, on condition that she pumps it in such a way that the milk goes to waste, such as into the sink or into a container with soap in it so that the milk is immediately ruined. It is true that expressing milk on Shabbat in order to feed a baby is prohibited by Torah law as a *tolada* of *Dash* (SA 328:34; above, 10:17). However, when the milk goes to waste, the prohibition is only rabbinic, and to relieve pain the Sages permitted it (SA 330:8). One may use a manual pump for this purpose or an electric pump attached to a timer that was set before Shabbat. On Shabbat, when the timer activates the pump, the nursing woman may use it to pump her milk (SSK 36:22 n. 63). If the doctors believe that it is necessary for a baby to have breast milk, and the mother tries not to miss any opportunity to pump during the week, then she may also pump on Shabbat for the baby, as this is a case of saving a life (see SSK 36:22 and n. 67).

8. OINTMENTS AND COMPRESSES

Even when using medicine is permissible, one may not apply topical medication (such as creams or ointments) to a bandage or a wound. If one applies ointment and smoothes its surface to spread it, he violates Torah law, as *Memare'aḥ* is a *tolada* of *Memaḥek* (*Shabbat* 75b; above, 18:6). It is also forbidden to place the ointment onto the body or the bandage without spreading it, out of concern that one will end up spreading it. Even if the bandage was prepared with ointment before Shabbat, one may not place it on the wound on Shabbat, out of concern that he will end up spreading it (SA 328:25).

However, to alleviate or prevent pain, the Sages allow one to place ointment directly on a wound or bandage, though one who does so must be careful to avoid spreading it. If the ointment was in a tube, he should place the tube directly on the wound. If it is in a container, one may apply the ointment using a tongue depressor or a spoon. The primary concern is that it should not be spread. When the bandage is placed on the wound, the cream will spread out along the sides. Nevertheless, as long as one does not smooth the surface intentionally, this is not prohibited (SSK 33:14; above, section 5).

Similarly, if one is in pain, he may place medicated cream on his skin and rub it in until it is completely absorbed. This is because as long as one wants all the cream to be absorbed, it is not considered *Memare'aḥ*. However, if one wants part of the cream to remain on the surface of the skin to make it smooth, applying the cream is prohibited by Torah law (*Da'at Torah* 328:26; R. Shlomo Zalman Auerbach cited in SSK ch. 33 n. 64; based on MA 316:24 and MB *ad loc.* 49; see above, 14:5, and *Harḥavot*).

If one is suffering from great pain that is weakening his entire body, he is considered a sick person, and one may treat him with compresses. Cloths that were dampened before Shabbat may be used for this purpose. If necessary, one may wet a completely clean cloth on Shabbat to use as a compress (see above, 14:4 and n. 2). In any case, he must take great care not to wring out the compress, whether in order for the water to reach the sore spot or in order to clean it after use (SSK 33:19; see *Harḥavot* here and above, 12:8, 10).

9. ADHESIVE BANDAGES, CLOTH BANDAGES, AND TREATING WOUNDS

One may use an adhesive bandage ("Band-Aid") to protect a wound or a sensitive area from the friction caused by clothing or other objects. Even one who is bothered by a mild ailment may do so, since an adhesive bandage does not cure but merely protects (SA 328:23).

Although one may not affix an adhesive bandage to paper or the like because of the prohibition of *Tofer*, affixing one to the body is not prohibited, because *Tofer* does not apply to the human body. Besides, adhesive bandages are meant to remain on the body for only a short time.

Le-khatḥila, one should try not to attach the ends of the adhesive bandage to each other and to avoid using an adhesive bandage to keep a cloth bandage in place. This is because some maintain that these cases are rabbinically prohibited, as sticking one item to another in such a manner resembles *Tofer*. If necessary one may be lenient and rely on those who maintain that since adhesive bandages are affixed temporarily, for a short period of time, one may do so just as one may tie a temporary knot that lasts only a short time.[5]

One may not cut a bandage or adhesive bandage to size, and one who does so violates the Torah prohibition of *Meḥatekh* (MB 322:18; above 15:10). If a bandage is too long, one should wrap it around the injury multiple times rather than cutting it. If one knows that he may need to bandage wounds on Shabbat, he should prepare bandages of various sizes before Shabbat. It is also good to prepare methods of fastening them with safety pins or an elastic sleeve, since it is preferable *le-khatḥila* not to use an adhesive bandage in order to keep a cloth bandage in place.

One may use a butterfly bandage to hold together the edges of a cut. This is because of two lenient opinions. First, some maintain that there is no prohibition of *Tofer* when it comes to the body. Second, some say that this type of bandage cannot qualify as sewing, since all it does is hold closed the edges of the cut, helping the wound close up on its own (SSK 35:25; see *Harḥavot* 27:2:4).

In order to stop bleeding, one may use a bandage (using a permissible method of tying) or antihemorrhagic sprays or powders (like Dermatol). These measures are not considered medicinal; they simply stop the bleeding (see SA 328:29). Additionally, one may place iodine on a wound in order to prevent infection (SSK 35:13).[6]

---

5. We saw above in ch. 13 n. 9 that according to Rabbeinu Yoel, Ra'avya, Rashbam, and others, the laws of *Tofer* are similar to the laws of *Kosheir*, and thus there is no prohibition of sewing something that will last for less than a week. Rabbeinu Peretz and *Mordechai* disagree, arguing that the two *melakhot* are not analogous, and the rabbinic prohibition of *Tofer* applies even to temporary attachments. In times of need, one may rely on the lenient authorities; see there. This is also the opinion of *Tzitz Eliezer* (8:15 and in the summary, 14:14-15). R. Shlomo Zalman Auerbach (cited in SSK ch. 35 n. 67) adds that even when the cloth bandage is later thrown away together with the adhesive bandage so that they stay attached for an extended period of time, this is not considered a permanent attachment, since it serves no purpose. We also saw above in ch. 13 n. 9 that it is not prohibited to remove the plastic strips protecting the adhesive on the tapes of a disposable diaper. The same applies to removing the plastic strips protecting the adhesive of an adhesive bandage.
6. *Orḥot Shabbat* ch. 20 n. 250 expresses surprise at SSK's permission to use Dermatol, maintaining that it is indeed medicinal. R. Shlomo Zalman Auerbach seems to maintain that Dermatol and iodine are not meant to heal, but simply to stop bleeding and

One may clean blood with a bandage or paper towel, even though this will color them red. Similarly, one may bandage a wound that has been treated with iodine, even though the color of the iodine will stain the bandage or paper towel. This is because this "coloring" is in fact a manner of soiling the material. Additionally, none of these items (bandage, paper towel, body) are meant to be dyed (SAH §302, *Kuntres Aḥaron*; MB 303:79 and 320:58; above 18:5).

If an adhesive bandage is irritating, one may remove it. When doing so, *le-khatḥila* one should try to avoid ripping out hairs, because of the *melakha* of *Gozez*. If there is no alternative, one may remove the adhesive bandage even if it is clear that this will rip out hairs, since one does not want this to happen and it is simply an ancillary effect of his action (SSK 35:30).

10. OPENING MEDICINE PACKAGES

When it is permissible to take medicine but it is packaged in plastic, paper, or cardboard, one may tear open the packaging in order to get to the medicine. Those who are stringent make sure to destroy the packaging, rendering it unusable for storing the medicine (above, 15:12). It is preferable to avoid tearing words on the packaging. *Be-di'avad,* if it cannot be opened without tearing words, it may still be opened, because one's intention is not to erase the letters, and the "erasing" happens through a destructive action (as explained above, 18:3).

When one may take pills that are inside a sealed plastic container, he may remove the cover, even though doing so breaks the temporary plastic seal connecting the cover to the container. This is not considered making a *kli,* because the container and cover were already finished products; they were simply attached to the plastic seal (above 15:13-14).

11. MEASURING FOR MEDICAL PURPOSES AND USING A THERMOMETER

When medically necessary, one may use a regular mercury thermometer to take someone's temperature. One may also use a manual blood pressure

---

prevent infection. In any case, even if they do heal, someone who is suffering would be permitted to use them, as I pointed out here in section 5 and n. 3.

monitor. Although without a significant need one may not measure things on Shabbat, as this is a weekday activity, it is nevertheless permitted for a mitzva or medical need (SA 306:7 and 328:43; above 22:6). It is also permitted to shake down a thermometer so that the mercury contracts (SSK 40:2).

Some rule leniently and permit a sick person to use a thermometer strip, which displays body temperature upon being placed on one's forehead's. They maintain that this is not considered *Kotev* since the numbers are already imprinted on the strip, and the temperature merely makes them visible for a short time, after which they disappear (*Yeḥaveh Da'at* 4:29). Others maintain that using this type of thermometer is rabbinically prohibited, considering it temporary writing (SSK 40:2). Since it is a rabbinic law, one may be lenient in a case of necessity (*Tzitz Eliezer* 14:30; see *Harḥavot* 18:4:4).

The *poskim* disagree about whether one may perform a medical test on Shabbat that causes color to appear. Some prohibit this on account of *Tzove'a*. Others permit it, as one is not interested in the color, only in the test result. *Le-khatḥila* one should be stringent, but when necessary he may be lenient, since this is a case of uncertainty regarding rabbinic law (see SSK 33:20, and *Harḥavot*).

12. PERMITTED ACTIONS

On Shabbat, one may perform therapeutic treatments that are not normally done with the aid of medications. Since there is no concern that one will come to grind ingredients, such treatment is not included in the prohibition of medicine on Shabbat. However, if there is no real need, even such treatment is prohibited because it is a weekday activity. But as long as a real need exists, for example when one is in pain, it is permissible (SA 328:43; MB *ad loc.* 136).

Therefore, one may apply pressure to an injury with a utensil or his hand to prevent swelling, as this is a type of therapeutic action that is not normally done with medications (*Ḥayei Adam* 69:5; MB 328:144; SHT *ad loc.* 104). Similarly, one may apply ice to an injury in order to prevent swelling and reduce the pain, because this is not normally done with medicine (SSK 35:35 and n. 92).

If one's eyes hurt, he may do eye exercises on Shabbat, because there is no medication that substitutes for these exercises. If one's eyes do not hurt, but he wants to strengthen his eye muscles, the exercises have the same status as physical therapy exercises: if one needs to do them several times daily, one may do them on Shabbat as well (as explained in the next section).

One may place an orthodontic retainer in one's mouth on Shabbat, as no medication can straighten one's teeth (SSK 34:29).[7]

One who has a stomach ache or an earache may place a hot water bottle on the affected area to relieve his pain (MB 326:19). Ice may also be used to relieve pain (SSK 33:15).[8]

One who has an earache may put cotton in his ears. This is not considered medicinal, since it does not heal the ear, but simply protects

7. SA 328:43 states that someone in pain may perform actions to alleviate an illness that is not normally treated with medication. Such treatments were not included in the Sages' enactment, since there is no concern in these cases that one will end up grinding ingredients for medicine. MB *ad loc.* 136 clarifies that when there is no pain, one may not administer such treatments because it is a weekday activity. Along the same lines, SA 306:7 permits measuring for the sake of a mitzva or for a medical need, even though measuring is normally considered a weekday activity. MB *ad loc.* 36 explains that healing the body is itself a mitzva. At first glance it would seem that placing a retainer in one's mouth should be prohibited because it is a weekday activity, as it does not alleviate pain. However, R. Shlomo Zalman Auerbach (cited in SSK ch. 34 n. 113) explains that it seems reasonable that the prohibition on weekday activities does not apply when results are seen only after a long period of time. This is also cited in *Orḥot Shabbat* 20:154. I maintain that administering treatments is considered a prohibited weekday activity only when not necessary. Since they can wait, undertaking them on Shabbat is considered a weekday activity. However, when there is a real need, then even if there is no pain involved, it is not considered a weekday activity. This can be inferred from the position of Radbaz and those who follow him (above, n. 3), namely, that the enactment banning medicines is less severe than a *shvut di-shvut*, which is itself permitted when pain is involved (above, 9:11). When it comes to treating sick people, the prohibition on weekday activities is even less severe than the ban on medication (as explained in MB 328:136).
8. *Shabbat* 40b states that one may not place a container of hot water on a person's stomach, due to the risk of spilling. Rashi and Ran explain that this is the reason for the prohibition on Shabbat as well, but *Tosafot* state that it is forbidden on Shabbat because of the ban on medicine on Shabbat. It would seem that according to Rashi and Ran, if the hot water bottle is sealed well, one may use it on Shabbat, whereas according to *Tosafot* it is still prohibited. MB 326:19 states that one may be lenient if there is a great need. Based on what we said in section 5, nowadays, when medicine is mass-produced, one may be lenient concerning all medicine for one in pain.

it from the wind (SA 303:15; SSK 34:9). One who wishes to soothe his throat may swallow a raw egg, as this is not considered a medicinal act (SA 328:38). One may put talcum powder into one's shoes to absorb sweat and foot odor or to soothe his feet. However, one who has athlete's foot may not put medicated powder in his shoes. If he is in pain, though, he may (section 5 above).

13. PHYSICAL THERAPY, MASSAGE, AND ACUPUNCTURE

Physical therapy exercises are often meant to restore function to limbs or muscles that have atrophied as a result of injury or paralysis. If it is not strictly necessary to do the exercises on Shabbat, one should not do them then, because this is a weekday activity. For example, if one is not always careful to do the exercises regularly during the week, one may not do them on Shabbat. Even if no equipment is used, since these exercises are undertaken with professional guidance, they are considered a weekday activity. One should instead exercise on Friday before Shabbat begins, and on Saturday night after Shabbat ends. However, if the exercises are indeed necessary for the patient, and during the week he takes care to do them several times a day, he may do them on Shabbat as well. One may even use equipment, as long as it does not require electricity to operate. These exercises have the same status as pills that must be taken for several consecutive days: one may take them on Shabbat as well (n. 4 above; *Nishmat Avraham* 328:93 in the name of R. Shlomo Zalman Auerbach).

One may do gentle stretches to loosen his back or neck or to refresh himself. This is not considered medicinal, nor is it considered a weekday activity. However, one may not do calisthenics, which maintain or improve one's fitness, as they are a weekday activity (see above, 22:8).

One may not give a professional massage to someone who is experiencing discomfort in his back or another limb. Since such aches are treated with pills and ointments, their treatment is included in the rabbinic enactment against medicine on Shabbat. In addition, a professional massage is considered a weekday activity. Nevertheless, if the ailment is truly painful, one may give a professional massage in order to relieve it. As we have already seen (section 5), since medications today are generally mass-produced, one who is in pain may use such medications. Certainly, then, one may provide treatments that do not involve medication at all. Furthermore, the prohibition on weekday activities does not apply when pain is involved.

One may always give a non-professional massage. Since it is not professional, it is not considered medicinal, nor is it considered a weekday activity. Even a professional masseur may give his family members a non-professional massage that is meant to be soothing. Since they are not in pain and the massage is not done in a therapeutic context, it is not prohibited.

Acupressure is a treatment in which one applies pressure to various parts of the head or body in order to relieve pain and restore the health and vitality of the body and its limbs. When there is no great need, one may not perform it on Shabbat, both because of the enactment against medicine and because it is a weekday activity. However, one who is in pain may undergo acupressure, either manually or with an instrument designed for this purpose.

One may not administer acupuncture on Shabbat even for one who is in pain, because the needles are *muktzeh meḥamat ḥesron kis*. However, a patient who needs acupuncture very badly may be treated. As we already have seen (n. 2 above), the Sages suspended their enactments for the sake of caring for a sick person. Even for a sick person, acupuncture is only permitted on condition that the treatment will not necessarily cause bleeding, which is prohibited by Torah law.

In circumstances where a professional may provide treatment (of pain or illness) on Shabbat, he may not accept payment for his services. However, if he provides treatment during the week as well, the Shabbat payment may be subsumed within the weekday payments (above, 22:12). When a professional is summoned to provide treatment on Shabbat, one may not discuss the arrangements for subsuming his fee. Rather, one may say that after Shabbat they will discuss the details that they may not discuss on Shabbat. This is because when necessary, the Sages permitted alluding to such matters (above, 22:3, 10).

14. SEEING A NON-OBSERVANT DOCTOR

If a sick person whose life is not threatened needs to see a doctor on Shabbat for an examination or treatment, he should try to visit a religious doctor who knows how to avoid *melakhot* that are prohibited by Torah law. If he goes to a Jewish doctor who normally desecrates Shabbat, there is a concern that he will cause the doctor to desecrate Shabbat. For example, the doctor might turn on a light in order to examine him, write down his personal information, or write a prescription for him. We have already seen that only rabbinic prohibitions are suspended for the sake of caring for a sick person who is not dangerously ill, but Torah prohibitions remain in force. Furthermore, just as one should give preference to an observant doctor, one should also give preference to a hospital that operates in accordance with *halakha*. In hospitals that do not operate in accordance with *halakha*, he may encounter Jewish staff members who will transgress Torah prohibitions on his account.

If it is not possible to see an observant doctor or visit a hospital that operates in accordance with *halakha*, one may see a non-observant doctor as long as he requests that the doctor refrain from desecrating Shabbat by Torah law on his account. If the doctor insists on writing in the normal fashion or on doing other *melakhot* that are prohibited by Torah law, the patient should forgo the treatment to avoid aiding Shabbat desecration. Under pressing circumstances, when the exam and treatment are extremely urgent, the patient may rely on the lenient position and accept treatment from this doctor.[9]

---

9. R. Shlomo Zalman Auerbach (cited in SSK ch. 40 n. 32) says that when one is entitled to treatment covered by his health fund or HMO, he is entitled to go to the hospital and is not responsible to prevent the doctor from violating Torah prohibitions. Just as a creditor has a right to bring his debtor to court even if the debtor threatens to curse him, blaspheme God, and swear falsely, the creditor may still take him to court. Similarly, one may accept the medical treatment to which he is entitled. SSK 40:10 rules this way in practice. This ruling can be combined with that of *Shakh*, which maintains that one does not have to worry about aiding the Shabbat desecration of a non-observant Jew who desecrates Shabbat regularly. However, according to *Ḥavot Yair* and most *poskim*, the prohibition of aiding Shabbat desecration applies even to him (*Pitḥei Teshuva*, YD 151:3).

In any case, many are stringent here because in practice, one who sees a non-observant doctor on Shabbat indeed causes him to sin. The Torah commands us to reprove our fellow Jew in order to help them avoid sin. Yet here the patient is aiding the Shabbat desecration of the doctor. Those who are stringent include *Zivḥei Tzedek*, OḤ 2:19; Ben Ish Ḥai in *Rav Berakhot, ma'arekhet lamed*, 3; and *Yesodei Yeshurun*. See *Harḥavot*.

Chapter Twenty-Nine

Eruvin

1. TRANSFORMING A PUBLIC DOMAIN

As we learned in chapter 21, one may transport items on Shabbat within a private domain (*reshut ha-yaḥid*) but not more than four *amot* within a public domain (*reshut ha-rabim*) and not from a public to a private domain and vice versa.

An *eruv,* however, transforms a *reshut ha-rabim* into a *reshut ha-yaḥid,* thus allowing people to transport items within that area without limit, as well as to transport items from homes and yards into that area, and vice versa.

An *eruv* has two components, one pertaining to the area that will be transformed into a private domain, and the other relating to the people who will live within the *eruv*'s boundaries. In order to define the area as a single private domain, it must be enclosed by a fence. However, this is not enough. The people who live within the area must also establish a partnership with one another. This is done by means of two meals worth of food that is owned collectively by everyone and from which anyone may partake. This communal food is called an *eruv* (literally "merging") because it merges or joins together all the homes and yards, turning them into a single private domain. Nevertheless, it has become commonplace to call the enclosure itself an *eruv* as well, and we follow this convention.

As we learned (21:2-3), there is a difference between a *reshut ha-rabim* by Torah law and a semipublic domain (*karmelit*), which is treated as a *reshut ha-rabim* by rabbinic law. In order to permit carrying in a *reshut ha-rabim* by Torah law, the area must be enclosed by a wall or fence at least ten *tefaḥim* high (approximately one meter),[1] and the gates that people use to enter the enclosure must be locked at night (SA 364:2).

However, a *karmelit,* considered a public domain on the rabbinic level, need not be enclosed by an actual fence. Rather, it is sufficient to surround it with *tzurot ha-petaḥ* (defined in the following section) to transform it into a *reshut ha-yaḥid* (SA 362:10-11).

2. *TZURAT HA-PETAḤ*

We have learned (21:8-9) that according to most *poskim,* today's streets are considered a *karmelit.* Thus, to permit carrying in the streets, it is sufficient to surround them with structures resembling doorways (*tzurot ha-petaḥ*), which form a kind of wall around them.

The basic form of a doorway is comprised of two doorposts with a lintel atop them. A lintel can be formed by laying a board across the top of two posts or running a string above the posts.

1. A *tefaḥ,* according to R. Ḥayim Naeh, is 3.15 in (8 cm). Ten *tefaḥim,* then, is 31.5 in (80 cm). He bases his calculations on Rambam's opinion regarding the size of a dirhem (a unit of mass derived from the Greek drachma coin). However, it has since been ascertained that a dirhem at the time of Rambam was more than ten percent smaller in volume than the Turkish dirhem with which R. Naeh was familiar. This means that R. Naeh's *shi'ur* is too large. Using the corrected measurements, a *tefaḥ* is 3 in (7.6 cm) and ten *tefaḥim* is 30 in (76 cm). Ḥazon Ish, basing himself on *Noda Bi-Yehuda,* maintains that a *tefaḥ* is 3.78 in (9.6 cm). The law accords with Rambam, whose opinion is accepted by the vast majority of *poskim,* taking into account the current knowledge about the size of the dirhem. Nevertheless, for two generations, people have grown accustomed to relying on R. Naeh's *shi'ur.* Additionally, some follow the stringent opinion of Ḥazon Ish. It would seem reasonable *le-khatḥila* to follow Ḥazon Ish when building an *eruv* (whether enclosed by a fence or *tzurot ha-petaḥ*), since sometimes the wire droops. When that happens, if the *eruv* was constructed based on a small *shi'ur,* its validity is uncertain. By following Ḥazon Ish, we avoid this problem. In addition, an *eruv* is meant to serve the entire community. *Le-khatḥila,* when acting on behalf of the entire community, it is more important than usual to try to meet the requirements of all the different opinions. In light of all this, I write generally that ten *tefaḥim* is approximately one meter (following Ḥazon Ish), even though technically one could follow the smaller, updated *shi'ur.* When there is a gap of ten *amot,* which can disqualify the *eruv,* one should be stringent and use the smaller, updated *shi'ur* of 4.56 m.

The main requirement for a *tzurat ha-petaḥ* is for the posts on the sides and the string or wire above them to be configured like a doorway. Since the lowest doorway is ten *tefaḥim* high, the poles of a *tzurat ha-petaḥ* must be at least that high to be considered valid for an *eruv*. The wire extended above them must also be at least ten *tefaḥim* above the ground. Accordingly, if any part of the wire droops lower than that, the entire area between the poles is considered breached, since there is no actual doorway in which any part of the lintel is lower than ten *tefaḥim*. And if the poles are more than ten *amot* (4.56 m) away from one another, the entire *eruv* is disqualified, as a breach of ten *amot* disqualifies an *eruv*.

Since the poles form the sides of the *tzurat ha-petaḥ*, they must be strong enough that a normal wind would not cause them to sway, and to support some type of door, even if only an extremely light one made of straw (SA 362:11).[2]

According to most *poskim*, there is no limit to how wide a *tzurat petaḥ* may be, as it can retain the basic form of a doorway even if it extends for a thousand *amot*. However, Rambam maintains that when most of the *eruv*'s perimeter is comprised of *tzurot ha-petaḥ*, no *tzurat ha-petaḥ* may extend longer than ten *amot*. *Le-khatḥila*, when possible, his opinion should be taken into consideration. However, in practice, since it is very difficult to enclose towns and cities using *tzurot he-petaḥ* that are limited to ten *amot*, we are lenient and do not limit the width of a *tzurat petaḥ* (SA 362:10).

The wire that is stretched between the tops of the poles must be secured well enough that it will not become detached in a normal wind. *Le-khatḥila*, when possible, it should be stretched taut so that it will not even sway in the wind or droop down below the tops of the posts, since lintels do not normally sway or droop. However, *be-di'avad*, even if the wire sways or droops, the *eruv* is kosher (MB 362:65; AHS 362:37).

2. The pole that is used to form the *tzurat ha-petaḥ* must look like a pole. Therefore, one should not use a wall as a pole for this purpose (MA 363:28). However, if the *tzurat ha-petaḥ* is parallel to a wall and continues where the wall leaves off, the edge of the wall can be considered a pole (Ḥazon Ish 70:15; see R. Elimelech Lange, *Hilkhot Eruvin* 4:12, p. 55).

3. ENSURING THAT THE WIRE IS STRETCHED ACROSS THE TOPS OF THE POSTS AND ELECTRICAL POLES

One must take care that the wire that serves as the lintel stretches over the poles, not alongside them, as in a *tzurat ha-petaḥ* the lintel sits atop the doorposts. Even if the post is low and the wire runs far above its tip (as with power lines), as long as the wire runs directly over the post, and the post is at least ten *tefaḥim* high, it is considered a valid doorpost, and the wire is considered a valid lintel. But if the wire is not directly above the pole, the *eruv* is invalid. If the pole is crooked, the wire must extend directly above the tip of the pole; if the wire is above any other part of the pole, the *eruv* is invalid (SA 362:11; MB *ad loc.* 64).[3]

Utility poles and the cables they support cannot serve as *tzurot ha-petaḥ*, because the cables generally do not pass directly over the poles, but alongside. In order to solve this problem, additional poles, each about a meter high, must be erected directly underneath the cables.[4]

---

3. When erecting a low pole underneath a wire that extends high above, one must ensure that there is nothing between the poles and the wire, such as an awning. This is the position of *Taz* and MB 363:112. However, some are lenient *be-di'avad*, including AHS 363:46 and *Meshiv Davar* 1:26.

   If a pole has a hole near the top, according to most *poskim* one can thread the wire through it. The wire is not considered situated on the side of the pole, since it is still situated above the section of the pole below it. Even though the pole continues above the wire, this is not a problem. This is the approach of AHS 362:32 and *Ḥazon Ish* 7:9. However, *Pri Megadim* and MB 362:64 are stringent. Since the pole continues above the wire, the wire cannot be considered situated above the pole. The same disagreement applies to a pole that has deep grooves, where the wire is wrapped around them in such a way that it is contained completely within the grooves. Those who are lenient consider the wire situated above the pole, while those who are stringent maintain that since the pole continues above the wire, the wire cannot be considered situated above the pole. In a time of necessity, one may rely on those who are lenient.

4. When several utility poles are situated in a straight line, it is enough to erect *eruv* posts underneath the cables of the two outlying utility poles. The poles in the middle are not considered doorposts, but only extra supports for the lintel. This is the opinion of most *poskim*, including *Divrei Malkiel* 3:16. Nevertheless, some are stringent and require placing an *eruv* pole underneath every single utility pole, because otherwise those who see them may mistakenly think that utility poles never need to be supplemented with *eruv* poles.

   What I have written concerning utility poles is the opinion of the vast majority of *poskim*. A lenient opinion maintains that only if one constructs a *tzurat ha-petaḥ*

4. FENCES, BREACHES, AND A *TEL HA-MITLAKET*

A fence that is ten *tefaḥim* high is considered a bona fide wall and is effective in transforming even a *reshut ha-rabim* by Torah law into a *reshut ha-yaḥid* (as explained above in 21:2-3). Even a chain-link fence is acceptable for this purpose. As long as each of the spaces between the wires is less than three *tefaḥim* wide, the fence is considered continuous, and it can transform even a *reshut ha-rabim* by Torah law into a *reshut ha-yaḥid.*

If a fence or series of *tzurot ha-petaḥ* encloses an area but has gaps in the perimeter, as long as each gap is less than ten *amot* wide and the combined width of all the gaps on any side of the perimeter is less than the combined length of the fence or *tzurot ha-petaḥ* on that side, the *eruv* is kosher (MB 362:45; however, AHS 362:23 maintains that the lengths to compare are those of the entire perimeter, not just one side). In contrast, if the unfenced section of any side of the city is longer than the fenced section on that side, or if there is a gap anywhere that is longer than ten *amot,* the *eruv* is invalid (SA 362:9).

If one side of the city consists of houses with yards enclosed by fences, with open space between the yards, then if the distance between each yard is less than ten *amot,* and the width of each yard is greater than ten *amot,* there is no need to enclose that side any further with a wall or *tzurat ha-petaḥ.* The fences surrounding the yards are considered walls, and the gaps of less than ten *amot* do not disqualify them.

If a city is encircled by a garden with terraces at least ten *tefaḥim* high, then it is considered walled, and there is no need to add another

---

but attaches the wire to the side of the poles does he show that he is not interested in constructing a valid *tzurat ha-petaḥ*. In contrast, if poles are erected for a different purpose, such as in the case of utility poles, and wires are attached to the sides of these poles, this does not show that one is not interested in a *tzurat ha-petaḥ*. Therefore, this opinion allows these poles to be used for an *eruv* (*Sho'el U-meshiv, Mahadura Kama* 2:88). Some are lenient because the settings over which electrical wires pass are tightly connected to the utility pole and are considered part of it, so the wires are above the pole in accordance with the lenient opinion in the previous note. Furthermore, according to some, Rif and Rambam maintain that even if the wire is situated at the side of the pole, this does not invalidate the *eruv*. This opinion is quoted in *Ḥelkat Yaakov* 1:200. In practice, we do not use utility poles for *tzurot ha-petaḥ* without first making the adjustments described above. See R. Elimelech Lange, *Hilkhot Eruvin* ch. 4 nn. 60, 66, and 67.

wall or *tzurat ha-petaḥ*. If only part of the city is enclosed by a terrace, then that part needs no additional wall.

If one side of a city is built on a hill, then if the hill is steep enough that it declines ten *tefaḥim* (30 in or 76 cm) every four horizontal *amot* (5.98 ft or 1.824 m), it renders everything above the slope a *reshut ha-yaḥid*. The Sages refer to such a hill as a *tel ha-mitlaket*, and it is considered a bona fide wall (SA 345:2).

If a town is surrounded by a fence, and the gate at the entrance road is wider than ten *amot*, then as long as the gate will be closed at night, the *eruv* is valid even when the gate is open (SA 364:2; *Melumdei Milḥama* §74). However, if the gate is generally left open at night, or if it merely serves as a barrier (or boom gate), which, even when closed, is not a proper wall, a *tzurat ha-petaḥ* should be erected above the gate.

5. FORMING A PARTNERSHIP USING TWO MEALS' WORTH OF FOOD

As we have seen (section 1 above), in order to transform a *reshut ha-rabim* or *karmelit* into a *reshut ha-yaḥid* in which carrying is permitted, it is not enough to enclose it in a fence or *tzurat ha-petaḥ*. A partnership must also be formed among all the residents in the enclosed area. This is accomplished by means of bread owned jointly by every resident of the enclosed area. It is not necessary to use bread made from one of the five species of cereal grains; rice bread is also acceptable (SA 366:8). If fewer than eighteen people live in the enclosed area, it is sufficient to have enough jointly-owned bread for each person to have the volume of one *grogeret* (dried fig). If there are exactly eighteen people, a volume of eighteen *grogarot* is required, the quantity considered the equivalent of two meals' worth. For a group of more than eighteen residents – even a thousand – the amount of bread required to form a partnership between all of them does not change, but remains uniform at two meals' worth.

The *poskim* disagree about the precise quantity of two meals' worth of food. The accepted ruling is that *le-khatḥila* the volume of eight eggs (about 13.5 oz or 400 ml) should be used, while *be-di'avad* the volume of six eggs (about 10.1 oz or 300 ml) is sufficient (SA 368:3). As mentioned above, this communal food is called an *eruv* (literally "merging") because through it everyone is merged or joined together, and their enclosed property is defined as a *reshut ha-yaḥid*.

Since the *eruv* bread belongs to all residents of the city, any of them may eat it whenever he wishes. If the *eruv* was eaten during Shabbat, the residents may continue to carry for all of that Shabbat. Since the *eruv* was there during *bein ha-shmashot* on Friday (when Shabbat began), the partnership was already formed. For the next Shabbat, however, a new *eruv* must be set aside.[5]

On a kibbutz or anywhere else where all the residents eat together in a communal dining hall, it is sufficient to erect a *tzurat ha-petaḥ* around the area. It is not necessary to put aside two meals' worth of food in such a case, since the food in the communal kitchen serves to form the general partnership necessary for an *eruv*.

6. SETTING ASIDE THE *ERUV* AND RECITING ITS *BERAKHA*

It is customary to use matza for the *eruv*, as it has a long shelf life and can continue to serve as the *eruv* for as long as it remains edible (SA 368:5). Common practice is to set aside a new *eruv* before Pesaḥ each year and to recite the *berakha* and the formula for setting aside the *eruv* of the

5. There are actually two types of "*eruv*" that transform a public domain into a private domain: *eruv ḥatzerot* ("merging of courtyards") and *shitufei mevo'ot* ("sharing of alleyways"). The purpose of an *eruv ḥatzerot* is to permit carrying in a *reshut ha-yaḥid* that is divided into areas owned by different people. The Sages decreed that one should not carry from a home belonging to one person to a home belonging to another, even when both homes are a private domains. Since they belong to different people, the area between them resembles a public domain. By setting aside an *eruv ḥatzerot*, the homeowners become partners, and may carry from one home to another. The food for an *eruv ḥatzerot* must be placed in one of the homes (SA 368:3), and it must consist of bread (SA 368:1). In contrast, a *shitufei mevo'ot* is more effective, because it transforms all the homes, yards, and streets into one domain, within which everyone may carry. Therefore, the food for a *shitufei mevo'ot* does not need to be placed in a home; a yard can suffice. It also does not have to consist of bread; two meals' worth of any food is acceptable. When a *shitufei mevo'ot* is set aside, there is no need for an *eruv ḥatzerot*. This is why nowadays the custom is to leave the *eruv* food in the synagogue; even though it cannot be considered a home, the *eruv* is valid, because it is in fact a *shitufei mevo'ot* (SA 368:3; 386:1 and BHL *ad loc.*). Nevertheless, since a *shitufei mevo'ot* can also serve as an *eruv ḥatzerot*, we make sure to use bread.

upcoming year (detailed below). In many communities, the rabbi is given the honor of performing this ritual on behalf of the community. Even if the residents forgot to set aside a new *eruv* before Pesaḥ, as long as the old *eruv* is still in existence, one may continue carrying throughout the enclosed area.

The *eruv* must be placed in one box or bag. The custom is to leave it in the synagogue or nearby, as the synagogue is a communal space.

Before setting aside the *eruv*, one must make sure that it belongs to all residents of the city. Therefore, the person charged with setting aside the *eruv* first lifts the *matzot* one *tefaḥ* with the intent to acquire them on behalf of all the city's residents. In order for him to acquire the *matzot* successfully, they must have previously belonged to a different person.

Before acquiring the *eruv* and setting it aside, the following *berakha* must be recited: "Blessed are You, Lord our God, King of the universe, Who sanctified us with His *mitzvot* and commanded us concerning the mitzva of *eruv*" ("*asher kideshanu be-mitzvotav ve-tzivanu al mitzvat eruv*"). Afterward, he should recite:

> With this *eruv* it shall be permitted to us (all the people living here in the town, city, or courtyard) to bring things in and out – from the houses to the yard and the yard to the houses, from house to house, from yard to yard, from roof to roof, from houses and yards to alleyways, and from alleyways to houses and yards in this city – for us, all who live here, and whoever joins us during all upcoming *Shabbatot* and holidays. (SA 365:15; MB *ad loc.* 83)

7. AN *ERUV* WHERE SHABBAT DESECRATORS LIVE

The *eruv*, the two meals' worth of food that all residents within the enclosed area own jointly, unites all the residents and renders the enclosed area a private domain, where carrying is permitted. However, all this is on condition that all the area residents, without exception, are partners in the *eruv*. If any one of them is not interested in participating, then the area can no longer be considered a single domain, and the *eruv* is invalid.

In light of this, it is problematic to implement an *eruv* in cities and towns whose residents include Jews who do not observe Shabbat.

Since they are not interested in an *eruv*, they and their homes are not included in the partnership of the *eruv*, which means the *eruv* cannot be valid. The same problem exists if a non-Jew lives in the area; since his home is not included in the *eruv*, the *eruv* is invalidated (SA 385:3; 382:1).

The solution is for the Shabbat desecrator or non-Jew to rent out his home for Shabbat to one of the Shabbat observers. This way his home will be included in the *eruv* as well. The problem with this solution is that it is almost impossible to implement in large towns, let alone cities. Therefore, it became customary to use a different solution – renting all the homes in the area from a city official who has the authority to enter every house in the city (SA 391:1).

Some argue that this solution is not viable today. In a democratic country, the mayor of a city does not have the right to enter the home of a private individual without a warrant. Still, the custom is to be lenient. After all, during wartime, the town major and the head of home front command may requisition homes of their choosing. They may even do so during training exercises. Therefore, these authorities have a share of ownership in all the homes, and one may rent their share from them before Shabbat for the purposes of the *eruv*.[6]

6. In Israel, a local rabbi generally acquires ownership from the mayor, as well as from the chief of police. Some also do so from the director of the local branch of the Ministry of the Interior, since in an emergency the police chief is authorized to enter any home, while the mayor and the representative of the Ministry of the Interior have authority over the streets. The terms of the acquisition grant the rabbi permission to leave things wherever he wants, making him a part owner of all places within the enclosed area. As a result, the *eruv* can include everyone in the area.

   It should be noted that we always tend to be lenient regarding the issue of constructing an *eruv* in a place where Shabbat desecrators live. This is because the prohibition on including non-Jews or Shabbat-desecrating Jews in an *eruv* is really a punitive stringency; technically, they may join with Shabbat-observing Jews to form an *eruv* partnership. The Sages wanted to discourage observant Jews from living in neighborhoods with Shabbat desecrators and non-Jews, so they penalized those who did so by forbidding such an *eruv*. However, if there is no alternative, we make use of any reasonable justification to be lenient and participate with all local residents in making an *eruv*. See *Ḥazon Ish* 18:9; AHS 391:4; *Menuḥat Ahava* vol. 3, p. 363.

8. AN *ERUV* THAT BECOMES INVALIDATED ON SHABBAT

Sometimes it becomes apparent during Shabbat that a wire from the *eruv* has snapped in a certain place, thus invalidating the *eruv*. Two questions then arise: 1) May the *eruv* be fixed on Shabbat? 2) If it turns out that the *eruv* cannot be fixed, do all the residents need to be informed that the *eruv* is down so they know not to carry?

Le-khatḥila, if a non-Jew is available, it is preferable that he fix the *eruv*. Although asking a non-Jew to do *melakha* for Jews on Shabbat is rabbinically prohibited, nevertheless, when there is a great need to save the masses from the prohibition of carrying on Shabbat, the Sages permitted asking a non-Jew to fix the *eruv*, even if this will involve *melakhot* that are prohibited by Torah law (MB 276:25; above 9:12).

However, if no non-Jew is available, a Jew certainly may not violate Torah prohibitions in order to fix the *eruv*. For example, if a pole has fallen over, a Jew may not stand it back up by jamming it into the ground. Similarly, if the wire has snapped, one may not tie it back together with a permanent knot, as tying this type of knot on Shabbat is forbidden by Torah law. However, the *poskim* debate whether one may tie a bow knot (the type used to tie shoelaces), as tying this type of knot on Shabbat is permissible.

Some argue that fixing the *eruv* on Shabbat is absolutely forbidden. Even though it is permissible to tie a bow knot on Shabbat, nevertheless in this case tying it would permit carrying on Shabbat. This means that by tying it, one constructs a *meḥitza ha-materet* (above, 15:4), which is forbidden on Shabbat. In other words, the Sages prohibited making a wall that serves to permit something that was previously halakhically forbidden. In this case, before one tied the knot it was prohibited to carry, while afterward it was permitted.

Others maintain that although the Sages generally forbade constructing a *meḥitza ha-materet,* nevertheless, in order to save the masses from sinning by carrying on Shabbat, one may create a *meḥitza ha-materet* by tying a bow knot. This is the common custom (*Responsa Mahari Ashkenazi* §13; *Panim Me'irot* 1:30; *Sho'el U-meshiv, Mahadura Tinyana* 1:89; SSK 17:34).

If the *eruv* cannot be fixed, this should not be announced publicly. This information is withheld out of concern that some people will carry anyway, desecrating Shabbat knowingly, and it is better that they transgress unknowingly rather than knowingly. The only people who should be informed are those who will definitely follow the *halakha* and refrain from carrying.[7]

7. This is the approach of *Maḥshavot Be-etza* §16. In principle, whenever there is a chance that people will listen, even if it is more likely that they will not, we do not say that "it is better that people transgress unknowingly rather than knowingly." As long as there is a chance that they will listen to reproof, we must reprove them (MB 608:3 based on Rosh). Accordingly, it would seem at first glance that the public must be informed that the *eruv* is down, as there is a chance that many people will follow the *halakha* and refrain from carrying. Nevertheless, R. Shlomo Zalman Auerbach explains (SSK ch. 17 n. 139) that carrying unknowingly in this case is considered even less severe than transgressing unknowingly in general; since people believe the *eruv* is still valid, as far as they know they are carrying permissibly. Thus, one who carries in such a situation is viewed as transgressing a rabbinic prohibition obliviously (*mitasek*). Therefore, it is better not to announce that the *eruv* is down.

Chapter Thirty

Teḥum Shabbat

1. GENERAL PRINCIPLES OF *TEḤUM SHABBAT*

The need to travel from place to place stems from man's deficiency: he cannot find his livelihood and meet his needs by remaining stationary. So he must roam and leave his place. But the idea of Shabbat is for every Jew to rest from his travails and worries, contemplate the inner perfection of creation, thank God for choosing Israel from all peoples and giving us His Torah, and delight in God and His goodness.

For this reason, the Sages ordained boundaries (*teḥumin*) within which one may walk on Shabbat, and beyond which one may not walk. One's *teḥum Shabbat* (Shabbat boundary) is determined by his *mekom shevita* – the place where he is spending Shabbat (literally "stopping place") – plus 2,000 *amot* in each direction (2,000 *amot* corresponds to 2,000 steps of an average person, approximately 0.57 mi or 912 m).[1]

1. According to R. Ḥayim Naeh's calculations, which are based on Rambam (with whom the vast majority of *poskim* agree), one *ama* is 18.9 in (48 cm), and 2,000 *amot* is 0.6 mi (960 m). According to Ḥazon Ish, one *ama* is 22.7 in (57.6 cm), and 2,000 *amot* is 0.72 mi (1152 m). Since it has been ascertained that the Turkish dirhem with which R. Naeh was familiar is larger than the dirhem used in Rambam's time, we should follow the more accurate calculation even though it results in a stringency. (Additionally, the *shi'urim* of volume need to be in sync with the *shi'urim* of distance, since the Sages said that the volume of forty *se'ah* can fit into an area of one *ama* by one *ama* by three *amot*.) Therefore, R. Ḥayim Beinish writes in *Midot Ve-shi'urei*

If one is spending Shabbat in a field (i.e., not in a city or town), his *mekom shevita* is defined as four *amot* squared. This is the amount of space one occupies when lying on the ground with his arms and legs outstretched.[2] He may walk 2,000 *amot* beyond that in each direction. If he is spending Shabbat in a city or town, the entire settled area is considered one place, and he may travel 2,000 *amot* beyond the city limits (see section 8 below).

According to Rambam and *Smag, teḥum Shabbat* restrictions are based on Torah law, though the Torah prohibition forbids one to travel more than twelve *mil* (24,000 *amot*, which is 6.8 mi or 10.944 km, almost eleven km) from his *mekom shevita*. This is based on the size of the Israelite camp in the wilderness, as the Torah states: "Let everyone remain where he is; let no man leave his place on the seventh day" (Shemot 16:29). However, according to Ramban, Rosh, Rashba, and most Rishonim, this verse does not refer to the laws of *teḥum* but rather to those of carrying in a *reshut ha-rabim*; all boundary restrictions (even beyond twelve *mil*) are rabbinic law.[3]

Torah 5:24 that according to Rambam, one *ama* is 18 in (45.6 cm) and 2,000 *amot* is 0.57 mi (912 m). In addition, the actual length of the average man's forearm (*ama*) is approximately 17.7 in (45 cm). See *Peninei Halakha: Berakhot*, ch. 10 n. 11. This is how we present every halakhic measurement. See above, ch. 29 n. 1.

2. According to SA 396:1, one's "place" is four *amot* by four *amot*, as it is with regard to carrying in a *reshut ha-rabim* or a *karmelit*. Rema writes that some maintain for the purposes of *teḥumin*, one's place extends four *amot* from the center in each direction, for a total of eight *amot* by eight *amot*.

3. The Sages were uncertain whether boundary restrictions apply above ten *tefaḥim*; perhaps, since people do not walk there, the prohibition does not apply there. In practice, when there is uncertainty pertaining to a rabbinic prohibition, the law follows the more lenient position. Therefore, regarding boat travel in oceans and rivers, where Rambam agrees that the prohibition is not a Torah prohibition (as such travel is not comparable to travel in the wilderness), as long as one is ten *tefaḥim* above the seabed, the *teḥum* prohibitions do not apply (*Eruvin* 43a; SA 404:1). According to SA 248:2, the ten *tefaḥim* above the seabed are measured from the bottom of the boat, while according to R. Eliezer of Metz they are measured from one's feet. SAH and MB 248:14 state that in times of need one may be lenient. However, if one is traveling at a height of more than ten *tefaḥim* above land, several *poskim* maintain that one should be stringent in accordance with Rambam and not travel more than twelve mil (Rema 404:1).

The Sages ordained that if one must travel beyond the *teḥum* on Shabbat – in order to attend a wedding celebration or a Torah lecture – he may make an *eruv teḥumin*, which extends his *teḥum* in the necessary direction (as explained below in sections 12-14). One who leaves his *teḥum* forfeits it and must remain within his four *amot* (as explained below, section 11).

2. SQUARING THE *TEḤUM*

The Sages established that one's *mekom shevita* on Shabbat is square, and thus his *teḥum* is square as well. This means that if he is spending Shabbat in a field, and his *mekom shevita* is thus four *amot*, the measurement is not made by drawing a circle around him with a diameter of four *amot*. Rather, to determine his *mekom shevita* we inscribe such a circle in a square with four-*ama* sides along the four cardinal directions, which adds space to his *mekom shevita* at the corners. Similarly, if one's *mekom shevita* is in a city or town, even if the area is round, we inscribe it in a square or rectangle, adding space at the corners (*m. Eruvin* 53a).

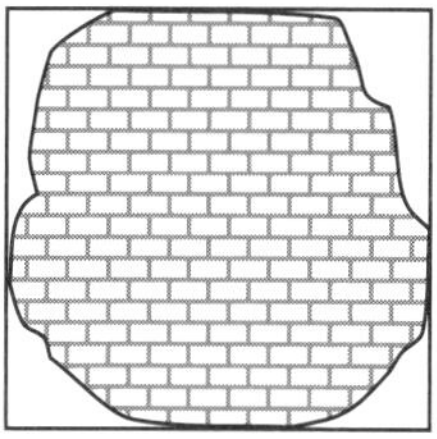

The diameter of the circle is 4 *amot*.

After squaring, the corners are added

Then 2,000 *amot* are measured in each direction. Once again we draw a square or rectangle, which once again grants him additional space in the corners.[4]

4. When measuring 2,000 *amot* from a city or town, according to Rambam and SA 398:5, we measure from the outermost homes or from the *eruv* (following the opinion of the Sages in *Eruvin* 57a). According to Rosh and Rema, one first adds the equivalent area of a *karpif* (an enclosed courtyard in front of the houses) to the city, which amounts to 70 2/3 *amot* (approximately 32 meters). This area is now considered part of the city. From there we measure 2,000 *amot* (following the opinion of R. Meir in the above *gemara*; see MB 398:21 and BHL s.v. "ve-khen"). As explained in section 8 below, when there are two settled areas adjacent to each other, SA agrees to the *karpif* rule.

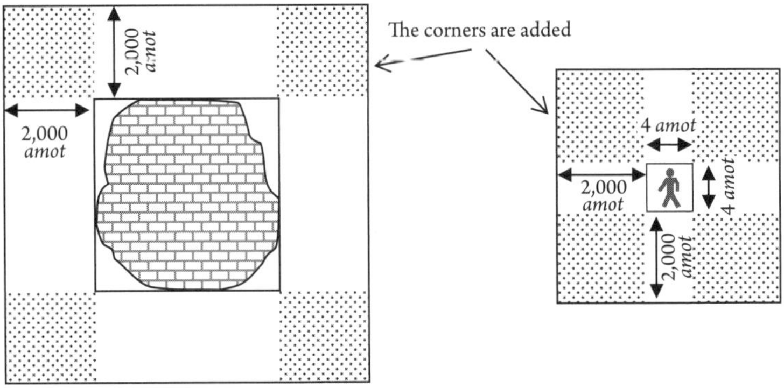

This rule, that we square off the city, is derived from the Torah's description of the area the Levi'im were given outside each of their cities:

> You shall measure off two thousand *amot* outside the city wall all around. You shall measure off two thousand *amot* outside the town on the east side (lit. corner; same applies to the other directions), two thousand on the south side, two thousand on the west side, and two thousand on the north side, with the city in the center. (Bamidbar 35:5)

The most straightforward explanation for why we square the *teḥum* is that it is extremely difficult to measure and mark off a circular boundary. One would need to measure 2,000 *amot* from almost each and every point of the city's perimeter. In contrast, when marking off a square boundary, only four measurements need to be made – one in each of the four cardinal directions. After that, a straight line can be drawn in each direction, and the result is the *teḥum*.

Additionally, this method reflects a spiritual reality. A circle represents the infinite, which has no beginning and no end. A person's life is circular and cyclical. His actions, wishes, and thoughts repeat themselves cyclically. Even his limbs are circular and cylindrical. This makes it difficult for a person to realize his aspirations. The way to solve the problem is to take one's "circular" infinite ideas, and give them a "square" finite framework that will help him put them into practice. This is the meaning of *teḥum Shabbat*, which is meant to provide a framework for absorbing the holiness and blessing of Shabbat. This is why each city belonging to the Levi'im who are charged with revealing faith in this world, is surrounded by a square boundary.

3. *TEḤUM SHABBAT* IS INDIVIDUAL

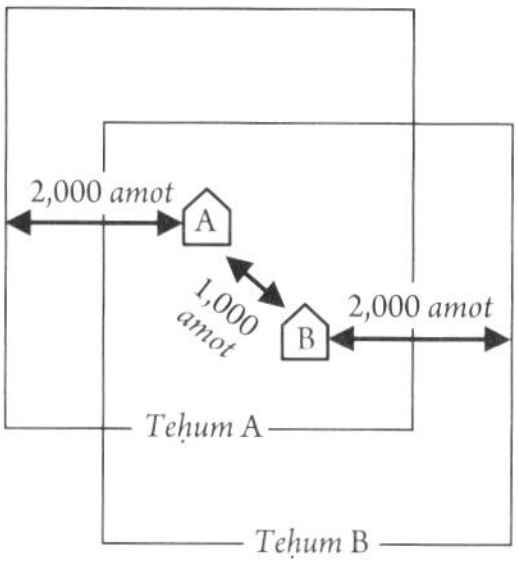

Teḥum Shabbat is specific to every individual, based on his location. For example, let us say that the homes of two neighbors (who do not live in a city) are located 1,000 *amot* apart from each other. Each neighbor has his own *teḥum Shabbat,* part of which overlaps with his neighbor's *teḥum Shabbat,* and part of which does not.

The laws of *teḥumin* apply to one's animals and belongings, and to Jews as well as non-Jews (see n, 12 below). Therefore, if one carried his *talit* to the edge of his *teḥum,* and his friend wants to borrow it but has a different *teḥum,* the friend may not carry the *talit* beyond its owner's *teḥum* (SA 397:3). If the *talit* is jointly owned, it may be carried only where their *teḥumin* overlap (*ibid.,* 397:9).

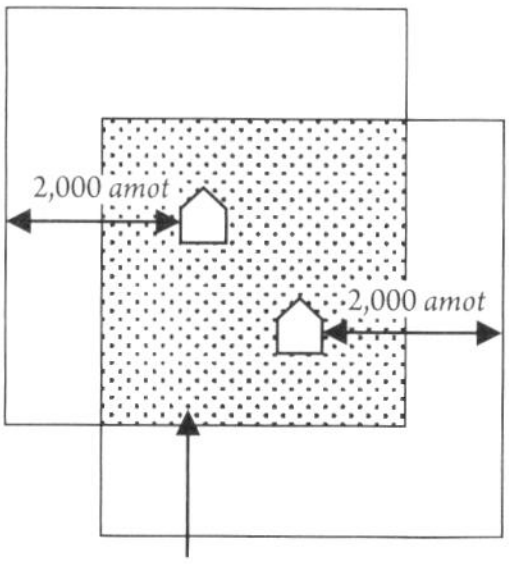

The overlap of the two *teḥumin,* where the *talit* may be carried

4. SPENDING SHABBAT IN OR OUTSIDE A CITY

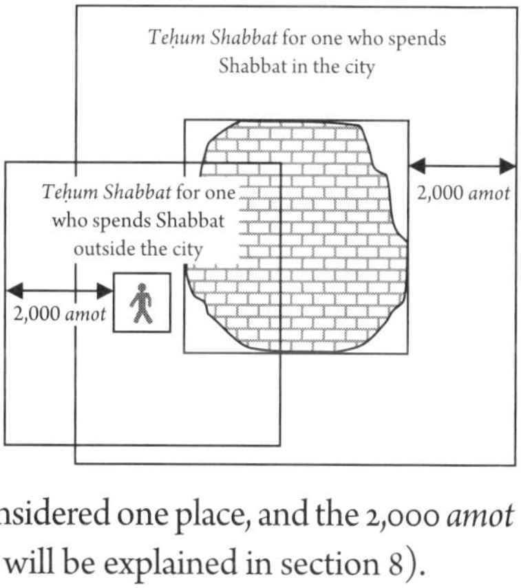

For someone who is spending Shabbat in a city or town, whether its residents are Jewish or non-Jewish, the whole area that is built up contiguously is considered one place, and the 2,000 *amot* of the *teḥum* are measured from its perimeter. Even if there is space between the homes, as long as they are surrounded by a fence or an *eruv,* the entire enclosed area is considered one place, and the 2,000 *amot* are measured from its perimeter (as will be explained in section 8).

All this pertains to one who spends Shabbat in the city or within its squared-off area. However, one who spends Shabbat in a field near the city is limited to 2,000 *amot* in each direction, and if his 2,000 *amot* terminate inside a city, his *teḥum* ends right there, in the middle of the city. We do not consider the whole city his four *amot*.[5]

5. MEASURING *TEḤUM* IN RABBINIC TIMES AND NOWADAYS

The Sages established rules for measuring the *teḥum Shabbat* as precisely as possible. First, they declared: "*Teḥum Shabbat* may be measured only with a rope that is fifty *amot* long, no more or less" (*Eruvin* 57b). If a longer rope were used, its weight would make it hard to pull taut, and the resulting measurement would be too short. If a shorter rope were used, one might pull it too tight, and the resulting measurement would be too long. Second, they required those measuring to hold the rope at chest height. If the person holding one end of the rope were to hold it at head level, while the person at the other end were to hold it at foot level, the resulting measurement would be too short (SA 399:1-3). Third, they said that when measuring an area that contains a valley, one person should stand on either side of the valley, so that they can measure the distance in the air. When measuring an area that contains a hill, tall poles should be set up so that the rope stretches above the hill. If the valley or hill is more than fifty *amot* wide, thus making it impossible to use a fifty-*ama* rope, the area should be measured with a four-*ama* rope. The person standing above should hold the rope at foot level, and the person standing below should hold it at chest level. If the slope is so

5. If a town is so small that the entire area is within his 2,000 *amot*, then the area of the town is skipped (the whole city is considered four *amot*), and his 2,000 *amot* continue from the far edge of the town (SA 408:1). Here is an example:

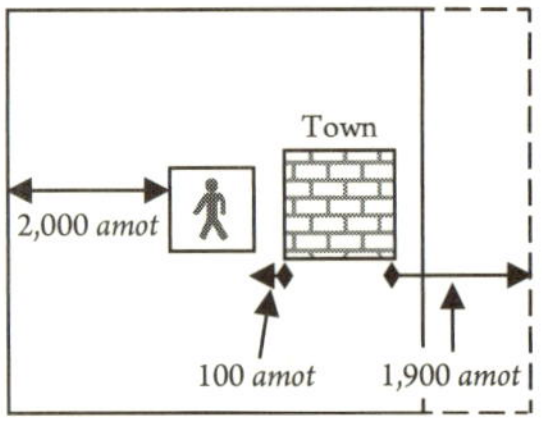

steep that it would be difficult to calculate the measurement this way, the measurement should be estimated. If the area contains a cliff, as long as the cliff is less than four *amot* wide, it is not taken into account at all (*Eruvin* 58a-b; SA 399:4-5).

The Sages added that for these measurements, we rely only on an expert who knows how to calculate distances properly. If two experts arrive at different measurements, we follow the measurement that results in a larger *teḥum*. Since the laws of *teḥum* are rabbinic, we follow the more lenient opinion (*Eruvin* 58b-59a; SA 399:7-9). If one happens to spend Shabbat in a place where *teḥum Shabbat* has not been calculated, and he needs to go somewhere for the sake of a mitzva, he may take 2,000 medium-sized strides, which is approximately 2,000 *amot* (*Eruvin* 42a; SA 397:2; MB *ad loc.* 5).

Today it is best to establish *teḥum Shabbat* using aerial maps or GPS devices, as these can measure distances with extreme precision. We should not insist on measuring in the way that the Sages established. After all, their whole purpose was to measure as precisely as possible, using the tools available to them, without terribly inconveniencing those charged with measuring. Now that we have methods of measuring that are both more precise and more convenient, we must take advantage of them.

6. THE CARDINAL DIRECTIONS AND SQUARING A CITY

As we have seen (section 2), we square a person's *mekom shevita* to determine his *teḥum*. If he is in a field (i.e., not in a city or town), his *mekom shevita* is a square with four-*ama* sides; if he is in a city, we inscribe the city in a square. From this square we measure 2,000 *amot* in each direction.

Let us add now that when we square the city, we do so based on the four cardinal directions (SA 398:3).[6] If the city already has corners

6. The city's residents may not decide to square the city in a way that does not follow the four cardinal directions just because they would like to add space in the corners in the direction they wish to go. This is because the law is unequivocal: the city must be squared in accordance with the four cardinal directions. This is based upon the procedure described for the Levite cities: "You shall measure off two thousand *amot* outside the city wall all around. You shall measure off two thousand *amot* outside the city on the east side, two thousand on the south side, two thousand on the west side,

that lend themselves to squaring in a way that does not follow the four cardinal directions, the squaring is done accordingly (SA 398:1).

Examples of squaring based on the four cardinal directions:

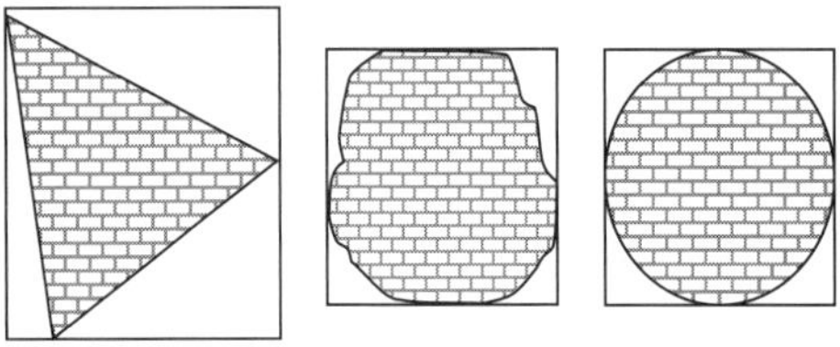

Examples in which it is agreed that the squaring does not follow the four cardinal directions:

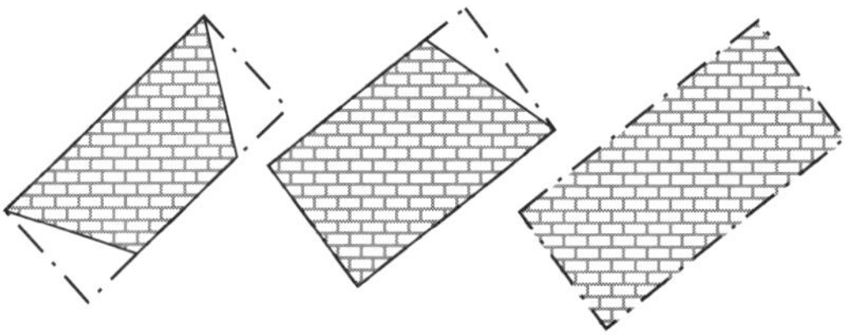

When a city's shape lends itself to squaring that does not correspond to the four cardinal directions, the *poskim* disagree how to square it. Some maintain that only when there is a compelling reason not to follow the four cardinal directions may one follow the layout of the city (SAH 398:3; *Ḥayei Adam* 76:14). However, most *poskim* maintain that if the shape of a city clearly lends itself to squaring in a certain way, we follow this squaring even though it does not correspond to the four cardinal directions (see n. 7). In cases of doubt, the local rabbinate or rabbinic authority should make the decision.

---

and two thousand on the north side, with the city in the center" (Bamidbar 35:5). We see that the verse follows the four cardinal directions. This understanding is implied in MT 28:7 and SA 398:3, and is also followed by MB 398:7 and *Ḥazon Ish* 110:23. Some maintain that the city's residents do have the right to decide to square their city in a way that does not correspond with the four cardinal directions. In such a case, every individual is bound by the group's decision (Rabbeinu Yehonatan, *Eruvin* 16a, s.v. "im"; *Perisha* 398:1; *Mirkevet Ha-Mishneh*, Shabbat 27:2; *Noda Bi-Yehuda, Mahadura Tinyana*, OḤ 51).

Examples of such intermediate cases in which a city's shape clearly lends itself to squaring in a direction other than the four cardinal directions include cases where one side of the city is straight from one end of the city to the other (figure 2) and cases where the perimeter of the city contains a right angle (figure 1, in which case we follow the directions of the right angle and not the four cardinal directions).[7]

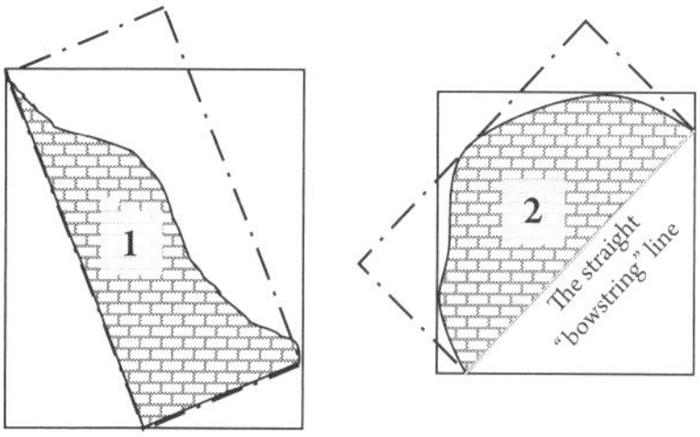

It is important to note that if one is spending Shabbat outside a city and his *mekom shevita* is limited to four *amot* square, he may choose to square his *mekom shevita* in whatever direction he wishes, and this will also determine how his 2,000-*ama teḥum* is squared (see section 12 below).

7. CASES IN WHICH WE DO NOT SQUARE A CITY

As we have seen, by squaring the city, we add space in the corners to the *teḥum*. However, the Sages pointed out that sometimes we cannot draw straight lines to square the whole city, because the resulting square would

7. In the city featured in figure 1, most Rishonim and Aḥaronim rule that it is squared based on the right angle (as is the case with a city that is shaped like an L, according to Rashba, Ran, Ritva, and Me'iri). In the city featured in figure 2, one side of the entire city is a straight line. The law in such a case can be derived from the case of a city that is shaped like a bow (section 7), where it is squared based on this straight line, or "bowstring" (Me'iri, *Eruvin* 55a). Ḥazon Ish states this as well in OḤ 80 and 110. Some maintain that in both the above cases, the city must be squared based on the four cardinal directions (SAH 388:3; *Ḥayei Adam* 76:14). Others maintain that in all doubtful cases, the city is squared in whichever way will add the least area to the city (*Ḥazon Ish* 110:23). The *halakha* follows the first opinion, that of the majority of *poskim*, and the figures above reflect this opinion. Nevertheless, when it is not clear if the perimeter of a city contains a right angle, the local rabbinate or rabbinic authority may decide to rely on those who rule that such a city should be squared based on the four cardinal directions.

include uninhabited areas that are too large to be considered subsumed by the city. Examples of this would be cities that are shaped like a bow or like an L. The operative principle is that if there are 4,000 *amot* between the two ends of the shape, that part of the city cannot be squared.

An L-shaped city:

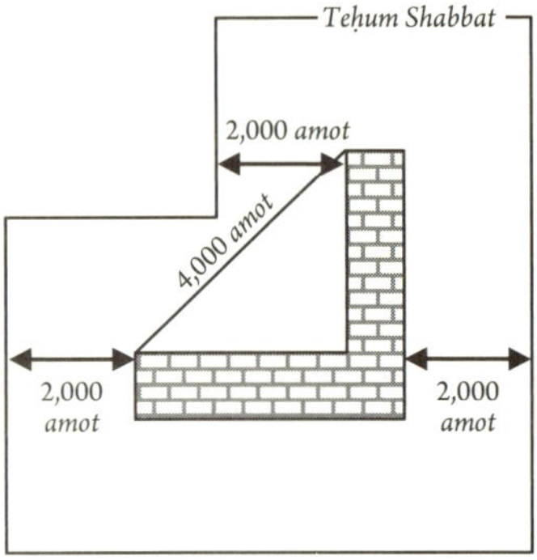

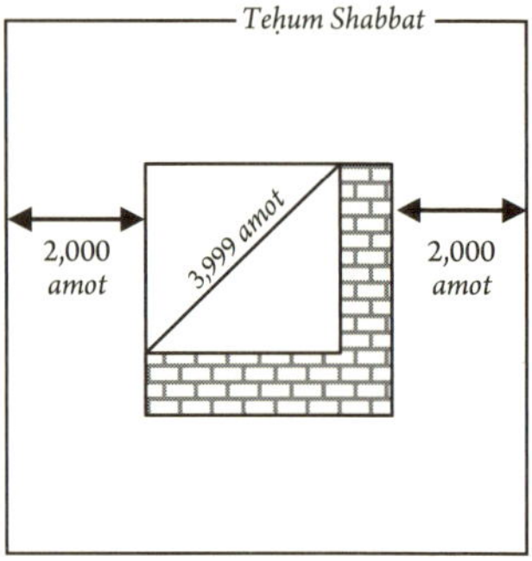

A bow-shaped city:[8]

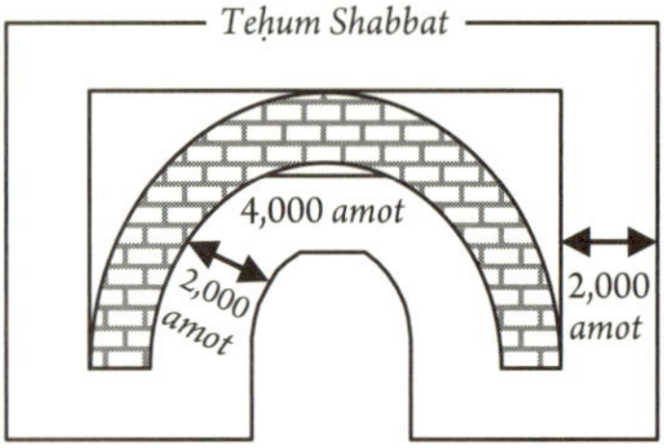

8. Rambam and SA 388:4 state, in disagreement with this diagram, that the 2,000 *amot* are measured from the edges of the inhabited homes. The resulting *teḥum* follows the curve of the bow. However, the diagram follows the opinion of *Tosafot* (55b, s.v. "ve-im lav"), Rosh, most Rishonim, and Rema that for the inside of the bow, where the arc narrows to less than 4,000 *amot*, we draw a "bowstring" from one end of the arc to the other and measure the *teḥum* as 2,000 *amot* from that straight line (see diagram). The *halakha* follows the majority of *poskim*, especially since the laws of *teḥumin* are rabbinic, so the *halakha* follows the lenient position. Although *Tur* has an even more lenient opinion, the rest of the *poskim* disagree, as detailed in BHL s.v. "ve-yesh omrim." Uncertainty still remains regarding how to measure the *teḥum* for the rest of the bow, where the arc widens to 4,000 *amot* and greater. It would seem that we can follow the position of Rambam and SA that the *teḥum* follows the curve, as displayed in the diagram. Ḥazon Ish maintains this as well (OḤ 110:10). See *Harḥavot*.

8. CONNECTING SETTLED AREAS

As long as the houses in a city are contiguous, meaning that they are not farther away from one another than the size of a *karpif* (a large courtyard, approximately 105 ft or 32 m long), they are considered part of one area for the purpose of assessing the *teḥum*. If they are separated from one another by more space than that, they are not considered part of one area, and each house's *teḥum Shabbat* is then calculated separately.[9]

If the houses in a city are contiguous, then even if one house is out of alignment, as long as it is not more than 105 ft (32 m) from the next house, the *teḥum*'s square or rectangle expands to include the unaligned house. If there are additional houses after this one, the *teḥum* expands to include them as well; this can continue even if it means that the *teḥum* extends outside the city proper for a distance that would take days to walk. As long as each house is not separated from the next by more than 105 ft (32 m), the *teḥum* extends to include them. However, if a house is more than 105 ft (32 m) away, it is not included within the rectangle.

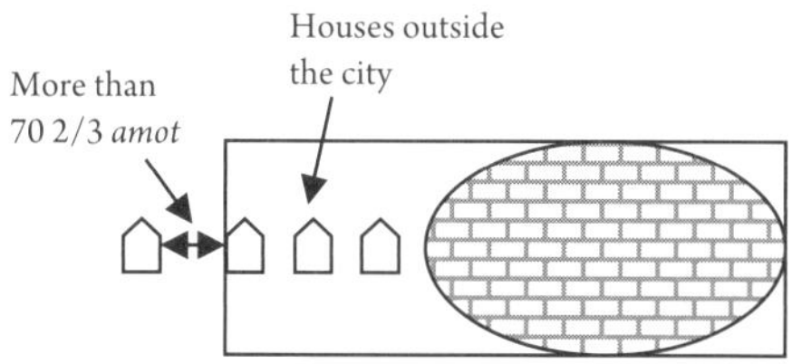

If the distance between two adjacent neighborhoods is greater than the size of two large courtyards (i.e., over 211 ft or 64 m), then each neighborhood is considered a town in its own right. We square each on its own, and then 2,000 *amot* are measured in each direction from that square. In contrast, if the distance separating the two neighborhoods is 211 ft (64 m) or less, they are considered one area and we square them

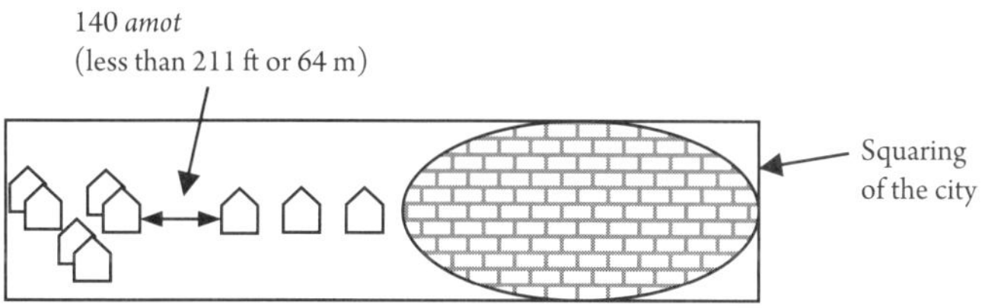

9. The *shi'ur* of a *karpif* is 70 *amot* and four *tefaḥim*. Following the updated calculation described in n. 1, this is 105.7 ft (32.224 m), and the size of two large courtyards is 211.4 ft (64.448 m). For the sake of simplification, we use the rounded-off measurements of 105 ft (32 m) and 211 ft (64 m).

together. There must be at least fifty residents living in an area for a group of houses to be defined as a neighborhood (*Eruvin* 60a). Even if there are fewer than fifty people, as long as the area contains three courtyards, each of which joins two homes together, or six homes, each of which has a courtyard, the area is still considered a neighborhood (MB 398:38; *Ḥazon Ish* OḤ 110:19).

If an area is enclosed by a wall or an *eruv*, all its homes and neighborhoods are considered one area. This is true even when the wall or *eruv* is farther than a *karpif*'s length from the last house, and even if there is a large distance between the homes and neighborhoods.

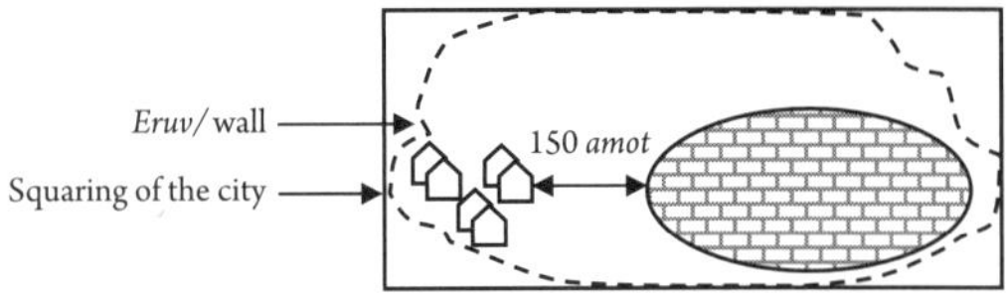

9. OVERLAPPING SQUARES

When the squares or rectangles formed around two cities overlap, even when there is no joint *eruv*, the overlapping area connects the cities. We draw a new rectangle around the entire area to include both cities. The residents of both cities may then walk 2,000 *amot* beyond the joint rectangle.

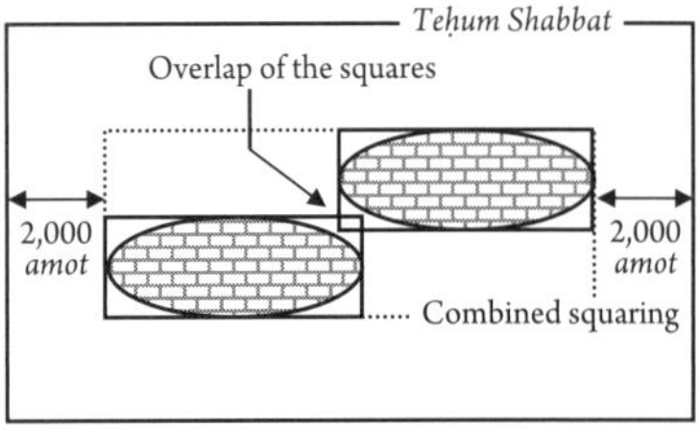

However, if the distance separating the corners of the two rectangles is greater than 4,000 *amot*, as we have seen (section 7), we do not square the entire area. Rather, each city is assigned a standard *teḥum* of 2,000 *amot* beyond its rectangle in each direction.

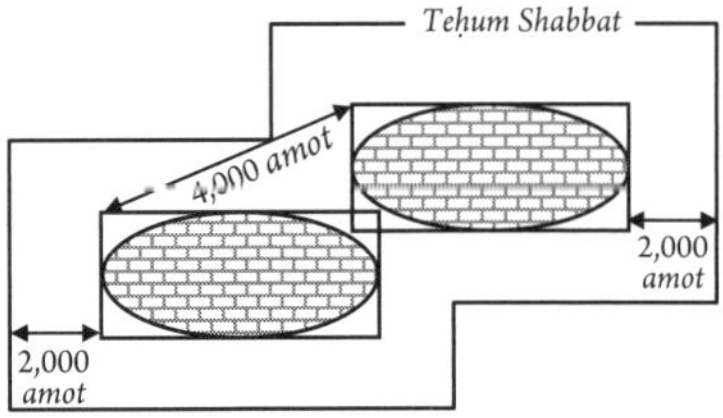

10. THE STATUS OF LARGE CITIES

If a highway within a city is more than 211 ft (64 m) wide and bisects the entire city, then the city is viewed as divided in two, and the *teḥum Shabbat*

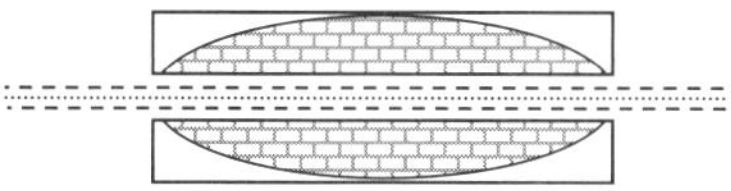

for residents of each of the two sections is calculated separately. This is also the case for a wide-open area such as a park or large garden. If it is more than 211 ft (64 m) wide and bisects the entire city, then the city is viewed as divided in two, and the *teḥum Shabbat* for each of the two sections is calculated separately.

At first glance, it would seem that the Ayalon Highway divides Tel Aviv into two cities. Nevertheless, since there is an *eruv* that encompasses all of Tel Aviv and the nearby cities, the *eruv* unites the different sections. Additionally, if a highway bisects a city but the rectangles drawn around each section overlap, then the overlapping area joins together the sections and we draw a new rectangle around the entire area, as explained above. Additionally, one could argue that since it is intended that all a city's residents will make use of a highway, park, or large garden, they are considered part of the city and do not actually divide it.

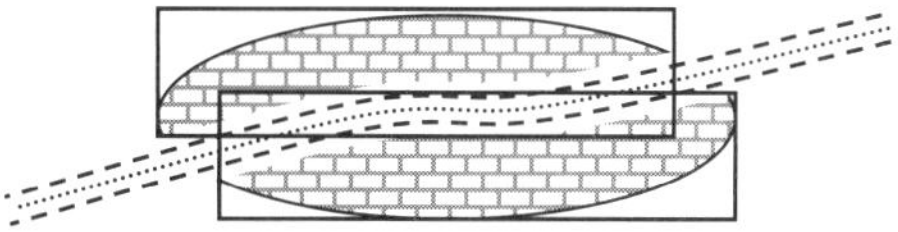

Others disagree, maintaining that these factors – an *eruv*, usage by all city residents, and overlapping rectangles – cannot join together the two sections formed by a highway or park that bisects a city. The primary position is the lenient one. However, it is proper to be stringent and avoid walking more than twelve *mil* beyond the highway, since some say that traveling beyond twelve *mil* is forbidden by Torah law (see section 1 above).[10]

10. As mentioned above, two cities or neighborhoods do not join together if they are separated by 211 ft (64 m), which is double the size of a city's outskirts (SA 398:7). Rema adds that if the entire length of a city is bisected with at least this much space, then the city is viewed as divided in two. Similarly, if a park that is more than 211 ft (64 m) wide stretches the entire length of a city, it divides the city, and each part is considered its own city. R. Ephraim Ariel Buchwald in his book *Kiryat Ariel* presents a ruling of R. Yosef Shalom Elyashiv that the Ayalon Highway, Namir Highway (north of the Yarkon River), and the Yarkon itself – each of which is over 211 ft (64 m) – divide Tel Aviv into five cities.

Nevertheless, for several reasons it seems that these highways and the river do not divide the city. First of all, the Tel Aviv *eruv* encloses all these parts, joining them together into one city. When the *halakha* speaks of a bisected city being divided in two,

11. TRAVELING BEYOND THE *TEḤUM* AND ITEMS ARRIVING FROM BEYOND THE *TEḤUM*

One who traveled beyond the boundaries of the *teḥum*, whether knowingly or unknowingly, forfeits his 2,000 *amot* and may now only move within his four *amot* (SA 405:1; n. 1 above). Should he need to move

---

it is referring to a situation in which the walls have been breached. If the city is walled, however, it is still considered one area. Furthermore, even if the *eruv* happens to be down and in practice one may not carry in the area, as long as the majority of the *eruv* is still standing, the city may still be considered one area. *Orḥot Shabbat* states this in ch. 28 n. 163 in the name of R. Shmuel Auerbach, who derives it from the laws of sacrifices (certain types of which had to be eaten within the walls of Jerusalem), for which a wall whose breaches cover less length than its standing parts is effective (*Tosafot*, BM 53b).

If the road bisecting a city is not straight, the rectangles drawn around each section can overlap, thus uniting the city even if there is no *eruv*. This opinion was expressed by R. Shalom Noaḥ Segal Weiss in *Tikun Eruvin* 2:5:39 (p. 211) and n. 156 (pp. 236-237). *Maḥazeh Avraham* OḤ 70 states that even if the rectangles do not touch each other, as long as the distance between them is less than 211 ft (64 m), they are considered joined.

Another justification for leniency is that the *shi'ur* of 211 ft (64 m) – double the size of a city's outskirts – was based on the standards in talmudic times. However, now that cities are much more sprawling, the entire area that serves the city's residents should be considered part of the city's outskirts. This can be derived from the law of a city that is situated next to a stream. If the bank of the stream that is closer to the city has a balcony that is four *amot* wide, the entire stream is considered part of the city, and the city's *teḥum* is measured from the farther bank. This would seem to be the case even when the width of the stream is greater than 211 ft (64 m). MB 398:46 cites Ritva (*Eruvin* 61a, s.v. "ve-Ra"Ḥ z"l") that since "this stream is in front of the whole city and is fit to be used by all the city's residents, we can consider it an extension of the city even though it is not habitable." We may also add the possibility raised by MA (398:13) that from the status of the stream we can extrapolate to any place that the city residents use. If so, urban highways are a part of the city even if they are very wide, since their purpose is to be used by the city's residents. This would also be the case with public parks and gardens. R. Michael Bleicher writes along these lines in *Teḥum Shabbat U-medidato*, p. 24. (Nevertheless, we see from Rema, cited at the beginning of this note, that the definition of a city is based on physical criteria, not on whether the two sections share a municipality.)

In practice, since the law is rabbinic, we may be lenient, whether based on the rationale that the city has an *eruv*, or on the rationale that the rectangles drawn around each section overlap. Each rationale is sufficient on its own, and they are even stronger when considered together. Even when distances greater than twelve *mil* are involved, where some Rishonim maintain that a Torah prohibition applies, we may be lenient based on these rationales. However, if there is no great need, it is proper to defer to the stringent opinion.

his bowels, he may walk to a place where he will be able do so privately. Afterward, he may distance himself from this place enough to avoid the foul smell, so that he may recite prayers and *berakhot*, but he may not move more than four *amot* from that spot (SA 406:1).

One who traveled beyond the *teḥum* knowingly and reached an area enclosed by a wall or *eruv* is nonetheless limited to his four *amot*. Even if he is now inside a house, he may not move more than four *amot*. In contrast, if he traveled beyond the *teḥum* unknowingly or under duress, he may walk freely within the enclosed area (SA 405:6; BHL s.v. "aval").

If one traveled beyond the *teḥum* in order to save a life, the Sages ordained that upon completing his mission, he may walk 2,000 *amot* in each direction. If this new *teḥum* overlaps his original *teḥum*, he may return home, and he retains his original *teḥum* as though he never left (*Eruvin* 44b). In certain cases he may even return to his original place regardless of *teḥumin*, as explained above in 27:10 and n. 12).

If one is traveling on a plane that, due to unforeseen circumstances, lands in an airport on Shabbat, his *teḥum Shabbat* is established upon his landing, and he may not go farther than 2,000 *amot* in any direction.[11] Since an airport is generally surrounded by a fence and often contains an area for sleeping, the whole airport is considered his four *amot*, and he can walk another 2,000 *amot* beyond it. However, if the airport is not surrounded by a fence, then his *mekom shevita* is established the moment the plane touches down. If the plane then taxies on the runway for another

11. See n. 3 above, which discusses the Sages' uncertainty about whether the prohibitions of *teḥumin* apply to airspace more than ten *tefaḥim* above land. The plane in this case has flown more than twelve *mil* on Shabbat; therefore, according to Rambam and those who follow his position, who maintain that traveling beyond twelve *mil* on Shabbat is prohibited by Torah law, one who lands on Shabbat should be stringent and stay within his four *amot*. However, according to most *poskim*, traveling beyond one's *teḥum* is never prohibited by Torah law, so we may be lenient cases of uncertainty. Therefore, we do not have to worry about *teḥumin* above ten *tefaḥim*. The passenger's *teḥum* is established only once his plane lands, after which he has 2,000 *amot* in each direction, as I wrote in the main text. In any case, even according to Rambam, since the passenger's arrival on Shabbat was unintentional, he may walk through the entire airport as long as it is enclosed by a fence (see Rema 248:4; MB *ad loc.* 32; *Yaskil Avdi* 8:20:62; *Yalkut Yosef* 248:4).

2,000 *amot*, he has gone beyond his *teḥum*, and he may not move any farther than his four *amot*. This means he must remain on the plane until Shabbat ends. If the crew or security personnel insist that he leave, or if he needs to leave in order to use the bathroom, he may do so. If he then reaches an enclosed area, he may move around within it, since the only reason he originally traveled beyond his *teḥum* is that he was forced to do so (SA 405:6). If his flight was for the sake of a mitzva, then even if the plane taxies for a full kilometer and the airport is not fenced in, he may still walk 2,000 *amot* from the airplane door (SA 248:4; MB *ad loc.* 32).

One whose boat docked on Shabbat may leave the boat and walk 2,000 *amot* in each direction. This is because until reaching the port, the boat was more than ten *tefaḥim* above the ocean floor, so *teḥum Shabbat* did not apply to it. Only once he sets foot on dry land is his *teḥum* established. If the port is fenced in, he may walk 2,000 *amot* beyond the enclosure (SA 404:1; n. 3 above).

One who traveled beyond his *teḥum* and then returned inside his *teḥum* unknowingly or due to circumstances beyond his control may still walk within his *teḥum* (SA 406:1). However, if he traveled beyond the *teḥum* knowingly, then even if he returned unknowingly, he forfeits his *teḥum*, though he may still walk throughout the city (SA 405:8).

Just as one may not travel beyond his *teḥum* on Shabbat, he also may not move his possessions outside the *teḥum*. If he took fruit beyond the *teḥum* unknowingly, even though they may not be carried more than four *amot*, they may be eaten. If he did so knowingly, the fruit may not be eaten (SA 405:9; MB *ad loc.* 52; see above, ch. 26 n. 6).

If a non-Jew brought fruit from outside the *teḥum* on Shabbat, as long as he brought them for himself or for another non-Jew, a Jew may eat the fruit. However, one may not carry them more than four *amot*. If the non-Jew brought the fruit into a home or a site that is enclosed by a fence or an *eruv*, one may carry the fruit within the enclosed area. In contrast, if the non-Jew brought the fruit for a Jew, that Jew and the members of his household may not eat the fruit until enough time has passed after Shabbat for the fruit to have been brought then (SA 325:8).[12]

12. Two sets of laws apply to objects that arrive from outside the *teḥum*. The first is the standard laws of *teḥum Shabbat*. Objects carried outside of their *teḥum* are considered

12. ERUV TEḤUMIN

If one wants to walk on Shabbat to a place that lies beyond his *teḥum*, he can render it permissible by making an *eruv teḥumin* before Shabbat, that is, by establishing his *mekom shevita* at the place where he puts the *eruv*. By placing this *eruv*, he merges the old *teḥum* (which would not have allowed him to go where he wants) with the new *teḥum* (which will allow

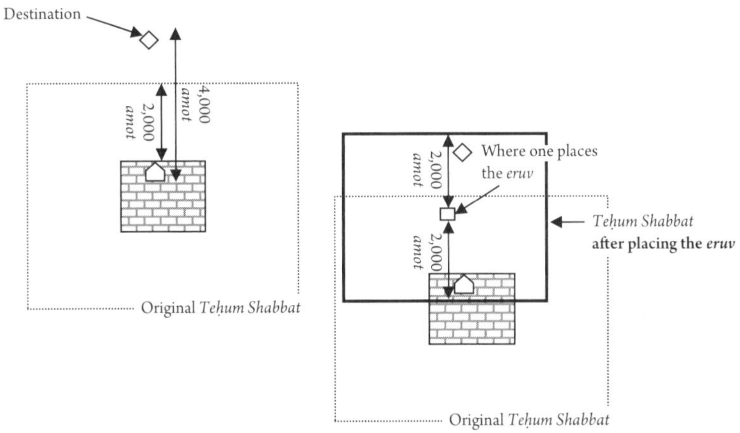

---

the same as people who left their *teḥum* unknowingly or due to circumstances out of their control, since objects have no will of their own. Therefore, if the objects arrived in an enclosed area, they may be carried throughout the enclosed area. However, if they were brought to a place that is not enclosed, they may be moved only four *amot*. If they are returned to their original place, they revert to their original status.

The second set of laws relates to benefiting from prohibited actions done on Shabbat, and the intent of the person transporting the fruits determines their status. If he did so knowingly, no one may benefit from his actions, and the fruit may not be eaten. If he brought them unknowingly, then since the prohibition itself is rabbinic, they may be eaten (*Pri Megadim*; BHL 318:1, s.v. "ha-mevashel"; see *Harḥavot* 26:4:1). If a non-Jew brought the fruit from outside the *teḥum* for himself or for another non-Jew, a Jew may eat them; but if he brought them for a Jew, that Jew and his household may not eat the fruit until enough time has elapsed for the fruit to have been brought to them permissibly after Shabbat.

The Sages established that the laws of *teḥumin* also apply to objects belonging to non-Jews, and such objects acquire a *mekom shevita* wherever they are when Shabbat began. If it was permitted to carry objects belonging to non-Jews without limit, people might mistakenly come to believe that objects belonging to Jews are also not subject to the laws of *teḥum Shabbat*. Ownerless items, however, are not subject to *teḥumin* restrictions (SA 401:1).

him to go there) – this is why it is called an *eruv* (which literally means "merging") *teḥumin*. However, the distance that the *eruv teḥumin* affords him in one direction is lost in the opposite direction. For example, if one places the *eruv teḥumin* 2,000 *amot* to the east of his home, he may now walk 4,000 *amot* eastward (2,000 *amot* from his home to the *eruv* and 2,000 *amot* beyond the *eruv*), but he may no longer walk westward at all.

There are two ways to shift one's *mekom shevita*. The first is by simply walking 2,000 *amot* in the desired direction before Shabbat begins and staying there for the onset of Shabbat. As long as one is there during the entire period of *bein ha-shmashot*, that becomes his place, and his *teḥum Shabbat* is now calculated from that point. He does not need to verbalize anything for this to take effect. It is enough for him to intend to establish his *teḥum* from that point. In contrast, if one is hiking in a field during *bein ha-shmashot* but does not intend to establish his *mekom shevita* there, his *mekom shevita* remains his home (SA 409:7; MB *ad loc.* 29).[13]

The second way is to set aside two meals' worth of food at that place and recite the declaration for making an *eruv teḥumin*, along with

13. The Sages allow a traveler who wishes to establish his *mekom shevita* someplace further along the way to do so by merely verbalizing this wish. This special leniency is effective as long as two conditions are met. First, it must be possible for him to reach that location before dark if he hurries. Second, at the moment when Shabbat begins, he must be within 2,000 *amot* of the location (SA 409:11). However, if he intends to establish his *mekom shevita* somewhere beyond his 2,000 *amot*, he loses his *teḥum* Shabbat, and he may not move beyond his four *amot*, since he cannot establish the desired location as his *mekom shevita*, as he is beyond its *teḥum*, and he cannot establish his current location as his *mekom shevita* either, since he pushed it out of his mind. This is the opinion of Rashba, Rosh (*Eruvin* 4:13), and *Tur* (409:11). However, according to Rambam, whenever one fails to establish his *mekom shevita* at his desired location, he establishes it at his current location instead. SA cites Rambam as a secondary opinion ("*yesh omrim*").

If one is traveling and wishes to establish his place verbally, he must specify the four *amot* that he intends as his *mekom shevita*. An example of such a verbalization might be "The four *amot* surrounding such-and-such tree trunk." If he did not delineate the area precisely, according to most Rishonim the entire uncertain area is included in his *mekom shevita*. If he said, "My place for Shabbat is under that tree," but half the tree is outside his 2,000 *amot*, he has not established a *mekom shevita*, and he is left with only his four *amot*. As mentioned in the previous paragraph, according to Rambam, whenever one does not specify his *mekom shevita* adequately, rendering his desired *teḥum* ineffective, his current location becomes his *mekom shevita* instead, and his *teḥum* is 2,000 *amot* from there. Under pressing circumstances, one may rely on this opinion.

a *berakha,* as will be explained in the next section. An *eruv teḥumin* should be made only for the purpose of a mitzva – for example in order to attend a Torah lecture or a mitzva celebration. If one makes an *eruv teḥumin* for some other purpose, it is still effective *be-di'avad* (SA 415:1).

When making an *eruv teḥumin,* one must place it within 2,000 *amot* of his home. This way his home will be within the *teḥum* of the *eruv,* and he may then walk from his home to the *eruv.* If his home is outside the *eruv*'s *teḥum,* the *eruv* is ineffective, and his *teḥum* is measured from his home.[14]

One can actually use an *eruv teḥumin* to travel 5,600 *amot,* not just 4,000 *amot.* Since the *mekom shevita* where he sets aside the *eruv* is temporary (unlike a city, as above in section 6), he may have in mind for the new *teḥum* created by the *eruv* to be oriented so that the square's diagonal faces his desired direction. He thus gains the additional corners.

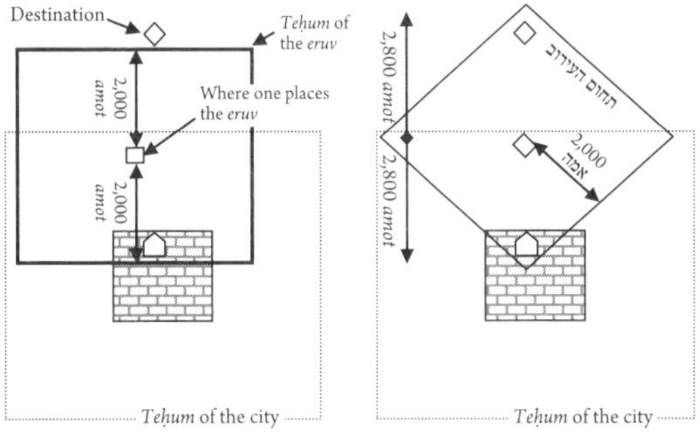

14. At first glance, it would seem that in most large cities, setting aside an *eruv teḥumin* is ineffective. After all, we saw in section 4 that when one is outside the city at the start of Shabbat, we do not include the whole city in his four *amot.* He may travel within the city only as far as his 2,000 *amot* allow. If so, when one's home is more than 2,000 *amot* from the *eruv* that one makes, the *eruv* is ineffective, and his status is the same as that of any other resident of the city. Indeed, this is how *Beit Me'ir, Maḥatzit Ha-shekel,* and *Olat Shabbat* understand SA 408:1, and so states *Eliya Rabba* 408:8 as well. According to MA and MB 408:3, 7, 10, SA agrees that one's *mekom shevita* in such a case is indeed the location where he set aside the *eruv.* Since he was in his home when Shabbat began, he may walk within the city in the direction of the *eruv,* but once he has left the city, he may not return home. According to Rema, since this person's home is in the city, if he placed an *eruv* outside the city, he has a connection to both places; therefore, in addition to the 2,000 *amot* granted him by his *eruv,* the whole city is considered four *amot* and he may walk freely within it. Even after he leaves the city, he may return to it and walk within it. BHL's discussion

13. PLACING THE *ERUV TEḤUMIN* AND RECITING THE *BERAKHA*

One who wishes to make an *eruv* by placing food must set aside two meals' worth of food. If bread is used, it must amount to the volume of six eggs, which is approximately 10.1 oz (300 ml). (Others maintain that it must amount to the volume of eight eggs.) If one wishes to use food that is eaten together with bread, it is sufficient to use the amount of that food that would normally be spread on or eaten together with six eggs' volume of bread (SA 409:7). If the *eruv* is meant to serve several people, two meals' worth of food must be left for each person. If a large number of people are involved and one would like to minimize the bulkiness of the *eruv*, he may use olive oil, chocolate spread, or peanut butter, as relatively small quantities of these foods are used with a large amount of bread. One may also use a *revi'it* (2.5 oz or 75 ml) of vinegar, which is enough to use as a dip or dressing for two meals' worth of vegetables (MB 386:35; 409:36). Drinks may also be used for the *eruv* as long as there are two

---

of this matter concludes with an endorsement of MA's understanding of SA (408:1, s.v. "raḥok"). However, many rule in accordance with Rema, including *Baḥ, Noda Bi-Yehuda* (*Mahadura Tinyana* 49), and AHS. SHT *ad loc.* 11 states that one should not object to those who are lenient in accordance with Rema. Since the laws of *teḥum Shabbat* are completely rabbinic, when necessary one may rely on Rema.

According to *Shulḥan Arukh*, the *eruv* he set aside is invalid, and he is left with the old *teḥum*, which is measured from his home. According to Rema and *Magen Avraham*, the *eruv* is valid; they disagree how far he may walk within his city.

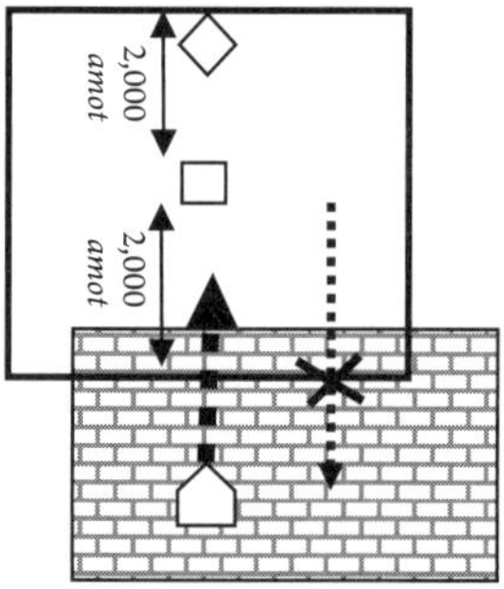

According to *Magen Avraham*, one may initially walk from his home to his new *teḥum*, but afterward he may not leave the new *teḥum* to return home.

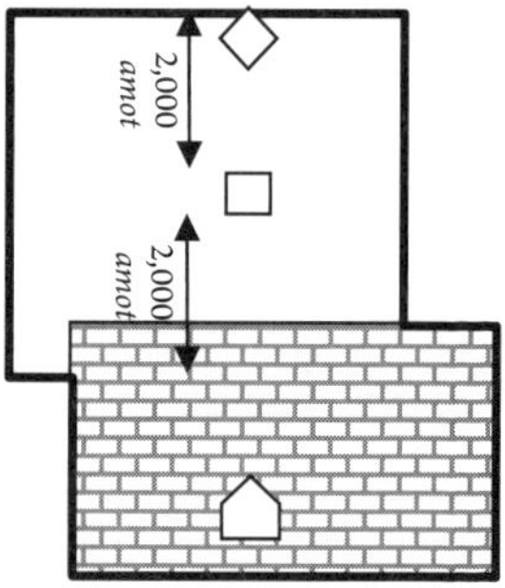

According to Rema, one may walk anywhere within the city as well as within his new *teḥum*.

revi'iyot (5.1 oz or 150 ml) per person (SA 386:6). Salt and water may not be used for the *eruv* (*Eruvin* 26a).[15]

The food must belong to the person who plans to make use of the *eruv*, as he uses this food to establish his *mekom shevita*. When the *eruv* is meant for several people, the food's owner must arrange for each person to acquire some of the food, making all of them partners in it. This is accomplished by means of third person, who lifts up the food with the intent to acquire it on behalf of all those who need to use the *eruv* (SA 413:1).

If the food set aside for the *eruv* was eaten before *bein ha-shmashot*, the *eruv* is ineffective. However, after *bein ha-shmashot* the *eruv* may be eaten, because once one has established his *mekom shevita* during *bein ha-shmashot*, it remains in effect for all of Shabbat (Rema 394:2). If the *eruv* was left in a place where it could not be accessed during *bein ha-shmashot* without transgressing a Torah law (for example, if a boulder would need to be rolled away to retrieve it), the *eruv* is ineffective (SA 394:3; 409:3-4).

When setting aside the *eruv*, one should recite the following *berakha*: "Blessed are You, Lord our God, King of the universe, Who sanctified us with His *mitzvot* and commanded us regarding the mitzva of *eruv*" ("*asher kideshanu be-mitzvotav ve-tzivanu al mitzvat eruv*"). One should follow this with the declaration: "With this *eruv* it shall be permitted to me to walk 2,000 *amot* from this place in every direction." *Bedi'avad*, even if he simply said: "This shall be an *eruv*," it is effective. But if he said nothing at all, he has not established an *eruv* (SA 415:4; MB *ad loc.* 15).

When the *eruv* is meant to serve several people, their names should be explicitly mentioned as part of the declaration. One must also take care that the *eruv* contains two meals' worth of food for each person who needs to rely on it (SA 415:4). If he would like the *eruv* to be effective for multiple *Shabbatot*, he should add at the end of the declaration the phrase "for all *Shabbatot* of the year." Then, as long as the *eruv* remains in existence, it is effective (MB *ad loc.* 16).

---

15. *Eruvin* 26a states that one may use a saltwater mixture for an *eruv*, and Rambam writes this as well (MT, Laws of *Eruvin* 1:8). However, based on the continuation of the Gemara, *Tosafot ad loc.* s.v. "aval" state that this is limited to a case in which oil is mixed in with the saltwater. SA 386:5 presents Rambam's opinion, and then cites *Tosafot* as a secondary opinion. MB *ad loc.* 29 states that the *halakha* follows the lenient first opinion.

An *eruv* may be placed by a *shali'aḥ* (emissary or proxy). However, a minor, a non-Jew, or one who does not believe in the mitzva of *eruv* cannot serve as a *shali'aḥ*. The *shali'aḥ* must recite the *berakha* and the declaration. If he said nothing, the *eruv* is not effective (SA 409:8). However, it is effective if the owner of the *eruv* declares: "With the *eruv* that my *shali'aḥ* is setting aside, I will be permitted to walk 2,000 *amot* from the *eruv* in every direction" (BHL s.v. "ve-yomar").

One cannot place an *eruv* on behalf of another without the other person's knowledge. One may place an *eruv* for his minor children, and the *teḥum* that it establishes is binding for them. Similarly, one may place an *eruv* for members of his household who are over the age of bar or bat mitzva. However, if upon hearing that there is an *eruv teḥumin* they object and state that they do not want it, the *teḥum* that it establishes is not binding for them. A child who is under the age of six is considered secondary to his mother, so an *eruv* that is effective for the mother is effective for her child as well (SA 414:1-2).

14. ESTABLISHING A CONDITIONAL *ERUV* FOR ALL LOCAL RESIDENTS

One may place an *eruv* conditionally. For example, if one knows that on Shabbat two Torah scholars will be lecturing in two nearby towns, but he has yet to decide if he will attend the lecture to the east, the one to the west, or neither, he places one *eruv* in the east and one in the west and stipulates in his mind that on Shabbat he will decide which *teḥum* to use, the one based on his home, on the *eruv* in the west, or on the *eruv* in the east. Once he has made his decision, though, he is bound by his chosen *teḥum*. If he did not make a conscious decision but merely started walking in accordance with only one specific *teḥum*, he has thus established his *teḥum* and may no longer change his mind and walk in accordance with a different *teḥum* (*Eruvin* 82a; SA 413:1; MB *ad loc.* 8).[16]

16. The Tanna'im disagree about this law. According to the Sages and R. Yehuda in the Mishna (*Eruvin* 36b), a stipulation is effective when placing an *eruv*, based on the principle of retroactive clarification ("*yesh breira*"). In this case, it means that when one decides which *eruv* he wants to use, it clarifies retroactively which of the two potential *eruvin* he set aside before Shabbat was the true *eruv*. The *beraita* mentions that some maintain that retroactive clarification is ineffective (*Eruvin* 36b and 37b).

One may volunteer to place an *eruv* on behalf of all residents of a locale. He then declares: "With this *eruv* it shall be permitted for all local residents and their guests to walk 2,000 *amot* from this place in every direction." Anyone who is aware of the existence of this *eruv* before Shabbat, even if he did not decide that the site of the *eruv* is his *mekom shevita*, may decide on Shabbat that he wishes to walk in that direction and may rely on the communal *eruv*. However, one who was unaware of the *eruv*'s existence before Shabbat may not rely on it (SA 413:1).

If there are so many local residents that the person placing the *eruv* cannot leave two meals' worth of food for each one of them, then as long as he knows that there will be no more than twenty people who will want to rely on the *eruv*, he may place two meals' worth of food for twenty people and declare: "With this *eruv* it shall be permissible for anyone who wishes to walk 2,000 *amot* from this place in every direction for all *Shabbatot* of the year." This allows all who are interested in relying upon his *eruv* to do so, on condition that they are aware of its existence before the Shabbat they rely on it (SA 413:1; BHL s.v. "le-khol eḥad"). It seems that when it is clear that someone will make use of the *eruv*, the *berakha* should be recited, but when it is uncertain whether anyone will make use of it, no *berakha* should be recited.

If one places an *eruv* unconditionally, his *teḥum* is determined by the location of the *eruv*. He may not change his mind and follow the *teḥum* measured from his home.

***

The Talmud in *Beitza* 38a cites the opinion of R. Oshaya that for Torah laws retroactive clarification is ineffective, while for rabbinic laws it is effective. This is the opinion of most *poskim*, including Rambam, Rabbeinu Tam, Rosh, Ramban, Ran, and SA YD 331:11. SA 413:1 and MB *ad loc.* 7 conclude similarly. Therefore, one may set aside multiple *eruvin* and then decide on Shabbat which *eruv* he will use to establish his *teḥum*. (Some disagree: Ri maintains that retroactive clarification is effective even for Torah laws, while Maharam of Rothenburg as quoted in *Mordechai* maintains that it is ineffective even for rabbinic laws.)

SA 413:1 uses the expression, "It all depends on his stipulation." This implies that if one places an *eruv* conditionally, such as by saying: "If the Torah scholar comes to the east, my *eruv* will be in the east," and then the Torah scholar comes to the east, the person's *teḥum* is set and cannot be changed.

May we all be privileged to accept *Shabbatot* joyously, to observe them properly, to become sanctified on them by remembering our faith, to spend them studying Torah, and to enjoy them through food and slumber. May our soul be illuminated by a twofold light, and may its light suffuse our entire week. May blessing extend to all of our works from the realm of Shabbat – *teḥum Shabbat* – and may we merit complete redemption, speedily in our day.

Glossary

Aḥaronim – halakhic authorities from c. 1500 CE until the present day

Al Ha-gefen – the *berakha aḥarona* recited after drinking wine or grape juice

aliya (pl. *aliyot*) – the calling of a congregant up to the Torah reading as a section of the Torah scroll is read aloud

ama (pl. *amot*) – a cubit; a standard halakhic measure of distance equaling c. 17.7 in (45 cm) and approximating the distance from the tip of the middle finger to the elbow of the average adult male

Amida – "The Standing Prayer"; also called the *Shemoneh Esrei*; the central prayer of each service, in which the worshiper stands as though in God's presence

Amora'im – sages of the Gemara (c. 200-500 CE)

Ashkenaz – a geographical region corresponding to modern-day Germany where the traditions that eventually became characteristic of European (Ashkenazic) Jewry coalesced in the Middle Ages

Ata Ḥonantanu – prayer added to the *Amida* of *Ma'ariv* of *Motza'ei Shabbat* that serves as a form of *havdala*

aufruf – the custom of honoring a groom on the Shabbat prior to his wedding by calling him up to the Torah and inviting family and friends to a celebratory *kiddush*

av melakha (pl. *avot melakha*) – primary category of *melakha* on Shabbat

avuka – lit. "torch"; a candle with at least two wicks that is customarily used for *havdala*

ayin ha-ra – the evil eye
Ba-meh Madlikin – the second chapter of Mishna *Shabbat* that many have the custom to recite at *Kabbalat Shabbat* on Friday night
basis le-davar ha-asur – a base for a forbidden item; an item that is rendered *muktzeh* itself because of the *muktzeh* item resting upon it
batel – rendered insignificant
be-di'avad – a level of performance that *ex post facto* satisfies an obligation in a less-than-ideal manner
bein ha-shmashot – the time between sunset and the emergence of stars, when it is uncertain whether it is night or day
beit din – rabbinical court
beit midrash (pl. *batei midrash*) – Torah study hall
beit satayim – unit of area equivalent to 5,000 square *amot* (about 1040 square meters, or a bit more than a quarter of an acre)
berakha – a formal blessing recited before eating or performing a mitzva, and on other occasions
berakha aḥarona – a blessing recited after eating or drinking
berakha le-vatala – a blessing in vain
besamim – fragrance used for one of the *berakhot* of *havdala*
Birkat Ha-mazon – known as the "grace after meals"; the *berakha aḥarona* consisting of four *berakhot* recited after a bread-based meal
Birkhot Ha-shaḥar – a series of *berakhot* recited each morning, praising God for meeting our most basic needs
Bishul – the *melakha* of cooking
bishul aḥar bishul – see *ein bishul aḥar bishul*
bishul akum – the prohibition on eating food cooked by a non-Jew
bitul – nullification
Boneh – the *melakha* of building
Borei Me'orei Ha-esh – the *berakha* recited over the light of a fire at *havdala*
Borer – the *melakha* of separating
brit mila – the ritual circumcision (*mila*) performed on the eighth day of a Jewish boy's life, when he enters into Israel's covenant (*brit*) with God
Dash – the *melakha* of threshing
davar gush – hot, solid food that possibly retains its heat even when transferred from vessel to vessel

davar she-eino mitkaven – an intentional action on Shabbat that results (though not inevitably; see *psik reisha*) in unintended Shabbat desecration

derekh akhila – the normal way to eat; the *halakha* is often lenient when one performs a *melakha* in this way

derekh melakha – the normal way to perform a particular *melakha*; the *halakha* is usually strict when one performs a *melakha* in this way

drasha (pl. *derashot*) – a communal sermon or homily given on Shabbat, usually delivered by the rabbi to his congregation and dealing with halakhic and theological matters

ein bishul aḥar bishul – the principle that there is no prohibition of cooking something that has already been cooked

Eretz Yisrael – the Land of Israel

eruv (pl. *eruvin*) – lit. "mixture"; see *eruv ḥatzerot* or *eruv teḥumin*

eruv ḥatzerot – a physical boundary that can transform a *reshut ha-rabim* into a *reshut ha-yaḥid*, allowing people to carry items within that area on Shabbat, as well as to carry items from another domain into that area, and vice versa; alternatively, the communal food that is set aside to join all homes and yards within the area, allowing it to be considered one *reshut ha-yaḥid*

eruv teḥumin – a means of establishing one's *teḥum Shabbat* before Shabbat begins, so that it includes a desired location that was previously beyond his *teḥum*; alternatively, the food that can be set aside at the place where one wants to establish his *mekom shevita* for this purpose

etrog – a citron, one of the four species used during the holiday of Sukkot

gabbai – the congregant in charge of running services in the synagogue, selecting prayer leaders, and calling people up to the Torah

garuf – a description for an oven that has been cleared of its coals, one of the two methods used to contain an oven's fire, eliminating the concern that one will raise the temperature; see *katum*

Ge'onim (sing. Gaon) – the leaders of the Babylonian *yeshivot* and authoritative interpreters of the Bavli during the latter part of the first millennium CE

Gemara – the part of the Talmud that interprets and expands upon the Mishna; compiled during the third-sixth centuries CE

ger – a convert

ger toshav – a non-Jew who takes upon himself the seven Noahide commandments

Gozez – the *melakha* of shearing

graf shel re'i – lit. "chamber pot"; a *muktzeh* item whose presence is so disturbing that the Sages permitted picking it up and removing it from one's vicinity

grama – causation; a *melakha* performed indirectly and not prohibited by Torah law

grogeret (pl. *grogarot*) – a dried fig; the volume of 18 *grogarot* is considered equivalent to two meals' worth of food, which is needed to establish joint ownership over an area enclosed by an *eruv*

haftara – a selection from the books of *Nevi'im* (Prophets) that is publicly read in synagogues on Shabbat, festivals, and fast days

Ha-gafen – the *berakha* recited over wine and grape juice

hak'hel – lit. "assemble"; the mitzva of assembling the entire Jewish people once every seven years to hear the king or leader of the nation read the Torah

halakha – the collective body of Jewish law; an individual Jewish law

Half-*Kaddish* – the *Kaddish* used to punctuate divisions and transitions within the prayer service

ḥalitza – levirate divorce; the shoe-removal ceremony by which a widow severs her connection to her late and childless husband's brother

ḥalla – the mitzva to give a part of a large batch of dough to a Kohen (nowadays it is burned instead)

ḥamar medina – lit. "the wine of the country"; a dignified beverage that people in one's locale drink as one would drink wine

Ha-mavdil Bein Kodesh Le-ḥol – the main *berakha* of *havdala*, commemorating the end of Shabbat or Yom Tov and the distinction between the sacred and the profane

ha-motzi – the *berakha* over bread

hanaḥa – "placing," putting food in a place where it will warm up; alternatively, one of the components of *Hotza'ah*, putting an object down after transporting it

hanetz ha-ḥama – sunrise

hashma'at kol – producing sound, an act that is rabbinically prohibited on Shabbat

hatmana – insulation; keeping a pot of food warm by enveloping it in wool or a different material to preserve its heat

havdala – the series of *berakhot* that marks the end of Shabbat and festivals

ḥazan – the person leading the congregation in prayer

haḥzara – returning fully cooked food to a heat source on Shabbat after removing it from there earlier on Shabbat

ḥesed – "loving-kindness"; one of God's attributes that we are enjoined to emulate

Ḥol Ha-mo'ed – the intermediate days of Sukkot and Pesaḥ, on which certain weekday activities are permitted

Ḥoresh – the *melakha* of plowing

ḥotalot – palm leaves used to protect unripe dates, which the Sages permitted cutting open on Shabbat, as the leaves are secondary to their contents

Hotza'ah – the *melakha* of carrying from one domain to another

Ḥovel – wounding or causing a loss of blood; a *tolada* of *Shoḥet*

ḥumash (pl. *ḥumashim*) – the Pentateuch; a term for Torah in printed form

irui – "pouring"; one of the ways taste is transferred; an intermediate phase between *kli rishon* and *kli sheni*

Kabbala – esoteric Jewish wisdom

Kabbalat Shabbat – the series of psalms and poems developed by the kabbalists of Tzefat (Safed) in the 16th century to usher in Shabbat on Friday night

Kaddish – a hymn of praises to God whose central theme is the magnification and sanctification of God's name

kalei ha-bishul – easily cooked foods that can become cooked even in a *kli sheni*

karet – extirpation, the most severe biblical punishment

karmelit – a domain where carrying on Shabbat is rabbinically forbidden

karpif – a large courtyard, approximately 32 m long; if houses in a city are not farther away from one another than this length, they are considered contiguous, part of one area for the purpose of assessing the *teḥum Shabbat*

katum – a description for an oven whose flame has been covered with ash, one of the two methods used to contain an oven's fire, eliminating the concern that one will raise the temperature; see *garuf*

kedusha (adj. *kadosh*) – holiness; transcendence (see 1:6)

Ke-gavna – a section from the *Zohar* that some have the custom to recite at *Kabbalat Shabbat* on Friday night

kevod ha-briyot – human dignity

kezayit – an olive's bulk, a standard halakhic measure of volume or weight

kiddush – an invocation of the sanctity of a holy day with blessings over a cup of wine

kiddush be-makom se'uda – the rabbinic requirement that *kiddush* be made at the place of the meal

Kidusha Raba – the *kiddush* that the Sages mandated be recited on Shabbat day

ki-le'aḥar yad – backhandedly, as one might perform a *melakha* on Shabbat without transgressing a Torah prohibition

kilkul (v. *mekalkel*) – a destructive action; a *melakha* performed in this manner is not prohibited by Torah law

kira – a type of mini-oven used in the time of the Sages that was heated by burning coals on its floor; modern ovens have the halakhic status of a *kira*

kli (pl. *kelim*) – vessel, implement, or utensil

kli rishon – the vessel in which food was cooked

kli she-melakhto le-heter – an object whose primary function is permitted; such an item may be moved on Shabbat for any reason, but not for no reason at all

kli she-melakhto le-isur – an object whose primary function is prohibited, and which thus may only be moved on Shabbat for a permissible activity or to use the space the object is occupying

kli sheni – the vessel into which hot food was transferred

kli shlishi – the vessel into which hot food was transferred after having been transferred to a *kli sheni*

ko'aḥ rishon – firsthand force; as in a *melakha* that happens close at hand to the person who initiated it, who is held completely responsible for the *melakha*

ko'aḥ sheni – secondhand force; as in a *melakha* that happens at a distance from the person who initiated it, causing the action to be considered *grama*

Kohen (pl. Kohanim) – a Jewish priest, descendant of Aaron, charged with performing the Temple rites and benefiting from certain privileges

Kore'a – the *melakha* of tearing

kos – goblet for *kiddush*

kos shel berakha – a cup of wine linked to the performance of a mitzva

Kosheir – the *melakha* of tying a knot

Kotev – the *melakha* of writing

Kotzer – the *melakha* of reaping

laḥatot ba-geḥalim – lit. "stoking the coals"; the motivating concern behind rabbinic enactments that forbid doing anything that might cause one to turn up a flame

Lash – the *melakha* of kneading

leḥem mishneh – the two whole loaves of bread/matza over which the *berakha* of "*ha-motzi*" is recited at Shabbat and Yom Tov meals

Lekha Dodi – a poem composed by R. Shlomo Alkabetz that is part of *Kabbalat Shabbat*

le-khatḥila – *ab initio*; a level of performance that satisfies an obligation in an ideal manner

lo titgodedu – the prohibition on factional disunity

lulav – a closed palm frond, one of the four species used during the holiday of Sukkot

ma'akhal ben Derusa'i – food that could be eaten in extenuating circumstances

Ma'ariv – the evening prayers

ma'aser – the tithe of one tenth of produce, given to Levi'im

Mafshit – the *melakha* of skinning

maftir – the person who reads the *haftara*, or at least recites the blessing on the *haftara*; alternatively, the *aliya* following the seven mandated *aliyot* that is given to the person who will read the *haftara*

Magen Avot – see *Me'ein Sheva*

Makeh Be-patish – the *melakha* of applying the finishing touch

marit ayin – "appearance"; an action that must be avoided because it may give a false impression of being a violation

Matir – the *melakha* of untying a knot

matza – unleavened bread eaten by Jews on Pesaḥ

Mav'ir – the *melakha* of lighting a fire

Me'abed – the *melakha* of tanning

Me'amer – the *melakha* of gathering

Me'ein Sheva – lit. "like seven"; the *berakha* recited by the *ḥazan* at the end of *Ma'ariv* on Friday night, which serves as a synopsis of the seven *berakhot* of the *Amida* of Shabbat

Mefarek – extracting; a *tolada* of *Dash* that involves removing one thing from another thing

megis – stirring hot food that is not fully cooked

Meḥatekh – the *melakha* of cutting

meḥitza – a wall or barrier

meḥitza ha-materet – a wall or barrier that renders something halakhically permitted, e.g., a *sukka* or an *eruv*

Meisekh – the *melakha* of warping threads on a loom

Mekadesh Ha-Shabbat – the *berakha* over the sanctity of Shabbat that is recited at *kiddush* and in the *Amida* of each of the Shabbat prayers

Mekhabeh – the *melakha* of extinguishing a fire

Mekhabes – washing clothes; a *tolada* of *Melaben*

mekom petur – a domain that is neither a *reshut ha-yaḥid* nor a *reshut ha-rabim,* in which one may carry objects on Shabbat by Torah law; since the rabbinic institution of the *karmelit,* this category only includes places that have no significant function

mekom shevita – lit. "resting place"; the place where one is spending Shabbat, which acts as the center of one's *teḥum Shabbat*

Melaben – the *melakha* of laundering

melakha (pl. *melakhot*) – productive work of the type prohibited on Shabbat and Yom Tov

melakha she-eina tzerikha le-gufah – a *melakha* that is done intentionally, but not for the sake of the object upon which it is performed

melaveh malka – lit. "accompanying the queen"; eating a meal on *Motza'ei Shabbat* in order to honor Shabbat at its departure

melekhet maḥshevet – lit. "skilled craft"; the Torah prohibits only *melakhot* that are performed in this manner, with intent and planning

melo lugmav – a measure of liquid; enough to fill the drinker's mouth with one cheek inflated

Memaḥek – the *melakha* of smoothing

Memare'aḥ – spreading a substance evenly upon an object; a *tolada* of *Memaḥek*

Men of the Great Assembly – a group of sages and prophets from the beginning of the Second Temple era (c. 500 BCE) who instituted several enactments that shaped the course of *halakha* and Jewish tradition

Menapetz – the *melakha* of combing wool

Meraked –the *melakha* of sifting

Mesartet – the *melakha* of marking animal skins

mevushal – cooked, as wine, possibly changing its status with regard to the laws of *kiddush* and the prohibition of *yein nesekh*

mevushal kol tzorkho – fully cooked, and thus no longer subject to the prohibitions of *Bishul*

mezid – performing a *melakha* knowingly

mezonot – food that is made from grain but is not bread, or the *berakha* recited on such foods

mezuza – the doorpost, or the parchment inscribed with specific paragraphs from the Torah that must be affixed to the doorpost of Jewish homes

mikveh – a ritual immersion pool

mil – a unit of distance; it takes 18 minutes (22.5 according to some, and 24 according to others) to walk a *mil*

milḥemet mitzva – a mandatory war, undertaken to conquer Eretz Yisrael or to save lives

milḥemet reshut – a discretionary war, undertaken to extend and expand the boundaries of Eretz Yisrael

Minḥa – the afternoon prayers

Minḥa gedola – 5.5 seasonal hours before sunset; the earliest time to recite the afternoon prayers

Minḥa ketana – 2.5 seasonal hours before sunset

minyan – a quorum of ten adult Jewish males required for certain religious obligations

Mishkan – Tabernacle; the portable dwelling place for the Divine Presence that was the center of Israelite worship before the Temple was constructed

Mishna – the earliest authoritative work of rabbinic literature consisting of legal statements and disputes arranged in 63 tractates and 6 orders, compiled in the third century CE

mitasek – performing a *melakha* while oblivious to one's actions

mitzva (pl. *mitzvot*) – commandment

Moḥek – the *melakha* of erasing

Mole'aḥ – the *melakha* of salting

Molid – creating a new entity on Shabbat

Motza'ei Shabbat – Saturday night after Shabbat ends and weekday activities are resumed

Motzi Me-reshut Li-reshut – see *Hotza'ah*

muktzeh – the prohibition on Shabbat on moving any item that has no purpose on Shabbat

muktzeh meḥamat gufo – *muktzeh* as a result of itself; items that have no use on Shabbat inherently

muktzeh meḥamat ḥesron kis – *muktzeh* as a result of monetary loss; items that have no use on Shabbat because they are valuable and one does not want them to break or become ruined

mumar – a Jew who regularly commits intentional transgressions

mursan – coarse bran that is difficult to make into a proper dough; it is questionable whether it is subject to the laws of *Lash*

Musaf – the additional service recited on Shabbat, Yom Tov, *Ḥol Ha-mo'ed*, and Rosh Ḥodesh, days on which the *korban musaf* was offered in Temple times

neshama yeteira – lit. "expanded soul"; the special connection between a Jew and God on Shabbat

netilat yadayim – ritual hand washing

neveila – an animal that was not properly slaughtered, the meat of which may not be eaten

nida – a woman who has menstruated and not yet immersed in a *mikveh* to purify herself

Nishmat Kol Ḥai – prayer of wondrous praise added on Shabbat and Yom Tov to the end of *Pesukei De-zimra*

noten ta'am bar noten ta'am – see *nat bar nat*

Ofeh – the *melakha* of cooking/baking

okhel – lit. "food"; in the context of the *melakha* of *Borer,* the desired part of a mixture

oneg Shabbat – the mitzva to make Shabbat a delight by experiencing pleasure and avoiding discomfort and suffering

Oreg – the *melakha* of weaving

Oseh Shtei Batei Nirin – the *melakha* of making two loops on a loom

pagum – "defective"; as a *kiddush* cup that is unfit for sacramental purposes

parsha (pl. *parshiyot*) – the weekly Torah portion that is read at the synagogue each Shabbat

pasul – ritually unfit

Pesukei De-zimra – the psalms of praise recited prior to *Shaḥarit* which prepare one for the *Amida*

pidyon ha-ben – a mitzva in which a Jewish firstborn son is redeemed from a Kohen with five silver coins

plag ha-minḥa – 1.25 seasonal hours before the end of the day; according to some, the earliest time that one can accept Shabbat on Friday afternoon

plata – a warming tray used to reheat foods on Shabbat

posek (pl. *poskim*) – a halakhic decisor or authority

Potze'a – the *melakha* of separating threads

psik reisha – an intentional action on Shabbat that inevitably results in unintended Shabbat desecration

psik reisha de-lo niḥa lei – an intentional action on Shabbat resulting in unintended Shabbat desecration that, while inevitable, is undesired

psolet – lit. "waste matter"; in the context of the *melakha* of *Borer,* the undesired part of a mixture

reshut – domain, for the purposes of the laws of *Hotza'ah* on Shabbat

reshut ha-rabim – public domain

reshut ha-yaḥid – private domain

Responsa – a genre of rabbinic literature that consists of rabbinic responses to halakhic queries

Retzei Ve-haḥalitzenu – the passage that is inserted into *Birkat Ha-mazon* on Shabbat during the third *berakha*

revi'it (pl. *revi'iyot*) – a liquid measure equal to a quarter of a *log*, calculated by most to be c. 2.5 oz (75 ml)

Rishonim – Jewish sages and halakhic authorities from the medieval era (roughly 1000-1500 CE)

Rosh Ḥodesh – the new moon; the one or two-day minor holiday that marks the beginning of each Hebrew month

rosh yeshiva (pl. *rashei yeshiva*) – head of a *yeshiva*

safek – a case of uncertainty or doubt

safek de-Oraita le-ḥumra – the principle that we rule strictly when in doubt about Torah law

Sanhedrin – the Jewish high court of 71 judges that sat on the Temple Mount

se'ah – a unit of volume; 40 *se'ah* is equivalent to one *ama* by one *ama* by three *amot*

se'uda shlishit (*shaleshudis*) – the obligatory third Shabbat meal

se'udat mitzva – a festive meal celebrating the fulfillment of a mitzva

Seder – the banquet on the first night of Pesaḥ that includes several special recitations, customs, and *mitzvot*

Seḥita – squeezing or wringing; a *tolada* of *Dash*

Shabbat ha-malka – the Shabbat queen; the personification of Shabbat itself

Shabbat Shalom – a customary greeting on Shabbat, especially to one's rabbi or the local rabbi

Shaḥarit – the morning prayers

shali'aḥ – proxy or agent

shalom bayit – peace in the home, i.e., domestic harmony among family members

Shamor – the negative aspects of Shabbat observance, namely, the requirement to refrain from certain activities

She-hakol – the generic *berakha* on food, recited on foods not included in the purview of any other *berakha*

hashhaya – leaving food that is not fully cooked on the fire before Shabbat, such that it will continue cooking on Shabbat

Shekhina – the Divine Presence in this world

Sheva Berakhot – the seven blessings recited at the conclusion of a meal in the presence of a bride and groom

shevita – cessation of work; the most basic expression of the nature of Shabbat

shi'ur – a standard halakhic measurement for weight, distance, or volume

shinui (pl. *shinuyim*) – performing a *melakha* on Shabbat in an irregular manner

shitufei mevo'ot – a shared alleyway; a type of *eruv* that transforms all homes, yards, and streets into one domain, within which everyone may carry

shki'at ha-ḥama or *shki'a* – sunset, when Shabbat begins

shnayim mikra ve-eḥad targum – lit. "twice Scripture, once translation"; the rabbinic requirement that every individual man supplement the communal Torah reading with a personal review of the weekly Torah portion

shofar – the ram's horn that we are commanded to blow on several occasions, especially on Rosh Ha-shana

shogeg – performing a *melakha* unknowingly; either one was aware that he was performing a *melakha* but forgot that it was Shabbat, or he was unaware that his actions were prohibited on Shabbat

Shoḥet – the *melakha* of slaughtering

shvut – rabbinic prohibition on Shabbat

shvut di-shvut – double rabbinic prohibition, which may be transgressed in certain circumstances

siddur (pl. *siddurim*) – a Jewish prayer book

simḥa – joy, a mitzva to experience on Yom Tov and possibly on Shabbat as well; compare to *oneg*

siyum masekhet – a *se'udat mitzva* occasioned by the completion of a tractate of the Talmud or an order of the Mishna

sofer (pl. *sofrim*) – Jewish scribe

Soter – the *melakha* of demolishing

sukka – a temporary hut constructed for use during the weeklong festival of Sukkot

Tanna'im – the rabbinic authorities in Eretz Yisrael during the first two centuries CE

targum – translation of the Torah, often referring specifically to Onkelos's Aramaic translation
tefaḥ (pl. *tefaḥim*) – a handbreadth; a halakhic measurement equal to c. 3 in (8 cm)
tefilin – phylacteries; black leather boxes and straps containing parchment scrolls, worn during weekday morning prayers
teḥum Shabbat – boundary surrounding one's *mekom shevita*, beyond which one may not travel on Shabbat
tel ha-mitlaket – a steep hill that descends ten *tefaḥim* (30 in or 76 cm) every four horizontal *amot* (6 ft or 1.82 m), rendering everything above the slope a *reshut ha-yaḥid*
teruma – a tithe of c. 2% of produce, given to Kohanim
teshuva – return or repentance; on Shabbat we return to the basic foundations of our faith
tikun – a constructive action; a *melakha* is only prohibited by Torah law when it is performed in this manner
Tofer – the *melakha* of sewing
Toḥen – the *melakha* of grinding
tolada (pl. *toladot*) – a secondary category of *melakha* on Shabbat
toldot ha-esh – objects that were heated by fire; one who cooks food using these transgresses a Torah prohibition
toldot ha-ḥama – objects that were heated by the sun; one who cooks food using these transgresses a rabbinic prohibition
Torah reading – the public reading of a set of passages from a Torah scroll
tosefet Shabbat – the time added before and/or after Shabbat to fulfill the mitzva of extending Shabbat into the week
Toveh – the *melakha* of spinning threads
Tzad – the *melakha* of trapping an animal
tzeit ha-kokhavim – the appearance of three distinct stars, marking nightfall for various halakhic purposes
tzitzit – four-cornered tasseled garments worn on a *talit* in fulfillment of a mitzva
Tzove'a – the *melakha* of dyeing
tzurat ha-petaḥ – a halakhic doorway used to surround an area to form an *eruv ḥatzerot*
uvdin de-ḥol – weekday activities, generally prohibited on Shabbat

Va-yekhulu – the Torah verses that first invoke Shabbat (Bereishit 2:1-3), typically recited three times on Friday night

Vi-yhi No'am – prayer recited in *Ma'ariv* on *Motza'ei Shabbat* (and other occasions) that begins with Tehilim 90:17 and includes all of Tehilim 91

Ya'aleh Ve-yavo – the paragraph inserted into the *Amida* and *Birkat Ha-mazon* of festivals on which *Musaf* is recited

yad soledet bo – hot enough to cause the hand to recoil, somewhere between 113°F (45°C) and (71°C)

yein nesekh – wine that is prohibited because it was touched by an idol-worshiping non-Jew

yeshiva (pl. *yeshivot*) – a school that is dedicated to Torah study; its students often live in dormitories

yibum – levirate marriage; the ceremony by which a widow marries her late and childless husband's brother

Yishtabaḥ – the concluding *berakha* of *Pesukei De-zimra*

Yom Tov – the festivals of biblical origin during which *melakha* is prohibited

yoshvei keranot – lit. "those who sit on corners"; idlers; alternatively, merchants and artisans who would not attend *Shaḥarit* services during the week

Zakhor – the positive aspects of Shabbat observance, namely, the requirement to mark it in specific ways, such as by reciting *kiddush*

zimun – the responsive passage recited prior to *Birkat Ha-mazon*, in which a leader invites two or more participants to praise God together

Zore'a – the *melakha* of sowing

Zoreh – the *melakha* of winnowing

Index

The numbers here correspond to the chapter, section, and note respectively.

behalf of the entire community, II:30:14; conditional *eruv,* II:30:14 and n. 16; without one's knowledge, II:30:13; establishing one's *mekom shevita,* II:30:12; minor, II:30:13; squaring the *teḥum,* II:30:12.
Etrog: for *havdala,* I:8:5.
Exam: studying for, regarding preparing for after Shabbat, II:22:15.
Exempt area: see *Mekom petur.*
Exercise: II:22:8 and n. 3; stretching, II:28:13.
Extending a person's life: regarding saving a life, II:27:3.
Extinguishing: see *Mekhabeh.*
Extracting: see *Mefarek.*
Eye drops: regular sick person, one who is suffering, II:28:5.
Eye shadow: I:14:4.
Eyes: eye drops, II:28:5; eye exercises, II:28:12.
Fan: regarding *muktzeh,* II:23:7.
Fasting: prohibition, I:7:2.
Faucet: detaching a filter or pipe from it, II:15:3; using a filtered tap, regarding *Borer,* II:15:3.
Fax machine: regarding *Kotev,* II:18:1.
Feathers: plucking, I:14:1.
Fertilizing: *tolada* of *Zore'a,* II:19:3; *tolada* of *Ḥoresh,* II:19:1.
Fetus: regarding saving a life, II:27:3.
Filament: II:17:1; in electrical appliances, regarding *muktzeh,* II:23:7.
Filter: installing in the sink, II:15:3; cleaning a sink filter, II:15:9, 12; regarding *Borer,* I:11:7; removing from the faucet, II:15:3; using a sink filter, regarding *Borer,* I:11:13.
Fingernail: torn off most of the way, regarding one who is suffering, II:28:3; clipping or biting, I:14:2.
Finishing touch: see *Makeh be-patish.*
Fire department: calling on Shabbat, II:16:5.
Fire: cooking with it or with something that was heated by it, I:10:2; regarding *Mav'ir,* II:16:2; extinguishing, II:16:6 and n. 2; minor extinguishing, II:24:4; danger of harm to the public, II:16:8; saving a life, II:16:7.
Fireplace: opening or closing the door near it, II:16:4.
Fish: for Shabbat meals, I:7:2.
Flies: closing a window when there are flies in the room, regarding *Tzad,* II:20:7 and n. 4.
Floor: drying water, I:13:5; cleaning and washing, II:15:9.
Flower pot: moving from its place, II:19:10 and n. 9; regarding *Ḥoresh,* II:19:1; regarding *muktzeh,* II:23:8; regarding *Kotzer* and *Zore'a,* II:19:10; opening shutters or a window near it, regarding *Zore'a,* II:19:3.
Flower: vase, II:19:9; smelling fragrant flowers when they are attached to the ground, II:19:8 and n. 7.
Folding: *talit,* I:13:9.
Food cooked by a non-Jew: for a regular sick person, II:28 n. 2.
Food: refrigerating or freezing, regarding preparing for after Shabbat, II:22:16; preparing for an animal, II:20:3; regarding *Kotev* and *Moḥek,* I:12:11; regarding *muktzeh,* II:23:3; regarding *Meḥatekh,* II:15:10; buying and selling, II:22:3; coloring on Shabbat, I:12:10 and n. 16; liquefying congealed food, I:12:12; finished cooking on Shabbat, regarding benefiting from *melakha*

Left-handed person: regarding *kiddush*, I:6 n. 9; regarding *Kotev*, II:18:2.
Lego: see Interlocking toy bricks.
Lekha Dodi: at *Kabbalat Shabbat*, I:5:14.
Lemonade: making, regarding *Dash*, I:12:8 and n. 14.
Lending money: II:22:4.
Lens: replacing a lens that fell out of a pair of glasses, II:16:8; cleaning contact lenses (soft and hard), I:13:7.
Lettering: Torah scroll/*tefilin*/*mezuza* script, cursive script, regarding *Kotev*, II:18:2.
Leveling the ground: II:15:2; regarding *Ḥoresh*, II:19:1.
Levirate divorce: see *Ḥalitza*.
Levirate marriage: see *Yibum*.
Lice: killing, II:20 n. 5.
Light bulb: prohibited to use by Torah law, II:17:1; removal from socket, II:15:3; reading by its light, II:15:3; instead of a *havdala* candle, I:8:6 and n. 4.
Light: turning on by a non-Jew, for a communal need, II:25:4; turning on by a minor, II:24:4; regarding benefiting from *melakha* performed on Shabbat, II:26:2 and nn. 2-3; regarding electricity on Shabbat, II:17:1 (see Electricity); electric light for Shabbat candles, I:4 n. 2; electric light for additional lighting, I:4:2; regarding benefiting from *melakha* performed on Shabbat, II:26:2; motion detectors that cause lights to go on, II:17:12, 14 and n. 12.
Lipstick: I:14:4.
Liquids: straining, I:11:11; coloring, I:12:10 and n. 16; regarding *bishul aḥar bishul*, I:10 n. 6.
Liver: making chopped liver, regarding *Lash*, I:12:7.
Lottery: for distributing portions of food, II:22:4.
Ma'akhal ben Derusa'i: regarding *Bishul*, I:10 n. 1; regarding *hashhaya*, I:10:15.
Ma'aseh Shabbat (benefiting from *melakha* performed on Shabbat): basic principle, II:26:1; when there is a dispute between the *poskim*, II:26:5; *melakha* performed by a non-Jew, II:25:1 and n. 2; *Hotza'ah* performed by a non-Jew, II:26 n. 6; objects carried outside of their *teḥum Shabbat*, II:30 n. 12; on *motza'ei Shabbat*, II:26:7-8; when benefiting is permitted, II:26:3; power outage, II:26:6; when the item itself is unchanged, II:26:4; *melakha* done by others with one's possessions, II:26:10; pot used to cook on Shabbat, II:26 n. 8; knowingly or unknowingly, on purpose or against one's will, II:26:2; in order to fulfill a mitzva, II:26:2 and n. 3; *melakha* performed by a minor, II:24:4.
Machine: electric, II:17:1; vending machine, regarding benefiting from *melakha* performed on Shabbat, II:26:10; running on Shabbat, I:2:9; washing machine, turning on before Shabbat begins, I:2 n. 3; regarding *muktzeh*, II:23:7; photocopier, II:18:1.
Mafshit (skinning): II:18:6.
Magnet: for attaching items (on the refrigerator, e.g.), II:15:3.
Makeh be-patish (applying the finishing touch): basic principle, II:15:1; examples, II:15:8.

on Shabbat, 11:26:7; benefiting after Shabbat from *melakha* performed by a non-Jew on Shabbat, 11:25 n. 3; riding on a bus, regarding benefiting from *melakha* performed on Shabbat, 11:26:8; performing *melakha* and eating before *havdala*, 1:8:8; Jew in Israel watching a television broadcast from outside Israel, 11:26:8; *tosefet Shabbat*, 1:3:2 and n. 3, 1:4 n. 5.

Mouse trap: 11:20:6.

Mouthwash: 1:14:7.

Mud: removing from shoes, 1:13:6; removing from shoes by rubbing against the ground, regarding *Ḥoresh*, 11:19:1; covering with straw, sand, or gravel, 11:15:2; regarding *Toḥen*, 1:12:1 and n. 1.

Muktzeh: basic principle, 11:23:1; principles, 11:23:2; *meḥamat isur*, 11:23:10; *meḥamat gufo*, 11:23:3, 13; *meḥamat ḥesron kis*, 11:23:4; *meḥamat mitzva*, 11:23:10; filament, regarding *muktzeh meḥamat gufo*, 11:23:7 and n. 8; non-*kli* item used for a prohibited activity, regarding *kli she-melakhto le-isur*, 11:23 n. 7; wet clothes that are hanging to dry, 11:23:10 and n. 10; rendering an object unsuitable for its normal use, 11:23:11; *graf shel re'i*, 11:23:12; creating a *graf shel re'i*, 11:23 n. 11; *basis le-davar ha-asur*, 11:23:5; moving a *basis le-davar ha-asur* permissibly, 11:23:6; *basis le-davar ha-asur ve-hamutar*, 11:23:6 and n. 5; moving a *basis le-davar ha-asur* indirectly, 11:23:14; animals, 11:20:3; pets, 11:20:5 and n. 3; apricot pits, 11:24:8; door handle that broke, 11:23 n. 13; moving an item with one's body, 11:23:14; moving an item for a permissible activity or to use the space it is occupying, 11:23:7; moving an item indirectly, 11:23:14; moving an item for a regular sick person, 11:28 n. 2; non-Jew moving an item, in order to prevent a loss, 11:25:4; item that broke on Shabbat and had been attached to the ground, 11:23:13; broken object, when there is a concern that one might fix it, 11:23 n. 12; *kli she-melakhto le-isur*, 11:23:7; *kli she-melakhto le-isur*, regarding *basis le-davar ha-asur*, 11:23 n. 5; *kli she-melakhto le-heter u-le'isur*, 11:23:8; *kli she-melakhto le-heter*, 11:23:9 and n. 9; one who picked up a *muktzeh* item permissibly, 11:23:15 and n. 15; modeling clay, 11:24:7; using an item without carrying it, 11:23:6; child who is carrying a *muktzeh* item, 11:23 n. 16.

Muscles: stretching, 11:22:8.

Musical instruments: 11:22:17.

Nail: regarding *muktzeh*, 11:23:7; hanging objects, 11:15:3; attaching to the wall, 11:15:3.

Napkins: folding into shapes, 1:13:9, 11:15:7.

Necklace: beaded necklace that broke on Shabbat, regarding *muktzeh*, 11:23:13.

Needle: acupuncture, 11:28:13; regarding *muktzeh*, 11:23:7.

Neighborhoods: connecting, regarding *teḥum Shabbat*, 11:30:8.

News: on *motza'ei Shabbat*, regarding benefiting from *melakha* performed on Shabbat, 11:26:8.

About the Author

Rabbi Eliezer Melamed is one of the most widely read Torah educators in Israel today. He learned in the Merkaz Harav Yeshiva in Jerusalem under the personal tutelage of Rabbi Zvi Yehuda HaKohen Kook *zt"l*. For twenty years, he taught Gemara and classes in *maḥshava* at the Bet-El Yeshiva. Invited to become the rabbi of the settlement Har Bracha, he established the Har Bracha Yeshiva, which he has headed since 1991. Under his leadership, Har Bracha has grown dynamically and become an example of an idealistic, Torah-based community, which is also integrally involved in the leading social, economic, military, and educational issues of the day.

Besides being one of the founders of, and the spiritual force behind, the weekly newspaper *B'sheva*, he writes the "*Revivim*" column which has garnered wide exposure and generated impact nationally. A partner in the establishment of the radio station Arutz 7, his daily halakha broadcast gained high listener ratings, and brought the light of Torah to a diverse listening audience throughout Israel.

His popular series of books, *Peninei Halakha*, written in a clear, concise, and in-depth fashion, in a language accessible to all, is part of his vision to familiarize the entire Jewish nation with the basics of Jewish law and faith.

The fonts used in this book are from the Arno family

Maggid Books
The best of contemporary Jewish thought from
Koren Publishers Jerusalem Ltd.